violence and american cinema

Previously published in the AFI Film Readers series,
edited by Charles Wolfe and Edward Branigan

violence and american cinema

edited by j. david slocum

routledge
new york and london

To my parents,

who taught me to put things together—

and supported my wanting to take them apart

Published in 2001 by
Routledge
29 West 35th Street
New York, NY 10001

Published in Great Britain by
Routledge
11 New Fetter Lane
London EC4P 4EE

Copyright © 2001 by Routledge
Routledge is a member of the Taylor & Francis Group.

Parts of "Violence in the Film Western" appeared previously in *Westerns: Making the Man in Fiction and Film,* by Lee Clark Mitchell. Copyright © 1996 and permission to reprint by the University of Chicago Press.

Printed in the United States of America on acid-free paper.
Typeset by Liana Fredley.

LIBRARY OF CONGRESS CATALOGING-IN-PUBLICATION DATA

Violence and American cinema / edited by J. David Slocum.
p. cm. — (AFI film readers)
    Includes bibliographical references and index.
    ISBN 0-415-92809-5 — ISBN 0-415-92810-9 (pbk.)
    1. Violence in motion pictures. 2. Motion pictures—United States.
I. Slocum, J. David. II. Series
PN1995.9.V5 V56 2000
791.43'655—dc21   00-038265

contents

Part Three: Hollywood Violence and Cultural Politics

contents

acknowledgments

This project began with an innocent letter to Edward Branigan and Chuck Wolfe, series editors of the Routledge/AFI Readers, lamenting the dearth of cinema studies resources on violence and film, and suggesting they consider a reader on the topic. They responded immediately and affirmatively, and urged me to draft a proposal. I did, and Chuck and, especially, Edward have been model editors and colleagues since. They have my gratitude for their unstinting (and often calming) support. Bill Germano at Routledge and Liana Fredley were likewise consistently patient and helpful.

I owe each of the contributors a debt, not only for their incisive work but their good-natured willingness to engage in an uncertain and lengthy process. Several waited fully three years to see their words in print and all remained steadfast and responsive. I am also grateful to Miriam Bratu Hansen and Robert Lang, who were committed to contributing until unforeseen circumstances made that impossible.

My fascination with and research on violence and film stems from a fateful conversation, prompted at the end of my doctoral exams, with Richard Sennett and Robert Sklar. With Juan Corradi, these mentors nurtured my attempts to explore a vast area of inquiry and I remain indebted to each of them. Among the many friends and colleagues who have contributed to my thinking about film violence, Martin Roberts, Amresh Sinha, and Jonathan Veitch deserve particular gratitude for helping to shape this volume. Special thanks are due to Carol Wilder, Chair of the Communication Department at the New School for Social Research, who encouraged me to initiate this project amid my many other responsibilities there; and to Catharine R. Stimpson, Dean of the NYU Graduate School of Arts and Science, who was unsparing in her support of this reader and the everyday efforts required to complete it.

This book would not exist without Amy Grace Loyd, whose patience and love sustained me from its inception.

acknowledgments

violence and american cinema: notes for an investigation

introduction

j. david slocum

In the early 1990s "new violence" came into vogue as a description for the contemporary productions of Quentin Tarantino, Abel Ferrara, and Oliver Stone. The term was subsequently adopted by popular critics and cultural commentators to characterize a range of films and other media productions, including rap music and popular fiction.[1] During the 1996 presidential election campaign, both Bob Dole and Bill Clinton made extensive public comments about what they perceived as the immorality of movie violence. Other public figures, political and popular, ranging from Michael Medved and Bill Bennett to John Grisham, likewise rang in with their opinions on the topic.[2] Later in the 1990s a spate of school shootings, culminating in the shooting deaths of fifteen at Columbine High School in Littleton, Colorado, forcibly renewed discussions about the role of violent films and other media in the development of American children and adolescents. While "quantitative" studies by social science researchers have accompanied such popular attention and concern, humanities and film scholars have undertaken the "serious" study of film violence haltingly. Few have attempted to relate contemporary films or controversies to broader contexts or histories, or to provide more sophisticated accounts of cinematic forms of violence. This lack is all the more conspicuous because of the large body of critical work in other disciplines, like anthropology, literary criticism, and art history, devoted to complex understandings of representations of violence.[3] The current volume aims to correct this lack by bringing together a set of original essays that explore the history and theory of American film violence.

Film scholars have traditionally treated violence as a secondary concern. They regularly include violence in considerations of given periods, genres, directors, stars, or oeuvres. Perhaps most familiarly, priority is given to sexuality over violence when the two subjects are addressed. Conventional studies of the early 1930s, the late 1960s, the early 1990s, film noir, the gangster film, the Western, Sam Peckinpah, Martin Scorsese, and Quentin Tarantino—to name a few of the most obvious—thus highlight violence even as they fail to thoughtfully explicate its functions and contexts. Likewise, analysts often characterize the defining operations of the institution of cinema or the medium of film as violent without adequately interrogating the various meanings and value of the term or the history and situation of its viewing. Even more layered accounts of public controversies cite film violence as a catalyst, a provocation, or a cause, but fail to contextualize the images in question. Violence, on the whole, tends to be employed as a lazy signifier, conspicuous but typically unexamined.

Conceiving of Violence and American Film

Violence is a notoriously expansive notion. While the term indicates an action or behavior that is harmful or injurious, the least elaboration quickly demonstrates the range of phenomena for which it is potentially relevant. Individuals, groups, and states undertake harmful actions against individuals, groups, states, animals, property, and nature. Harm can be physical, psychological, or even sociological (countering the bonds of community or the state). Even more, the *threat* of harm or injury can often be as disturbing as the act itself. And the act need not have an immediate cause or responsible agent: systemic or structural violence can emerge from conditions—like racism, sexism, homophobia, classism, or xenophobia—that inscribe a given set of social or cultural relations without necessarily clarifying the reasons for or consequences of specific actions. Still more basically, aggression, sadism, or destructive behavior can be viewed as the result of the psychological or physiological tendency of human beings or social groups—that is, of human nature.

Lurking behind many efforts to define acts of violence are the complex cultural processes by which some behaviors and actions are marked as "violent" and others not. The classical sociological distinction formulated by Weber between violence and coercive force relies on a standard of legitimacy that has deep social roots. The state retains a monopoly on the legitimate use of coercive force, whereas individuals who employ violence are allowed to do so only in extraordinary circumstances (self-defense, war) or they are judged criminals. More than simply producing straightforward categories of acceptable and unacceptable uses of force, the distinction between legitimacy and illegitimacy also suggests the power of language to name certain actions as violent while marginalizing or eliding others. A ready example is domestic violence—itself a revealing, mitigating term—which refers to violent actions that occur outside the public realm for which notions of legitimacy are most easily applied. Compared to the brutish actions of war, urban riots, or even injurious crimes, violent acts perpetrated in domestic spaces are typically viewed as lesser offenses and discussed through euphemisms like "abuse." Legitimacy as a critical category is thus crucial not only for the actions it validates as violent within a given culture but for the behaviors that it excludes from popular discourses of violence.[4]

Assessing the character of putatively violent actions across cultures and historical periods is more complicated still. The legitimacy of forceful action is very much in the eye of the beholder and subject to the shifting nature of contemporary cultural identities and allegiances. Actions motivated by attitudes toward race and ethnicity are in this way frequently open to varying and even contradictory interpretations; otherness also emerges as a guiding principle for comprehending how prevailing values are translated into cultural practices. Looking at violence across time can highlight some of what falls short in traditional views of violence. The philosopher Sergio Cotta contends that the prevailing twentieth-century approach to violence as an unavoidable structural feature of contemporary society represents a radical break from that of the nineteenth, when violence was seen as an immoral aberration that ran against the norms of culture and civilization.[5] Though in their reach they undermine more focused or concrete discussions, such sweeping theses are provocative.

The matter of representation further tangles considerations of violence. As Foucault argued, language itself communicates violence by giving a name to certain behaviors and constructing certain objects and subjects of violence.[6] The example of legitimacy given above illustrates the power of language to establish violence as a social or legal fact. Prevailing standards of representation go far in a given culture to produce and circumscribe violence. Whatever the inherent violence of language, of course, events or behaviors in the actual world retain their disturbing, often horrifying immediacy. The problem becomes reconciling—or more fundamentally, coming to terms with—the connections between representations of violence and concrete occurrences in the world. One can ask superficially whether representations cause these actual behaviors. But more thoughtful inquiry raises larger questions about whether or how understandings of violence bridge experiences of representations and actual life, about the pleasures of viewing barbarous images or committing actual incidents, and about the necessity to confront destructive tendencies in order to resist or at least comprehend them better. Especially in a modern society mediated by popular culture, these questions are complicated by spectators' losing track of the distinctions between representation and reality in everyday life.

Early cinema provided amusements whose immediate stimulations replicated the sometimes assaultive experience of modern urban society.

Leo Charney, in his essay here and elsewhere, relates the visual shock and visceral stimulation at the heart of early cinematic experience to an increasingly modernist sensibility.[7] Editing, the basis of film language, similarly relied from its beginnings on breaks between otherwise continuous images that have startling and visceral effects upon viewers. Eisenstein's notion of montage involves a collision between frames or images that, when edited in sequence, produce a distinctive and more intense response from viewers than the individual frames or images shown separately. The images themselves may or may not denote violence or produce certain effects for given audiences. Indeed, the threat of violence posed by a narrative can often be more powerful than any graphic single image in provoking viewer responses. Further, even images of blatant violence on-screen, physical or otherwise, beg for multiple and complexly determined responses from viewers: slapstick pratfalls and battlefield kills and acts of noir sadism and boxing matches and serial killings necessarily elicit different kinds of responses and call for different kinds of critical approaches. And while a special difference may exist between the less graphic displays of studio-era films and what Pauline Kael, writing about *Bonnie and Clyde*, called the cinema of "blood and holes," many of the far-reaching difficulties with defining violence adumbrated above have special resonance when discussing film violence generally. From the technical nature of the medium itself to the pleasures and anxieties it evokes in viewers, from its layered narratives to frequently graphic spectacles, cinema is thoroughly violent—even as that violence is difficult to explain simply.

The violence of mainstream Hollywood film typifies that difficulty. Narrative filmmaking practices during the classical period typically involved strictly linear narratives, centered on individual, white, psychologically well motivated male protagonists, moving through the resolution of public conflicts toward social integration and heterosexual coupling that reaffirmed prevailing ideological currents that were themselves grounded in national cultural myths. These narratives are presented through well-focused compositions, continuity editing, realistic settings, naturalistic lighting, and frequent reliance on generic story forms and recognizable star performers. Summarized initially and still most familiarly in Bordwell, Staiger, and Thompson's *Classical Hollywood Cinema*, these tendencies establish the bounds of images of conformity and nonconformity alike. Breaks from these norms, including images or suggestions of violence, thus may represent nonconformity, deviance, and transgressive behavior. Such images may mark violent actions deemed illegitimate but still acceptable to present as part of a mainstream cultural production.[8]

At the same time, individual images, scenes, or acts that are compelling and often viscerally engaging in themselves—spectacles—appear in varying and complex relationships to the narratives. In fact, the oscillation between narrative and spectacle, examined by Leo Charney and Marsha Kinder in the pages that follow, is pivotal to the exposition of American film as well as its repertoire of violent representations. Whether through masculine protagonists, public conflicts and resolutions, familiar genres, or integrated fictional narratives, this popular cinema employs certain images of violence and excludes others in the process of exploring and, for the most part, validating the prevailing ideology. That some forms of violence appear so consistently while others remain absent or implicit urges more careful study of the narrative strategies, production practices, and formal operations of Hollywood cinema.

A Century of Responses

There have, of course, been many instructive critical attempts to understand film violence. The following overlapping categories delineate some of the issues that have been central to previous attention and study—and that are crucial in this collection.

Social, Institutional, and Policy Debates

Predictably, most critical attention has taken the form of case studies and historical summaries of specific controversies concerning the regulation of film content.[9] Accounts of early cinema have emphasized the emergence of the medium amid a complex and primarily urban U.S. society increasingly populated by ethnic immigrants. "An aesthetic of astonishment" (film historian Tom Gunning's term for this conjunction of cinematic and social experience) conveys something of the disquieting power of cinema perceived by early opponents of the medium. Local lawmakers and social reformers, who typically saw in this power the potential to corrupt children or to incite uneducated (ethnic) working-class viewers, sought to limit film content and exhibition practices. Boxing films (either re-creations or actual footage of prizefights) were a continual topic of reformist debate nearly from the beginnings of cinema: in 1896 *The Corbett-Fitzsimmons Fight* became immensely popular and therefore a target of reformist concerns about its effects on viewers ranging from the growing middle class to women and workers.[10] As narrative films increasingly predominated U.S. film production toward the end of the first decade of the twentieth century and the place of cinema in urban life continued to expand, local lawmakers took a more active stance, closing theaters, arresting exhibitors, and condemning specific films as corrupting. (Prizefight films were banned in 1912.) In 1909 the People's Institute, a reformist group in New York City, founded the National Board of Censorship. With financial ties to the Motion Pictures Patent Trust, this group, which was shortly thereafter renamed the National Board of Review, reviewed and gave approval to individual productions. The board's guidelines were drawn from eight prohibitive standards: number four involved undue depictions of crime; number five prohibited the "unnecessary elaboration or prolongation of suffering, brutality, vulgarity, violence, or crime." This lack of categorical distinction between representations of crime and violence would be seen in a number of regulatory efforts in succeeding decades, including the formation of the industry's self-regulatory organization, the Motion Picture Producers and Distributors Association of America, in 1922.

Guiding these attempts were the dual negotiations of social values and of the cultural role of motion pictures in a still changing urban America.

Richard Maltby's essay in this volume examines the discourse of criminality at its most contentious moment, when in the late 1920s and early 1930s a sustained scholarly and public debate about the effects of film, especially on children, took place and produced predictably contradictory conclusions. In 1929 Joseph Holmes's study stressed the overall morality of film narratives, in which the moral forces of good triumphed in the end over immoral characters and acts, and accordingly found no evidence of harmful effects. Not surprisingly, Holmes's critics focused on individual spectacles—shootings, whippings, beatings, stabbings—whose immorality could not be redeemed or contained by the moral ending. The most famous work of the era was the popular summary of a nine-volume study sponsored by the Payne Fund. Henry James Forman's *Our Movie-Made Children* (1933) viewed children as "unmarked slates" requiring protection from the scope and power of motion pictures. Writing euphemistically, Forman's concern about the dangers of "movies in a crowded section" is a holdover from earlier, progressive reformers' unease regarding predominantly ethnic workers in urban areas.[11] As Maltby suggests by contrasting the illegitimacy of violent action with the legitimacy of the government's use of force in Howard Hawks's 1931 *Scarface* and throughout the gangster genre, criminal behavior on film became a register for exploring the shifting role of violence and its impact in a turbulent age.

Much popular and scholarly attention has been paid to the formulation and enforcement of the Production Code in the early 1930s. The Code itself emphasized the responsibility of filmmakers to make entertainment, to adhere to common standards of morality and decency, and not to violate the sensibilities of the audience. Yet most of the Code addresses social concerns about sexual impropriety, nudity, and the immorality expressed through deviant behavior. Its specific prohibitions regarding violence were vague: under the applications concerning "crimes against the law," the overriding concern with depictions of "murder" and "crime" is that specific details or techniques not be presented "to throw sympathy with the crime as against law and justice or to inspire others with a desire for imitation." With the cooperation of the studios, the Code succeeded in circumscribing images of violence so that their function remained instrumental, mostly validating existing values, and never excessively subversive of mainstream assumptions. The Code and its proscriptions also helped to negotiate the cultural role of movies, especially sound movies as they emerged in the Depression-era United States. Jonathan Munby has even argued that the engagement of cultural issues springing from images of brutality, killing, or cruelty was crucial for the resituating and legitimation of sound cinema.[12]

At no time was this apparatus, or its efforts at inclusion and exclusion, more active than during the Second World War, when an alliance between Washington, Hollywood, and American audiences carefully regulated how the horrors of war were represented.[13] The Production Code provided filmmakers with the parameters through which to present images of physical force or psychic trauma that could, in years of depression and war alike, emphasize for audiences the cultural negotiations between good, sanctioned actions and criminal or evil ones. The Office of War Information, the government unit charged with monitoring and collaborating with the studios in order to ensure their contribution to the war effort, was keenly aware of the dangers in presenting war in its full, intense, and graphic reality. Instead, the suggestion of brutal action and the incremental increase in depictions of violence against Americans throughout the war enabled filmmakers to contain these shocking images in familiar narratives with upbeat or at least reaffirming endings. Popular audiences nevertheless demanded increasingly direct images of violence, indeed of deaths and killings, when they concluded that sanitized images failed to reflect the experiences of their loved ones. Art historian George H. Roeder Jr. has noted that popular cinema was central to the overall "visual experience" of the war, which finally encouraged polarized ways of seeing the conflict between the Allied and Axis powers. He goes on to claim that it was precisely the consolidation of existing Hollywood storytelling practices that suited the government's political aims of maintaining morale while also underscoring the ideological differences between the United States and its German and Japanese enemies.[14]

With the end of the war and the breakup of the studio system, the Code and its underlying cultural assumptions were subjected to changes marked by increasingly graphic images of violence in films ranging from Westerns to crime and war films. Meanwhile, in the mid-1950s, the Kefauver Senate Subcommittee on Juvenile Delinquency investigated the putative influence of a string of films about teens and, specifically, their delinquency. Its hearings proceeded from familiar anxieties about the corrupting influence of movies and, increasingly, television, on postwar youth. "The predominance of brutality in both movies and television is making our Nation's youth insensitive to human suffering," the committee's report read. "They are becoming so accustomed to an overwhelming amount of crimes and violence that death and pain are becoming meaningless."[15] Partly seeking to avoid governmental action, Hollywood instituted a voluntary moratorium on the making of "j.d. films" in 1956.[16]

The 1960s and early 1970s was the golden age of American film violence, a fact understood by filmmakers and critics at the time and celebrated since. Cinematic expressions of the counterculture challenged classical Hollywood genres and their underlying cultural myths, like that of the masculine hero. Through the exaggeration of formulaic images of aggression, productions increasingly mirrored cultural preoccupations with violence. They also emerged from filmmakers' efforts to expand the bounds of conventional film practice with stylistic and narrative innovations. Even more, though, filmmakers sought to join in a broader discussion about the nature of human aggression and the impact of violent images. Thus Sam Peckinpah's stated aim was to undermine viewers' conventional vantage points for watching movie violence. By doing so, he sought to convey the horrors of the era to viewers inured by media to the real violence in society. Critics at the time responded to the unprecedentedly violent images and the larger public debates variously: some celebrated the stylized renditions of gore as breakthroughs or as appropriate to the moment, others saw them as necessary cultural documents, still others derided the films as base and indicative of a decline in both Hollywood cinema and U.S. society. At a moment of thoroughgoing change for society and cinema alike, the break between classical norms for representing aggressions with restraint and an emergent willingness to depict violence more graphically was lost on few observers.[17]

Despite the wide-ranging public and political debates on the topic, few extended scholarly tracts concerning film violence appeared at the time. Even as violence grew more and more prevalent in cinema and a society riven by civil rights disputes, generational conflicts, and Vietnam, increased efforts to make sense of it remained disjointed. During these years, policy makers increased their focus on the mass media, of which popular Hollywood cinema was only one component—and one secondary to television. Researchers sought to establish links between violent images and actual behavior, with varied but mostly undramatic results.[18] Violence in film was also subsumed for some under the broader moral threat of pornography. The eleven-volume report of the National Commission on the Causes and Prevention of Violence included one volume on media that devoted only six of its nearly four hundred pages to motion pictures.[19]

Throughout the later 1970s and into the 1980s, as the introduction of cable television, VCRs, and multiplexes reshaped the cultural role of cinema, the so-called Reaganite entertainment of the latter decade featured a return to mostly innocuous films with violence bolstered by special-effects technology and devoid of antiestablishment tenor. Violent film images were still regularly assailed by cultural critics and used to illustrate the depravity of a number of electronic media, including television and video games, but cinema itself was rarely analyzed on its own terms. Public discourse on the carnage in slasher films or action blockbusters thus ironically became excuses for positing "Hollywood" as a synecdoche for mass media or a culture industry that was increasingly shaped by other media. Inverting the effort of many in the late 1960s to plumb the depths of human aggression through an understanding of graphic film images, film and cultural critics of the 1980s and early 1990s generated scandals around individual productions that were alleged to represent more widespread moral turpitude and social decay. *Dressed to Kill*, *Year of the Dragon*, and *Basic Instinct* were among the movies seized upon as outrageous and then made the basis for establishing new standards of "appropriate" and "fair" representation without regard for the subsequent effects of such generalizing.[20]

The decade also saw continuing attempts by social scientists to identify the "effects" of screen violence on viewers and their behavior; while film remained in these studies a medium of concern secondary to television, the emergence of cable television and video cassettes provoked greater sensitivity among scholars and public policy makers to the meaning of violent images in specific media.[21] Still, most public debate remained narrowly cast and avoided the increasing cartoon violence of mainstream action films featuring hypermasculinized stars like Stallone and Schwarzenegger and spectacular special effects. An important subset of inquiries into media effects during the 1980s, involving attention to violent pornography, demonstrates the point. Attorney General Edwin Meese oversaw the production in 1986 of a report on obscenity and pornography that devoted a mere three out of its more than nineteen hundred pages to the mainstream film industry; rather than explore Hollywood filmmakers' tendencies to rely on images of sexuality or violence, the report dealt almost entirely with a marginalized "adult-only" film business.[22]

Briefly put, the guiding focus of most of the century's social and institutional attention to film violence has been on censorship itself or effects on viewers, or institutional modes of regulation, specific social concerns, or marginalized groups—all worthwhile projects, but rarely allowing for a more synthetic understanding of film violence. More recent disputes over graphic images involving homosexuals and ethnic or racial minorities acknowledge the complex issues and discourses at play in the exhibition and reception of violent images. As a consequence, some film scholars have begun to contextualize their attention to effects, as Stephen Prince's recent collection of readings from the past four decades, *Screening Violence*, demonstrates.[23] However, the vast majority of popular treatments of film violence have dealt superficially with claims of viewer effects and, especially, the threat of corruption or incitement to imitation. Cinematic, cultural, and historical contexts have been neglected in favor of assertions regarding individual films and the repetitive production of scandals that rehearse a narrow range of viewpoints.

Cultural and Ideological Interpretations

Other scholarly work has considered more directly how images and narratives of violence betray social dynamics of power, subordination, and subversion. They also evaluate how the film medium itself structures these dynamics and perpetuates given representations of gender, race, or social relations. Genre studies have explored the often defining presence of violence in gangster films, science fiction films, combat films, comedies, and, as detailed below, horror films. Assessments of individuals—from Sam Peckinpah to Clint Eastwood, Sigourney Weaver, and John Woo—and specific films—such as *In a Lonely Place, Psycho,* and *Bonnie and Clyde*—have similarly used discussions of film violence to shed light on cultural contests over the meaning of masculinity and femininity, race and ethnicity, and the body.[24]

Most efforts have been recent, and few predate the Second World War. Early chronicles of Hollywood, even those like Lewis Jacobs's *The Rise of the American Film* that aspired to connect cinema to social history, made only passing reference to images of violence in order to discuss the public debates and governmental (or industry self-) regulation that shaped the growth of the film studios.[25] The locus classicus of interpretation of social content in film, Siegfried Kracauer's *From Caligari to Hitler*, published in 1947, connects the tormented and fractured psychologies depicted in German films of the 1920s and 1930s to the devolution of society from which Nazism emerged.[26] At the same time, sociological and psychological studies of American cinema offered critiques of the myths and ideologies refracted in popular cinema.[27] Discussions of film violence in these works tended to apply myth and symbol analysis to film content in order to identify the anxieties, conflicts, and fears of the period.

Two examples are illustrative. In 1950 Hortense Powdermaker's ethnographic study of Hollywood recognized the centrality of violence to mainstream films (and introduced a term made familiar by Pauline Kael two decades later), noting that "South Sea natives" classify American movies into two broad types, "kiss-kiss" and "bang-bang," for those stories, respectively, about love and violence. She also weighed in on the question of effects, or, as it was still posed in the immediate postwar years, "catharsis," concluding rather unsatisfactorily that while productions featuring violence "provide a vicarious outlet . . . the basic insecurities of the individual are left untouched."[28] Robert Warshow penned essays on what he termed "the two most successful creations of American movies . . . the gangster and the Westerner: men with guns." In the former, Warshow saw an extreme, definitively American, and finally tragic individualism expressed through brutal gunplay. The latter featured a central heroic figure who expressed himself most clearly through violent action; such action suggested to postwar audiences anxious about "killing or being killed" that there remained a necessity and responsibility of "establishing satisfactory modes of behavior."[29] For both Powdermaker and Warshow, and for most writers of the period, representations of violence epitomized the popular cinema's process of mirroring conflicts—from Cold War paranoia and consumer culture anxiety to post–Second World War traumas and family tensions—pervading contemporary society.

Other critics viewed increasing images of film violence, and popular cinema more generally, as symptomatic of a developing mass culture and mass society. Gilbert Seldes, Dwight MacDonald, and Clement Greenberg were among the most vocal of those who, in the 1950s, scrutinized what they perceived as an increasingly impersonal society that offered standardized kitsch to its isolated members. Unlike traditional high culture's creation of art with human value, this mass culture provided few outlets for individual anxiety and little basis for community. The repetitive nature of Hollywood films made them consistent fodder for these arguments; for example, Seldes was led to criticize the uniform tempo of Hollywood editing (compared with the varied styles of European film cutting) and MacDonald to dismiss genre filmmaking as formulaic and lacking the potential for artistic significance.[30] American film violence figured in this critique as a predictable and frequently trivializing aspect of the manufactured mass commodity—and therefore one to be disparaged as infantile and sensationalistic.

By contrast, French critics saw Hollywood screen violence at the time not as contributing to the standardization of film production but as a means to undercut predictable formula and create original cinematic visions. Jacques Rivette observed in 1955 that "those punches, weapons, dynamite explosions have no other purpose than to blast away the accumulated debris of habit, to create a breach." The designation of many American film directors as auteurs also led writers in *Cahiers du Cinéma* to laud the tendency toward individual, heterodox filmmaking. Writing of

Samuel Fuller, Luc Moullet observed that cinema needs "madmen" willing to transgress traditions in the arts and to aspire to create work "comparable to the living model." The development of the notion of American film noir likewise depended on a recognition of darker visions of society and psychology that were expressed through brutal threats and action. However characteristic they may or may not have been of postwar films and directors, violent images and narratives bespoke for many French critics a creative attempt to engage the aesthetic traditions of Hollywood and to address new postwar realities.[31]

Critics in the United States, with only a handful of notable exceptions, moved further from any such embrace of screen violence as movie representations grew increasingly explicit in the late 1960s and 1970s. Pauline Kael thus championed *Bonnie and Clyde* and celebrated iconoclastic "movie brutalists" like Sam Peckinpah, Irving Kershner, and Jean-Luc Godard, whom she saw as operating against the encroachment of numbing mass culture.[32] Beyond popular critical estimations, however, surprisingly few extended interpretive studies emerged during years in which anthropological, sociological, and public policy studies of mass media and its content proliferated. One was *Violent America: The Movies, 1946–1964*, a collection of brief essays written by Lawrence Alloway to accompany a 1970 screening series at New York's Museum of Modern Art. As its subtitle imparts, however, the work's treatment of film violence stopped short of engaging the period and films that were most tumultuous and radical.[33] Thomas Atkins later gathered a small group of essays on "graphic violence on the screen" that discussed the popular appeal of violent movies (and "their graphic depictions of destruction and death in familiar urban environments"). He perceptively noted that despite the increase in numbers and "realism" of these images, "real and recreated" violence had been "one of the cinema's fundamental obsessions from the beginning."[34] At roughly the same time, writing in Britain, John Fraser considered violence in film, as in other media, by the standard of whether it disturbed viewers' complacency and comfort and, if so, to good, moral effect or not.[35]

In their groundbreaking social histories of film of the mid-1970s, Robert Sklar and Garth Jowett revised earlier accounts of Hollywood's development and resituated the representation of violence. Rather than simply being a contentious subject for policy makers or industry regulators, these images came to betray broader social antagonisms. Writing about Mack Sennett's slapstick films made during the First World War and the great influx of immigrants that transformed America's cities, Sklar observed, "Sennett's comedies, appearing in an era of strife and official violence, gave audiences their first glimpses of a social perspective that was to become one of the most emotionally powerful of Hollywood formulas—the anarchic individual pitted against disordered violent authority—which re-emerged in later periods of upheaval in the early 1930s and late 1960s."[36] Such a reading viewed violence as a manifestation of deeply rooted cultural conflicts and, crucially, suggested that the actions of social authorities—in Sennett's films, the police—could be construed as violent just as readily as those of individuals. In doing so, the analysis also exemplified the varied possibilities of more sophisticated approaches to the study of popular cinema and American culture.

Scholars from outside cinema studies also began to make contributions to cultural accounts of film violence. Political scientist Michael Rogin, for example, elucidates some of the founding images of otherness in Hollywood history. For him, *The Birth of a Nation*, *The Jazz Singer*, and *Gone with the Wind* establish a system of differences—between men and women and whites and blacks, enforced by physical violence or its threat—whose purpose was to guard against the breakdown of difference in contemporary society. American studies scholar Richard Slotkin has probably put forth the most detailed single survey of film violence in his cultural exploration of the myth of the frontier in movie Westerns. He sees in this popular genre "the redemption of American spirit or fortune as something to be achieved by playing through a scenario of separation, temporary regression to a more primitive or 'natural' state, and *regeneration through violence*."[37] Slotkin's monumental work assigns myth a guiding role in the formation and recapitulation of ideology as well as in the central function violence therefore assumes in both myth (especially as expressed in popular culture) and ideology.[38]

From both within and outside cinema studies, writers have paid special attention to the violent marking of otherness that takes place in horror films. Robin Wood's readings of the genre have been hugely influential and hinge on what he views as "the struggle for recognition of all that our civilization *re*presses or *op*presses."[39] Not surprisingly, critics have often used psychoanalytical approaches to plumb the dreamworld of these films and to examine the excess desires being displayed. The monster at the center of most horror movies accordingly comes to epitomize the eruption of anxieties of a given cultural moment: what Wood terms "the return of the repressed." Technology, workers, youth, race, and, especially, sexuality are among the ideological issues that return in monstrous form to threaten some sense of social or psychic normality. Consequently, the violence deployed by the monster—not to mention the actions taken by society to counter and sometimes defeat him—not only speaks to given cultural anxieties but offers yet another vehicle for exaggerating categories of cultural difference.

Gender serves as the most consistently exaggerated category of difference in horror cinema and much has been made of the genre's reliance on the monstrous male and victimized female. Barry Keith Grant, whose writing and editorial work provides a fine overview of the genre's roots in gender and sexual difference, observes that "probably the most common image in horror movies" is "the beast in the boudoir."[40] From *King Kong* and *The Island of Lost Souls* through *Psycho* and *Rosemary's Baby* to the *Nightmare on Elm Street* series and *Candyman*, and underlying the dozens of versions of film horror's greatest story, *Dracula*, the monstrous appearance of surplus male desire threatens women with subordination, abject surrender, or death. Typically this dynamic assumes direct physical form in which female characters succumb to carnal or capital violence.[41]

While gender difference is obviously manifested across cultures, these analyses tend to remain culturally specific. One of the difficulties in making sense of film violence around the world is the extreme variability of the contexts in play and the methodologies therefore in use. For her history of recent Spanish cinema, for example, Marsha Kinder relies on the tension between opposing generic modes of violence—sacrifice and massacre—to explicate the ideological negotiations between the Church and the Francoist government.[42] Stephen Prince argues compellingly of the samurai's historical sacrifice in several of Akira Kurosawa's period films.[43] Recent writing on Hong Kong action cinema, notably Tony Williams's readings of John Woo's films, likewise hinge on the defining presence of characters caught amid irreconcilable forces and committed to traditional sacrificial behavior.[44]

Indeed, across cultures, ritual sacrifice is a structure that produces and maintains social cohesion.[45] Put simply by Susan Mizruchi, who has historicized the development of sacrifice as a persistently privileged act in American literature and social theory, the sacrificial mode is one in which "the social is defined by what is *given up* in order to produce it."[46] During the Second World War, Hollywood productions dwelled on the peculiarly American negotiation between individualism and group interest as the basis for a heroic sacrifice to the greater values of defending the nation and preserving democracy. In the midst of actual war, these films depicted the brutality of combat with unprecedented directness. For instance, in *The World War II Combat Film*, Jeanine Basinger asserts the following about the beheading death of an African American at the hands of a sword-wielding Japanese soldier near the close of Tay Garnett's 1943 *Bataan*: "although we do not actually see the head fall, or blood spurt out, this is one of the most graphic and violent killings of the pre-sixties period of film history. Involving us as it does in the swift action, the effect, even today, is breathtaking. This death finishes out the bad news for minority figures in the film—for them are reserved the most brutish deaths."[47] Deaths, it should be added, that are consistently sacrificial—that is, serving as an underlying modality or logic through which violence occurs, narrative is comprehended, and the values of the larger society are affirmed.[48]

Anthropologists and social theorists have taken pains to posit sacrifice as a social form and ritual function.[49] Probably the most far-reaching exploration is articulated in the work of anthropologist and literary theorist René Girard on ritual sacrifice. Girard claims that the social function of sacrifice begins with the desiring of a single object by two individuals, self and other, who, in recognizing their shared desire, become doubles to each other. The more the self comprehends this doubling, or mimetic, process, the more the object loses significance and the rivalry with the other intensifies; the rivalry tends toward violent conflict and the individual differences of self and other disappear. Finally, both look elsewhere for redress, to a marginal member of the community, a scapegoat, who absorbs the violence of the rivalry and is expelled, thereby restoring the community of self and other.[50] Violence here is not produced by a need to release aggression but by a social imperative to overcome competition, discover kinship by confirming otherness, and affirm hierarchies (of central versus marginal individuals). From Westerns and melodramas to war films and courtroom dramas, such a mode of organizing experience and cultural forms has proven central to popular narratives, especially during the classical Hollywood period. One writer, James B. Twitchell, goes so far in considering the sacrificial thesis to assert "that the rise of entertainment violence in popular culture has co-opted much of the force of religion and jurisprudence. Mass media carry much the same ritualized content through culture."[51]

Like many writers on the cultural significance of Hollywood violence—from Jacobs and Warshow to Rogin and Slotkin—Twitchell, a literary scholar, is not a specialist in film. Neither is Jake Horsley, "an independent scholar and world traveler" whose recent two-volume overview of the U.S. "cinema of savagery, 1958–1999," ranges broadly over traditional disciplines.[52] Their studies, while varied and sometimes addressing cases of scandal and censorship described above, mostly rely on the reading of national myths, symbols, and ideologies in given productions and genres. Thus film characters and narratives are seen as popular representations of individualism, the melting pot community, the frontier, the modern city, and democracy, as well as racism, corporate capitalism, and the subordination of otherness. As violent images give shape to narratives and help draw individual characters, these acts of bloodletting come to epitomize, punctuate, revise, or subvert the underlying mythologies and symbolism. The result is a privileging of narrative tendencies in individual films and their relation to deeply held cultural standards and values.

Representational and Epistemological Analyses

A final group of critical writings has brought attention to some of the fundamental norms and practices by which mainstream cinema has been imbricated in an identifiable set of power relations. Most of these have appeared over the three decades in which film studies has been institutionalized in British and American universities. The resulting theoretical studies of narrative and spectacle, of spectatorship and reception, and of representational and epistemological issues have posited the thoroughgoing violence of American filmmaking. Debates still ongoing among feminist film theorists have conceptualized the violence against women immanent in classical Hollywood and conventional narrative cinema.

Much of the feminist film theory that developed rapidly in the 1970s had strong psychoanalytic bases. Classical narrative cinema was seen to repetitively restage the Oedipal drama from the masculine side, following the hero through his difficult separation from the mother to his eventual and triumphal identification with paternal authority. In her seminal work, most notably the essay "Visual Pleasure and Narrative Cinema," Laura Mulvey emphasized the problem of the female erotic in classical Hollywood: female viewers are presented with a choice of identifying with either a male protagonist or a secondary female character who, in Freudian terms, is defined by lack (or castration). The choice for female viewers is therefore between the sadism of a patriarchal figure that subordinates women or the masochism inherent in women subordinated to patriarchy. Moreover, classical cinema not only emphatically defined gender but did

14

so through spectacles of physical and emotional violence. As Mulvey wrote of the melodrama, "There is a dizzy satisfaction in witnessing the way that sexual difference under patriarchy is fraught, explosive, and erupts into violence in its own private stomping ground, the family."[53] Violence for Mulvey is grounded in sexual difference manifested both in film narratives and the viewing process.[54]

Some theorists responded by questioning essential gender categories and their implications for Mulvey's spectatorial model. In the horror film, for instance, where one might expect to find spectatorial identifications unfavorable to women (and corresponding to the consistently ghastly images of violence against women on-screen), Barbara Creed, Carol J. Clover, and others argued for more ambiguous and fluid models. Women viewers here can identify with the monster's gaze, or their point of view could be more changeable.[55] Other responses to Mulvey included finding instances of femininity rubbing against the patriarchal grain of classical practice, emphasizing the powerful role of women in the narrative development of classical cinema, and reintroducing the Marxian notion of a cinematic apparatus as a less gender-specific means for understanding spectatorship. Running through much feminist film criticism, however, was the presumption that beyond the cumulative exclusions and oppression imaged in mainstream narrative films, the greater potential aggression of these productions was to be located in the psychodynamics and viewing positions they propagated. Violence remained a means through which cinema subordinated women viewing.[56]

In the late 1980s Gaylyn Studlar mounted an original critique of Mulvey and other Freudian theoretical writings. Her writings built on the work of Gilles Deleuze, who had moved beyond the strict division of male and female in Freud's Oedipally dominated and father-centered theory, as well as the distinction between sadism and masochism. Deleuze instead shifted the locus of masochism to the infant's relationship with the mother in the pre-Oedipal stage of development. For Studlar, cinema creates a relationship between spectator and screen that draws upon and acts out the experience of infants relating to their mothers and to fantasy. Such relationships rely precisely on a separation of the individual from the cinematic or dream screen; furthermore, the recognition that that separation, and the ongoing desire to overcome individuation despite that recognition, is masochistic. The cinematic observer is doubly implicated in this mechanism. Studlar asserts that the pleasures of narrative film involve both secondary and primary identifications, in which the spectator is seduced by both the given "conflict and narrative predicament" and by the cinematic apparatus itself, which replays the desires and ambivalences of the pre-Oedipal stage. In this way, her theory potentially brings together the violence of specific film images or "external reality" with the perverse psychic pleasures of masochistic desire.[57]

Studlar's formulations are far-reaching in part because they are not limited to male or female spectators, as in theories with Oedipal presuppositions. The very nature and practices of the cinematic medium, she suggests, convey violence. Like the inherently assaultive and violative operation of film editing noted earlier, the psychic effects of the process of film viewing can be more striking and extensive than those derived from the actions or narrative being dramatized.

The camera itself has been likened to a gun with the power to destroy. It is the parallel at the heart of Stanley Cavell's notes on *The Rules of the Game* that he used to enlarge his revised edition of *The World Viewed*: when the society in Renoir's film succumbs to the accidents or inevitabilities of the gun, cinema reasserts its own powers to reorder the social action with the camera. Jim Hoberman incisively sees *Bonnie and Clyde*'s climactic ambush, in which the heroic couple suffers a bloody if stylized end, as an analogy of the camera's repetitive, disfiguring effect on actors and bodies—particularly resonant for the youth culture of the mid-1960s, as those bodies belonged to stars Warren Beatty and Faye Dunaway. Though not so straightforwardly developed, Deleuze evokes in theoretical writings about "lines of flight" a similar parallel between lines of perspective and bullets' tracking lines in gun films. The metaphor of the camera-gun can be traced back to the riflelike camera device developed by Etienne Jules-Marey in the early 1880s, so these assertions are relevant not only to recent special-effects films like *Eraser* and *The Matrix*, in which the bullets' lines of flight are central to the visualization of action, but also to the potentially signal role of guns in a fuller theorization of the visual experience of certain long-standing cinematic genres.[58]

This correspondence between camera and gun brings to mind discussions of cinema and war. Perhaps the first writer to cite connections between the shifting martial and perceptual experiences of war was Ernst Jünger, whose direct experiences of the First World War led him to glorify the experience of battle and view men as technologized by their bodies' empowerment by and susceptibility to modern military equipment.[59] More directly relevant here are arguments regarding the changing nature of military perception, especially as it is mediated or replicated by photography and film. Bernd Hüppauf has written of modern warfare's replacement of "a gaze of understanding and empathy with a growing sense of the tensions, and twisted connections, between the foreign and the familiar." Increasingly impersonal technologies and the distanced gaze through which one sees images of destruction empty those very images of meaning; in the process, the viewer becomes less active, simply another abstract component of the media landscape.[60] Paul Virilio similarly argues that "the history of battle is primarily the history of radically changing fields of perception" and he focuses on the contemporaneous innovations of First World War military technologies and early cinema.[61] These writers variously raise the spectre of fascism as an aesthetic and ideology basic to modern modes of perception, including those underlying cinema, that are capable of voiding conventional meaning from images of violence, and of dissolving individual identity in the fetishization of history and community.[62]

Related is a separate tradition, developed most acutely during the 1960s and 1970s by Third Cinema filmmakers and theorists, that characterizes a certain mode of cinematic practice and production as itself violent within underdeveloped societies. One of the most famous ideological formulations of new Latin American cinema, for instance, by Glauber Rocha, claims that the originality of this generation of filmmakers is their "hunger" and that "the most noble cultural manifestation of hunger is violence."[63] Violence here is not primitive but revolutionary, a natural response of the people when they become aware of their colonization and oppression. Adapting the ideas of Frantz Fanon, Rocha and others saw revolutionary film practices and representations as authentic and empowering expressions of resistance. Filmmakers thus became allied with revolutionary movements, and violence in this cinema affirmed the potentially transformative violence of the people seeking to overthrow the yoke of their colonial oppression.

U.S. films of more traditional kinds of war have also served as the basis for several recent film historians' efforts to integrate consideration of such theoretical concerns with other institutional and cultural analyses. When Tom Doherty opens his study of American film culture during the Second World War with a discussion of Leni Riefenstahl's "contributions" to the U.S. war effort, the claim is not simply that Hollywood filmmakers and their wartime partners in government learned formal strategies for creating propaganda from the renowned Nazi director. Rather, the point is that cinematic forms are inextricably linked to shifting regimes of perception and representation as well as to institutional prerogatives and cultural mythologies.[64] That those regimes, so strongly shaped by classical Hollywood, pervaded wartime experience is the subject of Dana Polan's *Power and Paranoia*. By examining the narratives of fiction films and social life during the 1940s, Polan describes the actual physical brutality of the battlefront and the manifestations of psychic violence pulsing on the home front both during and after the war.[65]

Other writers have sought to establish similar connections for historical moments and types of film. Research on the Cold War era, the 1960s and 1970s, and the 1980s has provoked much discussion about how film narratives and representations of violence illuminate (and occlude) relations between the overt aggressions of war or protest and the less obvious brutalities of ordinary persons and everyday life.[66] Thus during the postwar years, family melodrama and film noir ("blood melodrama," in Graham Greene's memorable phrase) depicted physical cruelties heretofore unseen in mainstream films only to suggest even greater emotional savageries and cultural contradictions. Excessive production values, extreme cinematography and lighting, abrupt, often stylized editing, existential and antiheroic protagonists, and fractured narratives created fictional worlds of loss, decay, nostalgia, uncertainty, and paranoia in which the more graphic images of violence seemed fitting.

Running through these periods and filmmaking strategies is the presumption of norms against which innovations or extreme variations define themselves, press, or transgress. Narrative norms, such as those of studio Hollywood adumbrated above, are among the most important because the structure, development, and coherence of classical narrative is perceived as a standard means through which dominant ideology perpetuates itself and recapitulates its guiding myths. The employment of narrative in mainstream cinema strongly inscribes and codes representations of violence, creating, as outlined above, ideological and formal frameworks for spectacles of destruction and death. When depictions of violence fall outside, run counter to, or exceed those normative frameworks, the acts mount both cultural and representational challenges. Much critical writing on film noir, for instance, couples the convoluted plots, frequent flashbacks and play with temporal ordering, and uncertain, often unredemptive closures with the altered gender roles, expanded and depersonalized consumer society, and repressive and reactionary politics of the postwar years.[67] As Paul Arthur's contribution to this volume surveys, the brutish acts featured in many of these films accordingly become markers and symptoms of these layered challenges to previous, culturally inflected narrative norms.

Generic norms, too, are subject to revision and subversion. Indeed, genres require ongoing revision to remain culturally relevant; it is precisely the tension between variations and normative structures that enables genres to exist and evolve. The question is, to what degree do individual films or periods alter the norms that are perceived to constitute a given genre. Writing in 1978, at the end of more than a decade of far-reaching revisions, John Cawelti observed that the significance of genres persists even when the cultural myths underlying them are inverted, nostalgically, or revealed as inherently inadequate and destructive. Cawelti concludes, in fact, that even when films express a "dark awareness" that inverting meanings of oppositions between criminals and society or family is a "mythical simplification," as happens in *Bonnie and Clyde* and *The Godfather*, they nevertheless reconfigure and extend their respective genres.[68] In both films, violence is centrally involved in this complex generic transformation. Illustrative are the symbolic invocations of genre offered in the balancing of family life and business at Connie Corleone's wedding, the reversal of traditional roles evident in the lighthearted treatment of the Barrow gang's destructive encounters with the law, and the self-consciously ritualized narrative closure afforded by the series of violent spectacles intercut with Michael Corleone's becoming his nephew's godfather. If genres are assemblages of cultural forms dependent upon longstanding cultural myths and reshaped by historical imperatives, these productions from the tumultuous 1960s and 1970s, like the Westerns that Lee Clark Mitchell incisively examines here, suggest that violence both marks prevailing coherencies and punctuates changes.[69]

Particularly when rendered through aggressive action, the violation of narrative or generic norms confronts viewers with both terror and a stimulating sense of possibility, even transcendence. Such an aesthetic strategy was most clearly articulated and practiced by Antonin Artaud in his "theater of cruelty," which sought to tear off masks of social convention in order to reveal the baseness and darkness beneath—thereby allowing viewers to engage these forces in the controlled setting of the theater.[70] Sporadically, that strategy has been deemed applicable to cinema. In 1971 a slight scholarly piece on the topic appeared in *Cinema Journal*. Four years later, Francois Truffaut collected pieces by his favorite critic, André Bazin, on the work of seven directors—Von Stroheim, Dreyer, Hitchcock,

Sturges, Buñuel, Hitchcock, and Kurosawa—and entitled it *The Cinema of Cruelty*. The contention is that these directors couple their narrative attention to sexual obsession and sadism with original, even radical formal revisions; the consequence is that viewers are at once made uneasy and enthralled. In the 1980s Will Rocket employed the notion of a "cinema of cruelty" to examine the formal and emotional effects of horror films rather than revisit more prevalent cultural and ideological interpretations.[71]

To read film violence and viewers' responses against specific cinematic and historical contexts is partly an exercise in cultural and ideological criticism. However, it also touches on some of the fundamental properties of cinema—the bond between viewers and on-screen representations, the truth claims made by the film text, and the standard of realism proposed to exist between on-screen representations and the actual world. On the one hand, such matters are more straightforwardly the province of documentary studies and attempts there to comprehend the codes and strategies by which texts establish truth claims and afford viewers privileged access to observable reality. On another, the study of how "fiction" and metaphor may make truth claims is the project of philosophers of language. This area of study is crucial to a fuller understanding of narrative film, for just as we believe that truths exist in Homer and Shakespeare and Dickens, it is relevant to Hollywood movies.[72] Yet throughout, these epistemological issues are precisely those that can enrich our understanding of films as different as *Psycho* and the Zapruder film and enable us to appreciate how central representations of violence can be to the medium of cinema.

Contemporary Orientations[73]

Over the last two decades, and especially during the 1990s, writers on film have reoriented the critical frameworks and revised the categories by which cinema generally and film violence specifically can be interrogated and understood. Much of this work has taken place under the rubric of postmodern criticism and theorizing. Some have self-consciously sought to develop new methodologies and approaches to violence in media-dominated culture. Others have claimed only to be addressing, in largely conventional fashion, the shifting status of contemporary society and filmmaking practices. Much of this writing derives from a willingness to reexamine, question, and subvert the assumptions underlying conventional accounts of film violence. Nearly every one of the central concerns already outlined—from otherness and sacrifice to censorship, cultural specificity, and conceptions of violence itself—has been reconsidered. Collectively, the variety and quality of recent critical efforts constitute a second golden age, after that of the late 1960s and early 1970s, of film violence scholarship.

History is indeed central. Robert Sklar has observed that "the question of historical memory has become the touchstone of movies' cultural power, as myths and dreams had been in the Great Depression and World War II."[74] The event whose memory has elicited the greatest critical attention is also among history's most horrifically violent. Debates about Holocaust films, especially *Schindler's List*, have been wide-ranging, but many have dwelled on the signal issue of how or if to represent genocidal violence.[75]

Thus Spielberg's decision to take a camera into the gas chamber at Auschwitz becomes for some a limit-case for imaging violence on film. In her essay here, however, Terri Ginsberg asserts that much of the popular debate about that film relies on familiar assumptions of potentially redemptive and sacrificial violence operating both within Spielberg's narrative and among contemporary critics. The greater role of movies in shaping popular understandings of the past, she suggests, does not perforce alter traditional and entrenched modes of understanding history or violence. Consequently, the twofold challenge for critics becomes to recognize the historical claims made by contemporary films in their depiction of specific events—including violent ones, large and small—and to remain aware of the use of representational forms and reception practices that may be familiar.[76]

History also furnishes, through reference to earlier films or cultural formations, a backdrop for the explication of recent movies. That backdrop tends to highlight or even to rest exclusively in the late 1960s and early 1970s. Paralleling the counterculture's challenges to traditional social standards and values, Hollywood created scenes of increasing violence that culminated in three films that epitomize for many the era's imagining of individual and social violence: *Bonnie and Clyde*, *The Wild Bunch*, and *A Clockwork Orange*. While other films are sometimes added, with *Psycho* (1960) and *Taxi Driver* (1976) adduced most frequently as beginning and endpoint, it is the central trilogy that carries most of the cultural freight for the period. As Marsha Kinder demonstrates in her splendid overview of the 1960s through the 1990s, these works remain central to our cultural imagination of violence and merit continued study as precursors to the graphic productions of our own time.[77] Others, though, while granting important similarities or precedents, emphasize a discontinuity between contemporary cinematic bloodletting and that of earlier productions. For critics like Christopher Sharrett, the achievement of filmmakers three decades ago was to subvert classical forms and demythologize popular cinema so that, in today's media productions, increasingly, traditional modes of structuring and comprehending brutish action, like that of sacrificial violence, no longer hold sway.[78] The question becomes to what extent contemporary films constitute a legacy of the past, especially the late 1960s and early 1970s, and to what extent a radical shift from that past.[79]

The answer, necessarily given in degrees, turns on one's position vis-à-vis postmodern culture. This new cultural condition, which results from the transition from an industrial order based on the production of goods to a social order based in communication and the circulation of signs, is increasingly dominated by those signs and images, which, moreover, themselves become a key reality for citizens. That transition is the nub, and, in cinema, it can be identified in a number of ways. One is in the transformation that took place in production practices and technologies between the industrial mass production of the studio era and the more flexible forms of independent production characteristic of New Hollywood and, perhaps again more recently, the conglomeration of media and information industries.[80] Another, more familiar, way is in the changes in films themselves. Some accounts have claimed the rise of an ideologically conservative and coherent cinema in response to New Hollywood's questioning of social institutions and of cinematic norms: the "post-modern American film," contends Robert Kolker, "has done its best to erase the traces of sixties and seventies experimentation."[81] A final transition involves the collapse of traditional cultural or aesthetic hierarchies and the concomitant exhaustion of given cinematic forms or modes of production. Exemplified by their use of intertextual references and pastiche, contemporary films appropriate styles and references freely from throughout film and media history, producing historically "depthless" movies whose simulation of and nostalgia for the past are based in existing representations rather than any attempt to re-create a "real" past.[82]

Accordingly, violence in postmodern cinema arguably loses depth and any meaning accrued through traditional relations to the real world. Even the most graphic instance of violence in these films potentially becomes like any other image, homogenized and emptied of meaning or seeming originality. National myths or cultural codes of representation are eroded, and other substantive meanings largely evacuated, leaving only the images themselves. For, indeed, as films become largely self-referential commodities, the concern is that they are increasingly intended for the spectator's consumption—regardless of "content." Attempts to critique this process, like Oliver Stone's excessive use of media pastiche in *Natural Born Killers* or Errol Morris's elevation of formal "documentary" qualities as subject for inquiry in *The Thin Blue Line*, largely fail as these texts, too, are emptied of meaning by the very familiarity and repetition of the forms they employ. More routine examples of violence in contemporary horror and action films merely rework and recirculate self-consciously spectacular images that tend to affirm, in their familiarity, the conservative status quo. Where theorists disagree is how far the claims of postmodern culture extend, and how thoroughly they can be applied to the diversity of today's filmmaking practices and the range of often contestatory and ambivalent contemporary film violence.

One critique of postmodern theorists is, in fact, that in the process of skeptically tracking the decline of traditional myths, the emptying of meaning from signs, and the collapse of traditional aesthetic boundaries, they erect a new overarching myth or alternative grand narrative of crisis and exhaustion. More illuminating for some have been local efforts to question the conventional cultural processes and politics of naming, category-building, and inclusion and exclusion. Looking at "censorship" in this way expands its meaning from a restrictive practice to a constitutive one, not only demarcating the socially acceptable and forbidden but determining what might be subject to such demarcation. Debates surrounding the gangster films of the early 1930s thus mark criminal violence as the subject of potential regulation while excluding consideration of other forms of violence, like the aggressive treatment of women on-screen or the structural violence of Depression-era economic oppression.[83] Genre can be seen to operate similarly: as Steve Neale argues, part of the generic project—that is, the ongoing refiguration of genres across time through multiple films—is the control and aggressive delimitation of forms that might be negotiated in some historical moments and marginalized in others.[84] Especially relevant to a discussion of violence and American cinema is an interrogation of the meaning of a national mode of film production or a cinema meaningfully separate from other media interests in today's increasingly globalized and technologized culture. While "Hollywood" representations are still widely circulated and influential, it remains necessary to question how and why these distinctions continue to be drawn.[85]

The reliance on Hollywood and other national cinemas in film and media studies has generated sophisticated inquiries into the politics of space and place, what recently has been termed "geopoetics." Writers from a Marxist tradition, like Fredric Jameson, have thus explored globalization and the complex negotiation between transnational economic, ideological, and cultural imperatives and local conditions. Elizabeth Goldberg's essay here exemplifies this mode of analyzing violence: even as U.S. productions purport to provide exposure to humanitarian and political abuses in Burma and South Africa, she asserts, they continue to privilege white Western protagonists and to mark non-Western locals, often through scenes of torture, as expendable and anonymous subjects. These explicit images come to code the violence of these places—and finally the places themselves—as a manifestation of far-reaching and persistent ideological conflicts.[86]

Investigations of the sacrificial rituals underlying so much popular cultural production have similarly resituated that mode of defining and explaining violence. Closely reading René Girard's theories, commentators have questioned the structural process of ritual sacrifice, especially in terms of contemporary models of identity and culture. Is, for example, the straightforward antagonism of self and other possible for individuals whose identities are contingent on and shaped largely by media? Can the psychic consequences of the mimetic process be construed as sadistic or masochistic and, if so, how might these desires affect the individual's social interactions? And how does Girard's notion of social ritual, in which violence is mounted collectively against a marginalized member in order to reaffirm collective bonds, relate to modern societies, much less to postmodern consumer societies in which community, consensus, and kinship arguably mean little?[87] The issue posed by rethinking Girard's work is not whether contemporary culture continues to feature sacrifice and scapegoating. Clearly, the straightforward structural employment of these forms and processes seems insistent and undeniable. The issue, rather, is whether ubiquitous media representations of bloodletting remain connected to shared myths that still shape and define the society and the viewer's place in it—or whether the myths have been destroyed, individuals diminished, and the society depoliticized, leaving popular narratives of sacrifice without conventional ritual meaning and defined only by their value as commodities.

Potentially more applicable to contemporary society is Georges Bataille's notion of sacrifice. His writings, in fact, range widely across different kinds of societies, including the bourgeois, and dwell on the dynamics of economies, broadly conceived, and of excess and expenditure in those societies. For Bataille, human sacrifice "restores to the sacred world that which servile use has degraded, rendered profane." Yet, unlike Girard, he believes that the sacred "is only a privileged moment of communal unity, a convulsive form of what is ordinarily stifled."[88] Sacrifice becomes a site of transgression, a way of introducing disequilibrium into a society of consumption; it is, for Bataille, a disruptive release of excess or irrationality in an ordered economy. In such a society, where conventional mythic sacrifice can no longer generate consensus or have shared meaning, bloody acts involving the body still retain some, brief ability to transgress the utilitarian role assumed by the individual and to introduce heterogeneity into social life.

This emphasis on the body epitomizes a recurrent strain of contemporary cultural theory with special resonance to film. What might be termed "body criticism" has explored the complex ways ideologies inscribe individual bodies and, in the process, define and delimit them. In his studies of insanity and the prison, Foucault believed that the physical body was the most determinative—even as it had been the most neglected—element in the making of history.[89] Feminist film theorists and critics of gay and lesbian film have embraced this approach as a means of explicating ideologically imposed definitions of gender and sexuality.[90] In *The Body in Pain*, Elaine Scarry takes a broader view, meditating on the bodily effects of war and torture, and examining, especially, "the unmaking of the world" that takes place when extreme pain deprives one of voice and expression.[91] Mark Winokur has briefly applied Scarry's ideas to his analysis of silent film comedy and produced an innovative account of Charlie Chaplin's use of torture to express freedom to early-twentieth-century audiences.[92] Elizabeth Goldberg's essay here, on more nearly contemporary films, first approaches torture through reference to Scarry's work.

Running through many of these body studies is the discourse of trauma. The writings of Mark Seltzer and Kirby Farrell address the putative shift to a new cultural formation (which Seltzer labels "wound culture") defined by technology and media; a signal consequence of this shift is the breakdown of traditional notions of personal identity and the increasing deployment of violent action in an attempt to differentiate self from other.[93] Because of its varied centrality to these many approaches to cultural and ideological inscription, the body has emerged as a potentially important component of the study of film violence.[94] Illustrative from cinema studies is Janet Walker's writing on the "textual trauma" complict in representations of incest in *King's Row* and *Freud*.[95]

It also returns us, in a way, to the beginnings of cinema and the initial, visceral reactions of theatergoers to early, often violent attractions. The foregoing sketch of contemporary critical orientations to film violence has been almost entirely critical and scholarly, holding up violent films as artifacts embodying cultural and ideological meanings. Amid recent violent productions and the proliferation of theoretical analyses (and bloody events in the actual world that implicate film violence), policy debates and behavioral studies nevertheless continue. Following the Columbine tragedy, for instance, the U.S. Senate Commerce Committee convened to hear testimony from media experts, including Henry Jenkins, on the possible effects of media on the two adolescent perpetrators. Cited at these hearings were some of the ongoing studies of the behavioral influence of media; while the focus of this work moves increasingly toward the violence in new media like video games and the Internet, the putative effects of television and film viewing continue to be researched.[96] Other perceptive efforts to comprehend film violence, to assess viewer responses, to describe its centrality to popular culture, and to explain its allure to nonscholarly audiences likewise continue to appear.[97] And even this expansive survey largely ignores the many historical, psychological, political, and philosophical studies of violence occurring in the actual world that could deepen our understanding of film violence.

As William Rothman observes in the opening essay of this book, the United States is not as violent a place as it once was. Can that be said of its mainstream cinemas and the narratives and spectacles of violence featured in it? Despite a surfeit of recent critical work on "new" film violence, we have not yet done enough work to enable us to make such a statement about violence—old or new—in Hollywood movies. This volume is a first step in that direction.

Notes

1. For one illustrative treatment of "new violence," see Michael Stein, "The New Violence, or Twenty Years of Violence in Films: An Appreciation," *Films in Review* 46, nos. 1–2 (January–February 1995): 40–48 (Part 1), and *Films in Review* 46, nos. 3–4 (March–April 1995): 14–21 (Part 2). Two collections that gather a variety of public comments and sometimes expanded discussions of the issue by film critics are, respectively, Karl French, ed., *Screen Violence* (London: Bloomsbury, 1996), which includes an exchange between Oliver Stone and novelist John Grisham; and Peter Keough, ed., *Flesh and Blood: The National Society of Film Critics on Sex, Violence, and Censorship* (San Francisco: Mercury House, 1995).

2. Following Bob Dole's attack on the entertainment industry, *Time* magazine published an ominously titled cover story, "Are Music and Movies Killing America's Soul?" *Time*, June 12, 1995, 24–39. The battle over standards within media conglomerate Time-Warner was one of the secondary stories, and devoted as much space to addressing violence in gangsta rap songs, music videos, and "real" lives of musicians like Tupac Shakur as in motion pictures. A book-length lament for the corruption of traditional values by media that received sustained popular attention during this time was Michael Medved, *Hollywood vs. America: Popular Culture and the War on Traditional Values* (New York: Harper Collins, 1992).

3. See, for example, Michael Gilsenan, *Lords of the Lebanese Marches: Violence and Narrative in an Arab Society* (London: I. B. Tawris, 1996); Ronald Bogue and Marcel Cornis-Pope, eds., *Violence and Mediation in Contemporary Culture* (Albany, N.Y.: SUNY Press, 1996); Jana Hewlett and Rod Mengham, eds., *The Violent Muse: Violence and the Artistic Imagination, 1910–1939* (New York: St. Martin's Press, 1994); Sara Louise Knox, *Murder: A Tale of Modern American Life* (Durham, N.C.: Duke University Press, 1998); Maria M. Tatar, *Lustmord: Sexual Murder in Weimar Germany* (Princeton, N.J.: Princeton University Press, 1995); and Hent de Vries and Samuel Weber, eds., *Violence, Identity, and Self-Determination* (Stanford, Calif.: Stanford University Press, 1997).

    Also relevant here is the massive three-volume encyclopedia on violence in America published in late 1999. The fifteen-hundred-page work contains nine separate entries on film by leading scholars: "Film: Overview," "Landmark Films," "Film Violence and Censorship," "Documentary Film and Violence," "Violent Genres," "Directors," "Animation," "Aesthetics of Violence," and "Representations of Gender, Race, and Ethnicity." Ronald Gottesman and Richard M. Brown, eds., *Violence in America* (New York: Charles Scribners Sons, 1999).

4. For his original definition of the state in terms of its monopoly on the legitimate use of force, see Max Weber, *The Theory of Social and Economic Organization* (New York: The Free Press, 1947). Much work on the relationship between the state and violence has followed, in the field of sociology especially, involving research into war, revolution, and the military.

5. Sergio Cotta, *Why Violence? A Philosophical Interpretation*, trans. Giovanni Gullace (Gainesville: University of Florida Press, 1985).

6. Michel Foucault, *Discipline and Punish: The Birth of the Prison*, trans. Alan Sheridan (1975; reprint New York: Random House, 1977); and Foucault, *Madness and Civilization: A History of Madness in the Age of Reason*, trans. Richard Howard (1965; reprint New York: Vintage, 1988). This issue is also addressed in Nancy Armstrong and Leonard Tennenhouse, eds., *The Violence of Representation: Literature and the History of Violence* (New York: Routledge, 1989).

7. See Leo Charney and Vanessa R. Schwartz, eds., *Cinema and the Invention of Modern Life* (Berkeley: University of California Press, 1995); and Tom Gunning, "An Aesthetic of Astonishment: Early Film and the (In)credulous Spectator," *Art and Text* 34 (spring 1989); reprinted in *Viewing Positions: Ways of Seeing Film*, ed. Linda Williams (New Brunswick, N.J.: Rutgers University Press, 1995).

8. David Bordwell, Janet Staiger, Kristen Thompson, *Classical Hollywood Cinema: Film Style and Mode of Production to 1960* (New York: Columbia University Press, 1985); for the discussion of containment of nonconformity, see especially "The Bounds of Difference," 70–84.

9. For two excellent historical overviews of the regulation of popular cinema, see Richard Randall, *Censorship of the Movies* (Madison: University of Wisconsin Press, 1968); and, Edward de Grazia and Roger Kendall, *Banned Films: Movies, Censors, and the First Amendment* (New York: Bowker, 1982).

10. For an introduction to his research into the early boxing film, see Dan Streible, "A History of the Boxing Film, 1894–1915: Social Control and Social Reform in the Progressive Era," *Film History* 3, no. 3 (1989).

11. Holmes's work is cited by Richard Maltby in this volume, page 123, note 39. Henry James Forman, *Our Movie-Made Children* (New York: MacMillan, 1933); "Unmarked Slates" is the title of chapter 8, and "Movies in a Crowded Section" is the title of chapter 15.

　　For a recent examination of the Payne Fund Studies, see Garth S. Jowett, Ian C. Jarvie, and Kathryn H. Fuller, eds., *Children in the Movies: Media Influence and the Payne Fund Controversy* (New York: Cambridge University Press, 1996).

12. Jonathan Munby, *Public Enemies, Public Heroes: Screening the Gangster from Little Caesar to Touch of Evil* (Chicago: University of Chicago Press, 1999), 15. Also relevant here is David Ruth, *Inventing the Public Enemy: The Gangster in American Culture, 1918–1934* (Chicago: University of Chicago Press, 1996). For a more general work on studio-era censorship and regulation, see Matthew Bernstein, ed., *Controlling Hollywood: Censorship and Regulation in the Studio Era* (New Brunswick, N.J.: Rutgers University Press, 1999).

13. An excellent overview of the regulation of wartime film production is Clayton R. Koppes, "Regulating the Screen: The Office of War Information and the Production Code Administration," in *Boom and Bust: The American Cinema in the 1940s*, vol. 6 of *History of the American Cinema*, ed. Thomas

Schatz (New York: Charles Scribners Sons, 1997).

14. For a fascinating survey of this incremental increase in graphic images of bat-tlefront violence, see George H. Roeder Jr., *The Censored War: American Visual Experience during World War Two* (New Haven, Conn.: Yale University Press, 1993).

15. Subcommittee on Juvenile Delinquency, *Report of the Committee on the Judiciary, United States Senate* (Washington, D.C.: U.S. Government Printing Office, 1957), 9.

   To address the issue of motion picture effects on juveniles, the standard text on delinquency of the 1950s still relied heavily on one of the resulting volumes of the Payne Fund Studies. See Herbert Bloch and Frank Flynn, *Delinquency: The Juvenile Offender in America Today* (New York: Random House, 1956), 210–12; the Payne Fund reference is to Herbert Blumer and P. M. Hauser, *The Movies, Delinquency, and Crime* (New York: MacMillan, 1933).

16. For one account of the Kefauver hearings and public perception of juvenile delinquency in a broader cultural context, see Thomas Doherty, *Teenagers and Teenpics: The Juvenilization of American Movies in the 1950s* (Boston: Unwin and Hyman, 1988).

17. See, for instance, the juxtaposition between the "traditionalists" and the "new men" in Roger Manvell, *New Cinema in the USA: The Feature Film since 1945* (London: Studio Vista/Dutton, 1968).

18. For two illustrative pieces coauthored by the leading scholar in this area, see Leonard Berkowitz and Edna Rawlings, "Effects of Film Violence on Inhibitions against Subsequent Aggression," *Journal of Abnormal and Social Psychology* 66, no. 5 (1963): 405–12; and Leonard Berkowitz and Russell G. Geen, "Film Violence and the Cue Properties of Available Targets," *Journal of Personality and Social Psychology* 3, no. 5 (1966): 525–30.

19. Robert K. Baker and Sandra J. Ball, *Violence and the Media: A Staff Report to the National Commission on the Causes and Prevention of Violence* (Washington, D.C.: U.S. Government Printing Office, 1969).

20. For a summary of these disputes, see Charles Lyons, *The New Censors: Movies and the Culture Wars* (Philadelphia: Temple University Press, 1997).

21. Two exemplary studies from the 1980s are Guy Cumberhatch and Dennis Howitt, eds., *A Measure of Uncertainty: The Effects of the Mass Media* (London: John Libbey, 1989); and Edward Donnerstein and Daniel Linz, "Mass Media, Sexual Violence, and Male Viewers: Current Theory and Research," *American Behavioral Scientist* 29 (May–June 1986): 601–18.

22. *The Final Report of the Attorney General's Commission on Pornography* (Washington, D.C.: U.S. Government Printing Office, 1986), 1: 278–80. For a history of violence in the hard-core industry written at the time, see Joseph W. Slade, "Violence in the Hard-Core Pornographic Film: A Historical Survey," *Journal of Communication* 34, no. 3 (summer 1984): 148–63.

23. Stephen Prince, ed., *Screening Violence* (New Brunswick, N.J.: Rutgers University Press, 2000).

24. For examples of director- and actor-based studies that address screen vio-lence, see Lawrence S. Friedman, *The Cinema of Martin Scorsese* (New York: Continuum, 1997); Robert Sklar, *City Boys: Cagney, Bogart, Garfield* (Princeton, N.J.: Princeton University Press, 1992); Paul Smith, *Clint Eastwood: A Cultural Production* (Minneapolis: University of Minnesota Press, 1993); and Lesley Stern, *The Scorsese Connection* (London: BFI, 1995).

   Sam Peckinpah's preoccupation with violence makes writing about his films and career particularly relevant. See especially Michael Bliss, *Justified Lives: Morality and Narrative in the Films of Sam Peckinpah* (Carbondale: Southern Illinois University Press, 1993); Marshall Fine, *Bloody Sam: The Life and Films of Sam Peckinpah* (New York: Primus, 1991); Stephen Prince, *Savage Cinema: Sam Peckinpah and the Rise of Ultraviolent Movies* (Austin:

University of Texas Press, 1998); Paul Seydor, *Peckinpah: The Western Films*, rev. ed. (Chicago: University of Chicago Press, 1997); and David Weddle, *"If They Move . . . Kill 'Em!": The Life and Times of Sam Peckinpah* (New York: Grove Press, 1994).

The vast corpus of critical work on Alfred Hitchcock also consistently addresses film violence. For a sampling of relevant full-length studies, see Tania Modleski, *The Women Who Knew Too Much: Hitchcock and Feminist Theory* (New York: Methuen, 1988); William Rothman, *Hitchcock—The Murderous Gaze* (Cambridge, Mass.: Harvard University Press, 1982); and Robin Wood, *Hitchcock's Films Revisited* (New York: Columbia University Press, 1993). The critical literature on *Psycho* and the later films, especially, turn on the director's imaginings of violence.

Notable book-length readings of individual films that address violence include Michael Bliss, ed., *Doing It Right: The Best Criticism on Sam Peckinpah's* The Wild Bunch (Carbondale: Southern Illinois University Press, 1994); Nick Browne, ed., *Francis Ford Coppola's "The Godfather Trilogy"* (New York: Cambridge University Press, 1999); Lester Friedman, *Arthur Penn's* Bonnie and Clyde (New York: Cambridge University Press, 1999); Steven Kellman, ed., *Perspectives on* Raging Bull (New York: G. K. Hall, 1994); Robert Lang, ed., The Birth of a Nation*: D. W. Griffith, Director*, Rutgers Films in Print (New Brunswick, N.J.: Rutgers University Press, 1994); Dana B. Polan, *In a Lonely Place* (London: BFI Publishing, 1993); Stephen Prince, ed., *Sam Peckinpah's* The Wild Bunch (New York: Cambridge University Press, 1999); Camille Paglia, *The Birds* (London: BFI, 1999); and Sandra Wake and Micola Hayden, eds., *The* Bonnie and Clyde *Book* (London: Lorimer, 1972).

25. Lewis Jacobs, *The Rise of the American Film* (New York: Harcourt Brace, 1939).

26. Siegfried Kracauer, *From Caligari to Hitler: A Psychological History of the German Film* (New York: Noonday Press, 1947).

27. Examples of these studies are Parker Tyler, *The Hollywood Hallucination* (New York: Simon and Schuster, 1944); Tyler, *Myth and Magic of the Movies* (New York: Simon and Schuster, 1947); and Martha Wolfenstein and Nathan Leites, *Movies: A Psychological Study* (Glencoe, Ill.: The Free Press, 1950).

28. Hortense Powdermaker, *Hollywood: The Dream Factory* (Boston: Little, Brown, 1950), 14 and 325.

29. Robert Warshow, "Movie Chronicle: The Westerner," in *The Immediate Experience*, intro. by Lionel Trilling (New York: Anchor, 1964), 89 and 105. See also Warshow, "The Gangster as Tragic Hero," in *The Immediate Experience*, 83–88.

30. For a one-volume anthology of readings on the subject, see Bernard Rosenberg and David Manning White, eds., *Mass Culture: The Popular Arts in America* (Glencoe, Ill.: The Free Press, 1957). The best starting place for MacDonald's film writing is Dwight MacDonald, *MacDonald on Movies*, intro. by John Simon (New York: Da Capo Press, 1981).

31. Jacques Rivette, "Notes on a Revolution" (Christmas 1955), trans. Liz Heron, in *Cahiers du Cinéma: The 1950s: Neo-Realism, Hollywood, New Wave*, ed. Jim Hillier (Cambridge, Mass.: Harvard University Press, 1985), 95. Luc Moullet, "Sam Fuller: In Marlowe's Footsteps" (March 1959), trans. Norman King, in *Cahiers du Cinéma: The 1950s: Neo-Realism, Hollywood, New Wave*, 149. See also Michel Mourlet, "In Defence of Violence" (May 1960), trans. David Wilson, in *Cahiers du Cinéma: The 1960s: New Wave, New Cinema, Reevaluating Hollywood*, ed. Jim Hillier (Cambridge, Mass.: Harvard University Press, 1986). The original elaboration of film noir was Raymond Borde and Étienne Chaumeton, *Panorama du film noir américain* (Paris: Editions de Minuit, 1955). For one account of the French origins of the film

noir category, see Marc Vernet, "*Film Noir* on the Edge of Doom," in *Shades of Noir: A Reader*, ed. Joan Copjec (New York: Verso, 1993), 1–33.

The early 1960s also saw the stirrings of attention to film and media violence among British writers, who would later develop approaches to the subject in the fields of mass communications and cultural studies. For an early example, see Stuart Hall and Paddy Whannel, "Violence on the Screen," in *The Popular Arts* (New York: Pantheon, 1965).

32. Kael's piece "Movie Brutalists" and her review of *Bonnie and Clyde* were reprinted in the aptly named collection *Kiss Kiss Bang Bang* (Boston: Little, Brown, 1969).

33. Tellingly, the museum's screening series was renamed "The American Action Movie, 1946–1964," when one of the film distributors refused to accept "Violent America." That the two distinct titles refer to the same series of films reveals precisely the sort of slippage of meaning related to violent films that marked the period. See Lawrence Alloway, *Violent America: The Movies, 1946–1964* (New York: Museum of Modern Art, 1971).

34. Thomas Atkins, ed., *Graphic Violence on the Screen* (New York: Simon and Schuster, 1976).

35. John Fraser, *Violence in the Arts* (London: Cambridge University Press, 1974). The other notable British study of the time was Stephen Brody, *Screen Violence and Film Censorship: A Review of Research*, A Home Office Research Unit Report (London: Her Majesty's Stationery's Office, 1977).

36. Robert Sklar, *Movie-Made America: A Cultural History of American Movies*, rev. and updated ed. (New York: Vintage, 1994), 109. See also Garth Jowett, *Film: The Democratic Art* (Boston: Little, Brown, 1976).

37. Richard Slotkin, *Gunfighter Nation: The Myth of the Frontier in Twentieth-Century America* (New York: Athenaeum, 1992), 12 (emphasis in original).

38. Among the titles by these writers relevant here are Michael Rogin, *"Ronald Reagan," The Movie, and Other Episodes in Political Demonology* (Berkeley: University of California Press, 1987); Slotkin, *Gunfighter Nation*; Slotkin, *The Fatal Environment: The Myth of the Frontier in the Age of Industrialization, 1800–1890* (New York: Harper, 1985); and Slotkin, "Violence," in *The BFI Companion to the Western*, ed. Edward Buscombe (New York: Atheneum, 1988).

39. Robin Wood, "An Introduction to the American Horror Film," in *Planks of Reason: Essays on the Horror Film*, ed. Barry Keith Grant (Metuchen, N.J.: Scarecrow Press, 1984), 171.

40. Barry Keith Grant, "Introduction," in *The Dread of Difference: Gender and the Horror Film*, ed. Grant (Austin: University of Texas Press, 1996), 5.

41. For two extended treatments of gender in the horror genre, see Rhona Bernstein, *Attack of the Leading Ladies: Gender, Sexuality, and Spectatorship in Classic Horror Cinema* (New York: Columbia University Press, 1995); and Carol Clover, *Men, Women, and Chainsaws: Gender in the Modern Horror Film* (Princeton, N.J.: Princeton University Press, 1992).

42. Marsha Kinder, "Sacrifice and Massacre: On the Cultural Specificity of Violence," in *Blood Cinema: The Reconstruction of National Identity in Spain* (Berkeley: University of California Press, 1993).

43. Stephen Prince, *The Warrior's Camera: The Cinema of Akira Kurosawa*, rev. ed. (Princeton, N.J.: Princeton University Press, 1999).

44. Two excellent examples are Tony Williams, "Space, Place, and Spectacle: The Crisis Cinema of John Woo," *Cinema Journal* 36, no. 2 (winter 1997): 67–84; and Williams, "To Live and Die in Hong Kong," *CineAction* 36 (1995): 42–52. See also David Bordwell, *Planet Hong Kong: Popular Cinema and the Art of Entertainment* (Cambridge, Mass.: Harvard University Press, 2000); and Lisa Oldham Stokes and Michael Hoover, *City on Fire: Hong Kong Cinema* (London: Verso, 1999).

45. The "ritual" conception of a film genre's social function is discussed in Thomas Schatz, *Hollywood Genres* (New York: Random House, 1981).

46. Susan Mizruchi, *The Science of Sacrifice: American Literature and Modern Social Theory* (Princeton, N.J.: Princeton University Press, 1998), 23 and 369 (emphasis in original).

47. Jeanine Basinger, *The World War II Combat Film: Anatomy of a Genre* (New York: Columbia University Press, 1986), 58. For other useful introductions to Hollywood films of the Second World War, including the representations of conflict and violence within them, see Clayton R. Koppes, *Hollywood Goes to War: How Politics, Profits, and Propaganda Shaped World War Two Movies* (New York: The Free Press, 1987); and Bernard Dick, *The Star-Spangled Screen: The American World War Two Film* (Lexington: University Press of Kentucky, 1985).

48. Sacrificial violence arguably operated on the home front as well as the battle-front. See Mark H. Leff, "The Politics of Sacrifice on the American Home Front in World War II," *Journal of American History* 77 (March 1991): 1296–1318.

49. The writing of Victor Turner is particularly instructive in engaging violence in film. See, especially, *The Ritual Process: Structure and Anti-Structure* (Ithaca, N.Y.: Cornell University Press, 1977); and Turner, *Dramas, Fields, and Metaphors: Symbolic Action in Human Society* (Ithaca, N.Y.: Cornell University Press, 1974). For an interpretation of performance and social rit-ual using Turner's ideas, see Richard Schechner, *The Future of Ritual: Writings on Culture and Performance* (New York: Routledge, 1993). A useful summary of essays appears in David Riches, ed., *The Anthropology of Violence* (New York: Basil Blackwell, 1986); see especially Riches's introduction, "The Phenomenon of Violence," and Brian Moeran's piece, "The Beauty of Violence: *Jidaigeki, Yakuza,* and 'Eroduction' Films in Japanese Cinema."

50. The basic texts by René Girard are *"To Double Business Bound": Essays on Literature, Mimesis, and Anthropology* (Baltimore: Johns Hopkins University Press, 1978); Girard, *Deceit, Desire, and the Novel: Self and Other in Literary Structure,* trans. Yvonne Freccero (Baltimore: Johns Hopkins University Press, 1976); Girard, *Violence and the Sacred,* trans. Patrick Gregory (Baltimore: Johns Hopkins University Press, 1977); Girard, *The Scapegoat,* trans. Yvonne Freccero (Baltimore: Johns Hopkins University Press, 1986); and in Robert G. Hamerton-Kelly, ed., *Violent Origins: Walter Burkert, René Girard, and Jonathan Z. Smith on Ritual Killing and Cultural Formation,* intro. by Burton Mack, commentary by Renato Rosaldo (Stanford, Calif.: Stanford University Press, 1987).

For an example and overview, respectively, of Girard's applicability to cinema, see Andrew J. McKenna, "Public Execution," in *Legal Reelism: Movies as Legal Texts,* ed. John Denvir (Urbana and Chicago: University of Illinois Press, 1996); and Andrew J. McKenna, "The Law's Delay: Cinema and Sacrifice," *Legal Studies Forum* 15, no. 3 (1991): 199–215. A more var-ied and ambitious attempt to test the use of mimetic theory in film critique can be found in the collected papers from the 1997 Graz conference on film and modernity; see Gerhard Larcher, Franz Grabner, and Christian Wessely, *Beiträsse-Zum Symposium Film and Modernity: Violence, Sacrifice, and Religion, Graz 1997* (New Brunswick, N.J.: Transaction, 1998).

51. James B. Twitchell, *Preposterous Violence: Fables of Aggression in Modern Culture* (New York: Oxford University Press, 1989), 46.

Massacre is a less well formulated logic of violence that nevertheless illu-minates some postclassical Hollywood and non-U.S. cinema—and the soci-eties from which they emerged. Tzvetan Todorov has argued that massacre reveals a weakness or desuetude in the social fabric rather than performing a social function; instead of publicly confirming otherness, massacre takes place in secret, often remotely, and only vaguely acknowledges the moral law. His notion of a "massacrifice" society also perhaps merits more thoughtful con-sideration than it has received, especially when addressing recent cinema and contemporary society. This third term literally brings together the character-istics of the other two: victims are selected individually and killed close to home, but the killing is committed without ritual and ultimately denied by a society that professes a coherent moral law but permits everything. One can imagine certain New Hollywood or more recent films—the *Godfather* films, *Reservoir Dogs*, or *Pulp Fiction* come to mind—for which such a category might be illuminating. See Tzvetan Todorov, *The Conquest of America: The Question of the Other*, trans. Richard Howard (New York: Harper and Row, 1984), 144 and 253.

52. Jake Horsley, *The Blood Poets: A Cinema of Savagery, 1958–1999*, vol. 1, *American Chaos—From "Touch of Evil" to "The Terminator"*; and vol. 2, *Millennial Blues—From "Apocalypse Now" to "The Matrix"* (Lanham, Md.: Scarecrow Press, 1999).

53. Laura Mulvey, "Notes on Sirk and Melodrama," *Movie* 25 (winter 1977–78): 53.

54. For her seminal and much anthologized essay, which initially appeared in the British journal *Screen* in 1975, see Laura Mulvey, "Visual Pleasure and Narrative Cinema," in *Issues in Feminist Film Criticism*, ed. Patricia Erens (Bloomington: Indiana University Press, 1990).

55. See Barbara Creed, "Dark Desires: Male Masochism in the Horror Film," in *Screening the Male: Exploring Masculinities in Hollywood Cinema*, ed. Steven Cohan and Ina Rae Hark (New York: Routledge, 1993); Barbara Creed, "Horror and the Monstrous-Feminine: An Imaginary Abjection," in *The Dread of Difference*, ed. Barry Keith Grant; Creed, *The Monstrous Feminine: Film, Feminism, Psychoanalysis* (New York: Routledge, 1993); and Clover, *Men, Women, and Chainsaws*.

56. Useful anthologies of essays by feminist scholars and theoreticians include Diane Carson, Linda Dittmar, and Janice R. Welsch, eds., *Multiple Voices in Feminist Film Criticism* (Minneapolis: University of Minnesota Press, 1994); Mary Ann Doane, Patricia Mellencamp, and Linda Williams, eds., *Re-Visions: Essays in Feminist Film Criticism* (Frederick, Md.: University Publications of America, 1984); and Constance Penley, ed., *Feminism and Film Theory* (New York: Routledge, 1988).

57. Gaylyn Studlar, *In the Realm of Pleasure: Von Sternberg, Dietrich, and the Masochistic Aesthetic* (Urbana: University of Illinois Press, 1988), esp. 177–93. Studlar primarily works from Deleuze's reexamination of Leopold von Sacher-Masoch and Richard von Krafft-Ebbing; see Gilles Deleuze, *Masochism: An Interpretation of Coldness and Cruelty* (New York: Braziller, 1971).

58. J. Hoberman, "'A Test for the Individual Viewer': *Bonnie and Clyde's* Violent Reception," in *Why We Watch: The Attractions of Violent Entertainment*, ed. Jeffrey Goldstein (New York: Oxford University Press, 1998); Stanley Cavell, *The World Viewed: Reflections on the Ontology of Film*, enlarged ed. (Cambridge, Mass.: Harvard University Press, 1979); and Gilles Deleuze and Félix Guattari, *On the Line*, trans. John Johnston (New York: Semiotext(e), 1983), reprinted in Deleuze and Guattari, *Dialogues*, trans. Hugh Tomlinson and Barbara Habberjam (New York: Columbia University Press, 1987). For a more recent and less theoretical collection of papers, see Murray Pomerance and John Sakeris, eds., *Bang Bang, Shoot Shoot! Essays on Guns and Popular Culture* (New York: Simon and Schuster, 1998).

59. For a helpful introduction to Jünger's writings, see Andreas Huyssen, "Fortifying the Heart—Totally: Ernst Jünger's Armored Texts," *New German Critique* 59 (spring/summer 1993): 3–23.

60. Bernd Hüppauf, "Emptying the Gaze: Framing Violence through the Viewfinder," *New German Critique* 72 (fall 1997): 15. For related works, see Hüppauf, "Experiences of Modern Warfare and the Crisis of Representation," *New German Critique* 59 (spring/summer 1993): 41–76; and Hüppauf, ed., *War, Violence, and the Modern Condition* (New York: Walter de Gruyter, 1996).

61. Paul Virilio, *War and Cinema: The Logistics of Perception*, trans. Patrick Camiller (London: Verso, 1989), 7.

62. The classic if brief statement of these dynamics in cinema is Susan Sontag, "Fascinating Fascism" (1975), in *Movies and Methods*, vol. 1, ed. Bill Nichols (Berkeley: University of California Press, 1976). See also Georges Bataille, "The Psychological Structure of Fascism," in *Visions of Excess: Selected Writings, 1927–1939*, trans. Allan Stoekl, with Carl R. Lovitt and Donald M. Leslie Jr. (Minneapolis: University of Minnesota Press, 1985); and, more generally, Richard J. Golsan, ed., *Fascism, Aesthetics, and Culture* (Hanover, N.H.: University Press of New England, 1996).

63. Glauber Rocha, "An Esthetic of Hunger" (1965), in *Theory, Practices, and Transcontinental Articulations*, vol. 1 of *New Latin American Cinema*, ed. Michael T. Martin (Detroit: Wayne State University Press, 1997), 60.

64 . Thomas Doherty, *Projections of War: Hollywood, American Culture, and World War II* (New York: Columbia University Press, 1993).

65. Dana Polan, *Power and Paranoia: History, Narrative, and the American Cinema, 1940–1950* (New York: Columbia University Press, 1986).

66. See, for example, Robert Phillip Kolker, *A Cinema of Loneliness: Penn, Kubrick, Scorsese, Spielberg, Altman*, 2nd ed. (New York: Oxford University Press, 1988); and Robin Wood, *Hollywood from Vietnam to Reagan* (New York: Columbia University Press, 1986).

   Studies of films and the Vietnam War constitute a special category. For three works contributing to inquiries into cultural violence during the time, see Michael Anderegg, ed., *Inventing Vietnam: The War in Film and Television* (Philadelphia: Temple University Press, 1991); Linda Dittmar and Gene Michaud, *From Hanoi to Hollywood: The Vietnam War and American Film* (New Brunswick, N.J.: Rutgers University Press, 1990); and Susan Jeffords, *The Remasculinization of America: Gender and the Vietnam War* (Bloomington: Indiana University Press, 1989).

67. Among the expansive literature on noir, much of which engages issues of violence and narrativity, see, especially, E. Ann Kaplan, *Women and Film Noir*, expanded ed. (London: BFI, 1999); Frank Krutnik, *In a Lonely Street: Film Noir, Genre, Masculinity* (London: Routledge, 1991); James Naremore, *More than Night: Film Noir in Its Contexts* (Berkeley: University of California Press, 1998); J. P. Telotte, *Voices in the Dark: The Narrative Patterns of Film Noir* (Urbana: University of Illinois Press, 1989); Polan, *Power and Paranoia*; Richard Maltby, "Film Noir: The Politics of the Maladjusted Text," *Journal of American Studies* (April 1984): 59–71; and Robert G. Porfirio, "No Way Out: Existential Motifs in the Film Noir," *Sight and Sound* (fall 1976): 212–17.

   For a fascinating meditation on the complicity of narrative in viewer fixation on violence and destructiveness in visual culture generally—indeed, in image-based narratives ranging from Assyrian palace reliefs to cinema—see Leo Bersani and Ulysse Dutoit, *The Forms of Violence: Narrative in Assyrian Art and Modern Culture* (New York: Schocken Books, 1985); and, in film, Bersani and Dutoit, "Merde Alors," in *Pier Paolo Pasolini: The Poetics of Heresy*, ed. Beverly Allen (Saratoga, Calif.: Anma Libri, 1982).

68. John Cawelti, "*Chinatown* and Generic Transformation in Recent American Films" (1978), in *Film Theory and Criticism*, ed. Gerald Mast and Marshall Cohen, 3rd ed. (New York: Oxford University Press, 1985), 517.

69. For a summary of contemporary thinking about genre and generic criticism—including discussions of the war film, melodrama, film noir, and horror film—see Nick Browne, ed., *Refiguring Film Genres: Theory and History* (Berkeley: University of California Press, 1998); and Wheeler Winston Dixon, ed., *Film Genre 2000: New Critical Essays* (Albany: SUNY Press, 2000).

70. The "theater of cruelty" is elaborated in Antonin Artaud, *The Theater and Its Double*, trans. Mary Caroline Richards (New York: Grove Press, 1958).

71. William Blum, "Toward a Cinema of Cruelty," *Cinema Journal* 10, no. 2 (spring 1971): 19–33. André Bazin, *The Cinema of Cruelty: From Buñuel to Hitchcock*, ed. and intro. by François Truffaut, trans. Sabine d'Estrée (New York: Seaver Books, 1982). The study of horror films is Will H. Rockett, *Devouring Whirlwind: Terror and Transcendence in the Cinema of Cruelty* (Westport, Conn.: Greenwood Press, 1988). For a brief discussion linking Artaud's drama to Sam Peckinpah's filmmaking, see Prince, *Savage Cinema*, 111–12 and 166–69.

72. My thanks to Edward Branigan for suggesting mention of this point.

73. Portions of this closing section appeared in my review of Christopher Sharrett's *Mythologies of Violence in Postmodern Media*, in *Film Quarterly* 54, no. 1 (fall 2000).

74. Sklar, *Movie-Made America*, 358.

75. The standard reader on Spielberg's film is Yosefa Loshitzky, ed., *Spielberg's Holocaust: Critical Essays on "Schindler's List"* (Bloomington: Indiana University Press, 1997). A collection that speaks to broader issues of historical representation is Saul Friedlander, ed., *Probing the Limits of Representation: Nazism and the "Final Solution"* (Cambridge, Mass.: Harvard University Press, 1992).

76. Two introductions to discussions of the relationship between film and history are Robert Rosenstone, *Visions of the Past: The Challenge of Film to Our Idea of History* (Cambridge, Mass.: Harvard University Press, 1995); and Robert Brent Toplin, *History by Hollywood: The Use and Abuse of the American Past* (Urbana and Chicago: University of Illinois Press, 1996). See, especially, Toplin's essay, "*Bonnie and Clyde*: 'Violence of a Most Grisly Sort.'" See also two special journal issues on film and history: *American Historical Review* 93 (1988): 1173–1227, and the electronic *Screening the Past* 6 (uploaded April 1999), http://www.latrobe.edu.au/www/screeningthepast/.

77. Others have identified discursive or cultural shifts that took place during the 1960s or 1970s that remain pertinent and even predominant. An example is the transformation in the 1960s of the cultural status of documentary representations of death that arguably made *Bonnie and Clyde* more acceptable at the time and continues to shape our viewing of graphic images of death today.

    See, for example, Vivian Sobchack, "Inscribing Ethical Space: Ten Propositions on Death, Representation, and Documentary," *Quarterly Review of Film Studies* 9, no. 4 (fall 1984); Bernie Cook, "Beyond Good Taste: Shifting Audience Expectations and the Uses of Explicit Film Violence in the 1960s," paper presented at 24th Annual Conference on Film and Literature, Florida State University, January 29, 1999; and Tom Mullin, "Livin' and Dyin' in Zapruderville: A Code of Representation Reality and Its Exhaustion," *CineAction* 38 (September 1995): 12–15. Much of this excellent *CineAction* special issue, "Murder in America," is bracketed by the Zapruder film of Kennedy's assassination in 1963 and Oliver Stone's appropriation and manipulation of that image thirty years later in *JFK*.

78. Sharrett addresses this question directly, and at one point in his afterword to *Mythologies of Violence*, he writes: "Neither the postmodern condition that increasingly reduces the subject to spectator and consumer nor the destruction of human life in real experience and within the culture of representation necessarily suggests any epistemological or historical breaks when we look at the roots of current assumptions and representational practices in American history and ideology" (414). Unmistakeable throughout both his introduction and afterword, however, is the implication of profound exhaustion, disaffection, apocalypse, and crisis in his characterization of contemporary culture—that marks it as separate and distinct from that of the 1960s and 1970s. Christopher Sharrett, "Afterword: Sacrificial Violence and Postmodern Ideology," in *Mythologies of Violence in Postmodern Media*, ed. Sharrett (Detroit: Wayne State University Press, 1999).

79. Stephen Prince, in his outstanding study of Sam Peckinpah, effectively

embraces both possible answers. After providing a focused and thoughtful exegesis of the director's works, which he identifies as the origin of "ultraviolent" filmmaking, he concludes that the violence of more recent films is superficial—and a break from the ambitious precedents set by the director; see Prince, *Savage Cinema*.

80. Regarding changes in production, see Michael Storper and Susan Christopherson, "Flexible Specialization and Regional Industrial Agglomeration: The Case of the U.S. Motion Picture Industry," *Annals of the Association of American Geographers* 77, no. 1 (1987): 104–17. Cited in John Hill, "Film and Postmodernism," in *The Oxford Guide to Film Studies*, ed. John Hill and Pamela Church Gibson (New York: Oxford University Press, 1998).

81. Kolker, *A Cinema of Loneliness*, xi. See also Michael Ryan and Douglas Kellner, *Camera Politica: The Politics and Ideology of Contemporary Hollywood Film* (Bloomington: Indiana University Press, 1988).

82. See Fredric Jameson, *Postmodernism: Of the Cultural Logic of Late Capitalism* (London: Verso, 1991). Jameson discusses *Chinatown* and *Body Heat* as examples of the intertextual nostalgia film, thus identifying the postmodern, at least in part, with the practices of New Hollywood.

83. The best example of this approach in film studies is Annette Kuhn, *Cinema, Censorship, and Sexuality, 1909–1925* (New York: Routledge, 1988). For two general introductions to this approach to cultural regulation involving violence across media, see Colin Sumner, ed., *Violence, Culture, and Censure* (Bristol, Penn.: Taylor and Francis, 1997); and Robert C. Post, ed., *Censoring and Silencing: Practices of Cultural Regulation* (Los Angeles: The Getty Research Institute for Art and the Humanities, 1998). A more general statement of this expansive approach to censorship is found in Sue Curry Jansen, *Censorship: The Knot That Binds Power and Knowledge* (New York: Oxford University Press, 1988).

84. Steve Neale, *Genre and Hollywood* (New York and London: Routledge, 2000). For an illuminating essay on the violent transgression of the conventional boundary-making properties of narrative, see Peter Brunette, "The Three Stooges and the (Anti-)narrative of Violence," *Comedy/Cinema/Theory*, ed. Andrew Horton (Berkeley: University of California Press, 1991).

85. One wonders, for instance, why Hong Kong cinema has been embraced by mainstream viewers and its forms appropriated by filmmakers while other cinemas featuring violence, like those of the former Soviet Union, eastern Europe, and, increasingly, the Middle East, have remained largely ignored. The broader question is whether the continued critical emphases on nations and cinemas are themselves examples of a postmodern nostalgia for a mythic clarity regarding cultural practice.

86. For several provocative essays developing the notion of "geopoetics," see the special issue of *Critical Inquiry* 26, no. 2 (winter 2000). Two discussions of the significance of place, nation, and cinema in contemporary global culture are Fredric Jameson, *The Geopolitical Aesthetic: Cinema and Space in the World System* (London: BFI, 1992); and Patrick O'Donnell, "Engendering Paranoia in Contemporary Narrative," in *National Identities and Post-American Narratives*, ed. Donald Pease (Durham, N.C.: Duke University Press, 1994).

87. Two trenchant commentaries on Girard's work are Paul Dumouchel, ed., *Violence and Truth: On the Work of René Girard* (Stanford, Calif.: Stanford University Press, 1988); and Andrew J. McKenna, *Violence and Difference: Girard, Derrida, and Deconstruction* (Urbana: University of Illinois Press, 1992).

Chris Sharrett has offered a sophisticated reading of Girard in relation to film; see his afterword to *Mythologies of Violence in Postmodern Media*, esp. 423–32. For an exemplary textual reading, see Sharrett, "The American Apocalypse: Scorsese's *Taxi Driver*," in *Crisis Cinema: The Apocalyptic Idea in Postmodern Narrative Film*, ed. Sharrett (Washington, D.C.: Maisonneuve

Press, 1993).

88. Georges Bataille, *The Accursed Share*, vol. 1, trans. Robert Hurley (New York: Zone Books, 1988), 55; and Bataille, "The Sacred," in *Visions of Excess: Selected Writings, 1927–1939*, trans. Alan Stoekl (Minneapolis: University of Minnesota Press, 1986), 242. See also Bataille, *Erotism: Death and Sensuality*, trans. Mary Dalwood (1957; reprint San Francisco: City Lights, 1986).

89. His basic texts on the topic are *Discipline and Punish*; *Madness and Civilization*; and *The History of Sexuality, Vol. I: An Introduction*, trans. Robert Hurley (New York: Vintage, 1978). For an application of Foucault's notion of technologies of the body to cinema, see Ken Morrison, "The Technology of Homicide," *CineAction* 38 (September 1995): 16–24; reprinted in Sharrett, *Mythologies of Violence in Postmodern Media.*

90. For an early example of "body criticism" in film study, see Lesley Stern, "The Body as Evidence," *Screen* 23, no. 5 (1982): 38–60.

91. Elaine Scarry, *The Body in Pain: The Making and Unmaking of the World* (New York: Oxford University Press, 1986).

92. Mark Winokur, *American Laughter: Immigrants, Ethnicity, and 1930s Hollywood Film Comedy* (New York: St. Martin's Press, 1996), esp. 106–12.

93. Mark Seltzer, *Serial Killers: Death and Life in America's Wound Culture* (New York: Routledge, 1998); and Kirby Farrell, *Post-traumatic Culture: Injury and Interpretation in the Nineties* (Baltimore: Johns Hopkins University Press, 1998). Useful introductions to what has emerged as another scholarly sub-field, of text-based "trauma studies," are Paul Antze and Michael Lambek, eds., *Tense Past: Cultural Essays in Trauma and Memory* (New York: Routledge, 1996); Cathy Caruth, ed., *Trauma: Explorations in Memory* (Baltimore: Johns Hopkins University Press, 1995); Cathy Caruth, *Unclaimed Experience: Trauma, Narrative, and History* (Baltimore: Johns Hopkins University Press, 1996); and Geoffrey H. Hartman, "On Traumatic Knowledge and Literary Studies," *New Literary History* 26 (1995): 537–63.

94. The most thoroughly formulated approach to the body in film is Steven Shaviro, *The Cinematic Body* (Minneapolis: University of Minnesota Press, 1993).

95. Janet Walker, "Textual Trauma in *King's Row* and *Freud*," in *Endless Night: Cinema and Psychoanalysis, Parallel Histories*, ed. Janet Bergstrom (Berkeley: University of California Press, 1999).

96. Jenkins's testimony can be found on the Internet; see Henry Jenkins, "Congressional Testimony on Media Violence," May 4, 1999, http://media-in-transition.mit.edu/articles/dc.html (posted June 16, 1999). An example of contemporary research is Martin Barker and Julian Petley, eds., *Ill Effects: The Media/Violence Debate* (New York: Routledge, 1997). A specific treatment of film is Amanda E. Pennell and Kevin Browne, "Film Violence and Young Offenders," *Aggression and Violent Behavior* 4, no. 1 (1999): 13–28.

97. Sissela Bok, *Mayhem: Violence as Popular Entertainment* (Reading, Mass.: Addison-Wesley, 1998); Jeffrey Goldstein, *Why We Watch: The Attractions of Violent Entertainment* (New York: Oxford University Press, 1998); Annette Hill, *Shocking Entertainment: Viewer Response to Violent Movies* (Luton, England: University of Luton Press, 1997); and W. James Potter, *On Media Violence* (Thousand Oaks, Calif.: Sage, 1999).

Part One:

Historicizing Hollywood Violence

one   **violence and film**

william rothman

America is a less violent place than it used to be (say, five or ten or twenty-five or fifty or a hundred or two hundred years ago). But Americans *believe* that violence is escalating out of control, that it is threatening the moral fabric of our society, and that the proliferation of violence in the mass media, especially the graphic violence in today's movies, is a cause, and not only a symptom, of this threat.

During the Nixon administration, the United States Surgeon General issued a report that appeared to lend scientific legitimacy to the widespread belief that violence in the mass media causes violence in society. The report concluded that mass media violence desensitizes people, makes them more hostile and aggressive and more likely to perform violent acts. In *Mass Media Violence and Society* (1975), Dennis Howitt and Guy Cumberbatch scrutinized the research cited by the Surgeon General's report and demonstrated that none of the data actually constituted evidence that media violence significantly affects violence in society. Social scientists had compiled voluminous statistics, yet by and large they had assumed, rather than shown, that media violence causes real violence. The book went further to conclude that the available data strongly supported the conclusion that media violence has no effect on, perhaps even reduces, the level of violence in society.[1] That conclusion seems quite unjustified, though. Indeed, thinking in statistical terms may well hinder more than help in clarifying the roles mass media play in the diverse forms of life lived by Americans today. Our readiness to allow human beings to be reduced to statistical abstractions, I suspect, plays no small part in American society's obsession with violence.

Since its beginnings, the American cinema has been dogged by the belief that movies are harmful to society. In the early years of the twentieth century, New York's mayor tried to close all the city's nickelodeons, citing the "fact" that those "immoral places of amusement" were "liable to degenerate and menace the good order and morals of the people." Chicago passed a law requiring films to receive permits before they could be exhibited. When two were denied permits, the Illinois Supreme Court upheld the Chicago edict, saying that those films "represent nothing but malicious mischief, arson and murder . . . and their exhibition would necessarily be attended with evil effects upon youthful spectators." The United States Supreme Court concurred, endorsing the proposition that films were "capable of evil, having power for it, the greater because of their attractiveness and manner of exhibition."[2]

As such language suggests, the belief among film's earliest critics that movies caused harm to society was inseparable from their puritanical sense that movie viewing was in itself immoral. That moral judgment, in turn, was inseparable from a Victorian sense, as we might call it, that movies and moviegoing were improper. In the darkened movie theater, after all, women—some unescorted—sat shoulder by shoulder with men of all classes, viewing salacious scenes steeped in violence and eroticism. Film's turn-of-the-century attackers were fighting a rear-guard action against a modern medium that they took—perhaps not wrongly—to be a threat to their moral values, which meant it was an affront to their sense of propriety. In America, the idea that movies have harmful effects has remained inextricably intertwined with the puritanical notion that movies are intrinsically immoral. And a Victorian moral outlook that equates what is morally right with what conforms to conventional social practices (especially sexual mores) remains deeply entrenched in American culture, as well. Victorian moralists are hardly fashionable intellectual company, and I draw the lesson that we need to question our own motivations for being so ready to believe that movies cause our fellow Americans, but presumably not us, to lose their moral bearings. Another lesson is that we need to attend more thoughtfully to the origins and history of film, and to the larger history out of which film emerged, so that we may stop drawing the morals of movies too hastily.

No one more fervently believed in film's capacity for evil than D. W. Griffith. Griffith's films were awesome demonstrations of the terrifying power of the new medium. Yet Griffith staunchly defended, against the attacks of Victorian moralists, his tapping into film's power. Griffith's early films couched his defense in terms of Victorian moral values. *The Drunkard's Reformation* (1909), for example, acknowledged that film was capable of intoxicating viewers and thus had the "power for evil." Yet he also believed, when he began his career as a film director, that the new medium possessed an unfathomable capacity to restore lost innocence. By the time of *The Birth of a Nation* (1915), however, Griffith had lost his faith in film's capacity for redemption, his faith that tapping into the powers of the medium could be justified within the framework of Victorian morality. In the last third of *The Birth of a Nation*, the vengeful Ku Klux Klan, whose agency the film endorses, is no moral force—it is a nightmare inversion of Victorian moral values, no more capable of restoring America's innocence than movies are capable of saving America's soul. The American nation was born with blood on its hands, Griffith had come to believe. And so was the American cinema. Griffith envisioned film as possessing the power to whip viewers into a frenzied state, to cause viewers to lose their moral compass and give in to what is base in human nature. In Griffith's vision, movies have a voracious appetite for violence, as human beings have; violence is internal to film's nature, as it is internal to human nature.

The view that movies are inherently violent is at the heart of so-called apparatus theories, which emphasize film's supposed ability to force malignant ideological effects upon viewers. Indeed, it is a view that has surfaced again and again in the history of what we call "film theory," bridging otherwise opposed theoretical frameworks. Sergei Eisenstein famously insisted that montage, with its percussive, violent power, was the essence of the film medium, and championed radically new kinds of films that would more fully exploit the medium's capacity to force its violent effects—visceral, emotional, intellectual—on viewers. Less famously, Eisenstein believed that every frame of every film had, as it were, the blood of the world on it, due to the violence of the camera's original act of tearing pieces of the world from their "natural" place. The idea that the camera is an instrument of violence was taken up, at least implicitly, by André Bazin (if the film image is a "death mask" of the world, must not the camera be implicated in killing the world?), for whom Eisenstein's ideas were otherwise anathema, and, in turn, by Stanley Cavell (in its transformation into the world on film, the world undergoes a metamorphosis, or transfiguration, so profound as to be akin to death and rebirth). And the idea that film is inherently violent comes up again and again, and in a number of guises, in my own writings. It surfaces, for example, when in *Hitchcock—The Murderous Gaze* I characterize *Psycho*'s author, Hitchcock, in the famous shower murder sequence, as unleashing murderous rage upon Marion Crane (Janet Leigh), and upon us, the film's viewers, or when, in my reading of that film, I suggest that Hitchcock is characterizing film—a characterization I embrace, at least rhetorically—as a medium of taxidermy.

Today's films are filled with images of arteries spurting, limbs mutilated or chopped off, faces exploding, flesh penetrated or torn, and so on. Thanks in part to the Production Code, such explicit, graphic images of violence, or of the effects of violence, were absent from the so-called classical Hollywood cinema, as were explicit, graphic images of sexuality. But there was violence, as there was sex, in classical movies. Without sex, after all, there could have been no romantic comedies or melodramas or musicals. Without violence, there could have been no gangster films, war films, Westerns, private eye films, or horror films. In classical movies as in Greek tragedies, however, violence was generally left for the viewer to imagine. When acts of violence and their effects were explicitly shown in classical movies, the camera refrained from dwelling on the gory details; the violence was not *eroticized,* as we might put it.

Two quite obvious distinctions complicate these matters.

First, when critics or theorists discuss film violence, they usually have in mind what we might call physical violence—killings, beatings, mutilations, and the like. Yet what we might call psychological violence, though lacking in gore, can be no less brutal and no less devastating to those subjected to it. In *Gaslight,* the Charles Boyer character does not set out to do his wife physical harm, but rather to drive her mad, to deprive her of a voice and, ultimately, even a mind of her own. Then, too, as Freud recognized, there can be violence in the most apparently innocent of actions. One might object that the violence in a joke or a slip of the tongue is merely symbolic, not real, violence. As Freud also recognized, however, a clear boundary between real and symbolic violence is difficult or impossible to draw. "Real" violence can have symbolic meaning, and "symbolic" violence can have real consequences. In the Ophuls masterpiece, after all, a mere letter from an unknown woman proves quite literally death-dealing (if, perhaps, redemptive).

Second, in fiction films, violence is generally simulated, not real. When a gunman shoots Liberty Valance, no one really dies, or, rather, no existing person dies. The most graphic images of violence (or of the effects of violence) are illusions created through the magic of makeup, tricks of photography and editing, and, increasingly, special effects. Violence in live action movies is generally no more consequential than the violence in cartoons, such as the violence Wile E. Coyote suffers from the machinations of Road Runner. When we view President Kennedy's head exploding in the Zapruder film, by contrast, the violence projected on the screen is, or was, real. And yet John Kennedy, no less than Liberty Valance, is shot to death on the screen—which also means he is first brought back to life on the screen—every time the Zapruder film is projected. Even in nonfiction films, death is not final, in the world on film, the way it is in the "real world," the one existing world into which we are born and within which we are fated to die. On the other hand, if Kennedy had not met his death in the violent way he did, the Zapruder film, as we know it, would not exist; real violence is a condition of that film's existence. Luis Buñuel kicked a goat down a cliff in order to create one of the most memorable shots in his documentary, or mock documentary, *Land without Bread.* In fact, the goat was already dead, but it *could* have been a living goat that Buñuel pushed to its death as a condition of his film's existence. And, in this regard, in the medium of film the distinction between fiction and nonfiction can be difficult, or impossible, to draw. In order to film a crucial sequence in *The Rules of the Game,* hardly a documentary, Jean Renoir directed a hunt in which dozens of rabbits were shot to death, the violence real, not simulated.

In writing about *Nanook of the North* in *Documentary Film Classics,* I argued that Flaherty's film equates filming with hunting. Such an idea often arises in discussions of nonfiction film. But if in *To Be or Not to Be,* the "great, great Shakespearean actor" played by Jack Benny does to Shakespeare what Hitler did to Poland, what Flaherty does to Nanook by filming him hardly compares to what Nanook does to the walrus he harpoons, butchers, and consumes. *Night and Fog* asserts that the cameras of the Allied liberators were akin to the cameras of the Nazis, which were integral to the operation of the death camps, as guns were. But are cameras *generally* like guns?

To be filmed, a person must be in the world, a creature of flesh and blood. Filming people in the world, the camera does no real violence to them. But it does reveal their mortality, reveals their vulnerability to violence. In the early years of photography, no one envisioned the making a photograph as a violent act. The introduction of Kodaks toward the end of the nineteenth century, which made it possible for photographers to go out into the world and take snapshots of whomever they wished, coincided with the adoption of the violence-tinged language now universally applied to photography (calling the photographer's act "shooting," for example, or speaking of a person's picture as something a photographer *takes*). The emergence of the idea that photography has a violent aspect, the idea that cameras are like guns, coincided with the birth of motion pictures, which itself coincided with the birth of what we call modernity.

It is a strange idea, implausible on the face of it. Primitive peoples, we once were told, naively believe that cameras steal souls. Is it less naive to believe that cameras are violent? Unlike guns, cameras do not break bones (except, we now know, for X-ray cameras). In doing their mysterious work, cameras cause no physical harm. To be sure, photographs can be *used* in ways that harm their subjects, but in and of itself taking a photograph, like taking a look, has no effect whatever on the world. We may well have reason to envision the birth of cinema, as we envision all births, as traumatic, violent. But every time the world is transformed or transfigured by being projected on a movie screen, every time the world is born again on film, re-created in its own image, the world no more suffers from the creation of its double than the cloned sheep suffers from the birth of Dolly. Furthermore, violence within the world on film, in and of itself, has no effect whatever on the real world. And insofar as film violence has no real consequences, it is not real violence at all.

Eisenstein insisted that films, to be true to their medium, should be made to have as violent an impact as possible; viewers were to be hit on the head, as it were, by a series of percussive hammer blows. Apparatus theories, too, insist that movies do violence to viewers, although they deplore, rather than celebrate, this condition. And yet the train pulling into the station that would crush us to a pulp if we fell under its wheels is divested of its power to wreak violence on us when it is transformed into a train-on-film. Hence the popularity of the often imitated Lumière film, which, like all the earliest films, vividly demonstrated to its original audiences a defining condition of the new medium, in this case the condition that the world on film differs from the real world by being exempt from real violence, by being unable to do violence to us and by being impervious to our capacities for violence. In *Hitchcock—The Murderous Gaze*, I argue that the shower murder sequence in *Psycho* declares Hitchcock's wish to murder the viewer, a wish it may well be natural for anyone to feel who makes the classical role of movie director his or her own. But that sequence also declares it to be a condition of the film medium that the movie screen shields us from the world on film, shields the world on film from us.

Because it is not real violence, it would not be possible for film violence to harm us were it not for the massive ways we involve movies in our lives. In particular, film violence would pose no danger unless it were capable of causing real violence, whether by desensitizing viewers to real violence and thus neutralizing their inhibitions to performing violent acts in the world, by making real violence seem attractive, or by some other mechanism.

Viewing an action sequence in a John Woo film, we take pleasure in the fusillade of images purporting to represent the impact of high-power bullets on human bodies. Why it is so pleasurable to view graphic images of violence (or of the effects of violence), how viewing such images can be pleasurable, is a perplexing question. However we might go on to answer that question, though, we can agree that viewing such images is, or at least can be, pleasurable. We have an appetite for film violence, an appetite that film violence feeds, and perhaps also creates.

Puritans would condemn our appetite for film violence, as they would condemn all our appetites, as sinful. Again, though, film violence would only be capable of causing harm if it had the power to lead viewers to crave real violence, not merely more film violence. Film violence would be capable of this if it had the power to lead viewers to believe, even if erroneously, that performing or suffering violent acts in the real world would provide the kinds of pleasures film violence provides, or, especially, that the pleasures of film violence were only pale substitutes for the pleasures attendant upon the "real thing."

Again, a John Woo film offers innumerable images purporting to represent bullets causing mayhem to human bodies. Evidently, millions of viewers all over the world have a taste for such images. Surely, though, that taste is far more readily gratified by viewing a John Woo film, in which camera placement, makeup, editing, and special effects ensure an optimal view of every bullet's bloody impact, than by getting one's hands on a high-powered rifle and raining bullets on human beings in the real world. (A taste for pornographic images is far more fully gratified by viewing pornographic films than by, for example, brutalizing and raping women.) If our appetite for film violence were simply an appetite for *images* of violence (or of the effects of violence), in other words, film violence would not be likely to lead us—unless we were woefully misinformed—to perform real acts of violence. But films do not simply present us with images of violence (or of the effects of violence). They also represent violent actions.

In the climactic moment of *Raging Bull*, Sugar Ray Robinson hesitates, exhilarated and terrified by what he feels called upon to do, by his own desire to do it, and by his opponent's desire to have it done, before finally delivering the haymaker that busts Jake LaMotta's face but miraculously fails to knock him down. We experience this violence as something one person does, something another person suffers. We experience vicariously—that is, we imagine so vividly that we all but feel—the agony and the ecstasy Sugar Ray feels, within the film's fiction, as his fist smashes into the flesh and bone of Jake's face. We also all but feel the pain and the sweetness only Jake feels, within the fiction, as his already battered face erupts in a shower of blood. We imagine ourselves in Sugar Ray's place, and in Jake's place. We imagine feeling what each alone, within the film's fiction, is capable of really feeling. That is, we imagine that we are not merely viewing but living this exhilarating, terrifying moment of violence. (It is exhilarating because it is terrifying, but it is also terrifying because it is exhilarating.) We imagine that we are living, and not merely imagining we are living, this moment. We might well find ourselves thanking our lucky stars, as we are viewing, that the medium of film separates us from the world Jake and Sugar Ray inhabit, that we are living our lives, not theirs. But we might well also find ourselves thinking, at this moment, that if it is so thrilling merely to be imagining that we are throwing this punch and feeling its impact, it must be infinitely more pleasurable to be living what we are only imagining. If it has the power to motivate us to think such a thought, as in this celebrated instance it surely has, then film violence is capable of stimulating, or even creating, an appetite for violence, a blood lust, that, we imagine, we can more fully gratify by performing or suffering real acts of violence than by merely viewing violence (or the effects of violence) on film.

There is a continuum between cases like this one, in which we experience violence on film as something a person does, as something a person suffers, hence as something we might wish to do or suffer and not merely view, and cases in which film violence is a mere abstraction with no power to move us to act or to suffer.

What Sugar Ray's punch does to Jake's face, within the film's fiction, one person does to another person. One's fist is part of one's body, part of oneself. But a fist is also a potentially lethal weapon of the blunt instrument persuasion. When Al Capone, in *The Untouchables*, smashes a flunky's head with a baseball bat, the bat is not literally part of his body. Yet within the fiction he can feel—and we can imagine feeling—the satisfying impact of wood on flesh and bone. What the bat does to this unfortunate man, Capone, swinging the bat, does to him. But when Chow Yun-Fat shoots a hapless bad guy, the havoc the bullet wreaks on the bad guy's body, within the fiction, is not something that Chow Yun-Fat does to him. To be sure, the bullet's impact immediately succeeds Chow Yun-Fat's pulling of the trigger, and it has its impact on the particular bad guy he has targeted. The bullet acts at a distance, though, so that when Chow Yun-Fat pulls the trigger, he can view the effect of the bullet's impact, but he cannot feel it, cannot feel it as something he is doing, the way Sugar Ray feels

43

his own punch or Capone feels the impact of the bat he is swinging. (Compare the images of Joan burning at the stake at the climax of Carl Dreyer's *The Passion of Joan of Arc*. Within the film's fiction, people must have built this pyre, bound her, and kindled the fire. But once their work is done, they, like everyone else, can only view as the flames, on their own, consume Joan's body.)

Nonetheless, within the fiction, presumably, Chow Yun-Fat feels his finger pulling the trigger, and feels the gun's action as the trigger engages the firing mechanism. He feels this at virtually the same moment he views the havoc the bullet wreaks on the bad guy's body. To that extent, Chow Yun-Fat feels the connection, as we might put it—and we vicariously experience his feeling of the connection—between his pulling of the trigger, which is something he does, and the violence the bullet causes, which is something the bullet does on its own, without human intervention. When he pulls the trigger, the violence follows automatically, the way a camera automatically takes a picture when someone presses the shutter release. A human being pulls the trigger, but a machine causes the violence, making it possible for the gunman, with no blood on his hands, to view, at a remove, effects that are, and are not, his doing.

When Chow Yun-Fat views the world through the sights of his gun, all it takes is for him to pull the trigger for his target to become a bloody mess. Until he does pull the trigger, though, there is no sign at all, in the world he is viewing, of the impending violence. But violence threatens the bad guy Chow Yun-Fat is targeting precisely because he is targeting him, because he is viewing him, at this remove, through this instrument of violence. At such a moment, too, we might find ourselves thankful that the medium of film separates us from the world projected on the movie screen, thankful that movies make it possible to experience violence only vicariously, thankful that film violence is not real violence. But, again, we might well also find ourselves thinking, as we are viewing, how much more pleasurable it would be to be pulling the trigger ourselves, how much more pleasurable it would be if the ensuing violence were real. Then we would be able to experience, and not merely imagine we are experiencing, the pleasure of making violence happen at a distance, without getting blood on our hands.

In fiction films, violence happens on cue, as if the camera were a gun, and the director, off-screen, were pulling the trigger. Violence the camera causes in this way is not real violence, as we have said. The camera is not a real instrument of violence. Movies call upon us to imagine that film violence is real violence, that no barrier separates us from the world on film, and that is one key to the pleasure we receive from them. But they also call upon us to acknowledge that the world on film is separated from us, hence that film violence is not real violence, and this, too, is a key to the pleasures movies provide us.

Viewing the world on film, a world separated from us by an unbridgeable barrier, can stimulate our appetite for living in the world. A danger of film violence, as I have suggested, resides in the power of movies to motivate us to think that the pleasures of film violence are pale substitutes for the pleasures real acts of violence might give us. Film violence is capable of motivating us to think that performing or suffering real acts of violence might make it possible to experience life more intensely, to make our mark, to be someone.

But living in the world can stimulate our appetite for movie viewing, too. As we go about the world, we feel removed, as if we were viewing our lives, not living them. How much better to be viewing a real movie! When we are viewing a movie, the conditions of the medium automatically place us outside the world on film, free us from the responsibilities of living within the world. Therein resides another, perhaps more insidious, danger of film violence. For if film violence can motivate us to think that real acts of violence might enable us to exist more fully within the world, it can also motivate us to think that real acts of violence might enable us to detach ourselves more fully from the world.

Some pundits say that when those two young men in Littleton, Colorado, undertook their terrible plan to blow up their high school and kill their fellow students, they were imitating acts of violence they had seen in movies, television shows, or video games. Others suggest that their goal, in killing, was to become immortalized by the media, like Bonnie and Clyde. But I picture them as undertaking, rather, to detach themselves from the world as they knew it, to reject the world endorsed by the media, a world of conformists and sports heroes and consumer goods. If censors had removed all representations of violence from the media, these alienated youths would have hated society more, not less. By their violence, they felt they were rejecting America as it exists, declaring that society's conventions were not the measure of their existence. They were rejecting conventional morality, too. Nonetheless, their violent act had a moral dimension. In their view, their commitment to being true to themselves made them superior—superior morally—to an America that lacked the moral standing to judge them, an America they felt it was their right, even their duty, to obliterate, at least symbolically. They felt they were elevating themselves above the fallen America they were condemning. Yet by embracing this view, they were unwittingly keeping faith with the moral outlook that has underwritten, and been underwritten by, American movies since their origins. Even during the period in which the Production Code forced them to follow the letter of the Victorian moral law, American movies rejected the spirit of Victorian morality. In particular, they rejected its equating of what is morally right with what conforms to society's conventions. In American movies, it is a moral imperative to quest for human fulfillment, even when that means refusing to accept the strictures of conventional morality; self-realization is a greater good than social acceptance. This moral outlook was not imposed on movies from the outside, like the Production Code, but is internal to the stories movies keep telling. It is the American cinema's inheritance of the transcendental philosophy of Emerson and Thoreau.

What movies are and what gives them their awesome power are mysteries that vexed America in the early years of film, and they have continued to vex our culture. What is it about the medium that is so frightening that it led film's earliest critics to believe—as so many continue to believe—that movies are "capable of evil, having the power for it"? And what is it about the medium that has enabled movies to walk a moral path? The field of film studies has been reluctant to address, or even acknowledge, such questions. Despite the high priority it accords to what it calls—always choosing a pretentious term over a more humble one—"historiography," the medium's origins and history remain obscure to the field. That is because so much of its research has been ideologically driven, designed to confirm conclusions dictated in advance by currently fashionable theories rather than to put those theories to the test by discovering surprising new insights into mysterious matters that we prefer to believe pose no mysteries to us.

Notes

1. Dennis Howitt and Guy Cumberbatch, *Mass Media, Violence, and Society* (New York: Wiley, 1975).
2. Ibid., 8, 10, and 11.

the violence

of a perfect moment

two

leo charney

There is a scene in the middle of "The Saint" that may, in time, come to be viewed as a critical moment in American movies. The Saint (Val Kilmer) and his young, blond, beautiful, poetry-reading, world-changing-scientist sidekick Emma (Elisabeth Shue)—in short, his girl—are rushing through watery tunnels in the bowels of modern Moscow. Our man is in a fix: the exits are blocked, and there are Russian-mafia goons coming up behind. Salvation arrives in the shape of a young, dark, beautiful, beret-wearing, gun-toting Russian art dealer who appears from the shadows, ushers him and Emma into a secret chamber, and tries to sell them some icons. When this attempt fails, she offers to lead them underground to the sanctuary of the American Embassy, pausing only to deliver an outrageous product placement for our hero's waterproof watch. As the action unfolded, I sat there with my jaw resting lightly on the floor, and I thought, This is it. This is what we have been heading for all these years. Here is a film that makes *no sense at all.*

—Anthony Lane

Boom

In the beginning of *Lethal Weapon 3* (1992), a building blows up. The filmmakers found a building, blew it up, and filmed it. You might assume that the movie goes on to tell the story of a drug cartel that blows up buildings or a mad bomber who explodes urban landmarks. This would be a false and conventional presumption, since the movie has nothing to do with bombers and the blowing up of the building has nothing to do with the rest of the movie.

Lethal Weapon 3's opening illustrates two things about movie violence: the enduring appeal of these singular moments when a building explodes, a car crashes, someone shoots or stabs or punches someone else; and the seemingly escalating decontextualization of those moments, their apparently increasing tendency in contemporary action movies to stand on their own, as if for their own sake, no longer the handmaidens of an orthodox cause-and-effect story. Beginning in the "cinema of attractions" of the early years of the century, cinema's visual and kinetic violence is measured in moments, which reach a peak of sensation and then wane, ready to cycle back toward the next one. The violent moment is a hypermoment, a hypostatized moment. Yet throughout film history, these moments of heightened violence have done battle with a corresponding impulse toward storytelling. While the representation of violence would seem to be on the side of spectacle, it also depends on the narratives that enclose and defamiliarize it, that allow violence to retain its kinetic impact and prevent it from becoming a string of meaningless sensation. But the defamiliarizing effect wanes by definition, and the thrills must arise faster and sooner; the stakes of attractions rise as their ability to shock fades, with the result that they become both more lavish and more dominant, leading to contemporary complaints that attractions, originally ephemeral films in themselves, are now taking over "films"—defined as classical narrative stories.

The hunger for kinetic sensations in cinema becomes like a century-long drug addiction in which you need more and more to accomplish less and less. As *Lethal Weapon 3* indicates, sophisticated, media-savvy audiences who surf satellite dishes, make cellular phone calls while watching rented videos, and absorb Monday-morning movie grosses cannot be trusted not to be bored at the very first moments of the movie; and the popularity of TV shows in which cars crash or lions sink their teeth into cheetahs demonstrates the extent to which efficient machineries of postmodern entertainment may increasingly omit as much plot as they can and cut right to a string of sensation, as in American action movies recut for foreign audiences to include only action scenes. In the words of Joel Silver, the producer of the *Lethal Weapon* films, "The rule of thumb is that in every reel of a movie—that means basically every ten minutes—if you're making an action movie, every ten minutes you must have an action beat. Something dramatic and jolting must happen." Daniel Waters, one of Silver's screenwriters, calls this strategy "'all good parts' film-making." In Waters's words, Silver "wants the white stuff in the Oreo cookies without even touching the black pieces. . . . What would be the climax in a normal movie is the next scene in a Joel Silver movie. . . . Joel's approach is 'Why do we have to set up so many building blocks to get to an explosive climax when you can have the explosive climax *right now* and have *another* explosive climax in the *next* scene?' . . . He's assuming that everyone's seen everything before."[1]

In an environment in which "everyone's seen everything before," the raising of the stakes of sensation characterizes the movement of peak moments of violence from their original context in a modernist cinema of attractions to the upping of the ante that accrues around them in and as a postmodern cinema of attractions that we call the action movie of the 1980s and 1990s. I will argue that this impulse arises from a sense of lost intimacy with present moments that characterizes film's first context of modernity, as reflected in a cinema of attractions, and is then reformed through the derealized landscape of cartoon violence to emerge into a contemporary action cinema. The force of violence externalizes and renders as a kinaesthetic effect the rolling hunger to face the present, to feel it and see it and re-present it. But as this effort fails, and fails over and over again as it can only do, the need to reassert it by force becomes more and more the domain of what could only be called a hysterical impulse. Violence becomes more and more intense in the effort to restore the possibility of having an effect, creating a shock, provoking a response—aspirations that arose in the first place only in response to the absence of immediate presence that cinema has continued to reaffirm. Violence, like sex, becomes a way to feel present; or, more accurately, to mime presence, to manufacture a sensation of presence in the face of the impossibility of presence. Moments of violence aspire to restore, or at least to represent, the moments of tangible presence that are otherwise unachievable, as if their very force could hurtle them into the inside of a present moment. Violence and sex become aspirations to attain the immediacy of that sensational moment, but the apotheosis of sensation can by definition never be reached, and the inability to assuage the loss only intensifies the drive to do so.

The cinematic violence of the contemporary American action film only externalizes this hunger for intimacy with presence that began, together with cinema, in turn-of-the-century modernity. As modernist thinkers consistently reminded us, each passing moment restages a scenario of loss, in which the moment of initial impression can never coincide with the successive moments in which cognition rationally categorizes those things that have already happened.[2] This ever lost moment of first sensation marks the horizon of all sensations, the utopian border against which the intensity of all other sensations can be measured and must inexorably fall short. As violence and cinema, and violent cinema, ceaselessly search for a tangible present, they ceaselessly reaffirm its unattainability, and the failure ceaselessly reinforces the need for the search.

We can understand the violence (and the sexuality) of American cinema only in its link to this modernist sense of the loss of tangible presence in whose context cinema arose and which its phantasmic form has ratified in perpetuity. But as this cycle waxes and wanes across the twentieth century, violence increasingly becomes the visible and kinetic externalization of a state of hysteria, directed toward the impossible possession of the present—directed, that is, toward immediate sensation as an unattainable fetish object. The fetish quality of the lost moment, together with its unre-capturability, leads toward a logic of insatiability that gains momentum as cinema ages and its shocks become more difficult to achieve. Violent action movies overcompensate for an increasingly diffuse media environment by emphasizing emphasis, underlining moments of kinetic impact so forcefully that eventually such contemporary action movies as *Twister* and *Armageddon* are criticized for substituting an unmediated onslaught of sensation for any kind of story at all. This devolution of violent moments marks a certain kind of nostalgia in the guise of a certain kind of effectivity. Contemporary action movies may trade on postmodern nostalgia for an imaginary past potential to make an impact, to cut through the diffusion of the Internet and three hundred satellite channels to feel the force of a simple explosion. But this nostalgia is based in a possibility of immediate sensation that was never there in the first place. Contemporary global action cinema's nostalgia for sensation brings together a century of film narrative conventions with a century of aspirations toward the sensational presence of violent moments.

Gone

In *Beyond the Pleasure Principle*, Sigmund Freud offered his now well known description of a "good little boy" with "an occasional disturbing habit of taking any small objects he could get hold of and throwing them away from him into a corner, under the bed, and so on, so that hunting for his toys and picking them up was often quite a business."[3] The child takes a reel on a string, pitches it over the edge of his cot, then pulls it back again, the two actions accompanied by words that Freud identifies as "fort" (gone) and "da" (there). Freud suggests that the fort/da game aims to re-present the mother's departure and return and thereby allow the child some measure of mastery over this traumatic possibility: "At the outset he was in a *passive* situation . . . ; but, by repeating it, unpleasurable though it was, as a game, he took on an *active* part" (16). The fort/da game becomes a model of Freudian repetition-compulsion, in which the re-presentation of potentially uncontrollable situations helps the subject attain some control over them, and it provides a paradigm for the use of re-presentation in the face of loss, as the child finds an arbitrary representational device to help him assuage the absence of his mother and soothe himself with a palliative fiction about her possible return.

But most important, the fort/da game is an act of violence. The game is a re-presentation, predicated on an effort to conquer loss, whose violence reiterates the force of the generative loss and the force of the futile effort to bridge it. The staging of violence displaces the child's affect but in so doing creates a free-floating emotional excess legible as violence, read back into the child's actions as hostility. Violence emerges only as a function of an act of re-presentation, but that re-presentation is in the first instance predicated on a loss for which it can never compensate. Freud suggests that the child may be expressing anger toward the mother for leaving him: "Throwing away the object so that it was 'gone' might satisfy an impulse of the child's, which was suppressed in his actual life, to revenge himself on his mother for going away from him. In that case it would have a defiant meaning: 'All right, then, go away! I don't need you. I'm sending you away myself'" (16). In the fort/da paradigm, the mother becomes the primal fetish object, alluring only in her absence. (Freud notes that the same boy staged a similar game a year later when his father was sent to fight in the First World War, though he seems to miss the point that it is therefore not the absence of the *mother* that is privileged but absence in general as a founding abyss across which the urge toward representations is built.)

The fort/da game in this way indicates the centrality of violence to the endeavor of papering fictions over a traumatic originary loss. Fort/da's violence—an aspect unremarked by Freud—entertains the child as a distraction from his feelings of loss, yet the child finds himself needing to repeat the game over and over again. The effort to assuage the loss fails, yet this failure only accentuates the urge to keep trying: the reiteration of the loss reiterates the impossibility of ameliorating it, a repetition that keeps circularly reinforcing its own impulse. As the loss becomes more and more definitive, the need for the re-presentation becomes keener, more hysterical, and a more and more forceful violence is needed to keep making a palliative and distracting effect. The narrative deployment of violence marks the gesture of trying to make the present present; violence presents the present, but it does so with an emphasis, an affective excess, that is the byproduct of the impossibility of its generative desire for presence, a desire that can be met only in the moment of death. Images of violence re-present an inchoate, an inarticulate and inarticuable, desire for an intimacy with presence. Representations of violence partially recontain this hysteria, make it manageable and readable, as they perpetually reaffirm it. The fort/da paradigm underlines this impulse for presence as one not only of the fetish but also of hysteria. The child strives to rein in a potentially hysterical response to his mother's absence through a symbolic re-presentation of her absence. He wreaks havoc, throws his toys around the room, deliberately makes life difficult for those around him. The violence and the representation restage an affectively forceful scenario that helps work off the child's potential hysteria while also helping to contain it.

We can understand the evolution of cinematic violence only as part of this cycle of hysterical aspiration toward the unattainable fetish of a pure presence. Film emerges out of the artistic, literary, and philosophical contexts of modernity as a means to recuperate the possibility of presence—a paradoxical hope since cinema also becomes the art that puts the moment in motion and thereby reaffirms its ephemerality. An unattainable text, a phantom, a film also only literalizes its defining logic of insatiability; if a film constantly remarks a horizon of unattainable presence, its deployment of violence and sex strives to keep re–pinning down that presence, mark its borders, render it readable. Cinema emerged as, on the one hand, an art form of empty presence, tacked together from shadow and light and noise and flicker and the spaces between evanescent instants of images; and as, on the other hand, an aesthetics of aggression composed from clashing frames and jarring jolts of time and space. Film narrative in this sense arose from two impulses that are radically incompatible, even directly contrary to each other: the effort to feel isolated moments of sensation and the effort to achieve narrative continuity. Narrative cinema arose at the shifting crossroads of these two potentially incompatible tracks: the attractions tradition of discrete violent sensations and the classical tradition of linear, cause-and-effect storytelling.[4] Both of these avenues emerged from their own specific crisis of presence: violent attractions from a shortfall of sensory presence, from an effort to compensate a loss of sensation with an excess of sensation; and classical narration from the shortfall of narrative and material presence intrinsic to the cinematic form of gaps and ellipses and flicker and shadow. The lockstep linearity of classical Hollywood narrative's cause-and-effect logic aims to paper over a film's holes of narrative, spatial, and temporal continuity, an effort openly visualized in the devices of continuity editing (match on action, shot/reverse-shot, eyeline match) that aspire, as if by wishful thinking, to render legible the discontinuities contained inside every film like land mines.

The emergence of cinematic form yoked together a modernist fall from presence with an impulse toward sensationalist sex and violence that aspired toward pure presence while it also aimed to compensate for its loss; and the cinema thereby became enmeshed in a seemingly ever-increasing spiral of violent representations that is at the same time always a quasi-nostalgic evocation of its origins. Since Bosley Crowther's tirade against *Bonnie and Clyde* in 1967[5] and continuing through the action movies of the 1980s, violence and kinetic sensation have become the fall guys for a perceived decline in coherent storytelling that implicitly defines "films" as conventional classical narratives. Lane's ironic description of *The Saint* in the epigraph reflects a widespread perception that contemporary American action films since *Star Wars*, *Jaws*, and *Raiders of the Lost Ark*—and definitively since the *Die Hard* series, the *Lethal Weapon* series, and their cousins and avatars since the early 1980s—have marked the descent of traditional film aesthetics into meaningless, strung-together pastiches of violence and sensation. In an emblematic review of *Batman and Robin*, David Denby described the film as "a void of meaning in the middle of violent sequences composed of shots thrown together from nowhere to nowhere without the slightest relation in space. Two years ago, I insisted that the comparable mess in *Batman Forever* was a sign that basic film aesthetics were collapsing, and . . . I find no reason to revise my opinion. When you have seen Schumacher's two *Batman* movies, you have seen The End."[6] In Lane's words about the same film, director Joel Schumacher "arranged various stunts to look something like a film."[7] But the description of contemporary action movies as stringing together "action beats" with less than classical attention to story and character must fail as both a historical and an aesthetic position. From the aesthetic perspective, Denby's criticism equates one privileged mode of classical Hollywood narrative with "basic film aesthetics" in general. As Lev Kuleshov demonstrated in his montage experiments of the 1920s, "shots thrown together from nowhere to nowhere without the slightest relation in space" probably define "basic film aesthetics" more foundationally than does the imposition of a plot.

From the historical perspective, what reviewers predictably identify as a deterioration in storytelling aesthetics can be more accurately described as an increased (re)privileging of kinetic sensations over linear storytelling. Accustomed to staging evaluation on the ground of plot coherence, reviewers implicitly reject the possibility that violent movies that "don't make sense" are simply a different kind of movie, with deep historical roots and evidently enduring audience appeal, no more or less divergent, and not necessarily better or worse, than experimental or foreign films. Movie reviewers who perceive the weakening of "traditional film aesthetics" correctly intimate that a balance of power has shifted in these films, as the devolution of movie violence in an amorphous media environment requires more forceful force to achieve violence's defamiliarizing effect. This kind of cinema must be seen not as a teleological forecast of cinema's end but as a reformulation, in the light of classical narrative traditions, of the sensationalistic attractions that marked the early years of cinema in what Tom Gunning has called "the cinema of attractions."[8] Typified by Edison's 1903 film of an elephant's electrocution, these shorts emphasized not cause-effect narrative or melodramatic theatrical plots but simply display: an electrocution, an apprehended criminal, microscopic bugs. "These early films," Gunning writes, "explicitly acknowledge their spectator, seeming to reach outwards and confront. . . . the scenography of the cinema of attractions is an exhibitionist one, opposed to the cinema of the unacknowledged voyeur that later narrative cinema ushers in."[9]

The attractions of early cinema stand as a utopian holding action against the disappearance of a tangible presence, a manufactured substitute for the possibility of that presence. Gunning has suggested that the attraction, in consonance with the culture of fragments from which it arose and to which it contributed, "seems limited to a sudden burst of presence . . . to the pure present tense of its appearance."[10] Yet this is of course not strictly true. Even the briefest attraction consumes substantially more chronological time and perceptual attention than either a "burst of presence" or a "pure present tense." We need to understand attractions less as representations of pure presence than as part of a widespread modernist impetus to compensate for the loss of that pure presence. Attractions were precisely *not* the manifestations of an instantaneous or momentary presence, and it is in that shortfall that they became central to the evolution of film narrative. Attractions aspired to the condition of pure presence; their brief action aimed to restitute the shock of a single moment. But they can only fail and they can only fail every time. In their briefness, in their puppy-dog eagerness to spark a response from viewers, attractions marked the first gesture of the cinematic endeavor to rescue the sensation of presence. Their ephemerality and their canny deployment of violence and shock may make them feel like an instantaneous present tense, may reawaken the viewer to the sharpness of a present perception, but this effort derives both its impetus and its success only on the ground of the generative loss of presence from which it arises. To the extent that present sensations were increasingly conceived by discourses of modernity as inconceivable and uninhabitable, such devices as photography and cinema were rushed into the breach to provide ersatz, but by definition failed, approximations of immediate presence.

The excitement of new cinematic technologies of kinetic pleasure could be given aesthetic form in the attraction: ephemeral; visual and kinetic rather than narrative; oriented toward the pleasures of sensation, voyeurism, and often violence. But while the cinema of attractions first accosted cinematically virginal viewers, a new cinema of attractions must contend with blasé audiences who have emphatically been around the block. In contemporary action movies, the power of attractions thereby arises not from the novelty of cinema but from the exhaustion of cinema. In the wake of *Jaws* (1975) and *Star Wars* (1977), the deployment of effects and attractions involves an effort not so much to fashion something new as to do battle against the increasing fading of cinematic affect in post-modernity. Miriam Hansen has suggested that this link between early and contemporary cinemas represents "a certain *déjà vu* effect" in which "contemporary forms of media culture evoke the parallel of early cinema."[11] While I share Hansen's perspective on the homology between these two periods, her analysis tends to reify "early cinema" and "classical forms" and "contemporary forms of media culture" as three distinct and static eras, and it thereby minimizes the ways in which the negotiation between an early tendency toward attractions and a classical tendency toward story-telling has been at every juncture indeterminate and in process. The coexistence of narrative and sensation is neither simply a new phenomenon nor simply the reiteration of an old phenomenon; the balance between the two elements has been in negotiation throughout the history of cinema. The apparent rise of violent action films represents neither apocalypse nor return of the repressed but one ceaselessly evolving stage in a relationship between sensation and storytelling that at most has defined the unfolding nature of American filmmaking from its first years and at least has run coterminous with that history. No film needs literal violence, since even a film with the most quiescent storyline is essentially violent in its form, an aspect of cinema best recognized by Sergei Eisenstein in the 1920s, who famously advocated "conflict as the fundamental principle for the existence of every artwork and every artform."[12] But as in the fort/da game, the representation of literal violence brings to the surface the same hunger for presence that gives rise to that violence. At this stage, the revalorization of violent sensations becomes a central element of contemporary cinemas as a gesture of defamiliarization for a newly jaded audience.

Crash

In her study of the links among trains, modernity, and early cinema, Lynne Kirby notes the genre of the train accident movie concentrated in the first decade of this century.[13] She reports that these Lubin and Edison shorts derived from the even more bizarre genre of the staged county-fair train wreck, for which she finds evidence as early as 1896 and as late as 1929. "Equating technological destruction with both pleasure and terror," she writes, "the 'imagination of disaster' [invoked by the public interest in watching train wrecks] says volumes about the kind of violent spectacle demanded by a modern public, and the transformation of 'shock' into eagerly digestible spectacle" (61–62). While discourses of modernity, exemplified by the writings of Walter Benjamin, conventionally associated modern life with the experience of shock, Kirby indicates how these putative shocks were already being packaged and consumed as entertainment at least as early as the late nineteenth century. In the tradition of Benjamin and Siegfried Kracauer, the shocks of modern life are ambivalent and double-edged: as they empty out a consistency and tangibility once imputed to experience, they provide in their place a heightening of experience, a vehicle of defamiliarization to make perception keener and awareness more aware.[14] The shocks of cinema and other modern forms of distraction, typified by the cinema of attractions, are enlisted to compensate for the perceived loss of the possibility of intimate experiences of tangible, sensory presence that could testify to the existence of a coherent, legible reality. Gunning's formulation of attractions, for instance, associates them with "a fundamental loss of coherence and authenticity" in modern life that calls up modes of shocking stimulation as "a response to an experience of alienation."[15] As people feel increasingly distant from the ability to feel things, they need more and more stimulation to wake them up. In the alienated environment of modern life in the late nineteenth and early twentieth centuries, the "loss of experience creates a consumer hungry for thrills" like attractions and train smash-ups that hold out the hope of restoring, even if just for a moment, a feeling of palpable sensation, of the tangible immediacy of a present event.

The crash becomes in this way an icon of the unique moment, the unreachable instant of pure presence, the horizon of immersion in the sensual presence of the present that we can never in fact attain. The collision of two cars marks, by definition, a single moment, but this horizon of possibility for an identifiable moment can only—in theory as well as in practice—be mapped against the horizon of death, the moment of the body's ecstatic, yet final, immersion in a pure present.[16] In *Crash* (1996), based on J. G. Ballard's 1973 novel, David Cronenberg allied this hunger to re-present an identifiable moment of pure presence to a wider thematics of contact, of damaged and neurotic characters who seek the consoling immediacies of both the moment of collision and the moment of death as means to feel present. Assembled from Taylorist fragments of the human body, *Crash* limns the insatiable desire for intimacies of presence—and the presence of intimacy—that links violence to sex to death to representation across the bodies of twisted cars, waste products of a technological century. It invokes the insatiability of a culture of the lust for presence, the search for something bigger and better. This aspiration is linked to an originary fall from pure presence and to the role of cinema as a tool to soothe and compensate for that primal loss. Like the moment of death and the moment of orgasm, the moment of violent collision becomes a fetish object, and people literally give their lives in the hope of approaching it. Violence becomes an effort to restore sensation, to feel something, which means to feel present.

The association of violence with the instantaneous form of the car crash underlines the logic of insatiability that governs the film's universe. Like the story of Icarus flying too close to the sun, *Crash* becomes a cautionary tale about trying to get too close to pure presence, and it implies a corresponding argument for preserving pure presence as a utopian horizon, an unreachable imaginary ideality. The film's four central characters couple and recouple with each other like figures in French farce, but none of their sex satisfies their lust for something deeper and more intimate, a presence beyond the ersatz momentary presences of sexuality and orgasm. They turn to having sex in crashed cars, but these cars can only bear the traces of a momentary collision that once happened; the pastness of the crash reiterates the uncapturability of the singular moment and thereby mockingly reasserts the jaded pastness of sensation that these characters are trying to evade. Vaughan, the film's catalyst, moves actively into the realm of trying to create crashes on the highway and re-create famous car crashes. We first see him stage a detailed reenactment of James Dean's fatal crash that he calls "the ultimate in authenticity." "The trio would meet for one moment," he announces about the victims of the Dean crash, "but it was a moment that would create a Hollywood legend." One of his colleagues re-creates Jayne Mansfield's fatal car crash, in which he cross-dresses as Mansfield and meets the same instantaneous end. "It's all very satisfying," Vaughan tells James, the film's impassive center, as they look at his photographs of famous crashes, technological traces of technological traces of a vanished moment of collision. "I'm not sure I understand why."

The film's action intertwines sex and death as markers of presence on the body. Cars are figured as vehicles of death and then vehicles of sex and as such become stand-ins for the human body, which like the car can register the instantaneous moment only through traces that retroactively testify to a lost presence. While these themes already exist in Ballard's novel, Cronenberg enhances them by shooting body parts as isolated fetish objects, as if they were themselves discarded pieces of wreckage. Cronenberg's camera seems to mock its capacity for continuity, encapsulating discrete body parts in the manner of single still frames. The film's remorselessly fragmentary shots create a cubist sense of disorientation, of bodies no longer linked to their material embodiment; this aesthetic links them to the cars, the film's other fetish object, while it unmoors the bodies from a stable corporeal presence. The hypothetical possibility that a pure present might occur literally begins (in lost moments of prerational sensation) and literally ends (in the moment of death) on the body. The alienation of cars and the alienation of other bodies only mask the more primordial alienation of and from my own body, which receives and perceives sensations before I can recognize them as "a body" or "a moment." We believe our bodies to be present, right here, but this mirage is merely the most persuasive apparition of presence—and probably, as *Crash* explores, the most seductive one. The visual and sensual plausibility of the body's presence arises only in the face of the body's radical otherness as the receptacle for sensations that we can never rationally "know," that we can only approximate after the fact. Cronenberg, after Ballard, finds his metaphor for this self-alienation in the otherness of automobiles, which circulate through the film as furiously as do the characters in their mechanistic coupling and recoupling. Sex with/in other people and sex with/in cars mingle together with mutual indiscrimination. As throughout his films, Cronenberg deploys the defamiliarizations of film technique in an effort to restore the body's otherness, but here his relentless corporeal fragmentation plays into a wider dissolution of taken-for-granted presence that governs the film's networks of insatiability.

In its potential perfection of presence, the crash sets in motion a logic of insatiability germane to the fetish, the pattern by which, as in such classic fetish dramas as *The Maltese Falcon* and *The Treasure of the Sierra Madre*, the possibility of attaining the object of desire only intensifies both the desire and its ultimate futility. *Crash* connects this hunger for a re-presented moment to the fetish of celebrity worship, a more glamorous mode of aspiration toward the unattainable. Vaughan's colleague goes so far as to lose his life dressed as Jayne Mansfield, and he thereby succeeds in the final, actual inhabitation of the present moment of death—although he succeeds only by literalizing (threefold) his alienation from his own body by dressing as a dead female movie star. The sex-in-crashed-cars theme of a film that almost no reviewer could resist calling "auto-erotic" drew the most attention at the time of the film's first release. "As much as *Crash* would have you believe it," Owen Gleiberman emblematically asserted, "there simply *is* no link between eroticism and car crashes."[17] But the characters' hunger to have sex in crashed cars functions only as a metaphor for sex in general, which in turn metaphorizes the sexualized desire to attain lost presence that would be called fetishization. The moment(s) of orgasm seem to offer our greatest possible intimacy with pure presence, the most immediate immersion in a purely sensual present, and in that sense, as the description of an orgasm as a "little death" implies, move the subject closer to that actual immersion in pure presence inside the moment of death. If the imaginary utopian moment of pure presence forms a horizon, and aspirations toward presence an asymptote in the direction of that unreachable goal, then the sensation of orgasm (which the film never in fact represents) marks a way station on that journey in the direction of death; sex and death and crashes—three modes of violence on the body— come together around this use of violence to substitute and compensate for an actual presence of presence.

The hunger for intimate presence that governs these characters' lives can be answered only in the moments of death that crashes memorialize and metonymize. The moment of death marks the ultimate, and only possible, reconciliation between the sensual moment of presence and the cognitive apparition of that lost moment. At the end of the film, having failed to create their own crash-deaths, James and Catherine lie inert in a field and ask each other: "Are you all right? I don't know. Are you hurt? I think I'm all right. I think I'm all right." The inability to know if one is all right, to know even if one is hurt, invokes the alienation from the body that grounds the hysterical aspiration toward intimacy in which all the film's characters are engaged. When Catherine asks James, "Are you all right?" and he responds, "I think I'm all right; I think I'm all right," the point is that they are disappointed. "Maybe the next one," they hope. The film ends not with the satisfying climax of death but with the failure to die, the falling short of the aspiration toward death. The moment of death stays in place as a horizon in the distance toward which the characters' activities can only aspire, and it becomes in this way only part of a chain of insatiability that defines the film's dissection of the violence of fetishization. The film's characters are continually enmeshed in a search for an authentic experience of presence: they seek it in sex, in violence, even, perhaps perversely, in the re-creation of violence. Their obsessive, ritualistic hungers for both sex and violence are only gestures toward this need for an authentic experience of present sensation. Death as the final horizon of immersion in an absolute present only literalizes this inability to inhabit the presence of a present. The unthinkable intimacy of being present inside the present marks the horizon against which the film's characters measure their desperate desires for closeness, and death in turn represents the final horizon of that insertion into an absolute presence. James and Catherine try and fail to reach the final apocalypse of collision between the body's first irrational moment of sensation and the ensuing rational moments that spin further and further away from that generative instant, moments that can meet only in the longed-for final collision of the moment of death.

Speed

The survival of attractions in mainstream narrative cinema has most often been associated with movie musicals; as Siegfried Kracauer, eagle-eyed for signs of modernist fragmentation, described musical numbers: "Penelope fashion, they eternally dissolve the plot they are weaving. The songs and dances they sport form part of the intrigue and at the same time enhance with their glitter its decomposition."[18] Kracauer sees this unravelling as part of an "eternal struggle for supremacy" (148) between what he calls film's realistic and formative tendencies, a perspective roughly shared by Dana Polan, who writes that "many postwar musicals . . . frequently figure narrative as a device for spectacle—that is, for a kind of showing off of form, a rejection of themes and meaningful mythologies for a new, non-signifying notion of art as endless, meaningless display."[19] Where Kracauer opposes formalism (spectacle) to realism (story), Polan associates spectacle with a resistance to content, with the presentation of "a world in which things only exist or mean in the way they appear."[20]

While Kracauer and Polan are clearly on the mark in connecting the survival of spectacle to the movie musical, I would suggest that the violent spectacles of a new cinema of attractions arise more specifically from cartoons, the bridge between an early comic/violent cinema of attractions and a contemporary comic/violent cinema of attractions.[21] As mainstream Hollywood cinema headed in the direction of conventional narrative, violent chase cartoons, epitomized by the Road Runner and Bugs Bunny series, accomplished two ends that led toward action movies of the 1980s and 1990s: they mingled comedy with violence, and they transfigured violence from something potentially "real" into something formulaic. These two endeavors were of course intertwined, since the representation of mayhem as humorous also derealizes it.[22] Animation's defamiliarizing form provides a license for bloody carnage unimaginable in "real" action, and this unreality has provided the crucial stepping stone toward making represented violence seem equally abstract or, in Polan's word, "non-signifying." Cartoons in which two animals (for instance, Road Runner and Wile E. Coyote) or an animal and a caricature (for instance, Bugs Bunny and Elmer Fudd) chase each other around and inflict carnage on each other, but in which the ending is always the same (one triumphs, the other is humiliated), bridge the formulas of early adventure serials and the formulas of latter-day action movies. In the new cinema of attractions, the violence of live-action movies has become no more "real" than that of cartoons; in Joel Silver's words, "These are formula movies. There are good guys and bad guys. And the bad guy does bad things, so the good guy chases him. . . . The bad guys can be aliens, the good guy can be a fish. But at the end of the movie—in this genre of movies—the bad guy loses and the good guy wins. And that has proved to be a commercially viable formula."[23]

The cartoonish quality of violence and the violent quality of cartoons engenders in action cinema a mingling of comedy and violence first initiated in slapstick and attractions.[24] The insertion of comedy into violence is in part opportunistic, as it leavens violence's edge, makes it more palatable and playful. But the link between comedy and violence arises more immediately from the modernist forms of presence and hysteria that I have associated with violence. No less than the violent effect, the humorous effect depends on the marshalling of the momentary, epitomized by the pie in the face; both humor and violence emerge from the unexpected momentary intersection between one thing and another, a collision that occasions an excess of affect, a spilling over of emotionality that may register as pleasure (somatically externalized as a laugh) or shock (somatically externalized as a scream or gasp). Humor provides a safety valve against the violence of violence, but each effect in fact defamiliarizes the other, as the violence renders the humor more surprising and the humor makes the violence more startling and unexpected.

The potential excess of the hysterical response can be lightened by this mixture of comedy and violence. Almost all contemporary action movies rely on the bantering tone set by such action figures as Bruce Willis in the *Die Hard* series, Mel Gibson (and later Joe Pesci) in the *Lethal Weapon* series, and Eddie Murphy in the *48 Hrs.* films. As Willis in *Hudson Hawk* and Arnold Schwarzenegger in *The Last Action Hero* learned, maintaining a jocular tone is a fine line that audiences evidently do not want pushed too far into comedy; both Schwarzenegger and Sylvester Stallone have proven famously unable to draw comparable audiences to see them in straightforward comedies, though the very fact that these action stars are making comedies, or that such comedians as Eddie Murphy and Martin Lawrence and Chris Rock make action movies, testifies to the fluid boundaries between the two genres. The success of such dry straight men as Willis, Gibson, and to some extent Schwarzenegger and Harrison Ford lies in their structural ability to make appalling levels of violence seem light and larky. If violence aspires toward sensory defamiliarization, these action stars function as *re*familiarization, as a de-defamiliarization engineered to make the violence seem derealized: "People come to the movies we do," as Joel Silver says, "and they come out having had a roller-coaster ride" (128). Willis and Schwarzenegger and Gibson and their highly paid peers function as no more (and no less) than live-action Road Runners.

Violent chase cartoons consist essentially of two elements: moments of kinetic violence, and running around before and after those moments of kinetic violence. For better or worse, this has increasingly become the pattern of such contemporary action movies as *Armageddon* (1998) or the infamously awful *Twister*, which presage what Owen Gleiberman has called "a movie future in which sensation is all, and people are just pretty props."[25] A cinema of violent attractions reaches an apotheosis in such films, but this success engenders a crisis of exposure, as if all the raiments mustered in Hollywood history to disguise a film's failures of presence were being increasingly stripped away like the emperor's new clothes. This hollowness becomes the very subject of a postmodern action experiment like *Speed* (1994), a film in which nothing happens, or, more exactly, in which the possibility that something may happen is all that happens. Nominally, *Speed* is about a Los Angeles city bus, full of passengers, planted with a bomb that will explode if the bus is driven below fifty miles an hour; the female bus driver and the male police officer negotiate the bus to safety and wind up in each other's arms. This storyline takes its shape from the deferral of the possibility of sex and the deferral of the possibility of violence: sex may happen and violence may happen, but we cannot be sure if they will happen, and so we keep watching. The film's austerely minimalist style takes its impetus from the stripping down of the narrative traditions that it intermingles: an attractions tradition of violent sensation (the initial bus explosion followed by scrapes along the way, subtended by the question of whether the bus will explode); a narrative tradition of heroes, villains, and linear storytelling; and a romantic comedy tradition of seductive climax as narrative denouement.

Speed becomes about the condition of waiting, of spectatorially hanging around, while it puts us in the lurid position of waiting to rubberneck. The film forces us to wait for the happy ending of sex and the jump-starts of violence. The possibility of narrative satisfaction intersects both violence (the possibility that the bus will explode or otherwise cause mayhem) and sex (the possibility, ultimately if briefly fulfilled, that the two main characters will come together romantically). In this process of reducing the contemporary action movie to its basics, like an aerodynamic aircraft stripped to its skeleton, *Speed*'s narrative logic becomes a logic of fetishization; or, more precisely, of an aspiration toward the condition of the fetish at the level of the narrative structure rather than simply as a premise of the story. The film responds to the exhaustion of narrative conventions by turning them into fetish objects, hung out in front of viewers like carrots on a stick; it plays with formulaic staleness less through overt defamiliarization than through the same kind of provocative teasing at a narrative level that its main characters exercise at a romantic level. The manipulation of the logic of the narrative fetish becomes, in *Speed*, both the story and the story's mechanism.

Speed indicates the next stage of the postmodern action movie toward a self-consciousness about its own devices of ersatz sensation. In the cinema of attractions, such events as the electrocution of an elephant sufficed for storytelling; at a time when cinema was relatively uncodified, the fleeting thrill of the attraction metonymized the thrill of cinema itself. *Speed* marks a moment when the thrill is gone, when explosions and sensations have to strive so strenuously to make a deep impact that they crowd conventional stories right off the screen. In contemporary cinema, the nostalgia for the comforts of simple sensation can hardly keep pace with the nostalgia for the comforts of familiar classical stories—depending on from whom the nostalgia arises. The accretion of violent shocks can occur only in relation to the exhaustion of the narrative conventions that they defamiliarize, and those violent sensations in turn become more and more familiar and require greater and greater emphasis to have an effect. A film as denuded as *Speed* or as self-conscious as *Crash* ultimately only foregrounds the situation of shock chasing absence from which cinema emerged, which it has memorialized in perpetuity, and which endures in spite of any nostalgic formulations of an idealized imaginary past in which audiences could feel authentically shocking shocks and genuinely sensational sensations.

Notes

Epigraph is from Anthony Lane, "Holy Fools," *The New Yorker*, April 14, 1997, 88.
1. Mark Singer, "The Joel Silver Show," *New Yorker*, March 21, 1994, 128 and 129.
2. For more detail on this characteristic modernist idea, see Leo Charney, *Empty Moments: Cinema, Modernity, and Drift* (Durham, N.C.: Duke University Press, 1998), esp. 30–42.
3. Sigmund Freud, *Beyond the Pleasure Principle*, trans. James Strachey, in *Standard Edition of the Complete Psychological Works of Sigmund Freud*, vol. 18 (London: Hogarth, 1955), 14.
4. This mode of storytelling is trenchantly described in chapters 2 though 4 of David Bordwell, Janet Staiger, and Kristin Thompson, *The Classical Hollywood Cinema: Film Style and Mode of Production to 1960* (New York: Columbia University Press, 1985).
5. Bosley Crowther, *New York Times*, August 14, 1967, 36.
6. David Denby, "Masquerade," *New York Magazine*, July 14, 1997, 48.
7. Anthony Lane, "Current Films," *New Yorker*, July 27, 1997, 18.
8. Tom Gunning, "The Cinema of Attraction(s): Early Film, Its Spectator and the Avant-Garde," *Wide Angle* 8, nos. 3–4 (1986): 63–70.
9. Tom Gunning, "An Aesthetic of Astonishment: Early Film and the (In)Credulous Spectator," *Art and Text* 34 (spring 1989): 38.
10. Tom Gunning, "'Now You See It, Now You Don't': The Temporality of the Cinema of Attractions," *Velvet Light Trap* 32 (fall 1993): 6–7.
11. Miriam Hansen, "Early Cinema, Late Cinema: Permutations of the Public Sphere," *Screen* 34, no. 3 (fall 1993): 200.
12. Sergei Eisenstein, "A Dialectic Approach to Film Form," in *Film Form*, ed. and trans. Jay Leyda (New York: Harcourt Brace, 1949): 46. On the evolution of Eisenstein's theory from conflict toward cooperation, see David Bordwell, "Eisenstein's Epistemological Shift," *Screen* 15, no. 4 (1975): 29–46.
13. Lynne Kirby, *Parallel Tracks: The Railroad and Silent Cinema* (Durham, N.C.: Duke University Press, 1997): 57–63.
14. See the two prominent explications of this theme, Walter Benjamin, "The Work of Art in the Age of Mechanical Reproduction," in *Illuminations*, ed. Hannah Arendt, trans. Harry Zohn (New York: Schocken Books, 1969); and

Siegfried Kracauer, "Cult of Distraction: On Berlin's Picture Palaces," in *The Mass Ornament: Weimar Essays*, ed. and trans. Thomas Y. Levin (Cambridge, Mass.: Harvard University Press, 1995).

15. Gunning, "An Aesthetic of Astonishment," 41.

16. The crash as the marker of an unrepeatable moment of death has been reinforced by the fascination with Princess Diana's fatal car accident and its three-fold response of hysteria, fetishization of the lost object, and the effort to reconstruct a scenario of the lost moment(s) of collision.

17. Owen Gleiberman, "Big Bang Theory," *Entertainment Weekly*, March 28, 1997: 51.

18. Siegfried Kracauer, *Theory of Film: The Redemption of Physical Reality* (New York: Oxford University Press, 1960), 213.

19. Dana Polan, "Brief Encounters: Mass Culture and the Evacuation of Sense," in *Studies in Entertainment*, ed. Tania Modleski (Bloomington: Indiana University Press, 1986), 179.

20. Dana Polan, "'Above All Else to Make You See': Cinema and the Ideology of Spectacle," in *Postmodernism and Politics*, ed. Jonathan Arac (Minneapolis: University of Minnesota Press, 1986), 61.

21. My formulation begs the question of whether attractions and spectacle are necessarily the same thing, a topic whose complexity expands beyond this discussion.

22. Matt Groening has both captured and parodied this aspect of classical cartoons in the *Itchy and Scratchy* segments of *The Simpsons*, in which two barely characterized animals inflict inconceivable violence on each other to Bart's and Lisa's inexhaustible amusement.

23. Singer, "The Joel Silver Show," 128.

24. On slapstick, see Henry Jenkins, *What Made Pistachio Nuts? Early Sound Comedy and the Vaudeville Aesthetic* (New York: Columbia University Press, 1992); and Eileen Bowser, ed., *The Slapstick Symposium* (Brussels: Fédération Internationale des Archives du Film, 1987), esp. Donald Crafton, "The Pie and the Chase: Gag, Spectacle, and Narrative in Slapstick Comedy."

25. Owen Gleiberman, "The Bugs of War," *Entertainment Weekly*, November 7, 1997, 54.

violence american style:

the narrative orchestration

three   # of violent attractions

marsha kinder

While writing on the cultural specificity of violence in the context of Spanish cinema, I was inevitably confronted by the question of what is culturally specific about Hollywood's violent representations. I avoided this question, partly because cultural specificity is far more difficult to perceive as an insider than as an outsider.[1] Yet I knew that whenever I did address this question, my starting point would be Sam Peckinpah: first, because his work provides a uniquely productive cross-cultural comparison with cinematic representations of violence in Spain; second, because his use of extremely violent representations in films like *The Wild Bunch* (1969) and *Straw Dogs* (1971) generated intense cultural debates at the time of their release, which resonated with larger social debates then in progress over whether violence should be considered a legitimate means of social-political change; and third, because, as Stephen Prince points out in *Savage Cinema*, he is "the crucial link between classical and postmodern Hollywood, the figure whose work transforms modern cinema in terms of stylistics for rendering screen violence and in terms of the moral and psychological consequences that ensue."[2]

The Cultural Reinscription of *The Wild Bunch*

Sam Peckinpah presents us with an intriguing paradox. This filmmaker who came to epitomize American excess in cinematic violence—particularly within the most American of all Hollywood genres, the Western— had at least partially adapted that approach from a Spanish film that was not well known in the United States, Carlos Saura's *La caza* (*The Hunt*, 1965). Not only does John Hopewell quote Peckinpah as saying, "Seeing *La caza* changed my life!" but also, according to Ricardo Franco, the Spanish filmmaker who directed *Pascual Duarte* (1975), one of Spain's most disturbingly violent films of all time, after seeing *La caza* Peckinpah wanted to do a film version of Nobel Prize–winner Camilo José Cela's 1942 post–Civil War novel, *La Familia de Pascual Duarte*.[3] In 1992 when I mentioned these two facts to Spain's most distinguished film editor, Pablo del Amo, who edited both *La caza* and *Pascual Duarte*, he told me he found them surprising, for he knew *The Wild Bunch* very well (since he was the one who, at the behest of Spanish censors, had reedited it to tone down the violence for its release in Francoist Spain), yet saw no similarities to *La caza*.[4] I also raised the issue with Carlos Saura in spring 1999 when he was in Los Angeles for the American Cinematheque retrospective of his work. He said that when he had met Peckinpah several years before in Hawaii, Sam told him that *La caza* was a major influence on *The Wild Bunch*, an influence that Saura (like Del Amo) was unable to see in the film. These reactions made me all the more intrigued with the question of precisely what Peckinpah had learned from Saura's film and how he had managed to culturally reinscribe it with American specificity to the point that it was unrecognizable even to these two "insiders" from Spain.

In *La caza* Saura uses the ritualized violence of the hunt, a favorite pastime of Franco and his political cronies, to substitute for the Civil War and its reciprocal savagery, which were then forbidden topics in Spain. The story follows a group of men—three former Civil War buddies who had fought on Franco's Nationalist side and one of their nephews—who go hunting for rabbits on a game reserve that had been a bloody battlefield in the Civil War. Although the film never mentions the war directly, the hunt and its setting lead the three veterans to reminisce about their wartime experience and old betrayals, memories that ultimately lead to an insane shoot-out in which they kill each other, leaving only the young man, in freeze shot, as the sole survivor. The opening image behind the titles immediately creates an atmosphere of repressed violence. We see a pair of caged ferrets restlessly pacing back and forth in a cramped space and hear a loud, pounding, percussive music, which makes their entrapment feel all the more oppressive. The camera relentlessly moves in to a tighter shot that intensifies their desperation, links the close-up with entrapment, and marks the ferrets as surrogate victims for the violence to come. Everything in the film—its claustrophobic narrative, its sporadic and carefully modulated release of violent movements, its spare landscapes, its emotional rhythms in dialogue and mise-en-scène, its percussive music and montage, its oppressive silences and ellipses, its interplay between extreme close-ups and long shots, and its blatant specularization of the violent gaze—move inexorably toward the final explosive shoot-out, heightening its intensity when it comes.

It was precisely this narrative orchestration of violence—with its varied rhythms, dramatic pauses, and cathartic climax—that had such a profound impact on Peckinpah rather than the number of thematic similarities that *The Wild Bunch* shares with *La caza*: the group of middle-aged male buddies as the focus, the gendering of violence as a sign of masculinity, the blatant specularization of the violence through visual apparatuses like binoculars and gun sights, the recriminating memories of past betrayals as a catalyst, the young outsider as the one whose impulsive shot unleashes the final suicidal battle, and the evocation of a war that is represented only indirectly (in Peckinpah's case, the First World War through the Germans and their war machines in the final massacre, and also Vietnam through the peasant resistance with which Angel is allied). While such thematic links ensured that Peckinpah could adapt this kind of orchestration to the Western genre, the life-changing lesson he learned from *La caza* (and applied not only to *The Wild Bunch* but to his other films that followed) was how to use violence to structure not merely an individual sequence but the stylistic and narrative design of the entire film—that is, to use representations of violence as a series of rhythmic eruptions that orchestrate the spectator's emotional response.

We sense it immediately in the syncopated sequence behind the titles, in which the wild bunch, disguised as soldiers, are riding into town for a bank robbery, and their movements, accompanied by a percussive drum beat, are periodically interrupted by a freeze frame that temporarily suspends the action and drains the color. Though we become impatient with those pauses—especially once we realize that these outlaws are heading toward a shoot-out with bounty hunters who await them in ambush—they give us more time to consider the moral ambiguities of the various groups assembled, not only the seemingly well-mannered bank robbers and the railroad's seedy bounty hunters (who are led by a former member of the wild bunch) but also the respectable hymn-singing townsfolk listening to a temperance union speech and the cluster of Anglo and Mexican children taking pleasure in torturing a scorpion, groups who may at first seem to be innocent bystanders but ultimately prove to be morally complicit. The pauses also lead us to become aware of our own complicity as spectators, for they make us realize how eager we are for the violent spectacle to be unleashed (which happens much sooner here than in *La caza* and with much more blood and slow-motion dazzle and with a richer orchestration of gunfire, screams, and shattering glass). The violence is unleashed by a clipped line of dialogue uttered by the outlaw leader, Pike Bishop (William Holden), just before Peckinpah's final directorial credit—a line that calls attention to the film's violent orchestration of motion and stasis: "If they move, kill 'em!" This kinetic dynamic—a temporary pause heightening the violent outburst—is repeated in both films just before the final massacre, when there is a strange moment of nervous silence and stillness before the climactic violence erupts with an excessiveness that far exceeds our expectations.

Although the structural dynamics of violence in the two films are similar, their meanings and emotional effects are totally different. In *Violence and the Sacred* (1972), René Girard argues that the sole purpose of all sacrificial violence (whether in art, myth, ritual, or religion) is the prevention of recurrent reciprocal violence, a theory that makes violence essential to social order. Girard treats violence as a performative language that speaks through an elaborate set of conventions that are codified by the social order it seeks to uphold. From this perspective, the key question is what kind of social order specific conventions are designed to defend, a question that makes the representation of violence a crucial issue for exploring cultural specificity.[5]

As I argued in *Blood Cinema*, in Francoist Spain the representation of violence was suppressed along with sex, politics, and sacrilege. The most graphic violence appeared in the films made in the 1960s and 1970s by the leftist opposition, who were eager to expose the violent legacy of the Civil War that was aestheticized and disavowed by the fascists. Thus, in the final sequence of *La caza* the ritualized violence of the hunt, which substitutes for the Civil War, is suddenly transformed back into a brutal image of modern massacre. It is not the violence itself that is glamorized or even condoned, but rather the cathartic act of exposing it as the legacy of fascism.

Conversely, in *The Wild Bunch* the excessive violence is orgasmic rather than cathartic, erotic rather than revelatory, for Peckinpah positions the spectator to desire rather than to fear its eruption. After the "big bang" opening of the bank robbery, we are left wondering with anticipation whether any subsequent violence can possibly equal or surpass that initial rush—a spectator response that is somewhat analogous to a drug experience, in recognizing that we are already partially hooked on a guilty pleasure. Rhetorically it is closer to the reaction we have to the shocking shower murder early in *Psycho* rather than to the periodic emissions of increasing violence in *La caza* that build slowly like Ravel's *Bolero*, yet in contrast to both of these films *The Wild Bunch* is not constructed on a rhetoric of fear. The only thing that is frightening in Peckinpah's film is having to face our own visceral response to the violence, which is like that of the children caught in the shoot-out who are thrilled by the violence that surrounds, endangers, and permeates them.

The excitement is at least partly dependent on those frequent pauses, which are most fully elaborated in the idyllic sequence in which the wild bunch visits Angel's peaceful home village. Like the weary gunmen, despite the pleasures of this respite we soon find ourselves itching to move on to the action. Whereas Saura (and other Spanish filmmakers of the leftist opposition) could use such pauses to allude subtly to the cultural repression that existed under Franco (allusions easily recognized by most Spanish spectators), Peckinpah, who lacked this cultural context, tailored them to the rhetoric of the Western genre (those dramatic build-ups to climactic gun battles in classic Westerns like *High Noon* and *Shane*) yet making them sufficiently hyperbolic so that they would be experienced as a new kind of narrative rhythm. Despite the stylization of its rhetoric, *The Wild Bunch* allows us no emotional distance; that's where Saura's rhythmic orchestration proves so effective, particularly when dialogized with conventions from another culture.

Unlike Saura, Peckinpah inflects the violence with a comic exuberance that can be found in American silent comedies, cartoons, and other popular forms of farce; for the violent outbreaks are repeatedly accompanied by an infectious laughter, which functions as another surrogate for sexual release. In the final sequence laughter is added to the mix of guns, music, and drum roll that accompanies the wild bunch on their final death march. The hearty laughter of Dutch (Ernest Borgnine, the character most strongly committed to the group) triggers the final blood bath and punctuates the final dramatic pause, which, like the idyllic visit to Angel's Mexican village, provides a brief moment to savor a nostalgic sense of belonging. His laughter initiates a knowing exchange of looks among the buddies, inaugurating a moment of masculine *jouissance* or expanded time that enables the wild bunch (and the audience) to look not only forward to the tragic massacre that brings their lives and narrative to an end, but also backward to earlier moments of laughter and male bonding (a movement actually visualized behind the final credits). This final movement reverses not only the structure of the narrative but also its meaning and tone, imbuing it with a comic resilience that disavows the finality of the violent ending.

With such changes, Peckinpah reinscribed Saura's orchestration of violence to address his own cultural context, justifying violence as a basic human response and the most honorable human choice in certain social-political circumstances. As he put it, "Those who have been too long oppressed by the violence of power are waking up, organizing and fighting for rights. Inevitably, the conflict can only resolve itself in violence."[6] In *The Wild Bunch* the question was not whether you die (for this is inevitable), or whether you kill innocent people (for no one in this film is innocent), but whether you are sufficiently committed to die for your own community. The film focuses on groups rather than individuals (the bounty hunters, temperance league, soldiers, Mexican army, peasant guerillas, and outlaws), an ethos visualized in the recurring signature widescreen shot of the wild bunch riding four or five abreast toward the camera. Both Pike and Dutch claim that this kind of commitment is what distinguishes humans from animals—a position that had political resonance in the cultural debates of the period and in the wake of 1968. You can find it not only in the writings of Frantz Fanon, who argued that free men must earn their freedom through violent revolution,[7] but also in actual choices then being made in the United States as to how to oppose the Vietnam War, racism, and other forms of social injustice—through militant action or passive resistance. As Prince points out:

By 1968 when Peckinpah . . . was working on *The Wild Bunch*, the Vietnam War was at its height, . . . with mass mobilization against the war producing crowds of 100,000 at demonstrations in New York and Washington, D.C.

During the first nine months of 1967, urban riots erupted in 128 cities. . . . From 1963–1968 more than two million persons participated in social protest. Civil rights demonstrations mobilized 1.1 million, anti-war demonstrations 680,000, and ghetto riots an estimated 200,000. Nine thousand casualties resulted, including some 200 deaths.[8]

Similar questions about violence were also being addressed in several European films of the late 1960s, such as Gillo Pontecorvo's *The Battle of Algiers* (1965), Jean-Luc Godard's *La Chinoise* (1967) and *Weekend* (1967), Joris Ivens's anthology film *Far from Vietnam* (1967), and even Ingmar Bergman's *The Shame* (1968)—reflexive films that generated controversy over issues of realism and representation. In contrast to these European films in which the links to current wars and political issues were explicit, the most violent American films addressed them within popular genres, with stories set in the past. By defining the Western as "a universal frame within which it is possible to comment on today,"[9] Peckinpah helped lead contemporary critics like Marilyn Yaquinto to conclude, "By 1969 director Sam Peckinpah gave us *The Wild Bunch*, supposedly a Western about a bygone era but the slaughter-on-screen was as fresh as anything ever filmed before."[10]

By now it should be clear that I am using this cross-cultural comparison between *The Wild Bunch* and *La caza* not to suggest that the former's narrative orchestration of violence was solely derived from Spain but as an entry into distinguishing how it functions with cultural specificity in American cinema of the late 1960s and beyond. For, despite differences in genre, the changes Peckinpah made in Saura's model are consistent with conventions found in *Bonnie and Clyde* (1967) and *A Clockwork Orange* (1971), and these are precisely the characteristics that Del Amo and Saura found so alien to Spanish cinema and that made these films seem so vitally new to American audiences at the time of their release.

American NOVA: The Narrative Orchestration of Violent Attractions

What these two films share with *The Wild Bunch* is a narrative orchestration of violence in which action sequences function like performative "numbers," interrupting the linear drive of the plot with their sensational audio and visual spectacle yet simultaneously serving as dramatic climaxes that advance the story toward closure. Because these violent numbers are so excessive, their rhythmic representation so kinetic, and their visceral pleasures so compelling, their cumulative effect provides a rival mode of orchestration that threatens to usurp the narrative's traditional function of contextualization through a seriality and an exuberance that render the film comic, no matter how painful, tragic, or satiric its narrative resolution may be.

The narrative logic that underlies this pattern of orchestration is perhaps most familiar (and innocuous) to us in musicals. Yet it has also been extended to other cinematic genres and regimes—perhaps most relevantly for our purposes by Linda Williams in her groundbreaking work on pornography, in which she persuasively shows how sex scenes function like musical numbers; and most powerfully by Tom Gunning in his influential work on the "cinema of attractions" as an alternative mode to narrative in early cinema, a mode that continues to survive not only in avant-garde texts (as he argued in that first formulation) but also in mainstream film genres like animated cartoons, musicals, disaster films, action films, and other hybrids.[11] Whereas Gunning claims that "the cinema of attractions directly solicits spectator attention, inciting visual curiosity, and supplying pleasure through an exciting spectacle—a unique event, whether fictional or documentary, that is of interest in itself," Mary Ann Doane argues that in early execution films (a popular subgenre of actualities) one finds a tension between narrative and violent attractions, which was intensified by the subject of death. In describing *Electrocuting an Elephant* (Edison, 1903) and *Execution of Czolgosz with Panorama of Auburn Prison* (Porter/Edison, 1901), she notes both their "intense fascination with the representation of death" and their narrativization of these killings as an "orchestration of guilt and punishment."

> The direct presentation of death to the spectator as pure event, as shock, was displaced by its narrativization. Technology and narrative form an alliance in modernity to ameliorate the corrosiveness of the relation between time and subjectivity. Perhaps death functions as a kind of cinematic ur-event because it appears as the zero degree of meaning, its evacuation. With death we are suddenly confronted with pure event, pure contingency, what ought to be inaccessible to representation (hence the various social and legal bans against the direct, nonfictional filming of death). Such a problematic is possible only where contingency and meaning, event and structure are radically opposed.[12]

In contrast to the singulative "ground zero" of death, the representation of violent iterations suggests a proliferating series that moves both forward and backward in time, as if denying the finality of death—a disavowal that is essentially comic. I am arguing that the tension between these rival orchestrations of violence—a rhythmic accumulation of discrete, serial events (beatings, murders, executions) versus their narrativization (in a unifying story of guilt and punishment)—is generated by a comic hybridization that is central to the American representation of cinematic action. Instead of the story merely anchoring the meaning and binding the emotional impact of the violence it contains, these recurring disruptive events resist narrative closure through a rhythmic orchestration of violent spectacle that inflects the story with a resilient seriality and comic exuberance until it is no longer certain whether the narrative is orchestrating the violence or whether the violent events are orchestrating the narrative.

The disruptive power of this tension is palpable in Prince's fascinating discussion of *The Wild Bunch* in which he blames the "kinetic montage" for undermining the narrative. After casting "Bloody Sam" as the "seminal practitioner" of a "savage" postmodern cinema, Prince earnestly tries to redeem him by distinguishing his moral vision from that of the "pernicious" postmodern films he helped spawn. To perform this feat, he celebrates Peckinpah's "melancholy framing of violence" in narratives that focus on suffering, a reading that unfortunately does not apply to *The Wild Bunch*. Thus, despite claiming that it and *Straw Dogs* are "Peckinpah's two films of hard brilliance and crystalline control in their cinematic design," Prince curiously concludes that *The Wild Bunch* is "an anomaly in Peckinpah's screen treatment of violence."[13] This torturous logic shows Prince struggling with the contradiction between traditional narrative contextualization and those violent "montage set pieces" it fails to tame—sequences that he acknowledges to be the most influential and innovative parts of the film but that he feels morally compelled to condemn. What I am arguing is that it is precisely this disruptive tension between the unifying narrative and these proliferating, comic violent attractions (rather than the attractions themselves) that is so characteristic of the American orchestration of cinematic violence.

The Violent Orchestration of Hybridization and Hysteria in Bonnie and Clyde

Preceding *The Wild Bunch* by two years, *Bonnie and Clyde* was the film that first popularized this violent narrative logic with mainstream American audiences. Like Peckinpah's Western, it had strong European influences. As is well known, screenwriters David Newman and Robert Benton had tried to get François Truffaut and Jean-Luc Godard to direct the film before turning to Arthur Penn, for they were partly inspired by the innovative use of the gangster genre (in films like Godard's *Breathless* [1959], *Band of Outsiders* [1964], and *Pierrot le fou* [1965], and Truffaut's *Shoot the Piano Player* [1960]); by the fast-paced, exhilarating motion of their characters, camera work, and narratives; and by the unpredictability of their violent events.

While exploring the mythic roots of the American gangster film, a genre that flourished in the 1930s and justified violence as a common social response to the impotence imposed by the Great Depression and by the economic inequities of capitalism, *Bonnie and Clyde* blatantly combines this form with conventions from the musical (another popular American genre of the 1930s that offered a different model for orchestrating violent attractions). The mixture is most blatant in the scene when, after committing their first murder, the Barrow gang escapes into a movie theater that happens to be showing Busby Berkeley's "We're in the Money" number from the classical American musical *Gold Diggers of 1933*, in which a chorus line of showgirls dance in front of huge gold coins bearing the words "In God We Trust." The film presents these two popular genres from the 1930s as opposite sides of the same coin: violent confrontation versus total escape. Both genres appealed to our nation at a time when it was deeply polarized and in extreme political crisis, which was also the situation in 1967 (the year of the film's release), when the nation was sharply divided over the Vietnam War. After quoting one of the film's screenwriters, Robert Benton, as saying that spectators at the time frequently speculated that the film was "really about Vietnam . . . really about Lee Harvey Oswald, really about police brutality," Yaquinto concludes:

> Within a year of *Bonnie and Clyde* real-life violence made the film's screen

blood look contrived. As the war in Vietnam continued to mushroom and antiwar sentiments reached an equally theatrical pitch, bloodshed was a nightly news event. Then came the assassinations of Bobby Kennedy and Martin Luther King as well as the street rioting outside the Democratic National Convention in Chicago. It must have looked as if no amount of screen violence could ever seem like overkill to a public feeding off a daily diet of carnage.[14]

This feeling of excessive violence in the film is intensified by the way it is combined with a driving comic energy. As in *The Wild Bunch*, the fusion of violence and laughter is orgasmic, for both function as surrogates for sex; but here that point is explicitly narrativized as compensation for Clyde's sexual impotence, which complicates the masculine gendering of violence and makes it more vulnerable to subversion by Bonnie and her parodic posturing with phallic guns and cigar. Instead of being confined to the exclusively male realm of the traditional gangster movie, farcical violence is all in the family, equally accessible both to the Barrow brothers and their wives. The combination of violence and laughter is amplified by the exuberant bluegrass banjo music of Flatt and Scruggs's "Foggy Mountain Breakdown," which pushes the comic exuberance to new extremes, turning this road movie into a Road Runner cartoon in which characters resiliently bounce back after every violent episode. After one successful bank robbery, there is even a brief cut to a farcical Keystone Cop–type chase scene in which harmless police cars roll over and nearly collide while the gang escapes across the state line. When the music is absent, the tone grows ominous and the violent consequences more serious, as in the playful bank job that ends with the first murder and in the hilarious encounter with Eugene and Vilma, which ends with the gloomy discovery that he's a mortician. When the situation and tone grow desperate, the laughter and violence become hysterical, which makes the action appear aberrational. The rhythmic alternation between silence and shrieking contributes to the film's sustained tension, implying that hysteria is always just below the surface of the action. The hysteria is amplified by Blanche, whose terrified screams run throughout the film and are as disturbing to the audience as they are to Bonnie.

The hysteria is most intense in the two-part shoot-out in which Blanche is blinded and Buck killed. Evoking the war film genre, an armored tank cautiously approaches the small motor cabin in which the Barrow gang is sheltered for the night (as if the police were troops entering a war zone held by the enemy). The gang escapes this confined space and flees to their cars, desperate to get back on the open road. Their flight is accompanied not by the comic banjo music but by a terrifying cacophony of orchestrated hysteria: the racing engines, the staccato firing of machine guns, Buck's painful moans, Blanche's blood-curdling screams and prayers, and C. W. Moss's quiet weeping. Finally they escape the noise and stop for the night in an open field, tumbling out of the car like toons. At dawn this brief interlude of darkness and quiet is ruptured by the police, shrieking like animals and setting the Barrow car ablaze, resuming the cacophony of gunfire, car crashes, and agonizing screams. When Buck Barrow finally dies, it is a welcome relief.

The alternation between silence and hysteria intensifies the violence of this sequence and of the entire film. Hysteria becomes the norm, punctuated only by moments of stillness and slow motion. Like the visit to Angel's village in *The Wild Bunch*, Bonnie's visit with her mother at the family picnic is a symbolic respite steeped in nostalgia, a utopian vision of the lost community to which the Barrow gang can never return. Like Peckinpah's Western outlaws, she and Clyde can find lasting solace only in the film's final massacre, which functions both as orgasmic climax to the series of hysterical violent events that precede it and as the pivotal point in the narrative where the hyperviolence turns tragic. The formal dynamics are reminiscent of the final *danse macabre* of Toshiro Mifune's Macbeth figure in Akira Kurosawa's *Throne of Blood* (1957), in which this tragic villain is killed by an army (who pierce his body with scores of arrows) and, despite his defeat, both the excessiveness of the overkill and the use of slow motion help imbue the murdered figure with an almost supernatural power. Similarly, the final massacre of Bonnie and Clyde by an army of lawmen (who riddle their bodies with scores of bullets) and its balletic representation in romanticized slow motion help transform these outlaw lovers into mythic figures worthy of tragedy, even though their own violent deeds are rendered comic through the accelerated rhythms of editing and music.

It was partly this mythic approach that led William J. Free to observe, "We recognize the subject—a gangster film—but the values presented on the screen are so different from our stereotyped expectations that we see the subjects in a new light," but it was also the way the violence rhythmically structured the narrative that led spectators to this difference in perception. Whereas Yaquinto concludes, "The film enabled the genre to use violence in a more literal manner—not just for the punctuation, but also to explore the brutality of violence itself,"[15] I am arguing that it was precisely this orchestration of violent punctuation that enabled the brutality to have such strong emotional impact and that made spectators feel the film was so "new."

Although *Bonnie and Clyde* combines familiar elements of the gangster genre and musical, this mythic ending helped it spawn a new subgenre of violent road movies featuring a heterosexual outlaw couple in search of justice, thrills, or fame—a genre that could be traced back to Fritz Lang's *You Only Live Once* (1937), Nicholas Ray's *They Live by Night* (1948), and Joseph Lewis's *Gun Crazy* (1949) but that owed its violent orchestration to *Bonnie and Clyde*. This was the subgenre that launched the careers of both Terrence Malick and Steven Spielberg in the early 1970s, with *Badlands* (1973) and *The Sugarland Express* (1974) respectively;[16] that was subsequently subjected to subversions of gender and sexuality both here and abroad in films like Alain Tanner's *Messidor* (1977), Margarethe von Trotta's *The Second Awakening of Christa Klages* (1977), Ridley Scott's *Thelma and Louise* (1991), and Gregg Araki's *The Living End* (1992); and that reached a new level of hyperviolence in the 1990s in films like Tony Scott's *True Romance* (1993) and Oliver Stone's *Natural Born Killers*

(1994), both based on screenplays by Quentin Tarantino. All of these films—and the critical discourse around them—look back with nostalgia to *Bonnie and Clyde.*

A Futuristic Vision of Violent Representation in A Clockwork Orange

The third film to become part of the raging debate over cinematic violence in this period was Stanley Kubrick's *A Clockwork Orange* (1971), which was bound to be compared with *The Wild Bunch* and *Bonnie and Clyde.* In contrast to the visceral complicity we experienced in response to the violence in those two earlier genre films, here we enjoy the ironic distance of satire, which mocks any easy identification with brutal popular heroes. In the opening shot the camera glides backward from a facial close-up of the punkish protagonist Alex (Malcolm McDowell) to a safe emotional distance, revealing the futuristic kitsch aesthetics of the Korova Milk Bar. The film is not personally threatening because we are not turned on by the violent spectacle or longing for its return, even if Alex is. Instead of functioning as a surrogate for sex, violence merely heightens or blocks Alex's erotic pleasure.

To orchestrate the violence, the film uses both nondiegetic musical scoring (as in its violent predecessors *The Wild Bunch* and *Bonnie and Clyde* and Kubrick's own *2001: A Space Odyssey* [1968]) and also fully staged song and dance sequences of rape and violence, which make the hybridization with the musical more corrosive. The fighting and ultraviolence are literally transformed into dance through musical orchestration, and the elegant pull-backs to long shots not only keep us from seeing any blood but also enable us to savor the artfully designed irony. The violent attractions are unified more by the music than by Alex's voice-over narration, particularly through the music's continuing incongruity with the brutal actions it accompanies. The film uses both slow-motion and speeded-up footage to heighten not the emotional intensity (as in *The Wild Bunch* and *Bonnie and Clyde*) but aesthetic stylization (particularly in the comical softcore scene in which Alex has sex with two young girls to the accelerated strains of the William Tell Overture). Such scenes reveal how dependent all representations are on the modulation of rhythm. These blatantly contrived manipulations of the image helped lay the groundwork for a reliance on special effects and multitrack sound design in the violent action films of the 1980s and 1990s, particularly once they were augmented by the increased compositing capacities of computer graphics and digitization.[17]

The film is not about the use of violence for social change but about the representation of violence and its consequences for subjectivity. The thematics don't emphasize allegiance to a group (for all groups in the film are equally corrupt—Alex's gang of droogs, his family, the police, the church, political parties, and so on), but rather the freedom of an individual to make moral choices, even when spawned in a violent, dehumanized culture. This larger scope of political-social corruption makes distinctions of law and order appear as deceptive as the artificial lines drawn between genres, which means all purebreds are suspect and all hybrids valued for their unique combination of choices. In this case we find a unique generic brew of political satire, science fiction, the musical, and the juvenile gang film, in which comic exuberance is not a matter of resilience but a scathing black humor to which virtually everyone in the film is subjected. The film evokes not a nostalgic sense of loss for values from the past, but satiric irony about utopian visions of the future.

Unlike the other two films, the nationality of *A Clockwork Orange* is also marked by hybridity. Although directed by Stanley Kubrick (a well-known Jewish-American filmmaker who emigrated to England) and financed and released by Warner Bros. (a major Hollywood studio), it was filmed in England with a predominantly British cast and was based on a popular British novel by Anthony Burgess (who spent many years working as a colonial in Malaya). Its protagonist is a marginalized Londoner who was later adopted as a cultural icon by a global youth culture.

In Burgess's 1962 first-person novel, the reader's experience is filtered entirely through the language of Alex (the brutish fifteen-year-old narrator), who, along with the droogs in his gang, speaks a strange patois that combines Russian and English. In learning Alex's vocabulary, we internalize his language and are inevitably drawn into complicity with his ultraviolent point of view. He literally puts his words in our mouth—a dynamic that merely exaggerates what happens in the process of reading any novel and thereby exposes the subversive potential of the first-person narrative. This process does not survive in the film because verbal language is no longer the dominant means of transmission in this medium. The patois sounds like merely another one of those British dialects or teenage jargons that are difficult to understand but not impossible to decipher, particularly with the aid of strong visuals and action.

As an alternative, Kubrick moves to reflexive commentary on cinematic spectatorship, where the audience's complicity is linked to the pleasure experienced while consuming violent audiovisual imagery. This process is particularly strong in the prison sequence, where in exchange for shortening his sentence, Alex agrees to undergo an experimental behavioral therapy (the Ludovico treatment) to eradicate the pleasure he takes in performing ultraviolence. Although this treatment is described in considerable detail in the novel, it is actually dramatized in the film, so that we spectators also partake in the experience. As Alex sits strapped in a straitjacket with his eyes held open by "lid-locks," a torturous contraption (worthy of the horror genre) that prevents him from shutting his eyes, he is subjected to a cinematic montage of "nasty bits of ultraviolence": realistic violence from a Hollywood-type action film with high production values and lots of hyperrealistic blood; a gang rape of a young woman from a teen-pic; and Nazi war footage showing Hitler, air battles, and bombings while Alex's beloved Beethoven's Ninth Symphony swells in the background. Unlike Alex we still have the freedom to close our eyes and are not conditioned to associate these images with a deathlike paralysis and nauseating terror; nevertheless, we are still forced to perceive other disturbing connections that make the noblest art complicit with evil. We are reminded that the same culture that created Beethoven also spawned

Hitler, who knew how to aestheticize brutality. And we are led to see how easily the cultural connotations of Beethoven's "Ode to Joy" and Gene Kelley's "Singin' in the Rain" can be modified and contaminated through montage, narrative recontextualization, and sound-image relations—a point Kubrick earlier demonstrated with Strauss's "Blue Danube" in *2001: A Space Odyssey*. Such reinscriptions across different cultures, media, and periods show the power of editing and meaning production at the point of exhibition and reception (rather than merely during production), a realization that potentially empowers not only fanatical Beethoven fans like Alex but also postmodernist artists who specialize in sampling and pastiche. This reinscription process also applies to Burgess's novel, whose story and language are retained but whose meaning and structure are reorchestrated through Kubrick's violent representations.

The film's shift of focus from violent behavior to representation, from social engineering to artistic reception, can best be demonstrated in the way Kubrick changes the murder that sends Alex to prison. This sequence is crucial because of its central position in the narrative, which is bisected by Alex's retraining in prison, with the second half mirroring the first and with each violent episode converting Alex's former role as perpetrator into that of victim, a reversal that shows us how easily our feelings toward a character can be manipulated even with emotional distance from the events. This structure positions the violent episodes as a series of discrete attractions, like guideposts along a narrative journey that can be recognized by a traveler moving in either direction. It also marks the murder that sends Alex to prison and the retraining he undergoes there as the two key points of narrative rupture, which are both pivotal to how the violent attractions should be read. Thus it is hardly surprising that these two central episodes are so explicitly focused on retraining spectators in how to respond to art. While this was also the case in the novel with respect to the prison episode, it was not so with the murder, which Kubrick ingeniously transforms.

Whereas in the novel the victim is a pathetic, lonely old "baboochka" living in a house in Oldtown swarming with cats and antiques, Kubrick turns her into a rich, skinny proprietor of a fashionable health farm who happens to be a collector of modernist art and who happens to specialize in sadomasochistic images that dehumanize the body. We first see her doing yoga exercises in leotard and tights, surrounded by her cats, who stand in for "pussy" in the sexual battle that ensues—a gendered duel in which artistic prostheses substitute for sexual parts. Alex and his droogs wear extravagant codpieces and long obscene phallic noses, radical costuming that not only prefigures the punk aesthetic but also parodies erotic high art. When the woman attacks him with a bust of Beethoven, he defends himself with her huge white sculpture of a detached phallus (which she calls "a very important work of art") and transforms it (rather than the small silver statue of a young girl used in the novel) into a deadly weapon. By being bludgeoned to death with her own pricey art piece, she is forced to face the material consequences of her own complicity with an elitist phallocentric culture. Although she uses the same language as did the old lady in the novel

("Wretched little slummy bedbug, breaking into real people's houses") and belongs to the same social class, here the elitism is intensified by her snooty upper-class accent and linked more directly to her taste for modernist high art. When the actual death blow is struck, there is a momentary substitution of a cartoon mouth for the scream we never hear, as if the murderous consequences are being aestheticized and thereby disavowed. But once outside the mansion, we are back in a male-driven Oedipal narrative, where the murder leads to Alex being temporarily blinded by his droogs and left alone between two sphinx statues to face the police and narrative consequences—exile in prison and a satiric redemptive return.

Unlike *The Wild Bunch* and *Bonnie and Clyde*, which are both set in the past, *A Clockwork Orange* looks forward not only because the story is set in the future but because it prefigured so many cultural trends to come. Although *Bonnie and Clyde* is still invoked in most critical reviews of recent outlaw road movies and a restored version of *The Wild Bunch* was rereleased in 1995, their representations of violence now seem relatively mild when compared with the hyperviolent movies of the intervening years. Yet Kubrick's film continues to attract new generations of fans who see it as a prime source for the punk aesthetic, the postmodernist sensibility, and a long line of bad-ass juvenile gang movies in which stylized costuming, speech, and gestures are an accepted mode of political action.[18] As Yaquinto puts it succinctly, "Kubrick's futuristic criminal meltdown, *A Clockwork Orange*, remains the nightmare vision about gang violence on either side of the Atlantic."[19]

Fast-Forward to the Super-NOVA of the 1990s

At this point I would like to leap ahead to the 1990s to consider how Hollywood's narrative orchestration of violent attractions has reached the point of super-NOVA, where violent spectacle is increasingly noisy and explosive, more blatantly stylized and parodic, more wildly humorous and energetic, and more specifically tailored to an adolescent male mentality. This rhetoric of violence has become increasingly dependent on expensive special effects, whose pyrotechnics rely on high-powered technology both in front of and behind the camera. The ability to afford and manipulate these concrete technologies of violence—both the weapons in the story and the cinematic apparatus on the set and in post-production—has become a sign of masculine mastery and comic empowerment. Here is how an outsider, French theorist Christian Metz, described the trend in the early 1990s:

> A considerable portion of American production tends to be combined with cinema for children. Very often, these films have a deep-seated and shrill vulgarity, a profound silliness, a disturbing attraction to violence. But . . . these films testify to an astonishing vitality of visual invention and of technological ingenuity, and to a vivacity of spirit in concrete things which is, as many continental people like to forget, a real form of intelligence.[20]

I want to examine how this super-NOVA comic intelligence functions in two hyperviolent films that generated as much controversy in the 1990s as the earlier ones did in the 1960s and 1970s—Quentin Tarantino's *Pulp*

Fiction (1994) and Oliver Stone's *Natural Born Killers* (1994), based on a Tarantino screenplay). Though clearly linked to the earlier three films, both carry the orchestrated violence and comic exuberance to a new level of stylization, hybridity, and reflexiveness and increasingly address the social consequences of living with violent representations. This reflexivity thereby enables them to comment on recent trends in the way violence is represented in action films of the 1980s and 1990s. Instead of asking whether violent action is warranted by moral or political circumstances, they are more concerned with how it is being orchestrated and amplified by popular culture. They show that violence has become synonymous with action, making its antonym not peace but boredom.

The Spectacle of Violent Subjectivity in Natural Born Killers

Natural Born Killers is a super-NOVA gone ballistic! It rivals the mainstream action movies of the 1980s and 1990s in sheer noise and thrills, but with an artistic brilliance that is both exhilarating and disturbing. This kaleidoscopic collage—of slanted angles, staccato cuts, jerky camera movements, distorting lenses, discordant voices, clashing styles, heavily layered soundtrack, subjective inserts, demented flashbacks, and abrupt shifts between black and white and color and live action and animation—creates a richly embroidered surface that unifies the film as pastiche. It also derails the fast-driving linearity of its plot, which moves forward as relentlessly as the Santa Fe train pictured in the opening montage. This paradoxical duality of constant flow and compulsive interruption is a defining characteristic of television, which the film targets as a primary source for our pathological subjectivity. The film also presents a rival cinematic form for that duality: the recurring shot of the outlaw couple (driving, fighting, or fucking) in one of their many vehicles, which instead of racing forward like the getaway cars of the Barrow gang, are strangely suspended (usually at a slanted angle and with artificial lighting) in front of a fake backdrop or dream screen on which a wild mélange of images from their cultural and personal reservoir of memories are rear-projected. Like thrill rides in an amusement park, these narrative vehicles may promise to put us "on the pathway to Hell," but the trip is visceral and interior.

The film addresses the question: What does it mean to grow up in a culture that is saturated with a constant flow of violent images from personal memory and media and constantly remixed into new kaleidoscopic combinations? This question is seen with respect not only to the film's notorious outlaw couple Mickey (Woody Harrelson) and Mallory (Juliette Lewis) but also their legions of teenage fans all over the world, who are increasingly homogenized by the same corrosive images. As one of them puts it in a TV interview, "I don't approve of mass murder but if I *were* a serial killer I would choose to be Mickey and Mallory."[21] This violent subjectivity is also shared by the media and cops on their trail. In fact, the flashback to the violent childhood of the murderous cop Jack (Tom Sizemore) features the same boy who consistently stars in Mickey's own recurring flashbacks to his painful childhood experiences, suggesting that the personal memories of both killers have been mediated by the same movie images. This process makes the word *natural* in the title ironic, inviting us to substitute the term *naturalized*.

In dramatizing this process of naturalization, *Natural Born Killers* alludes to all three films previously discussed: to *A Clockwork Orange* in its focus on violent subjectivity, to *Bonnie and Clyde* in its choice of the out-law couple road movie as the primary genre, and to *The Wild Bunch* in spe-cific allusions to the scorpion, which appears in the opening sequence of both films (and evokes the image of violent children) and to Peckinpah's final massacre, which is seen in excerpt in one of Stone's many montages of reprocessed violent imagery.

Like *A Clockwork Orange*, *Natural Born Killers* focuses on violent sub-jectivity in a totally corrupt culture yet grants us less emotional distance, for we are deeply immersed in the same cultural dream pool in which the film's homicidal lovers are spawned. This poisonous reservoir is comprised not of esoteric selections chosen by a discriminating yet brutal consumer like Alex, but an anarchic mixture of images broadcast daily to the masses with a volume and speed that make them far more dangerous and give new resonance to Alex's favorite term, *horrowshow*.

We are immediately confronted by this cultural reservoir in the mon-tage behind the opening credits. While listening to Leonard Cohen's apoc-alyptic "Waiting for the Miracle," we see a chain of discrete images of Americana whose meanings are narrativized by different genres: black-and-white shots of a desert, a coyote, and a rattlesnake suggest the iconography of the Western, whereas color images of a cup of coffee, a Santa Fe train, an American eagle, and a coffee shop sign evoke the road movie. These spe-cific images (particularly the rattler) snake through the rest of the film, their meanings constantly recontextualized in the scenes that follow.

Once inside the coffee shop, we see a black-and-white TV set, with the stations being changed by the waitress, evoking a more common form of montage that we daily experience on television: the images range from vin-tage series like *Leave It to Beaver* and *77 Sunset Strip* to monstrous facial close-ups of Nixon and Dracula. Once the actual story begins, the bom-bardment of choices continues: in Mickey's opening line, "What kind of pie do you have?"; in Mallory's selection of a song on the jukebox to accompany her erotic dance with the cowboy that literally morphs into murder; in her use of "eenie, meenie, miney, mo" to choose which of the two remaining victims they will murder; and in the alternation between black and white and color to represent this escalating massacre. The edit-ing pace is so fast and the pastiche so overwrought that we don't have time to shut our eyes or think about what we are seeing and hearing; we only have time to experience the exhilarating rush, to free-associate with the images, and to bounce between humor and horror.

The Kubrick sequence closest to this effect is the one in which Alex is subjected to the Ludovico treatment, but in *Natural Born Killers* the process is no longer experimental, and its effect is precisely the opposite—to enhance rather than extinguish the pleasure taken in violent imagery and to desensitize rather than arouse any discomfort over its consequences. Kubrick's retraining sequence was also replayed in Nicolas Roeg's satiric

78

sci-fi film, *The Man Who Fell to Earth* (1976), in the scene in which an alien, played by David Bowie, sits in front of a bank of television sets that bombard him with an accelerating montage of violent images, as he screams, "Get out of my mind!" Perhaps the British sources of these two movies make their marginal protagonists more resistant to these brutal media images, most of which hail from the United States, but in *Natural Born Killers* we're on home turf, where there's no way out.

Nowhere is this entrapment demonstrated with greater comic brilliance and horror than in the flashback sequence when Mickey and Mallory first meet and then murder her parents, not only her obscene, sexually abusive father (played by comedian Rodney Dangerfield) but also her apathetic mother, who is oblivious to the domestic incest and violence that permeate the household and who is brutally burned to death in her bed. Considered generically, this sequence plays like the obligatory scene in the outlaw couple movie where the young woman cuts her family ties so that she can run off with her lover on the road. Yet when compared with Bonnie Parker's nostalgic visit with her mother at the family picnic, it shows how far the genre has moved toward the horror film. Stone's sequence is more similar to the patricidal scene in Malick's brilliant outlaw road movie, *Badlands,* only here Stone substitutes outrageous humor for visual beauty as the antidote to the horror. Titled "I Love Mallory" and played like a TV sitcom, the sequence evokes *Married with Children* more than *I Love Lucy.* What is so uncanny about this flashback is that we seem to be seeing it from the inside—that is, viewing it through the shared subjectivity of Mickey and Mallory that has been shaped by television and sees everything, no matter how horrific, as a sitcom with an audience track, which (in case you're too numb or dumb) tells you exactly how and when to squeal with terror or delight. Yet the wild humor competes with the grotesquery of the violence, making us feel guilty whenever we laugh.

Though this double bind is a long way from *The Wild Bunch* (where it was visceral engagement with the violence rather than a humorous reaction that aroused our guilt), the fusion of laughter and violence can be found in many films of the 1990s—most offhandedly in Paul Verhoeven's *Total Recall* (1990), in which Schwarzenegger is left holding the bloody arms of the villain that are ripped off in an elevator fight scene (a scene that usually draws laughter from the audience); most disturbingly in Tarantino's *Reservoir Dogs* (1992), in which a long, drawn-out torture sequence (Michael Madsen cuts off the ear of his captive and dowses him in gasoline to burn him alive) is rendered hilarious through the dance number he teasingly performs for his victim—the 1970s hit tune "Stuck in the Middle with You"; and most brilliantly in Martin Scorsese's *GoodFellas* (1990), in which Joe Pesci tells Ray Liotta a violent story that may or may not be intentionally funny and purposely makes both him (and us) uncertain as to whether it's dangerous to laugh. Like Scorsese, Stone puts us in this double bind to show how the incongruous reaction is increasingly pervasive within our desensitized culture, particularly when the lines between all genres, tones, and feelings dissolve. This occurs very frequently on television, where with the zap of a button, you can jump from the TV movie of the week that deals with a social problem like incest to a serial comedy that plays the same domestic situation for laughs.

In the sequence where Mickey and Mallory go to a cheap motel with a kitsch log cabin interior, the film conveys their entrapment within this contaminated subjectivity, which is simultaneously bombarded by two screens compounding the violence: the little television screen (which Mickey manipulates with his joystick) and a blank white dream screen visible through the window on which violent sequences from films like *The Wild Bunch*, *Midnight Express*, and *Scarface* are intercut with personal memories from Mickey's abusive childhood. Substituting for the exterior, this reservoir of reprocessed images is the cultural landscape through which all other experiences are mediated; nothing exists outside it. What is so horrific is not the individual images themselves but the effect of their accumulation and inadvertent collisions within culture and consciousness—an assumption basic to montage (at least according to Eisenstein, who saw it as an alternative to narrative), where the primary resource is conflicting "attractions" and where the effect of the whole is always greater than the sum of its parts. Within this cultural dream pool all media, genres, and memories converge in pastiche, making it difficult to distinguish between inside and outside, subjectivity and culture, fact and fiction, good and evil, perpetrators and victims, exploitative complicity and satiric commentary.

This erosion of boundaries endangers not only the film's characters and viewers but also its director, who was subjected to the same kinds of attacks he was leveling against his exploitative TV journalist Wayne Gale (Robert Downey Jr.), whose live episode of *American Maniacs* sparks a prison riot and helps Mickey and Mallory escape. Although media exploitation was also depicted in *Bonnie and Clyde*, there it was still possible for Bonnie to manipulate the gang's image. But here, as in *A Clockwork Orange*, the media are part of a totally corrupt culture. As in *The Wild Bunch*, the only characters who escape the corruption are the indigenous Native Americans, but here no alliance with the protagonists is possible. Like the corrupt journalist Gale, the old shaman (Russell Means) joins the growing ranks of the couple's murder victims, with the only glimmer of hope being Mallory's emphatic refrain "Bad! bad! bad!" and Mickey's brief pangs of regret. Yet, in recognizing Mickey as the demon sent to kill him, the shaman lends credence to the killer's later insistence in his TV prison interview that murder is a form of "purity"—or in Doane's terms, a "pure contingency" with "zero degree of meaning." This "cinematic ur-event" resists being tamed not only by the shaman's dream and Gale's exploitative prison story, but also by Stone's satiric narrative.

The moral ambiguity in this film is very different from that in *The Wild Bunch* and *Bonnie and Clyde*, where it was more a matter of taking sides and remaining loyal till the end. Although Mickey and Mallory brag about their total commitment to each other, both their betrayals and hyperbole expose this position to ridicule, even during their improvised marriage ceremony, which is a weird mix of inventiveness and clichés. Symbolically set on a bridge with a sublime view, the ritual consists of Mallory transforming a long, diaphanous white scarf into a wedding veil, which gracefully floats down into the gorge below, while Mickey turns the ceremony into a blood wedding that unites them for life: the droplets of their hybridized blood morph into cartoon images of entwined snakes, which follow the white veil into the abyss and animate the graphic design on their wedding rings. Before we get too carried away by the beauty of the sentiment or ingenuity of the graphics, the mood is comically deflated by a passing truck full of screaming rednecks, who make the bride substitute "Fuck you" for "I do." Yet the film's ironic happy ending shows Mickey and Mallory still together on the road, cozily nested with their growing brood of kids in a comfy mobile home, an image of the American family that may be as terrifying as their earlier mayhem and murder.

Still, there is something invigorating about the film's comic exuberance, which reflects not only on Mickey and Mallory, who are as resilient, amoral, and wily as Road Runner and his pursuing coyote, but also on the breathtaking inventiveness of the film, with its richly textured cartoon aesthetic and its frenetically orchestrated violence. As if building on the cartoon cutaway from the central murder of the art dealer in *A Clockwork Orange*, Stone turns it into an aesthetic strategy that destabilizes every image, character, and moral position in his movie. It is these qualities that make the film celebrate the very culture it supposedly decries—a charge that was also leveled against all of the earlier films I have been describing.[22]

Pulp Fiction *as Database Narrative*

Pulp Fiction demonstrates how violent attractions are narrativized through genre and other paradigmatic choices. It does not merely "use" a combination of generic conventions (like the earlier films described) but is more about the process of hybridization itself. Although it reworks many ideas, images, characters, and lines from Tarantino's original script for *Natural Born Killers*, this film avoids Stone's directorial choice of an overwrought pastiche of convergence and instead relies on ellipses and segmentation to derail the linear drive of the narrative. By constructing a violent nonlinear narrative full of ellipses, Tarantino cracks open traditional genres to show how original variations can still be generated within the gaps. Building on the experimental elliptical narratives from the nonviolent films of Jim Jarmusch, his nimble narrative jumps present a low-tech form of compositing that stands in marked contrast to the expensive high-tech blockbusters of the 1990s. Black fades mark these temporal ruptures, emphasizing the story's segmentation; instead of syncopating the action (like the pauses in *The Wild Bunch* and *Bonnie and Clyde*), they become black holes in the narrative that give generic clichés new life.

This process is immediately introduced in the opening, when we are presented with a choice between two dictionary meanings for the word *pulp* that help define the film's approach to genre: "a soft, moist mass of matter," suggesting the malleability and contingency of Tarantino's basic material; and "a magazine or book containing lurid subject matter and being printed on rough unfinished paper," indicating the conventions of the genre and medium that help give it form. This word game is later resumed (with amusing cross-cultural inflections) in banal conversations about the gendering of the word *garçon,* and the distinctions between an American quarter-pounder and a Parisian "Royale with cheese." Such games show how the database structure of the dictionary can serve as an alternative to traditional narrative for contextualizing the meanings of words and images.

Once the pretitles teaser cuts to the diegetic world of a coffee shop, where a contemporary outlaw couple, Pumpkin (Tim Roth) and Honey Bunny (Amanda Plummer), are "plotting" a holdup, we are positioned within what appears to be a regular "story" but are once again presented with the process of making a selection from a database of choices: the target of their holdup (liquor store, bank, gas station, or restaurant), the ethnicity of their victims (Vietnamese, Koreans, or Jews), the tone of their scene (romance or terror), the intertexts that help define how we read it (*Bonnie and Clyde* and *Natural Born Killers* rather than *A Clockwork Orange* or *The Wild Bunch*), and the punctuation that brings it to a close (a freeze signaling ellipsis and segmentation). At the end of the credits, we hear what sounds like someone turning a radio dial, speeding across an array of stations and musical selections until (like a DJ) finding exactly the right song ("Jungle Boogie") that sets the film's emotional rhythms in motion (a process that dramatizes the way the film's vintage musical score was actually put together). Both sets of choices evoke *Natural Born Killers,* particularly the scene when Mickey lovingly calls Mallory his "Honey Bunny bride" and the opening coffee shop massacre where the waitress switches the TV set from one program to another and where there is a similar set of choices. But whereas Stone's embroidered visual texture and multilayered audio track evoke the pulsating cultural dream pool, Tarantino exposes its ulterior database structure.

"Jungle Boogie" is still playing when Tarantino's narrative jumps to the interior of a 1974 Chevy Nova carrying two killers—Vincent Vega (John Travolta) and Jules Winnfield (Samuel L. Jackson)—to their next encounter with violence, a new narrative vehicle that continues to offer more paradigmatic choices: not only in their dialogue regarding quarter-pounders and Royales with cheese or in their choice of weapons for their next hit, but also in the shift of genre from outlaw couple to gangster film. The rest of the film is structured as if Tarantino kept his hand firmly on that dial, constantly selecting from his personal archive of film-viewing memories which genre, character, setting, music, and dialogue to use for each elliptical pause in the narrative and precisely when to return to the stories already in progress on the syntagmatic plane.

What this implies is that database and narrative are not really alternatives (as Lev Manovich has argued[23]) but two sides of the same process, which is usually hidden from view: the databases are the normally unseen paradigms from which specific items are chosen and then combined (as a syntagma) to generate a specific sentence or narrative. But in this film both the paradigms and the process are blatantly apparent. According to Roland Barthes, this kind of "extension of a paradigm onto the syntagmatic plane" is a form of "semiotic transgression" around which "a great number of creative phenomena are situated" (particularly in the works of experimental nonlinear filmmakers such as Luis Buñuel, Peter Greenaway, Chris Marker, and Raul Ruiz).[24] But one rarely finds it used so blatantly in a successful mainstream film, especially one as violent as *Pulp Fiction*.

These dynamics grow complex in the sequence in which Vincent and Jules try to recover their boss's briefcase from a group of young thieves. We are confronted with a choice of whether to judge these characters by their dialogue or their actions (a choice equally relevant to the whole film, which could be judged by its innovative tone and orchestration or by its conventional plot and thematics). Although the drug war and resulting murder are familiar, Jules's steady stream of talk is not, for it ranges from amusing banter about fast-food to a long biblical quote about the path of the righteous man being beset by the tyranny of evil. Confronted with this contradiction, we must decide whether to force a synthesis, in which case Jules might be seen as "an exterminating angel" worthy of Buñuel. The consequences of this unique combination prove miraculous, for when we later cut back to this scene the fourth young thief (another member of the same paradigm, who had been hiding in the bathroom) fires bullets that pass right through the bodies of Vincent and Jules without drawing blood. Jules declares it "divine intervention" and decides to retire from his murderous trade. That is why it is Vincent rather than Jules who is later (in a subsequent sequence that precedes this flashback) murdered in another bathroom by the white boxer Butch Coolidge (Bruce Willis). Given the structure of this segmented narrative that frequently lurches backward and forward in time, another reason for getting rid of Vincent is that he is the brother of the white character named Vic Vega from Tarantino's earlier film *Reservoir Dogs*, whereas Jules looks forward to the African-American focus of his later crime film *Jackie Brown* (1997), in which Jackson has another juicy role as a killer, and Pam Grier replaces Travolta as the kick-ass comeback queen. For a reflexive filmmaker like Tarantino, his canon is merely another database that recontextualizes the meaning of any specific work.

The way this database structure is used to orchestrate violent events is perhaps best revealed in the sequence in which Butch the boxer is leaving town after having failed to throw a big fight for the black mobster Marcellus (Ving Rhames) but literally runs into him in the street. After both are hurt in the collision and the violence that follows, Butch flees into a pawnshop run by a twisted hillbilly sadist named Maynard and his redneck accomplice Zed (who both look like emigres from the back woods of *Deliverance*). Together with their leather-hooded love slave, the Gimp, they try to subject both Butch and his wily black pursuer to torture, rape, and murder. After managing to escape, the boxer gallantly goes back to rescue his former nemesis from, as they say in Griffith's *The Birth of a Nation*, "a fate worse than death" and, after subduing the kinky captors with a weapon chosen from their own pawn shop, leaves the murderous vengeance to Marcellus. Like the film's opening, this mind-boggling, hyperplotted sequence bombards the spectator with a series of multiple choices drawn from conflicting paradigms: the generic contextualization of the violence moves fluidly from boxing movie, to gangster film, to horror; the nature of the violence lurches from car crashes, to shootings, to torture, rape, and murder; and the weapons range from cars, to hammers, chain saws, baseball bats, swords, and guns. The forms of emasculation consist of a series of binary choices: betrayal or beating, feminization or dehumanization, rape or rescue, castration or killing. The sequence of rape victims is chosen by the same racist rhyme, "eenie, meenie, miney, mo," that Mallory used in the coffee shop massacre to decide which of the remaining victims to murder. But whereas she changed the offensive word in the concluding line from "nigger" to "redneck," Tarantino evokes it visually through the selection of Marcellus. The discursive register (against which all of these violent attractions are to be read) also keeps shifting from class to sexuality, gender, regionality, and race. By thrusting the boxer and gangster into this new homoerotic context, we are forced to consider them and their posturing hypermasculinity in a new light—particularly Willis's nickname "Butch" and Rhames's powerful black stud stereotype.

In Tarantino's film, moral issues comprise another handy database. Deciding which characters to root for is simply a matter of style and of how they are positioned in the narrative. Whereas similar dynamics in *A Clockwork Orange* made us question those narrative conventions, here they make us question moral distinctions. For, no matter how terrifying the situation gets for the characters, the comic excess of the reflexive hyperplotting renders the horror humorous for us spectators. The film provides an encyclopedic approach to violence that dazzles our senses with its spectacle of brutal and erotic attractions and tickles our fancy with its dialogue, but still grants us emotional distance. This film in which anything can happen (even miracles!) is more about narrative than about blood and guts, or good and evil. Its comic exuberance reassures us of the survival not of its resilient characters (not even Harvey Keitel's wily "Wolf," who specializes in "cleaning up" violent consequences, or "the comeback kid" Travolta, who is resurrected in flashback) but of popular genres that are still capable of generating innovative pulp fiction. As David Ansen put it, "The miracle of Quentin Tarantino's *Pulp Fiction* is how, being composed of secondhand, debased parts, it succeeds in gleaming like something new."[25]

This sense of "newness" is particularly strong on the register of race, where *Pulp Fiction* puts black and white characters in a range of oppositions—not only Vincent and Jules as contrasting partners and Butch and Marcellus as antagonists, but also Vincent and his boss Marcellus as rivals in a racialized Oedipal triangle involving his white wife, Mia (Uma Thurman). As Stanley Crouch argued in his *Los Angeles Times* review (which so pleased Tarantino that he asked this controversial African-American writer to accept his Best Director Prize for him at the 1995 National Board of Review Awards), his films show "the many miscegenations that shape the goulash of American culture and . . . how powerfully the influence of the Negro helps define even those whites who freely assert their racism" (an issue Tarantino has dealt with in other films he has written or directed, such as *True Romance, Reservoir Dogs,* and *Jackie Brown*).[26] What interests me here is the way Tarantino acknowledges how cinematic violence is increasingly used as an arena in which rival racial and ethnic masculinities vie for power.

Muscling in on the Action:
Ethnicity and Masculine Violence

The link between ethnicity and masculine violence is hardly new. As Robert Warshow observed in the early 1950s, a violent genre like the gangster film provided an effective means for various ethnicities (Italian, Irish, and Polish) to negotiate issues of power as they made their way into American mainstream culture.[27] A similar dynamic was also operative in the 1970s for ethnic minorities who were not recent emigres but were still struggling to get their share of the action.[28] The African-American community enjoyed considerable success with the emerging popularity of black independent action films, including Melvin Van Peebles's *Sweet Sweetback's Baadasssss Song* (1971), Gordon Parks's *Shaft* (1971), Gordon Parks Jr.'s *Superfly* (1972), and their blaxploitation sequels. This dynamic was also operative for later waves of immigrants in the 1980s and 1990s, but tended to be used as fresh material for individual auteurs rather than as a power move for an ethnic community, as in Brian De Palma's ultraviolent remake of *Scarface* (1983), with Italian-American actor Al Pacino as Cuban emigre mobster Tony Montana; in Michael Cimino's *Year of the Dragon* (1985), which many Asian Americans accused of being racist; and in James Grey's directorial debut, *Little Odessa* (1994), a marvelous film about the Russian mafia in Brighton Beach, with a stellar international cast including Tim Roth, Vanessa Redgrave, Maximilian Schell, and Moira Kelly, but no ethnic Russians. In the late 1990s, more challenging experimental auteurs like John Sayles and Jim Jarmusch would address the ideological implications of these issues by exploring how masculine violence is inflected with a diverse array of rival and hybridized ethnicities in popular Hollywood genres: white, Latino, African-American, and Native American ethnicities in Sayles's Western/melodrama *Lone Star* (1995); white and Native American violence in Jarmusch's philosophical Western *Dead Man* (1995); and African-American, Italian, and Japanese inflections in Jarmusch's gangster/martial arts hybrid *Ghost Dog, the Way of the Samurai* (1999). But to understand the full resonance of this hybridization, we need to turn back to the Reagan era of the 1980s, when Hollywood's action heroes appeared mostly lily white.

In the 1980s, as Hollywood action films grew more expensive and their cultural reach more global, "white" masculinity reasserted its dominance, even if some of the most popular new action heroes were Americanized imports—Arnold Schwarzenegger from Austria, Jean-Claude Van Damme from Belgium, and Mel Gibson from Australia, whose ethnicities disappeared as they were transformed into international superstars. Along with white home-grown action heroes (like Harrison Ford, Bruce Willis, Woody Harrelson, Tom Cruise, and even little Macauley Caulkin in those *Home Alone* comedies in which ultraviolence was performed against bumbling ethnic villains strictly for laughs[29]), these white imports and their Italian-American counterparts (Sylvester Stallone, John Travolta, Nicholas Cage, Al Pacino, and Robert De Niro) helped Hollywood perpetuate its cultural colonization of the world. It is unlikely that either Van Damme or

Schwarzenegger could have achieved superstardom in their respective native homelands of Belgium or Austria, because of the powerlessness of those national cinemas in the world market. The potency of American representations of violence is as dependent on economic penetration of the global market as it is on technology.

As the stakes grew higher and global competition more intense in the 1990s, there were new attempts by underrepresented minorities to muscle in on the action. Independent Latino filmmakers made their mark with Edward James Olmos's *American Me* (1992) and Richard Rodriguez's miraculously low-budget debut feature *El Mariachi* (1993) and its equally violent, more expensive mainstream sequel, *Desperado* (1995), which accelerated the successful Hollywood crossovers of two popular Hispanic imports—Spain's Antonio Banderas and Mexico's Salma Hayek. Functioning as both sequel and parodic remake, *Desperado* used myriad forms of doubling to amplify its cartoonish violence and ethnic stereotypes. In the opening bar sequence, when Steve Buscemi tells how he almost got killed in another town, he sets up the film as a hyperbolic retelling full of inset narratives, flashbacks, and performative numbers that literally double as music and violence, and wallow in the same kind of complicitous humor that Scorsese interrogated in *GoodFellas*. Arousing our expectations for Banderas—as the film's superviolent hero and primary object of desire— Buscemi authorizes us to enjoy his glamorized singing and killing without remorse. Carrying his guns and guitar in the same case, Banderas is positioned on-stage next to the unknown Chicano actor (Carlos Gallardo) from *El Mariachi*, whom he now replaces as star. He also replaces Peckinpah's Latino Angel, who, in this musical Western, no longer plays sacrificial victim but actually gets the guns, girl, and glory in the final massacre.

Augmented by the mainstream popularity of black superstars in hip-hop culture and basketball, the biggest ethnic challenges in cinematic violence in the early 1990s came from independent African-American filmmakers. Spike Lee's controversial crossover film *Do the Right Thing* (1989) pitted African Americans against Italians, a racial combination with box office appeal to most ethnic communities. It was followed in the 1990s by three powerful films by young independent black filmmakers that focused almost exclusively on black gangsta culture: Mario Van Peebles's *New Jack City* (1991), which launched Wesley Snipes as a star; John Singleton's *Boyz N the Hood* (1991), which advanced the movie careers of Cuba Gooding Jr., Larry Fishburne, and Ice Cube; and the Hughes brothers' *Menace II Society* (1993).

The Elliptical Verbal Rhythms of Menace II Society

Of these African-American films from the 1990s, *Menace II Society* performed the most original orchestration of violence—a stuttering, stacatto structure comprised of brief flashes of elliptical scenes punctuated by black fades. The narrative is as distinctive as the highly stylized rhythms of African-American speech that drive and define it, a connection the Hughes brothers learned partly from Spike Lee's *She's Gotta Have It* (1986) and *Do the Right Thing*.

Three of the film's murders are triggered by single lines of dialogue that are perceived as violating the masculine pride of the killers. In the opening liquor store shoot-out, which instantly turns the narrator Cain (Tyrin Turner) into an accessory to murder, the Korean proprietor's casual remark "I feel sorry for your mother" prompts O-Dog (Larenz Tate) to impetuously kill both him and his wife. In a flashback to a card game in the late 1970s, which functions as Cain's primal scene, an insult mouthed by one of the players, "Suck my dick!" leads Cain's father (Samuel L. Jackson) to shoot him point blank. And later a homeless man's desperate plea for a handout, "I'll suck your dick" (a variation on the previous mortal line), leads O-Dog to a similar homophobic overreaction, and he shoots him on the spot. These acts of murder—as well as the symbolic names of the characters (Cain and O-Dog) and the film's unifying voice-over narration— make us pay careful attention to the talk. In fact, the whole film is framed by the rhythm and stylization of speech. In the opening, before we see any images we hear a riff of black street talk, and at the end as Cain lies dying, with his syncopated heartbeat as back-up, his voice-over continues to define the structure and thematics: "You never knew what was going to happen or when." As we see pulsing flashbacks to brief excerpts from earlier scenes punctuated by black fades, we hear a replay of an earlier conversation: "My grandfather once asked me whether I wanted to live. . . . Yeah, I do—now it's too late." Not only do these final lines and flashing images imbue Cain's death with a tragic dimension (the way the stylized slow-motion massacre did at the end of *Bonnie and Clyde*) but they also make us realize that this film is all about timing.

While most of the violence is unpredictable, senseless, and almost incoherent in narrative terms, it plays as significant on the historical register, making the violent events in Cain's brief elliptical life seem almost inevitable. That's why the two flashbacks that immediately follow the opening liquor store murder are so telling: the first is to historic radio and TV coverage documenting the 1965 Watts riot, in which we see armored tanks rolling into the urban war zone, and the second is to the late 1970s, when Cain witnesses murder for the first time, committed by his drug-dealing father as his junky mother shoots up in a back room. Throughout the narration, Cain constantly calls our attention to the ironic timing of events: the drive-by shooting that kills his cousin occurs only a week after graduation, and his own murder happens just when he was leaving for Atlanta with his girlfriend Roni (Jada Pinkett) and her son Anthony and when the LAPD was closing in on him and O-Dog for the opening liquor store murder. With hindsight, the interruption of Cain's trip was predictable, for it was simply a matter of timing as to whether the gangbangers or the cops would get him first.

Yet the only specific act of violence that we are allowed to anticipate is the revenge killing against those who murdered Cain's cousin. And even there the "Love and Happiness" promised by the song they hear on the way to the drive-by (presumably the love for his cousin and the happiness in avenging his death) are not fulfilled. Instead, Cain tells us he merely learned that he was capable of murder and can do it again if he has to. This scene makes us realize that in this unending cycle of violence, the vengeful murder will also be done unto him when he least expects it. Thus, violent actions that might seem random and unpredictable in the short run of the brief elliptical scenes prove inevitable within the larger historical narrative.

As in *Pulp Fiction*, another American independent with a violent elliptical narrative, there are no expensive explosions or special effects. But unlike Tarantino's film, the violence here is never humorous or hysterical but rather a matter of history and survival, and the ellipses are not about narrative invention but about capturing the distinctive quality of life in a culture marked by violent, premature deaths. This elliptical structure is also reflected in the broken families—for Cain is raised by his churchgoing grandparents, who eventually reject him because of his violent behavior. More important, the recurring ellipses help emphasize the intense yearning for continuity across the truncated scenes and generations. We hear it from the women who are worrying about their children—both Eileen, whom Cain impregnates in a casual encounter, and Roni, who urges him to leave South Central with her and her son. We see it even more strongly in a few father figures who try to help the next generation to have a better, longer life. We hear it in the speech of Mr. Butler (Charles Dutton), who tells Cain, "Being a black man in America isn't easy, the hunt is on and you're the prey . . . all I'm saying is survive!" We see it even more powerfully in Cain's surrogate father Grenell, who, while serving life in prison, authorizes Cain to replace him as Roni's husband and Anthony's father: "Teach him the way we grew up was bullshit." And we even find it in Cain's final act, when he shields Anthony from the bullets. Both Grenell's unpredictable blessing and Cain's act of sacrifice radically rupture the traditional Oedipal narrative, for instead of a murderous rivalry between father and son they present a transgenerational male bonding, which is as romanticized as the one in *The Wild Bunch* and which represents one of the film's few glimmers of hope.

This male bonding is even extended across ethnicities, in the scene when, after badly battering Cain and his Muslim friend Sherif, two brutal white cops dump their bodies into territory controlled by a violent Latino gang, but instead of taking them out as the cops expect, they take them to the hospital, for they see them as moral allies struggling to survive the onslaught of the white man's violence, oppression, and exploitation. One can try to escape the violence, like Roni and Sherif, or totally embrace it without giving a damn for the consequences, like O-Dog (who is "white America's worst nightmare"), or waver between these two choices like Cain and still get caught in the crossfire. Yet none of these choices makes violence fun, as it is in *Pulp Fiction* and in most violent blockbusters of the 1990s.

The yearning for continuity is also seen in O-Dog's self-destructive obsession with duplicating, selling, and replaying the surveillance tape that recorded his liquor store murder. Although this obsession reflects the entrapping cycles of violence in the hood and ultimately can be used as evidence to capture and convict him, it also becomes a way of acknowledging and memorializing his brief life. Like the historic documentary footage of the 1965 Watts riot and like *Menace II Society* itself, it comes closer to documenting this segment of American life than does Frank Capra's maudlin classic *It's a Wonderful Life*, which Cain's religious grandparents, along with the rest of America, repeatedly watch every Christmas. Capra's film may be the source for the grandfather's question that Cain repeats at the end—Do you want to live?—but *Menace II Society* provides a far more compelling answer, especially for those living in South Central L.A.

Hong Kong's Choreographed Crossovers to Hollywood

In the 1990s new rhythmic orchestrations of violence were also provided by Hong Kong action stars—Jackie Chan, Chow Yun-Fat, and director John Woo, who were trying to muscle their way into Hollywood actions genres and the North American market to make their stardom truly global, particularly in the face of economic and political uncertainties raised by Hong Kong's restoration to communist China. Unlike Schwarzenegger and Van Damme, they were already celebrities within one of the few national cinemas that had succeeded in challenging Hollywood's dominance worldwide and even had a cult following within the United States (particularly with film buffs and college students). Unlike Banderas and Gibson (who also had American fans for earlier performances within their own national cinemas), before making the crossover their names were already synonymous with an orchestration of violent attractions. But, unlike the American films discussed thus far, whose narrative rhythms are based primarily on editing, music, and explosive special effects, the orchestration in Hong Kong action films relies heavily on the choreographed movements of the performers.[30]

Jackie Chan as Crossover Hero. This shift is easiest to see in the work of Jackie Chan, whose phenomenal mastery of martial arts (like that of his famous predecessor, Bruce Lee) is central to his films, while other characters merely function as back-up ensemble or chorus, like the props in the mise-en-scéne that this dancing bricoleur mobilizes as weapons to vary the action.[31] Because of the uniqueness of his talents as an acrobatic performer who does his own stunts, it is impossible to imagine any of his movies without him, which is not the case for the stars in the American films we have been discussing, no matter how brilliant their acting may be. The down side is that this limits the range of the characters Chan can play, for, despite his dazzling physical mobility in performing "impossible" feats, he is stuck in this persona that spectators follow from film to film. The only American film stars with this kind of uniqueness are Buster Keaton, Fred Astaire, and Gene Kelly, whom Chan acknowledges as key influences because they were primarily dancers rather than actors whose every move was choreographed.[32] In fact, Chan was rigorously trained as a dancer from the age of seven in the Peking Opera School and, according to him, "at 18 . . . became the youngest stunt coordinator in Asia."[33] As a result, the musical structure of his action films is blatant, perhaps most delightfully in *The Miracle* (1989), a gangster/musical hybrid written and directed by Chan that one critic describes as "a Hong Kong style remake of Frank Capra's *Pocketful of Miracles*" and that presents his best violent "numbers" as part of a dazzling night club performance.[34] The connection with comedy is also apparent, yet the laughter he evokes is not one of hysteria, irony, or orgasmic release as in the American films I've been describing but rather of comic delight in sheer mastery—the ability to perform seemingly impossible human moves before your eyes.

Chan's first American crossover film, *Rumble in the Bronx* (1996), was only a moderate box office success. Though directed by Stanley Tong and produced by Hong Kong production company Golden Harvest, Chan acknowledges, "we thought it was an American film but it was not."[35] Trying to tap into the African-American market, the film includes a cartoonish marriage between Chan's Chinese Uncle Bill (who had been living in the Bronx for thirty years) and his fat African-American fiancée. When Jackie is astonished to discover she's black, Uncle Bill says, "Welcome to America, my nephew," as if implying that racially mixed couples are a distinctively American phenomenon. Despite her friendliness, Jackie remains dubious and remains committed to his Chinese identity, which is immediately reinforced when he meets the first of his two Asian-American love interests. The emphasis on multiculturalism as an American characteristic is extended to the antagonists, an unrealistic rainbow assortment of bikers that includes a blonde named Angelo, a Latino, two whites, and two Chinese-Americans in need of reform.

Though Jackie and his producers were on the right track with the Chinese/African-American alliance, it was still relegated to a subplot; like his Hong Kong films, this movie was structured almost entirely around his martial arts action. After the film's release, when Jackie appeared as one of the presenters at the 1996 Oscars, he was paired with a huge African-American basketball star who teased him about his size and made him look dwarfish. If we was going to make it in Hollywood, Jackie still needed to find the right partner, for even Fred Astaire had his Ginger.

Jackie found that partner in Chris Tucker, his African-American costar in *Rush Hour* (1998), which made over $100 million dollars in the first month of its release, becoming the tenth top grossing film of the year.[36] He had finally mastered the North American market with a winning combination partly inspired by the success of mixed-race buddy-cop movies like *48 Hrs* and the *Lethal Weapon* series (in which Hong Kong action star Jet Li made his American debut, as a villain). Tucker and Chan imbued this action film with two contrasting modes of comic exuberance, which helped it appeal not only to Jackie's growing body of American fans but also to mainstream audiences. This successful combination of black verbal humor and Hong Kong martial arts action inspired not only the writing of a *Rush Hour* sequel but also the immediate addition of black comic Arsenio Hall as Samo Hung's black buddy on CBS's popular TV detective series *Martial Law*.

When asked to explain the success of *Rush Hour*, Chan emphasizes cultural specificity: "What made the movie so popular in America was that Chris Tucker did the verbal comedy, I did the action comedy."[37] And unlike *Rumble in the Bronx*, "the way it looked, the photography and the dialogue . . . everything was American."[38] Yet unlike *Lethal Weapon 4* (which it outperformed at the box office), *Rush Hour* featured Hong

Kong– rather than American-style action, for its young director, Brett Ratner, was a Chan fan who let him choreograph the fighting. Chan explains:

> In *Lethal Weapon 4* all the fighting scenes are similar to American movies— BOOM BOOM BOOM—big explosions. So when the movie started—*Rush Hour*—I went to the director and said, "Look, you have to promise me. Fewer explosions. Less violence. Fewer gunfights. Even if you have the gunfights don't show the blood. We want no special effects." . . . So the audience really can see something different than the typical American action movie. . . . American action movies have a lot of special effects, big explosions. . . . But they don't know how to choreograph all the fighting scenes. Everybody knows how to fight, I am proud of myself for knowing how to choreograph.[39]

Chan was keenly aware of not only the sharp contrast in "national" styles of violent representation, but also the fierce cultural competition in the lucrative action genre.

> I train very hard because I cannot use special effects. Even if I know how to use them, they will not be as good as Steven Spielberg or James Cameron . . . the only thing we can compare to America is action. People say, "Wow, Jackie's action is better than American." This is why training for me is very important.[40]

Even the nationality of the archvillain in *Rush Hour* is telling, for the mysterious Boss turns out to be British—a choice that not only alludes to Hong Kong's postcolonial legacy but also serves the marketing of the film: sufficiently Anglo to contrast with the Asian and African-American cultures being celebrated, yet sufficiently foreign to avoid alienating whites in the mainstream American audience.

The cultural alliance between Asian and African-American ethnicity is best dramatized in the comical scene outside the restaurant (where some of the most brilliant fight scenes will later be performed). Jackie and Chris exchange insider tips about the stylization of their respective ethnic moves (whether it's wordplay and dance or martial arts and cuisine). This exchange is like a dialogic dance between two cultural styles of orchestrating violent attractions—both very different from white mainstream culture, which is partly what makes them so appealing.

Wooing Hollywood. With John Woo's crossover, the situation was more complex. He already had his ideal partner in his signature hero Chow Yun-Fat (with whom he had been working since 1985), and his films already included American-style action with guns and explosions. However, they are still brilliantly choreographed, with cars, motorcycles, and actors moving fluidly between the balletic and the ballistic and with his expressive camera gliding from long shots and sweeping pans that highlight hyperviolence to static, dramatically lit close-ups that reveal complex homosocial relations within the equally excessive realm of melodrama and romance. Here is how Woo describes the nostalgia for a medieval Chinese chivalric code that he shares with Chow Yun-Fat in their creation of this hero, who is compatible not only with Bruce Lee's and Jackie Chan's optimistic martial arts mastery but also with the chivalric heroism that underlies the American pulp fiction of Raymond Chandler and Dashiell Hammet (but not Tarantino) and the Japanese samurai ethos of Kurosawa's action films of the 1950s and 1960s (a formative influence on Lucas's *Star Wars* saga):

> We both have the same kind of strong belief that we can make it . . . the same kind of hope, the same kind of heart, so we put this kind of feelings into the character. . . . We truly believe that even though we live in an evil world, if you can stand up with a stronger will, then you can't be beaten down. That's the true spirit of the Chinese knight.[41]

Woo was the first to cross over—moving to Hollywood in 1992 and making *Hard Target* in 1993 (a title bound to evoke his 1992 Hong Kong classic, *Hard Boiled*). Though the film advanced the Hollywood career of its Belgian-born star, Van Damme, it still left Woo in limbo. In his next film, *Broken Arrow* (1996), costarring John Travolta and Christian Slater, he was able to retain some of the homoerotic magic and moral ambiguity between the good guy and villain, but both narratively and stylistically it moved more toward Hollywood with less of his own Hong Kong stylization. Although his signature shot (of two guys sticking their guns in each other's faces) had already entered the language of American action plots (from Tarantino to popular TV series like *New York Undercover* and *The X-Files*), the verdict on Woo's bankability was still out. This changed with the Paramount release of *Face/Off* (1997), his first big Hollywood hit, which pitted two Italian-American superstars, Travolta and Nicholas Cage, against each other with the same kind of "emotional delirium" and homoerotic subtext that Chow Yun-Fat usually had with his closest buddy, a quality achieved here more through the plot (hero and victim actually trade faces) than through the camera moves or performance of the actors. Although the plot strained credibility, the film had the violent excess and the destabilizing of good and evil that complicated the best of Woo's Hong Kong films.[42] Now that he was established in Hollywood, it was time to bring on Chow Yun-Fat, but the debut had to be carefully orchestrated.

Chow Yun-Fat as Replacement Killer. The vehicle for Chow Yun-Fat's American debut was *The Replacement Killers* (1998), with Woo functioning as an executive producer rather than director (perhaps so that any box office success could be credited to the actor). Chow Yun-Fat plays a hired killer named John Lee, who refuses to assassinate the seven-year-old son of a cop, even though it puts his own family back in China in danger. The contract is a revenge killing since the cop killed the grown-up son of a Chinese crime lord named Wei during a drug bust in Los Angeles's Chinatown. Although the "replacement killers" of the title refer to the two assassins Wei hires to replace Lee, the title also reflexively refers to Chow Yun-Fat, who is being groomed to replace the Hollywood actors who have replaced him in Woo's Hollywood action films. But the film was a disappointment at the box office, grossing only $19 million and just making the one hundred list of top-grossing films of the year (in ninety-third place).[43]

As in the case of *Rush Hour*, the producers chose a talented young first-time director—Antoine Fuqua, who had established a reputation for visual pyrotechnics in directing music videos. And, as in *Face/Off*, they relied on an Italian-American costar, Mira Sorvino—perhaps thinking that the Italian connection could serve the same crossover function for the gangster genre that the African-American connection performed for Jackie Chan in comedy. Sorvino plays Meg Coburn, a female action figure who specializes in making forged IDs. Wearing a bare razor blade around her neck and always packing a gun, she substitutes for the male antagonist who usually is the homosocial object of Chow Yun-Fat's romanticized delirium. When the villain first sees Chow Yun-Fat with Sorvino, he tells him, "You picked the wrong partner," but also has to admit, "You two make a cute couple." Sorvino also substitutes for those Hong Kong female action stars who remain subordinate to heroes like Chow Yun-Fat (and Jackie Chan) but help affirm their heterosexual desirability within these homosocial plots. These actresses are increasingly used to energize and update Western action films—as in Olivier Assayas's stylized *Irma Vep* (1996), in which Maggie Cheung plays a postmodernist version of a notorious female phantom from French silent cinema,[44] and in the James Bond film *Tomorrow Never Dies* (1997), in which Michelle Yeoh is his strongest female playmate. Though Chow Yun-Fat never kisses Sorvino, she is obviously sexually attracted to him, and her unrequited desire helps ensure that this romanticized knight errant is the film's (and presumably our) primary object of desire—one that can be fulfilled only in future Hollywood features.

From the opening shots behind the credits, the film focuses on eroticizing Chow Yun-Fat's persona. He first appears as a man in black striding through a club full of dancers gyrating to a techno beat. Though his face is in shadows, the fragmented shots and distinctive stylization of his movements mark him as lead performer in this choreographed number, particularly when we see his triple image in a mirror shot. After shooting several Latino gangsters, he leaves Wei's marked bullet behind as a signature to the killing. Evoking a similar explosive shoot-out that he performed in the opening of Woo's *Hard Boiled*, this teaser might lead us to see an ironic shadow relation (like the one in *Face/Off*) between Woo and Wei, the good and bad controllers of the master plot who repeatedly cast Chow Yun-Fat in this role as killer.

Three scenes later Chow Yun-Fat is recoded as a good guy, for here we see him dressed in a light gray suit walking through Chinatown to get his next assignment, the one he fails to perform on moral grounds, with full awareness of the consequences. He goes to Sorvino to buy a fake passport for his transport back to China so that he can save his family from Wei's vengeance. The narrative is driven by a series of questions about his identity that also comment on the crossover: his morality (is this killer a good guy or villain?), name (is "John" an homage to Woo and "Lee" a link back to Bruce, associations that might help his acceptance in Hollywood?), and primary motivation (saving the American family or his own family back home?). Frequently posed in close-ups against artful Chinese backgrounds with a Hong Kong aesthetic or in heroic upward angles, he is defined primarily by his image and moves, and he says very little, which puts him in the Western tradition of strong silent heroes (like Gary Cooper and Clint Eastwood) and downplays the actor's limited English.

This verbal minimalism makes the fast-paced narrative more like a music video or electronic game—one structured by the syncopated rhythms of the violence, music, montage, and changing mise-en-scène rather than by plot or dialogue. Once this relentless pace is established, spectators know that violent action is never more than three brief scenes away. In most sequences we watch figures threading their way through visually rich, atmospheric interiors—sometimes filled with smoke, steam, incense, or fireworks; frequently lit in red or green; and usually shot in upward angle or in depth so that we can more fully savor the art direction. Providing the backdrop for the action, these spaces include a Buddhist temple, a photographic darkroom with dangling ribbons of drying film, a steamy car wash in motion, a movie theater showing animated violence, and an East L.A. tunnel covered with graffiti and filled with gangbangers. From the opening sequence, when Lee kills the gangsters in the club, the plot drives toward violent serial encounters with killers whose deaths never evoke a single flicker of emotion or regret. As in most violent video games, the primary goal is to exterminate as many bad guys as possible, without wounding innocent bystanders, an issue central to two of Woo's best-known films—*The Killer* (1989), in which Chow Yun-Fat is totally dedicated to the female singer he accidentally blinded in the film's opening shoot-out, and *Hard Boiled*, in which he carries a newborn (safely tucked under one arm) through the apocalyptic final battle with gangsters. In *The Replacement Killers*, this motif is reduced to a single incident in the garage shoot-out, when the bad guys mortally wound an anonymous woman in white who gets caught in the crossfire. Instead, the plot turns on Lee's refusal to assassinate the innocent child—the one good deed that licenses him to kill all the others.

The film targets young males whose masculinity was processed through those Manichean plots of the *Teenage Mutant Ninja Turtles* franchise (and who thereby already respect the Hong Kong film industry and its aesthetic) but who have subsequently moved on to more violent fare in cyberspace. At times the connection with electronic games is quite explicit, as in the video arcade scene in which the imported assassins are posed against the violent action of Altered Beast on the video screen. The film evokes the choreography of these violent games that rely primarily on continuous kinetic movement—running, jumping, rolling, kicking, punching—to create a visceral identification with the action, despite the comic hyperbole of its bloody consequences and its total lack of emotional resonance. These dynamics are perhaps best illustrated in one-on-one serial combat games like the notorious Mortal Kombat series, with its comic dismemberments, decapitations, exploding bodies, fountains of blood, and Vader-like voice-overs demanding "Fatality!"—a combination played out on a different comic register in those ultraviolent *Itchy and Scratchy* cartoons that make Bart and Lisa Simpson squeal with laughter.[45]

On the registers of ethnicity and gender, *The Replacement Killers* puts computer hardware in the hands of ethnic females (both African-American and Italian) but still assigns the mastery of guns primarily to males (which makes Meg all the more exceptional). This male mastery, however, is shared with other ethnic masculinities: with the Latino gangbangers from whose arsenal Coburn and Lee select weapons for their final battle against Wei; and with the tough Russian-American cop Zeedo (Michael Rooker), whom the plot sets up as Chow Yun-Fat's potential emotional antagonist but who is displaced by Sorvino. The homosocial relationship between Lee and Zeedo is drained of all homoerotic traces, for crossover action heroes must prove their desirability on the heterosexual front (a shift probably most blatant in the case of Banderas).[46] At one point, when Lee asks Meg whether the treacherous Latino, Loco, is her boyfriend, she replies, "I try to stick to my own species"—a line probably meant to convey her availability to Chow Yun-Fat, who (unlike the low-life Loco) is more than her equal in class, intelligence, loyalty, and fighting power. Yet, like Jackie Chan's reaction to his uncle's black bride in *Rumble in the Bronx*, this remark has racist overtones, for it elevates Chinese imports over home-grown domestic minorities.

In the final battle sequence in Chinatown, the film mobilizes the full arsenal of Chinese heroic connotations to imbue Chow Yun-Fat with greater global power. In preparing their getaway to Shanghai, Wei and his mob pile into their cars, but when the garage door opens, they face Chow Yun-Fat, who stands alone waiting to confront them. This shot evokes the lone Chinese student facing the tank in the Tianenmen Square massacre—an extraordinary image of Chinese heroism that was memorialized world-wide via satellite TV.[47] In the battle that ensues, Chow Yun-Fat literally performs like a dancer, using his whole body to imbue the two guns he is firing with greater gestural force. Like an action figure in a video game, he runs, jumps, leaps, spins, and rolls and makes other graceful acrobatic moves, discarding his weapons when they run out of bullets instead of paus-ing to reload. In this multitiered space of the Chinatown alley (which allows both horizontal and vertical camera sweeps to simulate the scrolling moves of a video game), he is backed up by Sorvino, who rides into the action in a fast-moving van, and the two of them alternate in one-on-one mortal combat against archvillains of their own rank and ethnicity. While Sorvino outstalks and outshoots Wei's chief deputy down in the kitchen of a Chinese restaurant, Chow Yun-Fat confronts the Boss on the more elevated tier of a fire escape, which enables the dead body falling in slow motion to be dis-played against a dynamic background of flashing light and falling rain. As if to remind us that Chow Yun-Fat is still the good guy, just before being shot, Wei tells him, "The boy will die, John . . . and your family." To which Lee replies, "Not in your lifetime," before blowing him away.

Despite its limited box office performance, *The Replacement Killers* is fascinating because of the way it reorchestrates diverse strategies of violent representation to ease Chow Yun-Fat's Hollywood crossover. Yet the pres-sure is still on Chow Yun-Fat, for, although he has made more than seventy movies in Hong Kong since 1976, he has not yet proven his box office appeal to Hollywood. He plays a character with greater range in his second Hollywood action film, *The Corruptor* (1999, directed by James Foley), an ultraviolent cop film that simulates the moral ambiguity, homoerotic sub-text, and playful tone of Woo's best action films. But what distinguishes this film is its emphasis on ethnicity. Not only does Chow Yun-Fat play the first Chinese detective in New York's Chinatown—one of the bravest and toughest on the force—but he is also a "dirty" cop who is paid by the Chinese ganglord to watch out for his own ethnic community. We specta-tors are positioned to identify with his white buddy (Mark Wahlberg), a young cop who at first seems to idolize him for his prowess as an action hero but who turns out to be an undercover Internal Affairs man sent to investigate and entrap him. Accusing Wahlberg of suffering from "yellow fever" (idolizing anything Asian, an accusation familiar to the film's execu-tive producer, Oliver Stone), Chow Yun-Fat at first rejects him, both on racial and generational grounds ("He's worse than white, he's green!"), but (as in *The Replacement Killers*) he ultimately becomes the "maternal" nur-turing hero who sacrifices himself to save the white boy. Despite the greater complexity of Chow Yun-Fat's character, *The Corruptor* was another box office disappointment, as was the big-budget *Anna and the King* (1999), which tried using Chow Yun-Fat's ethnic authenticity, glorious Asian loca-tions, and Jodie Foster's feisty feminism to update a remake of a tired colo-nialist romance. We may have to wait until Chow Yun-Fat is reteamed with Woo for his Hollywood crossover to be complete.

All of these ethnic crossovers reveal cultural reinscription in action. Like the comparison between *The Wild Bunch* and *La caza* with which this essay began, they help us see more clearly what is distinctive about the American inflection of cinematic violence, and how transcultural borrowings between Hollywood and other so-called national cinemas move in both directions. For, like the black independent films of the 1990s and the generic hybrids of Sayles and Jarmusch, these Hong Kong crossovers show how the pairing of ethnicity and masculinity can destabilize the national-izing of violence in the American action genre, preventing any such char-acterization from becoming monolithic and making room for a wider range of cultural inflections. They also highlight the rich stylistic variations that already exist within this narrative orchestration of violent attractions and challenge us to confront their complex cultural reverberations.

Notes

1. See chapter 4, "Sacrifice and Massacre: On the Cultural Specificity of Violence," in *Blood Cinema: The Reconstruction of National Identity in Spain* (Berkeley and Los Angeles: University of California Press, 1993).
2. Stephen Prince, *Savage Cinema: Sam Peckinpah and the Rise of Ultraviolent Movies* (Austin: University of Texas Press, 1998), 2.
3. John Hopewell, *Out of the Past: Spanish Cinema after Franco* (London: BFI, 1986), 76. Quoted in Carlos Balagu, "Entrevista con Ricardo Franco," *Dirigido por . . .*, no. 37 (October 1976): 14–15.
4. For more information about Del Amo, see Manuel Hidalgo, *Pablo G. Del Amo: Montador de sueños* (Festival de Cine de Alcala de Henares, 1987).
5. René Girard, *Violence and the Sacred*, trans. Patrick Gregory (1972; reprint Baltimore and London: Johns Hopkins University Press, 1977), 1–34.
6. Peckinpah, as quoted by Prince, *Savage Cinema*, 30.
7. Frantz Fanon, *The Wretched of the Earth* (New York: Grove Press, 1968).

8. Prince, *Savage Cinema*, 28.

9. Ibid., 34.

10. Marilyn Yaquinto, *Pump 'Em Full of Lead: A Look at Gangsters on Film* (New York: Twayne Publishers, 1998), 116.

11. See Linda Williams, *Hard Core: Power, Pleasure, and the "Frenzy of the Visible"* (Berkeley and Los Angeles: University of California Press, 1991); and Tom Gunning, "The Cinema of Attraction(s): Early Film, Its Spectator, and the Avant-Garde," *Wide Angle* 8, nos. 3–4 (1986): 63–67. In his marvelous annotated filmography (Smithsonian Institution Press, 1997), Charles Musser describes many such early violent attractions— including barroom brawls, boxing matches, bullfights, battles scenes, lynchings, and executions (both of real-life criminals like St. Louis murderer William Carr actually documented on film and of historical celebrities like Mary, Queen of Scots, Joan of Arc, and Jesus Christ in "realistic" historical reenactments).

12. Mary Ann Doane, "Screening Time," in *Language Machines: Technologies of Literary and Cultural Production*, ed. Jeffrey Masten, Peter Stallybrass, and Nancy J. Vickers (New York and London: Routledge, 1997), 142, 144, and 152.

13. Prince, *Savage Cinema*, 226.

14. Yaquinto, *Pump 'Em Full of Lead*, 114–16.

15. Ibid., 117.

16. For a discussion of these films and the genre, see my essay "The Return of the Outlaw Couple: *Badlands, Thieves Like Us*, and *The Sugarland Express*," *Film Quarterly* (summer 1974). Although the war film is beyond the scope of this essay, it is intriguing to consider that both Malick and Spielberg should return to ultraviolence in the same year (1998) and genre with *The Thin Red Line* and *Saving Private Ryan*. As in their earlier outlaw road movies of the 1970s, Spielberg's realistic representation of violence is still used to test what Americans are willing to sacrifice to salvage a fractured family, whereas Malick's stylized meditation on violence is more concerned with the interiority of those confronting fear and the unpredictability of death. While Spielberg's most stunning violent action scene is the Normandy landing that occurs right at the beginning of the film before we are sutured into emotional identification with any specific characters and can therefore be watched as pure horrific spectacle, Malick's comparable scene occurs after we have tuned in on the subjectivity of several characters through multiple voice-overs, which makes the unpredictability of the action more terrifying. While Spielberg's orchestration of his brilliantly realistic sequence makes full use of the soundtrack, whose base literally makes us tremble in our seats (at least in those theaters that are wired for digital surround sound), Malick's musical orchestration of the emotional motifs and visual imagery functions as an alternative to traditional narrative and, as a consequence, I find his film more innovative and ultimately more powerful.

17. For a brilliant analysis of the impact of developing multitrack digital technology and innovative concepts of sound design on aural spectacle and sound-image relations, see William Brian Whittington, "Sound Design and Science Fiction," (unpublished dissertation, University of Southern California, 1999). Whittington discusses films from the same period covered in this study—from groundbreaking works of the late 1960s and early 1970s like Kubrick's *2001: A Space Odyssey* (1968) and George Lucas's *THX 1138* (1971), to the proliferating *Star Wars* and *Alien* series launched in the late 1970s, to the two versions of *Blade Runner* (1982 and 1992) and *The Terminator* series of the 1980s and 1990s. Although he focuses specifically on science fiction, he claims that one can find a similar pattern in other popular Hollywood genres, including action films (from *Rambo*s to *Die Hard*s) and war films (from *Apocalypse Now* and *Platoon* to *Saving Private Ryan* and *The Thin Red Line*).

18. When the rereleased version of *The Wild Bunch* recently played at the Cinerama Dome in Hollywood, I stood in the long line of Peckinpah enthusiasts with my son Victor, a video game fan who was then fifteen and had never seen the film before. Though he basically liked it, he thought the representation of violence was surprisingly mild. This Halloween he chose to be Alex, and he and several of his friends have *Clockwork Orange* posters hanging on their bedroom walls.

19. Yaquinto, *Pump 'Em Full of Lead*, 231.

20. Christian Metz, *L'Énonciation impersonnelle, ou le site du film* (Impersonal Enunciation, or The Site of Film) (Paris: Méridiens Klincksieck, 1991), 161.

21. Those interviews came to mind when I read an account of Michael Fortier's testimony as star witness for the prosecution in the murder trial against Timothy McVeigh in the Oklahoma City bombing: "Well, if you don't consider what happened in Oklahoma, Tim is a good person. . . . He would stop and help somebody that's broken down on the side of the road. " Yet when Fortier went on to describe why McVeigh decided to detonate the bomb at 11 A.M. "because everybody would be getting ready for lunch," I thought back to the final massacre in *The Wild Bunch* even though McVeigh apparently had another action movie from the 1970s in mind—one that is generally not considered excessively violent. According to Fortier, "McVeigh used an analogy from the movie *Star Wars*, and characterized federal employees as 'individually innocent.' But because they are part of the evil empire, they were guilty by association." "McVeigh Ready to Die in Blast, Ex-Friend Says," *Los Angeles Times*, May 13, 1997, A13.

22. While Prince claims that Peckinpah changed his aesthetic strategies for representing violence as a consequence, Kubrick's response was even more extreme. According to Eric Harrison, "he yanked *A Clockwork Orange* out of theaters in England after it had shown for only a couple of weeks because critics said it glorified violence and an attorney used it to defend a client who had beaten up a tramp, saying the client had just seen the movie. . . . After that, it was shown only in film and theater schools." Eric Harrison, "Film Director Stanley Kubrick Dies at 70," *Los Angeles Times*, March 8, 1999, A18.

23. See Lev Manovich, "Database as a Genre of New Media," *AI and Society*, special issue on databases, ed. Victoria Vesna (forthcoming); and "Database: Semiotics, History, and Aesthetic," *Convergence*, special issue on cinema and new media, ed. Ross Rudesch Harley (forthcoming).

24. Roland Barthes, *Writing Degree Zero* and *Elements of Semiology*, trans. Annette Lavers and Colin Smith (Boston: Beacon Press, 1970), 86. See also Susan Suleiman, "Freedom and Necessity: Narrative Structure in 'The Phantom of Liberty,'" *Quarterly Review of Film Studies* 3 (summer 1978): 277–95; Suleiman was the first to note how this principle as theorized by Roman Jakobson could be applied to Buñuel's narrative innovations. For a discussion of how this operates in Buñuel's films, see chapter 6 of *Blood Cinema* and my essay, "The Nomadic Discourse of Luis Buñuel," in *Luis Buñuel's* The Discreet Charm of the Bourgeoisie, ed. Marsha Kinder (Cambridge: Cambridge University Press, 1999), 17.

25. David Ansen, "The Redemption of Pulp," *Newsweek*, October 10, 1994.

26. Stanley Crouch, "A High Point in a Low Age," *Los Angeles Times*, October 16, 1994, 5.

27. Robert Warshow, "The Gangster as Tragic Hero?" in *The Immediate Experience* (Garden City, N.Y.: Doubleday, 1962).

28. Although it is beyond the scope of this essay to deal with representations of violence performed by women, I must note the parallel challenge posed in the 1980s and 1990s on the register of gender by glamorous female stars playing non-monstrous, kick-ass roles in traditionally male-gendered action genres, usually directed by male auteurs—a role pioneered by Faye Dunaway in *Bonnie and Clyde* and by Pam Grier in the blaxploitation films of the 1970s.

Some of the most notable examples are Gena Rowlands in John Cassavetes's gangster film *Gloria* (1980) and Sharon Stone in Sidney Lumet's disappointing 1999 remake; Kathleen Turner in John Huston's comic gangster film, *Prizzi's Honor* (1985) and in John Waters's violent sitcom *Serial Mom* (1994); Susan Sarandon and Geena Davis in Ridley Scott's outlaw road movie *Thelma and Louise* (1991); Jodie Foster in Jonathan Demme's *The Silence of the Lambs* (1991); Sigourney Weaver and Winona Ryder in the *Alien* sci-fi series; Linda Hamilton in James Cameron's *Terminator 2: Judgment Day* (1991); Angelica Huston in Stephen Frears's noir thriller *The Grifters* (1990); Lena Olin in Peter Medak's gangster thriller *Romeo Is Bleeding* (1993); Demi Moore in Ridley Scott's war film *GI Jane* (1997) and in Brian Gibson's thriller *The Juror* (1996); and Jamie Lee Curtis in Kathryn Bigelow's cop movie *Blue Steel* (1990). In many of these films the violent behavior and buff bodies of these women are further eroticized by their male directors—a dynamic that is pushed to the point of parody in Oliver Stone's direction of Juliette Lewis in *Natural Born Killers*, particularly in her opening erotic murderous dance.

29. For a fuller discussion of these comedies, see my essay "Home Alone in the '90s: Generational War and Transgenerational Address in American Movies, Television, and Presidential Politics," in *In Front of the Children*, ed. Cary Bazalgette and David Buckingham (London: BFI, 1995).

30. The only Hollywood action genres with this kind of orchestration are swashbucklers and action musicals (like *West Side Story* and Michael Jackson's music video parody, *Beat It*), in which the moves of the performers are choreographed but the violence is stylized rather than excessive.

31. After Lee's death in 1973, Jackie Chan was groomed as his replacement, particularly in the early Hong Kong action film *New Fists of Fury* (1976), the sequel to Bruce Lee's *Fists of Fury* (1971). Chan literally replaces the kung fu master formerly played by Lee (whose huge facial close-up is prominently on display) by helping his sister restore their karate school to its former glory. At this point in his career Jackie Chan had not yet developed the inimitable comic persona that would dominate his future action films, soon enabling him to become as inimitable as Lee.

32. Two other possible exceptions are comics Jerry Lewis and Jim Carrey, whose cartoonish plasticity of voice, face, and gestures make them as unique as Keaton, Kelly, and Astaire.

33. As quoted by Rone Tempest in "Rolling with the Punches," *Los Angeles Times*, Calendar section, December 27, 1998, 39.

34. Tempest, "Rolling with the Punches," 38.

35. Quoted by Tempest, "Rolling with the Punches," 38.

36. *Daily Variety*, December 5, 1998, 74.

37. Tempest, "Rolling with the Punches," 39.

38. Ibid.

39. Ibid., 38.

40. Ibid., 40.

41. R. J. Smith, "The Coolest Actor in the World," *Los Angeles Times Magazine*, March 12, 1995, 14.

42. Treating Woo as a follower of Peckinpah, Prince acknowledges that he "has generated tremendous fascination among Western critics because of the sociological complexity of his work, a striking amalgam of Eastern and Western cultural, religious, and cinematic traditions and styles," yet Prince fails to take this moral vision seriously, dismissing Woo's representation of violence as "at best, an exercise in stylistic pyrotechnics." (Prince, *Savage Cinema*, 230).

43. *Daily Variety*, December 15, 1998, 76.

44. Although France has never successfully challenged Hollywood in the realm of male action heroes, that nation produced Luc Besson's phenomenal *Femme Nikita* (1990), an international hit movie that featured a manmade, high-tech female assassin, and that subsequently spawned a successful TV spin-off

(now on American cable TV) as well as a character in Raul Ruiz's multinational meta-narrative thriller *Shattered Image* (1998).

45. For a discussion of the cultural specificity of violence in video games, see my essay "Contextualizing Video Game Violence: From Teenage Mutant Ninja Turtles 1 to Mortal Kombat 2," in *Interacting with Video*, ed. Patricia M. Greenfield and Rodney R. Cocking (Norwood, N.J.: Ablex Publishing, 1996).

46. For a discussion of Antonio Banderas's crossover to Hollywood, see my essay "Refiguring Socialist Spain: An Introduction," in *Refiguring Spain: Cinema/Media/Representation*, ed. Marsha Kinder (Durham, N.C., and London: Duke University Press, 1997), esp. 5–8.

47. For a discussion of the cultural context of Woo's Hong Kong action films and their relationship to the changing political status of Hong Kong, see Tony Williams, "Space, Place, and Spectacle: The Crisis Cinema of John Woo," *Cinema Journal* 36, no. 2 (winter 1997): 67–84. For a discussion of Woo's representation of masculinity, see Jillian Sandell, "Reinventing Masculinity: The Spectacle of Male Intimacy in the Films of John Woo," *Film Quarterly* 49, no. 4 (summer 1996): 23–34; and Julian Stringer, "'Your tender smiles give me strength': Paradigms of Masculinity in John Woo's *A Better Tomorrow* and *The Killer*," *Screen* 38, no. 1 (spring 1997): 25–41. For a fuller study of Woo, see Kenneth E. Hall, *John Woo: The Films* (Jefferson, N.C.: McFarland and Co., 1999).

Part Two:

Revisiting Violent Genres

"clean, dependable slapstick": comic violence and the emergence of classical hollywood cinema

peter kramer

In contemporary debates about media violence it is often forgotten that, apart from constituting a problem, this violence is also a matter of tremendous skill (on the part of performers and filmmakers) and of sheer fun (on the part of audiences). A reminder of these basic facts can be found in James Agee's classic 1949 essay "Comedy's Greatest Era," which powerfully evokes the violent comedy of American silent cinema, concentrating on the "plain slapstick" of Mack Sennett in the 1910s and the more psychologically complex, character-based comedy of Charles Chaplin, Harold Lloyd, Harry Langdon, and Buster Keaton in the late 1910s and 1920s.[1] According to Agee, physical comedy, whether "plain" or complex, had its own "language." This language provided performers, whose task it was "to be as funny as possible physically," with a rich "vocabulary" that had been derived from the "accomplishments of the acrobat, the dancer, the clown and the mime." At the heart of the work of these performers were acts of violence, carefully broken down into distinct, easily recognizable, and "ferociously emphatic" gestures and moves, the precise execution and intricate combination of which was to be appreciated as the comedian's artistic creation, "a kind of poem . . . that everybody understands." When being hit on the head, for example, the comedian, rather than responding naturalistically, "gave us a figure of speech, or rather of vision, for loss of consciousness. . . . The least he might do was to straighten up stiff as a plank and fall over backward with such skill that his whole length seemed to slap the floor at the same instant. Or he might make a cadenza—look vague, smile like an angel, roll up his eyes, lace his fingers, thrust his hands palms downward as far as they would go, hunch his shoulders, rise on tiptoes, prance ecstatically in narrowing circles until, with tallow knees, he sank down the vortex of his dizziness to the floor, and there signified nirvana by kicking his heels twice, like a swimming frog."[2]

In the plain slapstick of Mack Sennett, such physical eloquence was situated in a narrative universe where all characters at any time might be the perpetrators or recipients of violent acts, or the victims of unintentional physical mishaps involving other people, treacherous objects, or simply a lack of control over their own bodies, always evoking the experience of pain without ever sustaining any serious injury: "Words can hardly suggest how energetically they collided and bounced apart, meeting in full gallop around the corner of a house; how hard and often they fell on their backsides; or with what fantastically adroit clumsiness they got themselves fouled up in folding ladders, garden hoses, tethered animals and each other's headlong cross-purposes." In many films these actions culminated in a final act of highly coordinated and all-embracing destruction, such as a chase: "a majestic trajectory of pure anarchic motion that bathing girls, cops, comics, dogs, cats, babies, automobiles, locomotives, innocent bystanders, sometimes what seemed like a whole city, an entire civilization, were hauled along head over heels in the wake of that energy like dry leaves following an express train."[3]

Crucially, for Agee, the screen action was mirrored by the systematic buildup and orgasmic release of comic tension in the auditorium. Agee identified four "main grades of laugh": the titter, the yowl ("a runaway titter"), the bellylaugh (pure pleasure), and the boffo ("the laugh that kills"). "An ideally good gag, perfectly constructed and played, would bring the victim up this ladder of laughs by cruelly controlled degrees to the top rung, and would then proceed to wobble, shake, wave and brandish the ladder until he groaned for mercy."[4] Thus, the spectator was as much a"victim" of the film's action as were its characters, both being physically subjected to the systematically executed on-screen violence, flirting with pain, yet always coming away from the violence unharmed. What Agee was interested in were not the precise historical circumstances and potential political meanings of slapstick's violent subversion of the social order on the screen and of the audience's physical restraint in the auditorium, but the apparently timeless mechanics of comic violence, the reduction of everything social and psychological to the physicality of objects and human bodies. This violent reductionism of silent comedy was a crucial yet all too easily forgotten aspect of the entertainment experience that the film industry provided for its audiences. Moreover, due to the skill involved on the part of performers and the pleasures generated on the part of spectators, for Agee it constituted one of the high points of all of film history.

Agee's essay still serves film historians well as a guide to a period when various forms of comic violence formed a ubiquitous and essential component of American film culture. By highlighting the plain slapstick of the 1910s as the foundation of later developments and the importance of Sennett's Keystone studio as the training ground for comedians, the essay focuses attention on the fact that filmic slapstick was a fully fledged cultural form and an important industrial practice at the very same time that what has come to be known as classical Hollywood cinema was institutionalized as a normative filmic style and dominant industrial mode of production in the United States.[5] It is immediately evident from Agee's writing that, while Sennett may have operated his own film factory broadly in line with the classical studio system, the stylized physicality, energetic chaos, and relentless attack on the audience so characteristic of slapstick films are at odds with the received conception of classical style, which, according to David Bordwell, embraces "notions of decorum, proportion, formal harmony, respect for tradition, mimesis, self-effacing craftsmanship, and cool control of the perceiver's response."[6]

How, then, did comic violence fit into American film culture of the 1910s, and, more particularly, how did it relate to the emergent classicism? I am going to address this question by taking a look at *The Butcher Boy*, a two-reel comedy produced and released in 1917, the very year that Bordwell, Staiger, and Thompson have chosen as the point at which Hollywood classicism is fully in place. *The Butcher Boy* is the first film that Roscoe Arbuckle, one of slapstick's superstars, made for his own independent production company (called Comique) after his departure from Keystone, and thus it is only one step away from the plain slapstick of the Sennett studio. *The Butcher Boy* is also the first film that Buster Keaton, one of the four masters of silent comedy that Agee designates, appeared in after a long and distinguished career in vaudeville; hence the film retains a close link to the theatrical performance traditions mentioned by Agee. My discussion of *The Butcher Boy* examines its violent comic performances and their celebration in the writings surrounding the film. I will also show that the film itself and its reviewers made gestures toward qualities usually associated with classicism, and suggest that these gestures primarily served a rhetorical function, constructing a respectable front for the basic pleasures of comic violence. In the second part of this essay, I will trace this rhetorical strategy back to the rise of extended dramatic films in the early 1900s, using contemporary writings about *The Great Train Robbery* (1903) as my main examples. I will show that early catalogue entries on this extraordinarily successful and highly influential film not only highlighted its violent attractions but also, rather prematurely, claimed a set of classical formal and stylistic qualities for it, which are at odds with the actual experience of viewing the film. This suggests that, right from the beginnings of extended filmic storytelling, the film industry's discourse about stylistic norms served not merely as a prescription for filmmakers, but also as a rhetorical smokescreen for audiences, obfuscating the very attractions that were at the heart of their entertainment experience. With the emergence of classicism, the attractions of violence were indeed increasingly subordinated to narrative (both within individual films and within movie theater programs), yet, as *The Butcher Boy* demonstrates, they have remained a much more important component of mainstream American cinema than most contemporary discourses and later academic accounts of Hollywood classicism were willing to acknowledge.

Executing Comic Violence: Buster, Fatty, and *The Butcher Boy*

On April 8, 1917, the *New York Morning Telegraph* announced that the vaudeville performer Buster Keaton would from now on support leading film comedian Roscoe "Fatty" Arbuckle in a new series of two-reelers, starting with *The Butcher Boy*.[7] The paper defined Keaton's performance specialty as the ability to take excessive amounts of physical abuse from his father in their long-running stage act, related his promise that he would take even more such abuse from Arbuckle, and invited, albeit with a lot of irony, the readers' sympathy with his sufferings: the audiences "who were wont to sympathize with him" in vaudeville "will have much greater reason to feel compassion for him" in the movies. The paper stressed the difference between Keaton's diminutive stature and Arbuckle's bulk, which was the precondition for Arbuckle's "ability to slam him about harder." While the paper thus clearly assumed that readers would relish Arbuckle's violence, it also focused their attention on the skill and the emotional appeal of the supporting comic at the receiving end of this violence, reminding them that for the enjoyment of comic violence its victims were just as important as its perpetrators, vicarious suffering as important as vicarious triumph. Most important, the paper unquestioningly presented acrobatic violence as the very essence of the work of comedians such as Keaton and Arbuckle.

A look at Keaton's first appearance in *The Butcher Boy* shows how the film delivered on the promise made in the announcement. The first half of the film is set in a grocery store, with Arbuckle playing the eponymous butcher boy, who deals with pieces of meat, knives, and other tools of his trade in the highly skillful manner of a juggler, and interacts with his boss, coworkers, and customers with good humor, but without proper decorum and respect. While he is always hinting at his latent aggression and potential for violent action with grimaces and playful little slaps, initially he is holding back. Then Keaton enters the store as the last in a series of customers, carrying a small pail to be filled with molasses. First, however, he examines a couple of brooms, and his skillful handling of these objects immediately establishes him as a juggler on a par with Arbuckle, thus setting up their subsequent violent encounter as the interaction of two trained acrobats. The brief interlude also shows that the young man Keaton plays is easily distracted from the task at hand, which helps to explain why, immediately after he has placed his order with Arbuckle's clerk, he departs from the counter to observe a game played at the back of the store, forgetting to point out that his money is in the pail. He only tells

Arbuckle after the pail has been filled, and then gets distracted again, failing to realize that, as an act of revenge, Arbuckle temporarily pours the molasses into his hat to get at the money.

Arbuckle's action gives rise to the first extended sequence of systematic violence in the film, which is thus psychologically and socially motivated both by the clerk's resentment against the customers he has to serve and by the inattentiveness and stupidity of this last customer (it is also physically motivated by the fantastic sticking power of molasses). The various incidents of this violent sequence are connected in a mechanistic cause-and-effect chain that is clearly delineated for all to see and understand; yet the sequence is also driven by the aggressive impulses of the clerk, who is given the chance to abuse his customer (and at the very end also his boss) while he appears only to do his job and offer help. This is what happens: When Keaton puts on his hat, it sticks to his head. While trying to pull it off, he throws the pail of molasses he has just bought to the ground. When Arbuckle comes to the rescue and manages to pull the hat off, Keaton falls to the floor, and when he gets up his oversized shoes are stuck in a puddle of molasses spilled from the pail. After unsuccessfully trying to get his foot off the floor, Keaton is again helped by Arbuckle, who first pulls one leg, then the other and then his whole body, before pouring boiling water onto the shoe, which, judging by his facial expression and gestures, causes the customer a lot of pain. Finally, Arbuckle leans against the counter and uses both feet and all of his formidable strength to push Keaton away. The shoe gets unstuck and Keaton stumbles backward across the store and out the door, knocking over the shopkeeper who was about to enter, and tumbling down the steps outside.

The sequence, which is the first in a series of similar comic set pieces, features a wide range of situations and activities that can be called violent, irrespective of the real or apparent intentions of the people involved: a man hurt or physically restrained by objects (the hat sticking to his head, the shoe sticking to the floor), a man distorting his own body (pulling his own legs), a man causing pain to another with the help of an object (the kettle filled with boiling water), a man using his own body to do damage to that of another (pulling him with his arms, pushing him with his feet). These various forms of violence methodically realize the destructive potential of the everyday world the film's audiences inhabit outside the movie theatre, the hidden power of objects as well as the latent aggressions of people, and in the process these incidents highlight the vulnerability of the human body and the fragility of the social order. Yet all this takes place in the safety of the movie theater, contained within the action on the screen, performed by trained and seemingly invulnerable acrobats, which allows the audience to respond with laughter rather than with fright. While *The Butcher Boy* includes minor violent incidents in its work setting right from the start, as a slapstick comedy it is expected to build up toward scenes of densely packed, carefully choreographed, and slowly escalating violence such as the one just analyzed, inviting the audience to join in equally escalating laughter.

Quite fittingly, the first of these scenes is focused on Keaton, whose ability to take excessive abuse had been announced as his specialty. Later in the film, Keaton has several more opportunities to take spectacular falls displaying the kind of physical poetry that Agee was so good at describing. Keaton's efforts were appreciated by the reviewer of the trade paper *Motion Picture News,* who stated that the vaudeville comedian made his film debut "by taking an amazing amount of punishment," and did so with such vigor that real injury was a distinct possibility, if it were not for his supreme skills: his falls "are not fake and would mean a broken neck to any one not in perfect physical shape."[8] Again, acrobatic violence was seen as a perfectly legitimate device that, together with all the other comic devices of the film, was understood to be in the service of the audience's enjoyment, a point reiterated several times in the review: a dog's performance in the film is "excruciatingly funny"; the supporting comedians make Arbuckle's antics "doubly enjoyable"; and, finally, "we cannot imagine a person in any picture audience who will not enjoy every foot of the two reels."

However, complementing its emphasis on the audience's enjoyment, the review also pointed out that the film's violent comedy had to be balanced with other qualities to make it acceptable as entertainment. A closer look at these required qualities reveals them to be central to the notion of Hollywood classicism. First of all, incidents of comic violence had to be integrated into a coherent narrative. *The Butcher Boy* attempts this mainly by introducing a romantic relationship between Arbuckle's character and the store owner's daughter, which gives rise to conflicts both with her father and with a rival clerk. This in turn motivates two escalating fights between the romantic rivals, first in the grocery store and then, in the second half of the film, in the boarding school where the daughter is sent to keep the peace in the store. While these two fights, which gradually spread across the settings in question and involve everyone present, exemplify the "pure anarchic motion" of slapstick climaxes that so fascinated Agee, both halves of the film end with older authority figures (first the store owner, then the principal of the boarding school) asserting themselves and taking charge again after their domain has temporarily been thrown into complete disorder by the fighting youth. Thus, comic violence is framed by the final reestablishment of social order, and also by the main protagonist's overarching goal of romantic fulfillment. The end of the first half of the film appears to terminate the romance of the butcher boy (he weeps after his loved one has been carted off to the boarding school), yet his activities in the second half (he enters the girls' school in drag and manages to escape from it with his loved one) result in the romance's happy conclusion, when the couple decide to get married. For the *Motion Picture News* this construction was sufficient: "The story has enough consistency to satisfy even the most old-fashioned stickler for 'plot.'" Rather than taking this claim at face value, it is more appropriate to see it as a rhetorical device, an assurance to exhibitors and their prospective audiences that there was more to *The Butcher Boy* than mere slapstick and the explosive laughter it provoked. While the review's emphasis on narrative coherence probably did not reflect the ways in which the film actually engaged its audience, it helped to deflect attention from the centrality of comic violence in the film.

That comic violence in itself constituted a problem and hence required justification or obfuscation becomes obvious elsewhere in the critical reception of *The Butcher Boy*. For example, in the first sentence of its review, the *Motion Picture News* declared, "the new Fatty Arbuckle comedies are going to cross the tape first in the race for clean, dependable slapstick that will always get the money." Dependability no doubt referred to the film's ability to generate laughter, while the demand for cleanliness signaled that there were boundaries of good taste that were not supposed to be transgressed in the pursuit of laughter. As it turned out, different people drew these boundaries differently. *Variety*, for example, was impressed by the "serious, earnest way" in which Arbuckle performed in this film, noting that as a consequence "the comic effect is all the more forceful," yet the review ended with an ambiguous statement: "While there is some slapstick, the comedy is recommended."[9] The fan magazine *Photoplay*'s much more negative review spelled out the likely meaning of this slight criticism, by noting the "enormous and almost painful labor in this play," that is its focus on physical processes rather than characterization and narrative development: "The piece needs more repose and less violence to make it really funny."[10] Thus, while all reviewers acknowledged that the primary function of Arbuckle comedies was to make people laugh, they varied in their estimation of the extent to which this aim could and should be achieved through the hard physical labor of violent comedy. Comic violence therefore always needed to be contextualized, by being situated first within a film's narrative framework and second within a publicity and critical discourse about the film's respectability.

Slapstick stars such as Roscoe Arbuckle, together with publicity agents and advertising people, worked hard to project a "clean" image for themselves and their films, while also assuring customers that the films would dependably deliver the required laughs. When in September 1916, several months before the release of *The Butcher Boy*, Roscoe Arbuckle had announced his imminent departure from Sennett's Keystone studio to set up Comique, he had assured his fans that he would continue with his characteristic physical performance, while also, however, making it more respectable: "I'm going to stick to slapstick. I'd be foolish not to, seeing that I built my reputation on it. . . . But it will be a little nicer, you know."[11] Arbuckle also declared that "it is the aim of his concern to produce serious plays also," and he hinted at the possibility that at some point in the future he might withdraw from acting in comedy shorts altogether to continue his performance career in full-length dramatic features.[12] Arbuckle's statements also foregrounded the multiple roles he played in the production of his films, as performer, director, producer, and entrepreneur. Thus, the publicity for Arbuckle's upcoming series of two-reelers highlighted his status as a respectable and multitalented filmmaker, playing down his identification with violent comic performance.

In sharp contrast to such deflections, the trade advertisements that the films' distributor, Paramount, aimed at exhibitors in the spring of 1917, highlighted the promise of laughs arising from the comedian's violent antics as the films' main appeal for audiences. In an ad for *The Butcher Boy*, for example, a picture of Arbuckle pointing at a safe while smiling at the reader was captioned with the question: "Do you want to fill that up?"[13] An ad for the second film in the series, *A Reckless Romeo*, highlighted the particular appeal of comedy as opposed to drama, hinting at the positive mood it would noisily spread across the auditorium: "A laugh is worth twenty sighs in any market." The ad asserted that there was no better way to create a successful show than to "tickle your patrons to death."[14] Here, then, the central importance of comedy for cinema programs, the primary function of comedy to generate laughter, and Arbuckle's success at fulfilling that function were acknowledged without any reservations. Comic violence was not in any way presented as a problem; instead it was metaphorically extended, much like Agee suggested, into the auditorium as a pleasurable attack on spectators. In doing so, the ads echoed the article in the *New York Morning Telegraph*, which alerted Buster Keaton's vaudeville fans to his film career, promising them an extension of the spectacular violence and punishment characteristic of his stage work.

These examples suggest a divergence between a discourse of effectivity primarily driven by a concern for audience pleasures and industry profits, and a discourse of respectability.[15] While in its internal communications the film industry was sometimes concerned with effectivity only, in its address of the public the industry, its most prominent practitioners, and its critics more often felt the need to present a respectable front, arguing that there was more to comedy than violence and laughter, namely good storytelling and sound aesthetic and moral judgment. These divergent discourses about film entertainment can be traced back to the early 1900s, and they are crucial for understanding the emergence and nature of Hollywood classicism.

Positioning Comic Violence: Violent Attractions and Hollywood Classicism

In November 1908, at the very beginning of the period that Kristin Thompson has characterized as "the transitionary phase toward the classical cinema,"[16] W. Stephen Bush expressed his strong concern in the leading film industry trade paper *Moving Picture World* about the impact of comedy's dominance in motion picture programs: "The public, having been so long and often invited to laugh at the things thrown on the screen by the operator, is inclined to laugh too much, and if you laugh at a thing all the time you begin to despise it, or at least to hold it in light esteem. Thus a portion, at least, of the public have come to look upon the moving picture as a mere toy."[17] Bush's concern is understandable in light of the fact that before 1908 the majority of fiction films copyrighted in the United States were comedies, at least seventy percent in 1907 and a much higher percentage in the preceding years.[18] However, noting the drastically increased emphasis on dramatic films in 1908 (rising to about seventy percent of the fictional output),[19] Bush was happy to report that, as far as the public's perception of moving pictures was concerned, "the work of conversion . . . is fully under way." To complement this work, film comedy had to change as well. Bush noted the film manufacturers' traditional emphasis on the comedy of physical mishaps and violent action: "Time was when a chase, a fall into water, the upsetting of wagons and pushcarts, the stumbling over sticks and fences, made up a very considerable portion of the funny moving picture."[20] While such physical comedy was highly effective, the industry now needed "something newer and better in quality of fun," such as adaptations of classic comic plays and novels or cute and lively child comedians or parodies of dramatic genres, anything that might have engaging characterization and an interesting story, so as to demonstrate that film was more than a merely playful medium, that like the legitimate stage and literature it could engage audiences in a serious fashion.[21]

Thus, the transition from what Thompson and others have called "primitive" cinema (up to 1908) to the classical cinema (from 1917), is closely linked to the subordination of violent comedy to the newly dominant genre of drama, and to comedy's transformation into a more dramatic genre. After 1908, there was indeed a continuing decline in comedy production, and also a shift in emphasis toward more character-based and narratively complex comedy. However, from 1911 comedy production revived and again numerically equaled the output of dramas; and, within its more complex narratives, comedy also largely returned to the violence of old, especially with the founding of the Keystone Film Company in 1912.[22] Slapstick's revival was made possible by, among other factors, the consolidation of an exhibition practice that assigned dramas, initially one-reelers (about a thousand feet) but from 1910 increasingly multiple-reelers, the role of the featured attraction on film programs, in relation to which the much shorter comedies functioned as support acts.[23] This exhibition practice, which highlighted the serious and legitimate part of the film program as the main attraction and downplayed the attractions of comedy as a mere sideshow, worked in conjunction with an extensive discourse, in advertisements and publicity as well as in the narratives and iconography of the films themselves, about the respectability, the artfulness, and the positive moral influence of the filmic medium.[24] Together, programming and the surrounding discourse assured the public that, while the basic pleasures of comedy were an indispensable part of most film shows, the main purpose of these shows was the powerful and lasting impact arising from the featured drama.

The model for this strategy to hide the essential appeal of comedy behind the featuring of, and debate about, drama can be found in exhibition strategies that emerged as early as 1902 through 1904, when multishot dramatic films first made an impact on the film programs presented, as one item on a bill of many diverse acts, in vaudeville theaters and other venues of variety entertainment. At this time, most narrative films produced in the United States were single-shot comic scenes typically featuring the transgressive actions and sometimes also the punishment of a bad boy, tramp, or similar figure, or a combination of such scenes into a multishot film of one to three minutes' length.[25] In an attempt to shift larger quantities of film and also to raise the profile of the filmic medium as a whole, producers and distributors suggested that for each film program an extended drama such as *The Great Train Robbery*, which could be around eight hundred feet long (ten minutes or so, depending on projection speed), should be used as a "Headline Attraction" or "feature film."[26] As a 1904 Kleine catalogue put it, "These long films admit of special advertising, that is to say, special emphasis on one subject, which is more effective than equal emphasis on a number of shorter films."[27] While the film program should include both the featured drama and various short subjects (comedy, trick films, actualities), the emphasis on drama, in the actual program and in the advertising for it, served to raise the overall tone, promising to engage the audience in a deeper and more sustained fashion than could be achieved by shorter films with their series of rapidly changing attractions. In fact, it was noted that the sophisticated pleasures of film drama had required some learning on the part of spectators: "The public has been educated to appreciate these long films which tell an interesting story." The main quality, apart from "photographic excellence," that the audience had learned to appreciate was the drama's tight focus on "continuous action" from shot to shot (unlike the largely self-contained action of each shot characteristic of most comedies): "There should be no lagging in the story; every foot must be an essential part, whose loss would deprive the story of some merit; there should be sequence, each part leading to the next with increasing interest, reaching its most interesting point at the climax, which should end the film." This "analysis of what a perfect film should be" was presented as an ideal and not as the reality of the average drama. However, it was noted that *The Great Train Robbery* had become such a huge success precisely because "it accurately follows" this ideal. Throughout the film "the observer finds his interest rising," getting ever more involved in the action and being taught a moral lesson along the way: "He sees inexorable fate bearing down upon the malefactors, pursuing them with irresistible force, until with heavy hand it strikes them down."[28]

Here, then, in a 1904 catalogue, is the basic outline of a form of filmic storytelling that would later develop into Hollywood classicism. Or rather, here are the beginnings of a *discourse* about the ideal of classical narration in the cinema. The catalogue text contains most of the elements that David Bordwell has identified as central to "Hollywood's own discourse . . . in trade journals, technical manuals, memoirs, and publicity handouts" from the 1910s to the 1960s about its filmmaking.[29] According to Bordwell, these elements are that "Hollywood cinema sees itself as bound by rules that set stringent limits on individual innovation" (the catalogue does not discuss *The Great Train Robbery* as a unique work but as a model for future filmmaking, an exemplification of a set of rules); "telling a story is the basic formal concern" (the catalogue says so as well); "the Hollywood film purports to be 'realistic'" (the catalogue's concern about "photographic excellence" signals an interest both in visual beauty and in the visibility and recognizability of the real world in front of the camera); it "strives to conceal its artifice through techniques of continuity and 'invisible' storytelling" (the entry emphasizes continuity and narrative drive); "unity is a basic attribute of film form" (the entry insists on the overriding objective of storytelling, which unifies its "parts" and for which "every foot" should be "essential"); and, finally, "it possesses a fundamental emotional appeal that transcends class and nation" (the catalogue emphasizes the film's power to engage the "interest" as well as the emotional and moral faculties of any spectator).[30]

The importance of this match between a 1904 catalogue and Hollywood's later discourse about its own classicism is not to do with timing; it does not suggest that the classical period started in the early 1900s. Instead the importance of this match lies in the insight it facilitates, into the relativity of classical principles and into the strategic function of the industry's discourse about these principles. For today's viewers of *The Great Train Robbery*, the film does not come across primarily as an invisibly narrated, efficiently presented, perfectly unified and emotionally engaging story; in fact, it probably appears just as artificial, digressive, disjointed, and emotionally detached (except for intentional and unintentional comedy and the impact of violent action) as *The Butcher Boy*. Of course, this is not to say that, at the time, audiences did not get caught up in the story to a much larger extent than would appear to be possible from today's perspective. However, there is evidence that the film's main appeal arose from the individual attractions contained within its narrative. For example, the Edison catalogue entry for *The Great Train Robbery* describes the film as "sensational" and refers to real-life crimes that had recently "shocked" the public, thus enhancing the shock value of the crimes in the film; it also highlights the "thrilling scene" on top of the speeding train.[31] Finally, and most famously, the entry describes the last shot of the film under the heading "Realism" as follows: "A life size picture of Barnes, leader of the outlaw band, taking aim and firing point blank at each individual in the audience. . . . The resulting excitement is great." Forgotten is the morality of the narrative conclusion of the film in the previous shot ("all of the robbers and several of the posse bit the dust"); instead the catalogue promises pure sensual and emotional stimulation. Furthermore, it undermines any sense of clear-cut narrative closure or moral conclusions by suggesting that this shot and its stimulating effect "can be used either to begin the subject or to end it, as the operator may choose."

At first sight, this suggestion merely demonstrates the flexibility of exhibition practices in this period. However, I think it has much wider ramifications, precisely because it is accompanied by a fully fledged discourse about the narrative cohesion, artistry, and morality of *The Great Train Robbery*. Rather than seeing the film as a transitional work (between an exhibition-led and a producer-controlled cinema, between a cinema of attractions and a cinema of narrative integration, between primitivism and classicism),[32] I would like to propose that the mobilization of the divergent discourses of effectivity and respectability in the making and marketing of *The Great Train Robbery* provided a model for mainstream narrative American cinema as a whole. Seen in this light, the catalogue suggestion to reposition the shot of the outlaw appears as the explication of one of the basic tenets of American filmmaking, namely that the generation of "excitement," by whatever means necessary, has been its primary objective, running parallel to, yet being hidden behind and occasionally at odds with, complex narrational procedures and their associated aesthetic and moral qualities.[33] Arguably, it was the huge success of *The Great Train Robbery* and similar extended narrative films in the early 1900s that allowed the audiences of variety shows to see their film-viewing experiences in a different and more respectable light, to rationalize their varied responses (such as laughter, amazement, suspense, shock, anger) as a formally coherent and morally sound experience. This in turn made it possible that, rather than continuing to be seen merely as one of many acts on the variety bill of vaudeville theaters and other venues, film projection could emerge as an entertainment institution in its own right during the nickelodeon boom of 1905 and 1906.[34] At this point, hundreds and then thousands of theaters turned the one- or two-reel variety turn into the whole show, carrying over the division between the featured drama and a support program of actualities, trick films, and violent comedy suggested by the Kleine catalogue in 1904, and also, following the successful model of *The Great Train Robbery*, adopting the divergent discourses of respectability and effectivity as a rationale for their operations.

The emergence of classical Hollywood cinema over the next decade did not alter these fundamental parameters, although it did extend the length of the overall film program and of each of its component parts, and it elaborated narrational procedures and the surrounding advertising, publicity, and critical discourses so as to disguise the basic exchange of money for sensual and emotional stimulation underpinning the institution of cinema. As a result, by 1917 the featured drama would, on the whole, avoid pure stimulation of the kind afforded by the gunman's attack on the audience in *The Great Train Robbery*. However, short comedies such as *The Butcher Boy* could blatantly contravene the dominant discourse of respectability by continuing to indulge in violent action on the screen with the explicit intention to induce violent laughter in the auditorium. So when at the narrative and moral conclusion of *The Butcher Boy* Arbuckle's character, who is on his way to get married, turns around (in full drag) and winks at the camera, he reveals himself to be a professional entertainer who directly communicates with his audience, much like the gunman at the end of *The Great Train Robbery* stepping out of the fiction and addressing every single spectator. And what Arbuckle is communicating to his audience is perhaps that, irrespective of the narrative and moral demands of the fictional world he has inhabited and of the wider world in which his film has to make claims to some kind of respectability, it has all just been a comic turn and great fun for him, and, he hopes, for them as well. Like the shot fired by the gunman directly at the camera in *The Great Train Robbery*, ideally *The Butcher Boy* has been a direct attack on the spectator, giving rise to the pure excitement of escalating laughter.

The Persistence of Violent Attractions

In 1917, at the very beginning of what is commonly defined as the classical period of Hollywood cinema, the textual strategies of Roscoe Arbuckle's *The Butcher Boy* and the discourses surrounding the film point to the problematic yet irrefutable presence of exciting violence (on the screen) and violent excitement (in the auditorium) at the heart of American film culture during its first two decades. With few exceptions, the film industry and its critics did their best to deny the existence of this double violence or to acknowledge it only with a call for more refinement. They also managed to relegate it to a subordinate position on film programs (an isolated scene in a dramatic feature, a short comedy or animated cartoon presented merely

as a support act) and to hide the fundamental effectivity of violent entertainment behind the increasing narrative sophistication of films and a
powerful discourse, directed both at industry insiders and the American
public at large, on the respectability, the aesthetic cohesion, and morality
of the industry's filmic output. It is perhaps unfortunate that film historians have often taken this discourse at face value, paying attention mainly
to the films that the industry and its critics highlighted (dramatic features
rather than comedy shorts, newsreels, or cartoons), and finding in those
films mainly the qualities that the surrounding industrial and critical discourse has emphasized. It is the great achievement of James Agee not to
have been fooled by the dominant discourse of respectability and instead
to have cut through the pronouncements on, and the skeletal framework
of, narrative and morality, so as to engage directly with the effectivity of
slapstick's comic violence. Once this breakthrough has been made, there is
a lot of scope for taking Agee's work on silent film comedy further into an
investigation of the persistent presence of entertaining violence in
American cinema across the century, from the slapstick clowns of its early
decades to the action heroes of its final decades.

Notes

This essay was completed with the help of a fellowship from the Amsterdam School
for Cultural Analysis, Theory, and Interpretation. I also would like to thank David
Slocum and Lee Grieveson for their very helpful comments on earlier drafts.

1. James Agee, "Comedy's Greatest Era," in *Agee on Film* (London: Peter Owen, 1963), 2–19.
2. Ibid., 3.
3. Ibid., 5–6.
4. Ibid., 2.
5. David Bordwell, Janet Staiger, and Kristin Thompson, *The Classical Hollywood Cinema: Film Style and Mode of Production to 1960* (London: Routledge and Kegan Paul, 1985).
6. Ibid., 3–4.
7. "Papa Joe's Worthy Succesor" (*sic*), *New York Morning Telegraph*, April 8, 1917, unpaginated clipping on sheet 28 of the Locke Collection Envelope no. 887A (LCE), Billy Rose Theatre Collection (BRTC), New York Public Library at Lincoln Centre, New York. Compare Peter Kramer, "A Slapstick Comedian at the Crossroads: Buster Keaton, the Theater, and the Movies in 1916/17," *Theatre History Studies* 27 (1997): 133–46.
8. George M. Smorey, Review of *The Butcher Boy, Motion Picture News*, April 28, 1917, 2683. See also the review of the later Arbuckle comedy *Out West*, in which Keaton "is continually getting the worst of a series of comedy tumbles" (*Variety*, January 25, 1918, 42) Also see the review of *The Butcher Boy* in the *New York Morning Telegraph*, April 15, 1917, unpaginated clipping in Arbuckle file (MFL+n.c.2754, 10–79), BRTC: Keaton was "drawn from vaudeville to do his spectacular falls before the camera."
9. Review of *The Butcher Boy, Variety*, April 20, 1917, 24.
10. Review of *The Butcher Boy, Photoplay*, July 1917, 134.
11. Quoted in *Chicago Post*, September 26, 1916. See also "Arbuckle to Quit Keystone Studios for Own Company," *Cleveland Plain Dealer*, October 3, 1916. Both are unpaginated clippings in the Arbuckle file, BRTC.
12. *Chicago News*, September 27, 1916; and unidentified clipping by Kitty Kelly, dated September 27, 1916; both in the Arbuckle file, BRTC.
13. *Motion Picture News* 15, no. 16 (1917): 2400.
14. *Moving Picture World*, May 26, 1917, 1214. See also the ad for the third film

in the series, *The Rough House*. "The name is descriptive, the story is there but you forget it in the rush of action. A twentieth century howitzer or 14 centimeter siege gun isn't in the same class." *Motion Picture News*, July 7, 1917, 3.

15. See Henry Jenkins, *What Made Pistachio Nuts? Early Sound Comedy and the Vaudeville Aesthetic* (New York: Columbia University Press, 1992), 48–58.

16. Bordwell, Staiger, and Thompson, *The Classical Hollywood Cinema*, 159.

17. W. Stephen Bush, "The Place and Province of Humor in the Moving Picture," *Moving Picture World*, November 28, 1908, 420–21.

18. Eileen Bowser, *The Transformation of Cinema, 1907–1915* (New York: Scribner, 1990), 179; and Robert C. Allen, *Vaudeville and Film, 1895–1915: A Study in Media Interaction* (New York: Arno, 1980), 151, 159, 181, and 212–13.

19. Bowser, *The Trasformation of Cinema*, 179; and Allen, *Vaudeville and Film*, 212–13.

20. For a systematic analysis of the comedy output of American manufacturers see Peter Kramer, "Bad Boy: Notes on a Popular Figure in American Cinema, Culture, and Society, 1895-1905," in *Celebrating 1895: The Centenary of Cinema*, ed. John Fullerton (London: John Libbey, 1998); Davide Turconi, "'Hic sunt leones': The First Decade of American Film Comedy, 1894–1903," *Griffithiana*, nos. 55–56 (September 1996): 151–215; and Richard Arlo Sanderson, *A Historical Study of the Development of American Motion Picture Content and Technique Prior to 1904* (unpublished Ph.D. dissertation, University of California, Los Angeles, 1961).

21. Bush, "The Place and Province of Humor." For a fuller discussion of the campaign against physical comedy that also takes into account reformist concerns about nickelodeon audiences and the competition between American and foreign manufacturers, see Peter Kramer, "The Fall and Rise of Slapstick Films: Physical Comedy in American Cinema, 1907–1913," in *The Birth of Film Genres*, ed. Leonardo Quaresima, Alessandra Raengo and Laura Vichi (Udine: Forum, 1999).

22. Kramer, "The Fall and Rise of Slapstick Films."

23. On feature films, shorts, and movie theater programs, see Bowser, *The Transformation of Cinema.*, chs. 8, 11, and 12.

24. See, for example, William Uricchio and Roberta E. Pearson, *Reframing Culture: The Case of the Vitagraph Quality Films* (Princeton: Princeton University Press, 1993).

25. See Kramer, "Bad Boy"; and Turconi, "Hic sunt leones."

26. Entry on *The Great Train Robbery*, *Edison Films*, Supplement No. 200, Edison Manufacturing Company, Orange, New Jersey, January, 1904, 5–7; "About Moving Pictures," *Complete Illustrated Catalog of Moving Picture Films, Stereopticons, Slides, Films*, Kleine Optical Company, Chicago, Illinois, October 1904, 30–31; both reprinted in George C. Pratt, ed., *Spellbound in Darkness: A History of the Silent Film* (Greenwich: New York Graphic Society, 1973).

27. "About Moving Pictures."

28. Ibid.

29. Bordwell, Staiger, and Thompson, *The Classical Hollywood Cinema*, 3.

30. Ibid.

31. *Edison Films.*

32. See Tom Gunning, *D. W. Griffith and the Origins of American Narrative Film: The Early Years at Biograph* (Urbana: University of Illinois Press, 1991); and Charles Musser, *The Emergence of American Cinema: The American Screen to 1907* (New York: Scribner, 1990), esp. ch. 11.

33. See Richard Maltby with Ian Craven, *Hollywood Cinema: An Introduction* (Oxford: Blackwell, 1995), esp. ch. 1; and Dirk Eitzen, "Comedy and Classicism," in *Film Theory and Philosophy*, ed. Richard Allen and Murray Smith (Oxford: Clarendon Press, 1997).

34. See Richard Abel, "'Pathé Goes to Town': French Films Create a Market for the Nickelodeon," *Cinema Journal* 35, no. 1 (1995): 3–26.

five   **the spectacle of criminality**[1]

richard maltby

In May 1931 a crowd of fifteen thousand New Yorkers watched the "Siege of West 90th Street" from behind police barricades, as Francis "Two Gun" Crowley, a nineteen-year-old bank-robber and double murderer, exchanged fire with the police until he was overcome by tear gas. During the gun battle, Crowley wrote a letter "to whom it may concern," claiming that "the new sensation of the films" had inspired him to go around "bumping off cops."[2] Crowley was electrocuted before he could discover that he had, in return, inspired Hollywood, but within a year of the event, newspaper reviews reported that many of the incidents in Howard Hughes's *Scarface* were "based on actual happenings," including "the St. Valentine's Day massacre of seven gangsters; the murders of Big Jim Colosimo in his café and Tony Lombardi in his flower shop; the shooting of Legs Diamond in a hospital, and the police bombardment of Francis 'Two Gun' Crowley's stronghold."[3]

The month after Francis Crowley achieved his moment of fame as a "gangster," Winslow Elliott, the twelve-year-old son of a banker in

Montclair, New Jersey, was accidentally shot and killed by his sixteen-year-old playmate, William Harold Gamble, as Gamble acted out a scene from *The Secret Six*, MGM's principal contribution to that season's cycle of gangster films.[4] Elliott's death escalated an already strident public discourse linking the public spectacle of crime to the movies, providing the press with the opportunity, as the *Literary Digest* put it, "to harp again on the type of pictures which are said to pervert the mind of youth."[5] Among those demanding the suppression of these movies was an unexpected authority, Al Capone, who declared:

> "These gang pictures—that's terrible kid stuff. Why, they ought to take them all and throw them into the lake. They're doing nothing but harm to the younger element of this country. I don't blame the censors for trying to bar them. . . . these gang movies are making a lot of kids want to be tough guys and they don't serve any useful purpose."[6]

In response to calls from newspapers and parents' associations for a boycott of gangster pictures, the film industry's trade association, the Motion Picture Producers and Distributors of America (MPPDA), declared that the cycle was already coming to an end. Publicly, MPPDA president Will H. Hays claimed that "the screen has done much in recent months to 'debunk' the gangster by removing his mask of mock-heroism and focusing public attention upon the grave dangers of his rule," while at the same time acknowledging that a continuation of the cycle "was not in the interest of the widest possible entertainment program."[7] Privately, Hays sought to use the publicity surrounding the death of Winslow Elliott to persuade Hughes to modify the script of *Scarface,* the last picture in the cycle, then just entering production.[8] Over the next few months, that publicity would also contribute to the attempts by MPPDA officials to redeem *Scarface* by providing it with a defensible educational message: that the solution to the gangster problem lay in the passage of strict gun control legislation.

The gangster movies of the early 1930s are conventionally interpreted as particularly privileged instances of Hollywood's "Golden Age of Turbulence," during which their "charismatic, antisocial heroes obviously fulfilled a public need."[9] Critics disagree, however, about whether that need was for "something like an Alka-Selzer for the headaches of the depression," or for "a form of cultural catharsis."[10] Opinions vary as to whether "the comparison between the gangster and the grasping, well-organized business tycoon, ... held to be responsible for the Depression *must have* been obvious" to Depression audiences, or whether "the public *must have* been ready . . . to admire disproportionately those whose business it was to provide citizens with liquor."[11] This writing has, however, taken too literally the hyperbole of the Warner Brothers studio publicist who claimed that while the contemporary value of gangster pictures was entertainment, "their priceless ingredients [*sic*] for future historians is their truth."[12] Few of the critics making claims for these movies' cultural resonance have investigated the conditions of their reception, and one could read the entire corpus of genre studies of the crime film without encountering any acknowledgment that their exhibition met with widespread protest in 1931. Ironically, the dominant critical paradigm has accepted and inverted the perspective of conservative moral reformers, valorizing as subversive "the fashion for romanticizing gangsters" that some contemporary critics complained of.[13] If the editor of the *Christian Century* had, for instance, read John G. Cawelti's comment that one of the gangster hero's "most endearing traits was that he never became assimilated into an upper-class lifestyle but remained an unregenerate barbarian," he would have had his—and Al Capone's—very worst fears about the effects of the movies on the minds of the young confirmed.[14]

The critical reduction of the gangster to a "loose metaphor"—of social bandit or "monstrous emblem of the capitalist"—also fails to recognize the extent to which the brief cycle of gangster movies made during the 1930–31 production season was part of a broader representational strategy within Hollywood during the early Depression, by which overtly retrospective accounts of the excesses of the previous decade were staged as melodramatic reenactments of the rise and fall of moral chaos.[15] Through such a strategy, Hollywood participated in a more general cultural attempt to account for the crisis as an effect of the alleged permissiveness of the Jazz Age.[16] The gangster pictures borrowed the rhetoric of contemporary press editorials demanding an end to "the reign of gangdom" to denounce their protagonists. *The Public Enemy*'s final title, for instance, declared that "'The Public Enemy' is not a man, nor is it a character—it is a problem that sooner or later, WE, the public, must solve." Critics have noted the disparity between such stated intentions and the effect produced by the performances, particularly, of Edward G. Robinson and James Cagney, of legitimizing the gangster's antisocial position. From this perspective, occasionally endorsed by production anecdotes, it is argued that the rhetoric contained in such captions is an empty and largely cynical gesture.[17] This argument displays a naive misunderstanding of the politics of Hollywood's representation. The industry had too much at stake, both politically and economically, to do what its most trenchant critics were accusing it of doing. The history of the cycle reveals that the industry fully recognized the need to counter accusations about the detrimental effect of these movies; their publicity campaigns clearly acknowledged that the only acceptable justification for their existence was that they increased public awareness of the gangster problem by dramatizing it.[18] Reviews of *Scarface* regurgitated studio publicity in claiming that "it does not glorify the gangster . . . no human being could sit through this 'brilliantly told tale of the effect of lust for power upon a small mentality' without being rudely awakened to the danger confronting the country."[19]

No one who saw *Little Caesar* or *The Public Enemy* in 1931 saw them in a cultural vacuum. The movies' rhetorical deployment of the trope "the business of crime" echoed the observations of contemporary cultural critics such as Walter Lippmann and Waldo Frank, of Chicago's criminals and businessmen, and of innumerable journalists. In these various accounts, the metaphorical and material relationships between business and crime were often seen as far more intricate than merely "an implicit condemnation of the amoral marketplace values that dominated the preceding decade" or a romanticization of criminals as "social bandits who robbed bankers and gave to the poor."[20] Rather than exploring or expanding the metaphor, in many ways the movies operated deliberately to close down its significances; their ideological activity is perhaps as clearly revealed by the obvious subjects—civic corruption and the repeal of Prohibition—that they do not discuss as by the material they did include.

The notoriety of these movies did not arise explicitly from the violence of their representation. Just as it is anachronistic to view the gangster as "a parody of the American Dream," it would be equally anachronistic to explain the objections to the gangster pictures as having to do solely or even mainly with their representation of violence.[21] Until at least the early 1960s, public discourses surrounding motion picture censorship did not make a categorical distinction between the representation of violence and the representation of criminal activity. In the press response to Winslow Elliott's death, for instance, or in Henry James Forman's sensationalized summary of the Payne Fund Studies, *Our Movie-Made Children*, the representation of heroic criminality on the screen was understood as being a potential source of inspiration to the weak-minded, but little attention was paid to the issue of violence in and of itself.[22] Significantly, the word *violence* does not occur anywhere in the multiple texts of the Production Code; the concept now signified by that term was subsumed under the code's discussion of "brutality" and "gruesomeness." Along with hangings, electrocutions, third-degree methods, branding, surgical operations, the sale of women, and cruelty to children or animals, brutality and gruesomeness were identified as "Repellent Subjects" that "must be treated within the careful limits of good taste."[23] Writing in 1937, former MPPDA employee Olga Martin observed that without this restriction:

> movie audiences would be exposed to such visual details . . . as disfigured, dismembered, bloodstained and mutilated bodies, close-up views of dying men, and hair-raising details of inhuman treatment. The Code, however . . . bans such details from the screen, permitting their introduction into a picture only by way of indirect suggestion.[24]

The Code also stipulated that criminal activity "shall never be presented in such a way as to throw sympathy with the crime as against law and justice or to inspire others with a desire for imitation." Methods of crime, including the techniques of murder, were to be presented in a way "that will not inspire imitation," the use of firearms was to be restricted to essentials, and brutal killings were not to be presented in detail.[25] Like the stipulations on repellent subjects, these requirements were duplicated from the code's precursor, the "Don'ts and Be Carefuls," adopted by the MPPDA in 1927 as a codification of the subjects known to provoke action by state and municipal censorship boards. Although the Code omitted the earlier document's explicit mention of its concern with "the effect which a too-detailed description of these may have upon the moron," it expressed the same concerns that the representation of crime must be constructed in a way that would discourage imitation.[26]

The representation of what would now be called violence was in practice fairly precisely codified by the conventions of state and municipal censorship established during the 1920s. These conventions determined, for example, that a character could not normally shoot another character in a two-shot; the image of the gun being fired had to be separated from the representation of its impact by a cut. The rationale behind the studios' adoption of such conventions of representation had less to do with any assumption that the segmentation of the action might produce a distancing effect on the viewer than with the protection offered to the narrative by dividing the action into two shots. A shooting could be represented by either half of the action—the image of the perpetrator or that of the victim—whereas if the whole action was contained in a single shot, a censor's deletion might remove or obscure a key plot event. Authorial criticism frequently makes reference to the inventive discretion of Classical Hollywood's auteurs in their representation of violence: Gerald Mast, for example, suggests that at the beginning of *Scarface*, the camera shows Tony Camonte's (Paul Muni) murder of Big Louie Costillo (Harry J. Vejar) in shadow so that director Howard Hawks can "begin the delicate balancing of point-of-view that allows this story to be told . . . distanced by the murder's shadowy indirectness, . . . we do not come to loath or detest the man who performs it."[27] The inventiveness may be the auteur's; the discretion, however, belonged to the institutions regulating Hollywood's regimes of representation.

These conventions of elision contained the appearance of violence, ensuring that it was not a particularly acute issue in the regulation of film content in the early 1930s. Concerns about the representation of violence had, however, formed part of a broader disquiet about the representation of criminality as a pleasurable spectacle since the first censorship ordinance was passed in Chicago in 1907.[28] Newspapers and reformers argued that the screen's imitation of reality was inherently dangerous because it might inspire incompletely or inadequately socialized viewers—paradigmatically, the delinquent adolescent—to imitate the behavior they saw on the screen.[29] This deviant viewer—William Harold Gamble and his ilk— remained the principal focus of censorial concern, and from its foundation in 1922 the MPPDA was vigilant in its pursuit and debunking of such characters whenever they appeared in courtrooms or newspapers. It also sponsored and publicized opinions denying any relationship between pictures and delinquency.[30]

The 1927–28 production season saw the first cycle of gangster movies, triggered by the commercial success of *Underworld* (Paramount Famous Lasky, 1927). Anticipating public complaint, the MPPDA solicited the opinions of various experts in the fields of criminology and psychology, including Dr. Carleton Simon, a psychiatrist for the New York police, associate editor of the *Police Journal*, and author of a pamphlet "Crime and the Motion Picture." Simon stated categorically:

> I do not believe that any legitimate melodrama of crime, any detective story or any motion picture dealing with the life of underworld characters has ever been the sole incentive to or motivation of criminal behavior. . . . the great mass of medical and psychological observation is set against the possibility that the witnessing of a motion picture could be an effective stimulus to behavior previously inconsistent with the individual's standard of conduct.

On the contrary, he asserted, the so-called crook picture might well serve a useful purpose of social control by "supplying a vicarious escape for vestigial emotional reactions that have no normal outlet in the highly artificial life of our modern cities."[31]

This first cycle was short-lived. By the end of October 1928, Colonel Jason Joy, director of the MPPDA's Studio Relations department, believed it to be over, partly because of the "protests which have come from responsible sources and partly because the fans have become satiated with the subject."[32] The cycle had, however, brought the association into its first confrontation with independent producer Howard Hughes. His production company Caddo's first production, *Everybody's Acting* (1926), had been a surprise hit, and its second, *Two Arabian Nights* (1927), had won Lewis Milestone an Academy Award for best direction. While Hughes was embroiled in his First World War air epic *Hell's Angels,* Caddo made two other pictures for release in the late summer of 1928, *The Mating Call* and *The Racket.* Caddo adapted *The Racket* from a play by Bartlett Cormack without consulting Joy, and did not show the final version to the MPPDA reviewers before it was sent to the New York censors. The picture preserved Cormack's depiction of the collusion between gangsters and city politicians in a thinly veiled version of Chicago, and it was this, rather than any representation of violence, that provoked the New York board to propose a number of cuts and caused censors in Chicago and Portland, Oregon, to ban the film entirely. Caddo's response was to threaten legal action and give the issue as much publicity as possible. The *New York Sun* gave Cormack space to declare that if *The Racket* appeared "toothless in spots . . . the public should know that it was the New York State censors who pulled the teeth, not Hollywood." Politically motivated censorship, claimed Cormack, would not allow "the public to see a sub-title wherein a decayed District Attorney tells a gangster, 'We can't carry you and this election both.' . . . But the whole meaning of *The Racket* is destroyed by the cutting of the gangster Scarsi's tirade against the D.A. and the political machine that is about to destroy him to save his own perspiring neck."[33]

Such publicity increased the intransigence of the New York board, and it required the intervention of MPPDA secretary Carl Milliken to persuade Cormack that the deletions were "necessary from a public relations standpoint," while Hays and Paramount's New York office urged Hughes not to pursue his protest, since the picture was being exhibited successfully in its censored form, and nothing short of court action would bring about the reinstatement of the eliminations.[34] Paramount's New York branch manager, M. S. Kussell, who had steered the picture through the New York board, felt that the eliminations were quite reasonable, since the board had warned him when they passed *Underworld* that they would eliminate suggestions of collusion between criminals and politicians. "If we are to continue to make pictures glorifying crooks," said Kussell, "we must expect some eliminations."[35]

Cormack was right to claim that the elimination of scenes depicting political corruption itself constituted an act of political censorship, but none of the participants approached the issue as a matter of principle. The MPPDA was not itself involved in dissuading its member companies from explicit political commentary, although had Joy been consulted during production he would certainly have encouraged Caddo to delete the material subsequently eliminated. Even within the MPPDA, opinions varied as to the appropriateness of the screen as a site of social commentary. Milliken's assistant Arthur DeBra regretted the deletion of *The Racket*'s political commentary, since its inclusion would have established that the movie was indicting "our gang ruled political system" in the same terms as the "nearsighted clergymen" who condemned it.[36]

This first gangster cycle provoked a hostile reaction among articulate sections of the public, which had the effect of exaggerating the quantity of such pictures in circulation. Milliken identified the cycle as amounting to twenty-nine pictures out of a total of three hundred produced by the major companies in the first half of 1928. In a letter to the mayor of Louisville, Kentucky, who had proposed a censorship ordinance to prevent the showing of crime pictures, Milliken also explained that the MPPDA had hired Dr. Frederick L. Hoffman, an international expert on the incidence and causes of homicide, to discuss the possible effects of pictures on the commission of crime, in order "to settle in our minds how to produce this type of story . . . to secure the impression of reality and at the same time guard against the dispersing of criminal technique." So far, no public authority had suggested that any picture provided the criminally inclined with any useful information about the methods of crime, since "in every criminal process some gap is left in the technique which guards against its imitation."[37]

At the end of the cycle in late 1928, Milliken viewed the public relations difficulties caused by the representation of crime as a far less serious problem than those caused either by profanity or by the independently produced sex hygiene pictures that violated the industry's code. Joy's office was now able to forecast public reaction to pictures "with amazing accuracy," and as long as member companies ensured "that each picture showing a crime theme is correct in its attitude forming influence, I do not believe there is any serious danger of influential adverse criticism based merely upon the number of such pictures.[38]

In April 1929 Columbia University professor Joseph L. Holmes published the results of a two-year study into the effects of motion pictures on children. Holmes found no evidence of harm, a result he attributed to a combination of the consistent presence in pictures of a "highly moral ending, the ultimate punishment of the sinner," and the children's poor memory of the movie, even immediately after they had seen it.[39] When, in the same month, economist and business statistician Roger W. Babson published a "special letter" in which he asserted that "such studies as I have made lead directly to the movies as the basic cause of the crime waves of today," Milliken published a thirty-page rebuttal that identified several major errors in Babson's statistics before demolishing the logical bases of the inferences he had drawn from them.[40] He also contrasted Babson's opinions with those of a range of expert jurists, psychologists, and sociologists, including Holmes, and detailed a number of cases in which juvenile crime had been erroneously attributed to movie influence by a judge or a newspaper. In every case investigated, the cause was to be found not in the movies but in an individual's "history of imbecility or unwholesome home environment and training."

Pictures, argued Milliken, were consistent in their demonstration of the punishment of evil. Of the thirty-eight "underworld" pictures produced in 1928, the principal villain was killed in fourteen, arrested by the police in nineteen, and reformed by the love of a good woman in the remaining five. The "new art" of the motion picture was "the first of the great forms of human expression to develop and make effective a definite policy for shaping its representations of dramatic fiction and editing its records of news events to the end that their effect upon community life shall be wholesome and constructive rather than harmful." Milliken pointed out that in stark contrast to the press, newsreels never featured current crime scandals, because the newsreel companies, "under the guidance of Mr. Hays," exercised "conscious self-control":

> The chief objection to portraying actual crime in the News Reels, as compared with imaginary crime shown in entertainment pictures, is that in real life punishment is neither swift nor certain, and, when it occurs at all, would not be seen in the same picture with the crime itself. In the crook story as shown on the screen, on the contrary, punishment follows quickly and certainly after the offense. Furthermore, current crime stories in the News Reels would tend to feed the criminal's abnormal lust for publicity and to make him a hero surrounded by a halo of romance, thus setting a bad example to the youth in motion picture audiences. Psychologists agree that glorification of actual crimes and criminals, with names and details, might well inflame one type of abnormal mind.[41]

Milliken's document represents a high point of self-confidence in the MPPDA's assertion of the superiority of its facts and statistics—he presented figures tabulating the seating capacity of various cities against their crime rates, for instance—and also of the logic of its arguments. That logic relied in part on the assumption, explicit in Carleton Simon's analysis of movies and in Holmes's conclusions, that the movies' narrative morality was the governing consideration in any assessment of their effects. The industry's principal defence against the accusation that it told evil stories was that, as Milliken's statistics proved, the movies consistently showed that in the end crime did not pay. Those concerned with demonstrating the cinema's ill effects would have to focus on a different aspect of the movies: on scene and spectacle, rather than on narrative.

Milliken's account of the newsreel's representation of crime stood in stark contrast to the way in which the press made the performance of organized crime an acceptable public spectacle for much of the 1920s. Owen Garrison Villard, editor of *The Nation*, observed that in October 1926 the *New York Daily Graphic* devoted ten times as much space to crime reporting as it did to foreign news.[42] Beginning with the funeral of Big Jim Colosimo in Chicago in May 1920, big gangster funerals became media events, while police raids and gangland wars supplied the melodrama on which the tabloids and sensational magazines thrived. Al Capone achieved national prominence not because he was particularly successful in his chosen field of endeavor, but because he so assiduously courted media attention. The press creation of "Scarface Al Capone" was itself a site in the battleground over the institutions of representation during the 1920s, and one exacerbated by the spread of the urban daily press: between 1925 and 1930, rural subscriptions to city newspapers doubled.[43] To the consternation of provincial Protestant culture, Capone, in his yellow and purple suits, appeared a daring, stylish figure in media consumed by the urban working class in the 1920s. Fred D. Pasley, Capone's biographer and one of the scriptwriters on *Scarface*, called him "the Horatio Alger lad of Prohibition . . . the gamin from the sidewalks of New York, who made good in a Big Shot way in Chicago."[44]

In the second half of the 1920s, voices in the dominant culture expressed increasing concern that the media were presenting the gangster—archetypally Capone—as a heroic role model, particularly for the children of immigrants, alienated from their parents' world by the superficial Americanization they acquired through their consumption of mass media. In his 1927 study of boy gangs, Chicago School sociologist Frederick Thrasher argued that

> The more rapid this type of assimilation, the more rapid will be the disintegration of family control. While it is true that the children of the immigrant quickly learn English in the schools and in their association on the streets and elsewhere, they also become acquainted with the more racy and the more vicious aspects of American life through the sensational newspapers and cheap magazines, through the movies and other types of commercialized recreation, and through contacts with vice, crime, and political corruption in their own chaotic milieu. . . . There can be little doubt that knowledge of criminal activities and technique is often disseminated through the newspapers, many of which seem to thrive best by featuring crime news and playing it up for its last shred of emotional appeal.[45]

In 1929 Progressive reformer Jane Addams expressed concern about "the effect of all this law-breaking upon the young. There is no doubt that a spirit of adventure natural to boys in adolescence has been tremendously aroused by the bootleg and hijacking situation. It is as if this adventurous spirit were transferred from the Wild West into the city streets."[46]

As Carl Milliken suggested, however, the movies contributed little to the representation of the gangster—factual or fictional—as an American archetype during the 1920s. Even in the 1928 cycle, gangsters appeared most frequently in romantic melodramas set in an underworld milieu (*Underworld*, 1927; *While the City Sleeps*, 1928), or in detective mysteries revolving around concealed identities and disguise (*Bitter Sweets*, 1928; *State Street Sadie*, 1928). When they did appear, they were more likely to be represented as gamblers or jewel thieves than as bootleggers.[47] While "crook-society melodramas" such as *Broadway after Midnight* suggested the interpenetration of the upper- and underworlds, they represented these worlds as coexisting in a dangerous and sad city of the imagination constructed according to conventions little different from those of the "mysteries of the city" novels of the 1840s and 1850s.[48] Nick Scarsi's eliminated observations about collusion between criminals and politicians in *The Racket* were the commonplaces of contemporary commentaries that identified bootleggers, racketeers, and speakeasy operators as the labor force of a business run by "respectable" brewery owners, law enforcement agencies, politicians, and public officials. But as the eliminations themselves implied, such comments were all but excluded from the movies.

In February 1931 Walter Lippmann commented that the shooting of Jack "Legs" Diamond had "amused New York for a few days and shocked it very little," not only because Diamond's life did not seem particularly precious, but more because the shooting seemed no more real than a murder in an Edgar Wallace novel.[49] The melodramatic world of urban criminality appeared radically divorced from the life of "the ordinary householder in American cities." The tabloid melodrama of gang warfare served as a convenient distraction from the practical realities of liquor-related crime and from a municipal *realpolitik* in which city government was frequently an exercise in barely concealed corruption. As Waldo Frank observed in 1929, the performance of crime had become part of the society of the spectacle, "a cult so potent and popular that it outdoes politics and vies with sport in its rank in the public prints":

> Of course, this idolatry cannot be admitted in a jungle so thick with moral relics. So the crowd creates a huge professional class of criminals—entertainers who grow yearly more self-conscious of their "mission." To cooperate with them in their trials and exploits there is an almost equally large group of crime reporters. Both news accounts of actual trials and fiction about crime conform with our mechanical ideal of art.[50]

While Prohibition was a subject of constant discussion in the 1920s, it was not a dominant political issue. A tolerant contempt for the law circumvented any great need to campaign for repeal. Liquor-related crimes, along with other activities now constructed as "organized crime"—prostitution, illegal gambling, and racketeering—were viewed, in Lippmann's phrase, as "service crimes." The underworld, he argued, lived "by performing the services which convention may condemn and the law prohibit, but which, nevertheless human appetites crave":

> We find ourselves revolving in a circle of impotence in which we outlaw intolerantly the satisfaction of certain persistent human desires and then tolerate what we have prohibited. Thus we find ourselves accepting in their lawless

forms the very things which in lawful form we intended to abolish but with the additional dangers which arise from having turned over their exploitation to the underworld. . . . we are all so much addicted to lawbreaking that the existence of a great underworld which lives on lawbreaking is not wholly alien and antagonistic to the working assumption of our lives. . . . The underworld is what it is largely because Americans are too moral to tolerate human weakness, and because they are too great lovers of liberty to tolerate the tyranny which might make it possible to abolish what they prohibit.[51]

In a similar vein, Frederick Thrasher argued in the conclusion to his study of gangs in Chicago that the publicity given to crime "has done little more than create a general public tolerance of crime and racketeering and a feeling of resignation on the part of the average citizen to the existence of the gangster, the racketeer, and the corrupt politician as a necessary evil in American community life. This widespread public lethargy is an important element in the total problem."[52] This framework of public morality permitted Capone to claim in 1931, "I'm just a businessman. . . . My rackets are run along strict American lines. This American system of ours—call it capitalism, call it what you like—gives each and every one of us a great opportunity, if we only seize it with both hands and make the most of it. . . . I've made my money by supplying a popular demand. . . . "When I sell liquor, it's called bootlegging. When my patrons serve it on silver trays on Lake Shore Drive, it's called hospitality. . . . Why should I be called a public enemy?"[53]

Capone's claims to be a capitalist (in 1930 he moved into the milk distribution business because it was more profitable than beer distribution) formed part of a rhetorical debate over the boundaries between crime and business that was in large part occasioned by Prohibition.[54] Public attitudes toward the spectacle of criminality, however, began to change drastically in 1929. This was partly the result of the Hoover administration's much more strenuous attempt to enforce the Prohibition law, but it also reflected the growing perception of American business that Prohibition had not produced the expected benefits of increased productivity and an expansion of the consumer market, while corporate taxes were shouldering a burden better borne by liquor taxes. More generally, by the late 1920s "the excited sense that taboos were going to smash, that morals were being made over or annihilated, and that the whole code of behavior was in flux," had, according to Frederick Lewis Allen, departed in favor of "signs of stabilization" in manners and morals. Inevitably, the Crash created "a general sense that something had gone wrong with individualistic capitalism and must be set right."[55] In the post-Crash repudiation of the previous decade business spokesmen used the frequently drawn analogy between organized crime and conventional American business to blame government interference and the anti-trust laws for the corruption of American corporate business and to reassert the morality of incorporation and oligopoly. In a manner quite different from that implied by Robert Warshow in his essay "The Gangster as Tragic Hero," the gangster in this account became a scapegoat of the early Depression years, a significant part of the sin that

127

was being expiated after the Crash. The widespread collusion between legitimate business and racketeering came increasingly to be seen as a corrupt mutation of modern business enterprise. Many sections of business, argued the executive director of the Employers Association of Chicago, unable legally "to organize themselves for rational control of competition, have developed a positively criminal philosophy, and have created an economic monstrosity the acts of which have run the whole scale of crime."[56] American capitalism, he argued, must at all costs resist the incorporation of American crime, or else there would shortly be established "a new aristocracy in business, traceable in its beginning to a criminal class."[57]

The early 1930s thus saw a redefinition of the boundaries of criminality, partly through a revised understanding of what constituted racketeering and what constituted restraint of trade, and partly through a reassertion of ethnic stereotypes as an explanation for crime.[58] Richard Gid Powers has argued that the period's "civic war on crime" was "a symptom of a more general fear: that under the impact of the depression, American society would no longer be able to enforce the rules that held it together."[59] The cultural function of the gangster and racketeer changed very rapidly: "no longer envied or admired as the fascinating middleman," he was "the symbol of all that was going wrong in a complex, frightening, and increasingly impersonal world."[60]

As the most prominent representative of organized crime, Capone—the media creation of Scarface Al Capone, King of the Rackets—became the most prominent target of a new wave of aroused bourgeois reform sentiment and changing press and public attitudes. As he declared after his sentence for tax evasion, "Publicity—that's what got me." In part, he brought it on himself: the St. Valentine's Day massacre in 1929, was, in a notable apocryphal phrase, "lousy public relations."[61] Perpetrated three weeks before Hoover's inauguration, it brought the intervention of federal law enforcement agencies, called in by Hoover at the behest of a group of Chicago businessmen. In May 1929 Capone was arrested for carrying a concealed weapon, and sentenced to the maximum term of one year's imprisonment. By the time of his release in March 1930, the Chicago Crime Commission had coined the term *public enemy*, and named Capone "Public Enemy No. 1." The phrase was taken up by newspapers across the country. In June 1930 *Chicago Tribune* reporter Jake Lingle was murdered, provoking a national press campaign against outlawry that was not diminished by the revelations of Lingle's extensive connections to organized crime. In the second half of 1930 the gangster melodrama acquired a new hero, who courted the press as assiduously as Capone. Eliot Ness's highly publicized campaign of wrecking raids on Chicago speakeasies, gambling joints, and brothels was principally intended to undermine Capone's prestige and to encourage the press to present Ness as "Capone's nemesis, the representative of Good in a triumph against Evil."[62]

By January 1931, when the Wickersham Committee reported indecisively on repeal, most Americans were agreed that "there was no logic left in Prohibition," compelled by the wets' argument that Prohibition was unenforceable and served only to aid organized crime.[63] The spectacle of gangsterdom, the public performance of criminality, the fact that "the very criminals who are making millions out of American citizens walk openly through the streets, or drive through the streets in their magnificent automobiles," had ceased to be the acceptable price of Prohibition.[64] Instead, the popular press invoked a melodramatic framework in which "every major crime was turned into a test of whether America and its values could survive the depression."[65] In November 1930 Chief Justice John P. McGourty of the Chicago Criminal Court declared that "the time has come when the public must choose between the rule of the gangster and the rule of the law."[66] The *Saturday Evening Post* declared: "before any other question is worth settling, we must get a decision on who is the Big Shot in the United States—the criminal or the Government."[67]

In March 1931 New York's flamboyant Mayor Jimmy Walker, as gaudy a symbol of Jazz Age urban decadence as Chicago's Big Bill Thompson, was charged with malfeasance and negligence of civic duties on the day after Capone was indicted for income tax evasion in Chicago. A week previously, *Collier's* magazine had published an article entitled "How to Wreck Capone's Gang."[68] In 1931 press coverage of Capone was preoccupied with his sequence of court appearances and his litany of denial that he was still active in the rackets. In April, Thompson was decisively defeated in the mayoral election by Democrat Anton J. Cermak, who had unified anti-Prohibition sentiment among the city's working-class ethnic groups into what became the city's Democratic political machine.[69] In the aftermath of his election, the local press echoed the new determination to improve the city's national image. The *Chicago Tribune* declared that Thompson had "given the city an international reputation for moronic buffoonery, barbaric crime, triumphant hoodlumism, unchecked graft and a dejected citizenship . . . he leaves office and goes from the city the most discredited man who has ever held place in it."[70] In October Capone was tried and convicted of tax evasion, and sentenced to eleven years' imprisonment. His parting comment to the press was, "It was a blow below the belt, but what can you expect when the whole community is against you?"[71]

The community was, however, hardly satisfied with the outcome. Press coverage of the gang wars and the ineffectual responses of local law enforcement had represented the gangs as "formally organized armies belonging to underworld states," beyond the control of law, posing both a political challenge to state authority and a moral challenge to the cultural order of the United States and its confidence in its system of values.[72] According to Powers, Capone's prosecution for the technical crimes of contempt and income tax evasion did not satisfy the public demand for "a poetic justice that took into account moral, and not merely legal, guilt," and for a symbolic punishment that would demonstrate the victory of order.[73] By one of those coincidences that makes synchronism the organizing principle of cultural history, Capone's cultural nemesis made his first appearance in the New York *Daily News* and the *Chicago Tribune* on October 12, 1931, five days before the verdict in the Capone trial: not Eliot Ness but Dick Tracy, comic strip prototype for J. Edgar Hoover's G-Men. Tracy's first adventure began with the murder of his girlfriend Tess

Trueheart's father by minions of Big Boy, the Capone-like boss of an unnamed city that might be Chicago. Tracy swears vengeance and joins the police force to pursue a "single-minded, meet violence-with-violence war on crime," meting out the melodramatic justice to the nation's public enemies in the funnies that the public looked for in vain in the news pages.[74]

Nineteen thirty-one was, then, the best of times and the worst of times for the motion picture industry to release films about gangsters. The subject could hardly be more topical, but the pictures were released into a climate of outspoken press condemnation of the metropolitan civic corruption it had tolerated and even celebrated in the previous decade. The gangster was fictionalized at the same time that he was being removed from his position as a representative of anti-Prohibition sentiment by ethnic politicians such as Cermak and Fiorello La Guardia.[75] Capone's demise in public reputation provided his biographers with the sense of an ending, which they could then embellish. The gangster narrative, in which the reassertion of moral order is enacted, became an overtly fictional form at the moment when its closure could be established. Between 1929 and 1931, seven books devoted wholly or partly to Capone were published, interweaving fact and fiction in the conversion of a no-longer-acceptable celebrity into a fictional character who shared an identity with a Chicago criminal. W. R. Burnett's *Little Caesar* was published in 1929, Dashiell Hammett's *Red Harvest* in 1929 and *The Glass Key* in 1931; in March of that year one MPPDA official reported that "literary agents are telling authors that gang stories are the only sure fire sellers."[76] The handful of gangster pictures depicting the rise and fall of a rugged individualist who calls himself a businessman thus borrowed their narrative from other institutions of representation, and dramatized it at the moment when the downfall of its most publicly prominent representative was being realized.

In contrast to Milliken's earlier claims that movies avoided feeding criminals' "lust for publicity," several pictures released in 1930 explicitly drew attention to the parallels between their fictional events and news stories. Universal's *Czar of Broadway* was based on the life of Arnold Rothstein, although Joy's office warned the studio not to make any reference to Rothstein in its advertising. Fox, however, actively encouraged exhibitors to tie their promotion of *Born Reckless*, released in May 1930, to "the periodic underworld outbreaks in the various large cities of the country" by pasting the headlines from "sensational gangster stories from the newspapers . . . as an irregular 'frame' around the stills on your display boards, particularly if there is any local trouble with criminals," or persuading their local newspaper to run feature stories, if possible ghost-written by the local police chief, suggesting "that gangsters are largely products of environment—in other words, are 'born reckless.'"[77]

Although Fox claimed that *Born Reckless* was "the first picture that really explains the underworld, presenting "the modern racketeer *as he really is*— neither a callous, cold-blooded, inhuman shooting machine, nor an impossibly sentimental moron, but a cool, fatalistic product of environment, thoroughly human in his impulses, but living and dying by his own inflexible code," neither it nor *Czar of Broadway* have received much attention in accounts of the gangster genre. Conventionally, these accounts erroneously suggest that Hollywood produced something close to a tidal wave of gangster movies throughout the early 1930s, and then compound the error by claiming that the three pictures they discuss—invariably *Little Caesar*, *The Public Enemy*, and *Scarface*—were typical of the "genre." In fact, the "classic gangster film" as conventionally identified was the product of only one production season, 1930–31, and constituted a cycle of fewer than thirty pictures, comparable in duration and scale of production to movies with a newspaper background produced in the same season, or imitations of *Back Street* made the following season.[78]

Four pictures were released late in 1930, of which only *The Doorway to Hell*, the first picture to borrow heavily from Capone's biography, enjoyed substantial box office takings. Its early-season success, followed by that of *Little Caesar* in January 1931, triggered a series of imitations in a pattern typical of the industry's exploitation of a topical cycle. Warner Bros. released *The Finger Points* in February, Columbia *The Last Parade* in March. *City Streets* (Paramount) and *The Public Enemy* (Warner Bros.) were released in April, *Quick Millions* (Fox) and *The Secret Six* (MGM) in May, but none of the pictures released after April performed with any notable success at the box office.[79] By April 1931 there was a growing volume of exhibitor complaint that audiences had already surfeited on gang pictures, in part because some theaters had played a series of gangster pictures in succession. There was also evidence of "a vast growing resentment against the continued production and exhibition of this type of picture." Jason Joy felt that the fanaticism of "those in places of authority . . . to stop the further flow of these pictures" came from "their desire to rid the country of gangsters, but the actual release of their energy is focused upon the picture itself."[80]

The strongest criticism directed against movies like *The Doorway to Hell* and *The Last Parade* was that they surrounded the gangster "with romance and glamour," implying that he was "in reality a brave fellow with a heart of gold." Although he "has to die at the end to satisfy the censor . . . he usually dies nobly, even when he is executed."[81] Journalist Eileen Percy complained in February 1931:

> Our gunmen are presented to us in such a manner that we find ourselves
> pulling for them in spite of ourselves, due to the subtle persuasion of the
> drama. . . . We want no falsely romanticized impressions about our vicious
> characters, no element which might contribute toward the building up of
> some future Napoleon out of the overemphasized power of some scum of the
> Chicago gutters. We want gang pictures. But we want them as propaganda
> against rather than for. We should have our main figure villified in such a
> manner that we can settle down to a pleasant evening of hating him right roy-
> ally for the cowardly thing that he is, and cheering lustily when he is finally
> knocked for a loop.[82]

More specifically, the casting of romantic male stars—Lew Ayres, Gary Cooper, and Jack Holt, "dean of our typical heroes"—as gangsters threatened the moral clarity of the movies' narratives, making it difficult to "tell the hero from the heavy."[83] The script for *The Doorway to Hell* had described the protagonist Louis Ricarno as "the type of man women love and men admire," and in an assessment of the picture for the MPPDA Carleton Simon expressed concern that Ayres portrayed the Capone-style gang leader as "a young man of fine features whose looks belie the character he assumes." He feared that because of his appearance, Ricarno might be viewed as "a hero/villain, a most dangerous possibility in the creation of sex appeal and concurrent sympathetic attitude which is close upon the borderline in the glorification of the criminal type."[84]

The industry responded to this criticism by constructing a twofold defence of the gang pictures, claiming that their pictures were produced "within the social safeguards imposed by the motion picture Production Code,"[85] and that their narratives provided a moral lesson, while the central performance "debunked" the gangster using "the deadly weapon of ridicule" to remove from "the bandit and the gunman every shred of false heroism that might influence young people."[86] The most conspicuous form of ridicule was the increasing use of ethnic stereotyping in casting, and what most clearly distinguishes the celebrated "classic" gangster trilogy from the rest of the cycle is that their protagonists' performances are conspicuously marked by signs of ethnic identity. While Edward G. Robinson had already played gangster roles in the Broadway production of *The Racket* and in his first three films for Universal and Warner Bros. before *Little Caesar*, it seems likely that Warner Bros.' acquiescence in the debunking strategy influenced the decision to cast James Cagney rather than Edward Woods in the lead role in *The Public Enemy*.[87]

The debunking strategy may well have succeeded in reducing the gangster's conventional romantic appeal, but in two other respects it was a clear failure. The industry had in the past been frequently criticized for its use of national stereotypes by both foreign governments and American ethnic organizations, and the association between ethnicity and crime was a particularly sensitive issue. *Little Caesar* provoked the wrath of New York congressman Fiorello La Guardia, who threatened to mobilize congressional support for pending federal censorship bills.[88] Subsequent films released in 1931 largely avoided repeating the offense, but Robinson's performance, and to an even greater extent Cagney's in *The Public Enemy*, provided a set of easily imitated gestures and mannerisms that supplied the advocates of reform ample superficial evidence of the movies' doleful influence on the young.

Quoting from Frederick Thrasher and Paul Cressey's Payne Fund survey of a predominantly Italian neighborhood in New York, Henry James Forman reported a preference for gangster pictures among adolescent males, many of whom "were observed to imitate Cagney in dress and mannerisms on the ground that he was 'tougher' (on the screen) than Edward G. Robinson."[89] While some younger children claimed to be deterred by Hays's "insistent message" that "you can't get away with it," Thrasher and Cressey had also found adolescents with enough practical experience of criminality to recognize the repressive artificiality of narrative closure when they saw it. As one explained, "Sure, I like Little Caesar and Jim Cagney, but dat's de boloney dey give you in de pitchers. Dey always died or got canned. Day ain't true."[90] Forman's use of Thrasher and Cressey's report was extremely selective, but they did establish that local theater managers thought that the popularity of gangland pictures came from the boys' sense that they were stories of their own environment, and that some believed Cagney and Robinson themselves to be local boys "made good in a Big Shot way" in the movies.[91] While the concern these reports engendered was not explicitly directed at the representation of violence, it was similar to the concerns exhibited in later periods by those who wished to repress the representation of violence: a concern with the misuse of representation by delinquent viewers who were not convinced by the repressive function of narrative. Forman's pseudovernacular specifically identified the delinquent viewers in question as urban ethnic youth.

By the end of March it had become clear that the performative appeal of the gangster protagonist to some sections of the audience provided too many opportunities for public opposition to be worth the box office risk. The "prairie-fire of protest" against gang films had led censor boards to view all crime pictures with increasing hostility, and the MPPDA, already uncomfortably aware of the threat to the industry posed by the Payne Fund studies, took action to curtail the cycle and to modify those pictures not yet released so as to minimize their potential for harm.[92] In mid-April, for instance, Fox's *Quick Millions*, a fictionalized biography of Bugs Moran, underwent revisions little more than a week before its New York opening.[93] The association was, however, obliged to defend films already in production or distribution as best it could. It hired August Vollmer, "the foremost police reformer of the day," to provide authoritative comments asserting "that films which have dealt with the subject of crime within the social safeguards imposed by the motion picture Production Code were deterrents, not incentives, to criminal behavior."[94] But where the association had previously distanced the industry from the worst excesses of the tabloid press, Hays was now forced to argue that "the efforts of the press to expose the menace of the gangster, and the public sentiment aroused through the dramatization of this problem on the screen, have done much to uphold the forces of law and order."[95] The relative weakness of this position was compounded by the MPPDA's public relations output failing to make a clear distinction between crime and gang films. The MPPDA press release reporting Hays's statement that the production of gang films was being curtailed referred to pictures dealing with "current crime conditions," and Hays was widely reported as having promised to end "crime pictures." This, in turn, was taken as a confession of fault. "[W]e retreated so far as publicity was concerned, in a complete rout," one of the association's officers put it later. "Criticism against us—against our good faith, against our efficiency, against the quality of our product—is rampant and widespread. . . . The censors feel that they can go to almost any length and that on a showdown the public will accord us scant support."[96] On April 14, the day after six scenes had been eliminated from *Public Enemy* before it was deemed acceptable for release in New York, Lamar Trotti reported the gist of a lengthy conversation with Dr. James Wingate, then head of the

New York Censor Board, to Hays. Wingate was of the opinion that pictures showing the police doing their job efficiently were suitable and even beneficial in establishing a wholesome regard for the law. When crime films showed the police as ineffectual, however, they added to what Wingate felt was the dangerous breakdown in respect for law that had been brought about by Prohibition. "Gangster pictures which show one gangster, or gang, shooting and killing the other, while one gets away" were particularly undesirable, since they carried the risk that children in the audience would identify the gang leader, rather than the police, as the hero.[97] On April 20, Vollmer and Hays met with studio heads to discuss some specific changes to the gangster pictures then in production, and to establish a practical distinction between what constituted "the proper treatment of crime" in pictures and plot lines and treatments that overemphasized the gangster's role in American life.[98] Stories in which the gangster was the central character, and scenes of intergang conflict such as those Wingate had objected to, were to be avoided, although this effective prohibition on the production of further gangster pictures would not apply to stories on which commitments had already been made.[99] The studio heads also agreed to stagger the release of the few remaining pictures in the cycle.[100] Of these, by far the most dangerous was *Scarface*.

Howard Hughes undertook *Scarface* in January 1931, in the wake of the financial successes of *The Doorway to Hell* and *Little Caesar*, hiring Howard Hawks to direct and a string of writers, including Ben Hecht, W. R. Burnett, and Capone's biographer F. D. Pasley, to adapt Armitage Trail's novel.[101] From Joy's first conference on the project with Hughes and Hawks in early March until late May, when a final script was submitted, MPPDA officials attempted to dissuade Hughes from producing the film, pointing out the scale of public objection to gangster films, and the comments by official censor boards that they would not pass any more gangster films. From the outset, the fact that the picture was the closest the industry had come to a biography of Capone was the major difficulty. Joy argued that while the industry claimed the right to produce "purely fictional underworld stories," it recognized the danger in portraying "actual contemporary happenings relating to differences in our government, political dishonesty and graft, current crime or antisocial or criminal activities." Such portrayals could only add to the public prominence of notorious individuals, and create in many viewers a desire to imitate their behavior, if only to secure a comparable notoriety. Capone, he suggested, was "the most contemptible and the most dangerous" of these figures, and "the motion picture industry has no right to exploit his name and methods before millions of people merely for the sake of entertainment. Any picture dealing with this man would, regardless of its content, be bound to create for him more importance as a successful individual than as a dangerous civic problem."[102]

A script was completed in late May, and Hays immediately obtained Carleton Simon's opinion. Simon noted the likely hostility of both Italian and Jewish groups to their representation in the script, and suggested that "A great many of the shooting scenes that serve no purpose except to vent the ruthlessness of the gangster can be wisely deleted and fist fights substituted." Most important, he wanted the ending revised so that the detective, Guarini, "get his man." As written,

> Scarface is endowed with humane kindly qualities especially as applied to the welfare of his sister. He is also given super human power in escaping a barrage of bullets. This should all be readjusted, otherwise it crowns the criminal with a halo, spiritual in his kindliness and courage of a physical nature which would readily lend itself to the charge of so-called "glorification of the criminal".[103]

Joy shared Simon's opinion, viewing the story as the "greatest gangster problem so far." On June 4, he wrote to E. B. Derr, production manager of Hughes's Caddo company, that the script contained a considerable number of unacceptable elements, of which the most dangerous concerned the presentation of Camonte as heroic, particularly because of his resemblance to Capone:

> It is inevitable that the audience's sympathy will be won by him because the only crime for which he is taken is one which the audience will consciously or unconsciously condone, namely the killing of the man who betrayed his sister. In addition, there is the fact that Camonte is shown as a home-loving man, good to his mother and protecting his sister. . . . Would it not be possible to give Camonte's mother some strong lines at the proper place in the story indicating that she was utterly opposed to that kind of business and emphasizing the fact that a life of crime always ends badly not only for the criminals themselves, but for those who love them and are dependent upon them.

It was also necessary, Joy argued, to change the ending, replacing Camonte's final "gesture of bravado when he deliberately walks into the police gunfire" with a scene in which he "becomes a cringing coward," while Guarini "becomes even more a fearless and efficient policeman who could be made to walk into Camonte's blazing arsenal to capture him alive."[104] Joy's assistant, John V. Wilson, also pointed out to Hughes that domestic censor boards invariably deleted shots of machine-guns in the hands of gangsters and shootings that were "too cruel and gruesome," and suggested that Hughes "keep the camera off the assailant and the victim, in each case, while the murder is being done."[105]

During production in June and July, Joy was in regular—at times daily—discussion with Derr and Hawks over modifications to the script and the shooting of various sequences, but the real obstacle came from Hughes's desire to make the picture "as realistic as possible." Hughes only allowed Hawks and Derr to modify the treatment after Joy had told him that the picture as initially shot stood no chance of passing any censor board and therefore of playing in more than fifty percent of the English-speaking market.[106] Hughes's apparent enthusiasm for including "inferences of incest" made the picture "look worse and worse to us, from a censorship point of view," and Joy proposed changing "the idea of a protective brother-sister relationship . . . to that of jealousy . . . and to imply a situation in which Scarface was planning to use her for ulterior motives."[107] By the end of July,

Joy's work on the script had, he felt, ensured that "the individual details of the picture will be as nearly Code and censor proof as possible."[108]

Before shooting was completed, however, the already high level of criticism directed against gang films by a press anxious to transfer public opprobrium away from their own representation of crime was intensified by the reaction to Winslow Elliott's death, which included repeated allegations by such public figures as New York police commissioner Edward P. Mulrooney that gang pictures encouraged juvenile crime.[109] The Protestant religious press exploited the incident to encourage support for Senator Clarence Dill's resolution for a congressional investigation of the motion picture industry, and the operations of the MPPDA in particular.[110]

At the beginning of September, just after principal photography on *Scarface* was completed, Joy reported that four gangster pictures remained in production, with a fifth, Universal's *Homicide Squad*, about to enter distribution after having undergone a number of changes suggested by the Studio Relations Department. It had also acquired a foreword by Commissioner Mulrooney and a dedication to "The Police Force of the Land—Vigilant-Courageous-Ready—Soldiers of Society Warring Against the Criminal, the Lawless, the Evil."[111] Joy's office had suggested changes to Columbia's *The Guilty Generation* and RKO's *Bad Company* that would make them "useable," and if United Artists followed their advice on *Corsair*, it would escape classification as a gangster picture. Joy did not believe that any of the companies would initiate any more gangster pictures, but he argued that the association should make public the distinction they were drawing between a gangster picture centered around "gangster warfare and [the] ruthless struggle between rival gangs with little or no implication of law or order," and a "legitimate crime picture," such as *The Star Witness*, in which "the conflict is between law on the one hand and the criminal or criminals on the other hand of which the gangster is only a part." In such stories, "the criminal and underworld is the heavy and the representatives of right living and those on the side of the law assuming the heroic roles."[112]

Joy's staff previewed *Scarface* on September 8, after which they argued strenuously for a complete revision of the ending, replacing the existing shoot-out with the police with a scene in which Camonte "turns yellow." Joy's assistant, Lamar Trotti, also suggested a further substantial modification, in part inspired by the Gamble-Elliott killing:

> An entirely new thread will be run through the picture shifting its meaning as follows: the gangster is a great man as long as he has a gun; once without a gun, he is a yellow rat. The final message of the picture will be—not to let criminals get possession of guns. It is in line with much of current thought on this problem. Mr Hawks was enthusiastic about the suggestion and will attempt to develop it and then sell the idea to Mr Hughes.[113]

Trotti's idea became the focus of the MPPDA's attempt to save Hughes and his investment from himself. Trotti drafted several press releases for the movie, which he proposed publicizing as the "First and Last Gangster

Picture," claiming that it endorsed "an ever growing body of public opinion . . . that there should be uniform States firearms laws to prevent the hoodlum from slipping across the border of one State and returning armed to the slaughter."[114]

By this stage Hughes was primarily concerned with protecting his investment so that it could at least be released, preferably in time to coincide with Capone's upcoming trial. He eventually agreed to both the revised ending and the insertion of the anti-gun theme, at a cost of an additional $25,000.[115] At the end of September, Joy informed Hays that he thought these revisions gave the movie "a right to live in spite of the prevalent, panicky opposition to gangster themes":

> What Hawks has done is to insert in about ten places in the picture scenes and dialogue pointing up the idea that Scarface is a killer as long as he has his guns. When he first gets hold of a machine gun there is a dramatic scene that fairly knocks you out of your seat emphasizing the fact. Than at the end he is caught. Without his gun he goes yellow, becomes a cringing, crying, pleading rat.

These sequences, together with "a strong, forceful foreword," which emphasized that the story was "woven from actual incidents taken directly from the news columns of our daily papers," provided the basis for Joy's defence of the movie as "worthwhile propaganda as well as entertainment. . . . For the first time, therefore, a gangster picture strikes at the very heart of what more and more people believe to be the answer to the gangster problem, namely the passage and enforcement of more stringent anti-gun laws."[116]

On September 29, the Board of Directors of the Association of Motion Picture Producers (AMPP), the West Coast subsidiary organization of the MPPDA, passed a resolution prohibiting any further production of "gangster" pictures.[117] As had happened in April, several pictures underwent revisions, and a number of projects were shelved. By that date, Joy claimed to have seen *Scarface* in various forms twenty times, and told Hays that Hughes had agreed to turn over supervision of the advertising campaign to the Studio Relations Department. In early October, Joy went east to negotiate the passage of a group of crime pictures, including the three remaining gangster pictures, *Bad Company*, *Homicide Squad*, and *Scarface*, through the New York censor board. Caddo undoubtedly hoped to capitalize on the publicity surrounding Capone's trial then taking place in Chicago, but neither the timing nor the endorsements of the movie that Trotti had gathered from police authorities on the West Coast helped its case. In mid-October the board passed the other two pictures but rejected *Scarface*.[118] Caddo and the MPPDA immediately began negotiating a further raft of changes, which included a new ending in which Camonte was tried and executed. Hays and a jury of the MPPDA board viewed the picture in early November 1931 under the provisions of the 1930 Resolution for Uniform Interpretation of the Production Code, and concluded that it also remained in breach of the Code. Hays was, however, reluctant to commit himself to a specific set of modifications that would make the picture acceptable. Joy told Hughes, Derr, and Hawks on November 9 that "it would be necessary to so modify the picture as that the ordinary intelligent person in the audience might leave the theatre with a definite impression of the anti-gun angle and no feeling at all that the gangster has been glorified."[119] A week of conferences followed before Hays, Joy, and Hawks succeeded in persuading Hughes to agree to a further revision of the brother-sister relationship and the inclusion of more anti-gun propaganda. The title was also now in dispute, and Hays also insisted on the elimination of all mention of the name "Scarface" in the dialogue: the picture, he said, "must not be known as the biography of America's public enemy number one, a convicted felon."[120] The association clearly hoped to postpone the picture's release until the immediate publicity surrounding Capone's trial had dissipated, and the protest against gangster pictures had diminished in the face of their absence from the screen.

The most extensive change was proposed by Joseph Breen, future director of the Production Code Administration, then working as one of Hays's executive assistants. Breen suggested an elaborate framing device, set in a juvenile court, in which a judge delivers a lengthy speech on the prevention of juvenile crime, before showing the picture to his audience of convicted delinquents as a warning "of what is in store for you—unless you draw up sharply now—before it is too late. . . . My purpose to let you see, with all its horrible and horrifying details, just what the life of your gangster hero really is." The picture's plot was to be interrupted at least once by a return to the court for the judge to stress the narrative moral, and Breen's version concluded with a further lecture on "the inevitable fate that waits upon those who become drunk by the power of the pistol."[121] While Breen's cumbersome device was not taken up, a scene performing a comparable function, staged in the office of a newspaper editor, was shot by Richard Rosson, Hawks's second-unit director.[122]

The picture was reconstructed in December, and the MPPDA saw a version they thought acceptable, now called *Shame of the Nation*, on December 24, 1931.[123] Hughes claimed to have spent $100,000 on revisions and retakes to make the picture acceptable. Having made substantial losses on at least three of his four previous pictures, he seems to have decided in early 1932 to quit the film business, undoubtedly to the relief of the MPPDA, since he had been by far the least cooperative producer with whom they had dealt.[124] The headaches over *Scarface* were not yet over, however. Hughes was anxious at least to retain the original title, and after two months' discussion of alternatives, Caddo announced in late February that it would be released under the title *Scarface*.[125] By then United Artists, the company through which Hughes was releasing the picture, was effectively prepared to cut its losses. Believing that the movie would not pass any censor board, Joseph Schenck, president of United Artists, wrote to Hays advocating that Hughes be allowed "to get what he can out of the picture in the spots where there is no censorship and where local authorities permit him to run it."[126] Although he continued negotiating with the Studio Relations Department about releasing an acceptable version, Hughes and his press agent, Lincoln Quarberg, devised a publicity campaign for the film, in keeping with Schenck's strategy, emphasizing

Scarface's challenge to "political censorship." Having abandoned his involvement with production, Hughes was testing the MPPDA's authority as well as its patience.

On March 2, 1932—by an unfortunate coincidence the day after Charles Lindbergh's twenty-month-old baby was kidnapped—there was a press screening at Grauman's Chinese Theater in Los Angeles. The version shown—and as a result the version reviewed in the trade press—was the one seen by Joy's office on September 8, 1931. While Hughes suggested to Schenck that UA release that version in territories without censorship, Schenck assured Hays that there was no question of UA's releasing any version other than that agreed to in December, which was still held to be in conformity to the Code.[127] Quarberg's publicity campaign did, however, wring two concessions out of the MPPDA. In mid-March Joy recommended to Hays that the ending shot in October, in which Camonte turns "yellow," be substituted for the execution scene.[128] At the end of the month, Hays also reluctantly acceded to the use of the title *Scarface*.[129] This version was, however, still not acceptable to a number of the state censor boards. In late March it was rejected by the New York board and the Massachusetts boards, which controlled Sunday showings. In April only the Ohio and Virginia boards passed it without making any further deletions.[130] Maryland passed it in mid-May after deleting parts of seven scenes, all involving gunfire.[131] Although Caddo issued press releases claiming that Hughes was bringing a court action to challenge the New York censor board, and insisting that the film would be released uncensored, it was in fact undergoing further editing revisions to produce a version the board would accept.[132] This version, titled *Scarface the Shame of a Nation*, was finally approved in late May. It used the December execution ending, and had substantial portions of dialogue, several shooting incidents, and much of the material involving machine-guns deleted from it. Quarberg put out press releases claiming that New York had passed the original version in preference to fighting Hughes in the courts; Hughes telegrammed Hays asking the MPPDA not to contradict Caddo's publicity.[133] The Pennsylvania board eventually passed a version with even more eliminations than the New York version; the Kansas board did not pass it until July 1933, and a substantial number of foreign censors, including Australia and most of the Canadian boards, rejected it altogether. It was also rejected by the Chicago censors.[134]

When eventually released, *Scarface* grossed $600,000, which Tino Balio estimates may have been enough for the film to break even.[135] To that extent, Hughes's publicity campaign may have been successful in at least limiting his losses on the project. The film's release briefly reinvigorated Protestant protest against movie representation of crime, sustained by the publication, in the September 1932 edition of *McCall's* magazine, of the first synopsis of Henry James Forman's *Movie-Made Children*.[136] But, as Jason Joy explained in his valedictory observations to Hays in September 1932, concern about the representation of crime had by then almost entirely given way to concern over the representation of sex. The Legion of Decency campaign in 1933 and 1934, preoccupied as it was with sex and sacrilege, exhibited no concern at all with the representation of crime.

The problem created by the gangster film took place in a much more specific period than that described in conventional histories of the genre, and in relation to a quite specific set of external events. The movies themselves were part of a wider discourse of condemnation of gangsterdom. In its various public forms, that discourse was a subject of controversy, but during the period in which the pictures were released, both press and film versions of that discourse were obliged to represent themselves as firmly repudiating any glamorization of organized crime. Even Lincoln Quarberg, in his spurious public challenges to the institutions of censorship, was obliged to argue that *Scarface* provided "an honest and powerful indictment of gang-rule."[137] The *Lewistown Sun* review managed, ironically, to encapsulate the successes and failures of the MPPDA's work on the picture when it suggested that Hughes had defied not only the Hays office, but also "Uncle Sam, the underworld, political censors and powerful politicians charged with gangland connections." It compounded the irony by declaring, "It does not glorify the gangster as charged by the Hays office," and then justifying its claim by quoting the police captain's speech, inserted at the MPPDA's insistence: 'It was all right to glorify the badmen of the early West. They had a code. They were not afraid to shoot it out in the open. But what is colorful about a crawling louse?'"[138]

When *Scarface* finally reached state and municipal censor boards, they did eliminate some of its scenes of violence, but they did not differentiate between scenes inserted as spectacle, such as the "reign of terror," and scenes inserted at the MPPDA's suggestion as part of its anti-gun theme. Even then, the issue at stake was not violence or the explicitness of its representation, but the need to contain the performative appeal of the gangster protagonist to the delinquent viewer. Not even the simian exaggerations of Paul Muni's performance and the absurd interpolations of Vince Barnett's farcical character Angelo could guarantee to debunk the gangster's public image among the urban, ethnic working class who already knew Capone as "that almost fabulous Chicago Robin Hood, that twentieth-century Cid Campeador."[139] It was, however, precisely these caricatured signifiers of ethnicity that led the Italian ambassador and fifty Italian-American organizations to denounce *Scarface* as a "libel on the Italian race."[140] However topical or potentially lucrative the subject might have been, the industry was unable to negotiate the contradictions required of an adequate representation of the gangster. Instead, it took concerted and largely successful action to abandon production in the face of public opposition. Had *Scarface* been produced by a major studio, the project would either have been abandoned in April 1931 before shooting commenced, or drastically rewritten, with a policeman as hero. Only someone in Hughes's financial position could have resisted the pressures to compromise to the extent that he did. As it was, the sequence revisions to the movie constituted an only partially successful attempt to salvage a commercially viable object that would not cause major damage to what Hays called the "organized industry."

Within days of *Scarface*'s opening, the body of Charles Augustus

Lindbergh Jr. was discovered, intensifying the public denunciation of criminality and the anxiety over a breakdown in standards. The *New York World-Telegram* editorial comment was typical:

> God knows why little Charles Lindbergh was murdered, but indirectly the wicked, wanton, causeless crime can be attributed to the wise-cracking, jazzed-up, hypocritical age in which we live—an age that pays racketeers for protection, that elects crooks to office on the ground that they are smart politicians, that outlaws bootleggers, buys their goods at exorbitant prices, and then claps them in jail when they fail to pay income taxes on the profits they make.[141]

For at least a year before these events, it had only been possible to represent the gangster as a scapegoat for the Depression. In movies released after *Scarface*, this scapegoating went much further. The last movies in the gangster cycle were more properly vigilante stories: in *The Secret Six* and *Beast of the City* gangsters protected by corrupt lawyers or politicians are finally eliminated by the extralegal action of concerned citizens; in *This Day and Age* gangster Charles Bickford is kidnapped by a group of idealistic high school students and tortured into confession. James Wingate, who had replaced Joy as director of the Studio Relations Department, reported to Hays in February 1933 that a scene in *The Woman Accused* in which the hero horsewhips a gangster into changing his testimony got a round of applause at the movie's preview. "It is evidently the sense of the public," reported Wingate, "that a little of this rough justice might well be meted out to such public enemies."[142] Almost the only uncontroversial element of William Randolph Hearst's 1933 picture *Gabriel over the White House* was its representation of gangsters, who are eventually court-martialed and executed by firing squad.

More generally, the public understanding of the metaphorical relationship between business and crime shifted in the early 1930s. Whatever outlawed desire the nostalgic memory of the Prohibition gangster has come to service in the cultural unconscious since 1948, Al Capone, in his various fictional guises, served neither as tragic hero nor as social bandit in 1932. In the cultural catharsis of the early Depression, the gangster was a scapegoat villain, an embodiment of guilt to be expiated, in the name of freedom from fear itself, by any means necessary. The gangster pictures contributed to that scapegoating, and in particular to the scapegoating of an ethnic stereotype of criminality. To some extent, like many other movies in the early 1930s, they should be seen as attempts to negotiate a strategy of representation, by which a transgressive spectacle could be contained within a repressive narrative structure. The gangster movies, however, were a failed attempt at such a strategy, since their reception deemed them inadequate representations of public hostility to the spectacle of criminality, and made the movies a collateral target for the denunciations and anxieties that spectacle of criminality was attracting through other media.

On a number of occasions in the remainder of the decade, the Studio Relations Department and its successor, the Production Code Administration (PCA), revisited the subject of crime in motion pictures, making several rulings about specific aspects of the representation of violence that then functioned as amendments to the Production Code.[143] After the Lindbergh case, restrictions were placed on the movies' treatment of kidnapping. In March 1934 the MPPDA Executive Committee agreed not to sanction the production of a picture based on the life John Dillinger, and this decision was subsequently interpreted as applying to the biographies of all notorious contemporary criminal figures.[144] After the passage of federal legislation requiring the registration of machine-guns and rifles in 1934, the PCA took "machine guns, sub-machine guns or other weapons generally classified as illegal weapons" away from criminals.[145] When companies returned to the subject of crime in 1935, in a cycle of pictures celebrating the G-Man, several rulings were introduced to protect the movies from serious mutilation by censor boards, particularly in Britain and Canada.[146] These prohibited any representation of "law-enforcing officers dying at the hands of criminals," "excessive" brutality or gunplay, and "action suggestive of wholesale slaughter of human beings, either by criminals, in conflict with police, or as between warring factions of criminals."[147]

Deprived of narrative centrality by the September 1931 decision of the AMPP, the gangster drifted to the margins of representation and, increasingly, surrendered his essential characteristics. In December 1935 Breen spelled out the detailed implications of the AMPP's decision three months earlier that "Crime stories are not acceptable when they portray the activities of American gangsters, armed and in violent conflict with the law or law-enforcing officers."[148] *Bullets or Ballots* would have to "keep away entirely from those incidents and details which are usually associated with 'gangster pictures.'" Its racketeers were to be

> of the suave, well-educated, well-dressed, polite type—more like successful bankers or businessmen than like gangsters. There will be no showing of guns, and no gun battles with police. . . . where, for storyline, it is necessary to "bump off" two or three of our racketeers, this will be done either by suggestion or in dialogue, but not in any brutally murderous fashion. . . . The police will be triumphant and will succeed eventually in bringing the criminals to justice. . . . The characters now called Schultz, Waxie, Coll, et al., should be definitely cast away from the usual gangster types and more emphasis should be placed on the manner in which the rackets are conducted, rather than along the activities of gangsters who conduct them.[149]

Toward the end of the decade, a number of pictures sought to rehabilitate the 1920s gangster either by placing him within a self-consciously historical narrative or releasing him from a long prison term into contemporary society, and giving him an opportunity to atone. Cagney reprised his *Public Enemy* performance in *Angels with Dirty Faces* in late 1939, but Robinson preceded him by two years in an MGM picture called *The Last Gangster*, based on a story cowritten by William Wellman. Robinson plays gang leader Joe Krozac who is convicted of tax evasion after organizing the killing of three rivals. While he is imprisoned in Alcatraz, his wife Talya (Rose Stradner) leaves him and remarries newspaper editor

Paul North (James Stewart). Released after ten years, Joe refuses to tell his old gang where he had hidden money. They kidnap Joe's son, who has been brought up without knowing his real father's identity. Joe manages to free him and return him to Talya, but he is then killed in a struggle with a former gangster, who threatens to reveal the boy's true identity. The original story, which had been titled *Public Enemy's Return*, underwent substantial modification to remove it from the gangster category, deleting details of both Joe's gangster activity and his successful career as a banker and "champion for law and order and Americanism" in California after his release. Breen insisted that

> the suggestion of luxury enjoyed by the criminal Joe. . . be toned down or changed possibly to the suggestion of very bad taste. . . . Those characters which suggest Italian names or nationality are to be changed, the slaughter of the criminals in scenes 12 to 15 to be entirely deleted. . . . The scene in which the editor shows Cesca [later renamed Talya] the photographs of the criminal activities of her husband are to be toned down quite considerably. The scene showing the brutalizing of Joe and the boy Paul are to be toned down to a minimum.[150]

During production, the PCA insisted on a series of detailed changes to the action. On viewing the completed picture, they required two further cuts to reduce the sound of machine-gun fire in the first murder and to considerably shorten the montage scene in which Joe is tortured by his gang, "to eliminate all shots of Robinson being hit by pieces of the rubber hose . . . by removing the sound of the blows and putting music over this scene we have softened it. We have deleted several of the boy's cries off screen at the end of the torture scene."[151]

The representation of violence was continually at issue in the gangster pictures of the 1930s, but it was never the principal issue at stake. By as early as April 1931 the industry had recognized that pictures featuring a gangster protagonist were unacceptable to censorship authorities and public opinion groups. Gangsters continued to appear in pictures, but as increasingly marginal characters in other people's plots. In keeping with Hollywood's practice of generalizing stereotypes to avoid offending any specific group, gangsters were rendered ethnically indeterminate: the character called Joe Atori in *Public Enemy's Return* became *The Last Gangster's* Joe Krozak, his wife Cesca became Talya, just as the rival gangster that James Cagney confronts in a spaghetti restaurant in *The Roaring Twenties* is called Nick Brown.[152] Their actions, including their violent actions, were moved off-screen, in the name of minimizing any appeal their representation might continue to hold for delinquent viewers. Action was, however, understood as being subsumed within character, and the industry's principal concern remained the inappropriate appeal of characters and stars. That concern was enacted in the plot of *Angels with Dirty Faces*, when Father Jerry (Pat O'Brien) persuades Rocky (James Cagney) to sacrifice his public reputation by turning "yellow" at his execution, so that the Bowery Boys will no longer see him as a hero. What delinquent viewers made of

Cagney's heroic cowardice is not recorded, but the action encapsulates the irresolvable contradictions of Hollywood's representation of the spectacle of criminality throughout the 1930s.

Notes

1. This essay draws on and reconsiders material previously published in three earlier essays: "Tragic Heroes? Al Capone and the Spectacle of Criminality, 1948–1931," in *Screening the Past VI: Australian History and Film Conference Papers*, ed. John Benson, Ken Berryman, and Wayne Levy, (Melbourne: La Trobe University Press, 1995); "'Grief in the Limelight': Al Capone, Howard Hughes, the Hays Office, and the Politics of the Unstable Text," in *Movies and Politics: The Dynamic Relationship*, ed. James Combs (New York: Garland, 1993); "A Short and Dangerous Life: The Gangster Film, 1930–1932," in *Prima dei Codici 2: Alle Porte di Hays (Before the codes 2: The gateway to Hays)*, ed. Giuliana Muscio (Venice: Fabbri Editori, 1991).

2. Quoted in James D. Horan, *The Desperate Years* (New York: Crown, 1962), 44.

3. *Lewistown (Maine) Sun*, April 23, 1932.

4. *New York Times*, June 26, 1931.

5. *Literary Digest*, July 25, 1931, 20–21.

6. Al Capone, July 29, 1931, quoted in John Kobler, *Capone: The Life and World of Al Capone* (London: Coronet, 1973), 313.

7. Will H. Hays to Joseph Melillo, June 11, 1931. Will H. Hays Papers, Indiana State Historical Society, Indianapolis (hereafter Hays Papers). See also "Hays Calls Gang Film a Crime Deterrent," *New York Times*, June 27, 1931, reprinted in *The New York Times Encyclopedia of Film, 1929–1936*, ed. Gene Brown (New York: Times Books, 1984), n.p.

8. Lamar Trotti to Jason Joy, 26 June 1931. *Scarface* file, Production Code Administration Archive, Margaret Herrick Library, Center for Motion Picture Study, Academy of Motion Picture Arts and Sciences, Beverly Hills (hereafter PCA).

9. Robert Sklar, *Movie-Made America: A Cultural History of American Movies* (New York: Random House, 1975), 175; Jack Shadoian, *Dreams and Dead Ends: The Gangster/Crime Film* (Cambridge, Mass.: MIT Press, 1979), 22.

10. Shadoian, *Dreams and Dead Ends*, 16; Garth Jowett, "Bullets, Beer, and the Hays Office," in *American History/American Film*, ed. John E. O'Connor and Martin A. Jackson (New York: Ungar, 1980), 68; and Richard H. Pells, *Radical Visions and American Dreams: Culture and Social Thought in the Depression Years* (Middletown, Conn.: Wesleyan University Press, 1973), 271–72.

11. Jowett, "Bullets, Beer, and the Hays Office," 68–69; Shadoian, *Dreams and Dead Ends*, 20–21 (emphasis mine).

12. Warner Bros., *Blondie Johnson* press book, 1933, quoted in David Ruth, *Inventing the Public Enemy: The Gangster in American Culture, 1918–1934* (Chicago: University of Chicago Press, 1996), 5.

13. *Time* review of *The Public Enemy*, quoted in Jowett, 69.

14. John G. Cawelti, *Adventure, Mystery, and Romance: Formula Stories as Art and Popular Culture* (Chicago: University of Chicago Press, 1976), 60.

15. The phrase is Francis Ford Coppola's: *Godfather II* "was always a loose metaphor, Michael [Corleone] as America." Quoted in John Hess, "*Godfather II*: A Deal Coppola Couldn't Refuse," in *Movies and Methods*, ed. Bill Nichols (Berkeley: University of California Press, 1976), 82; and

Shadoian, *Dreams and Dead Ends*, 6.

16. For a more extensive discussion of this strategy, see Richard Maltby, "*Baby Face*, or How Joe Breen Made Barbara Stanwyck Atone for Causing the Wall St. Crash," *Screen* 27, no. 2 (March–April 1986): 22–45.

17. One conspicuous exception to this general interpretation is Jonathan Munby's recent account, which argues that "the rhetoric of civic responsibility" enunciated in these titles "comes to form a frame narrative, as it were, which attempts to impose a preferred reading on the rest of the text." Munby also argues that such an imposition "had to compete with a range of other meanings, including precisely a rejection of moral and civic norms." Jonathan Munby, *Screening the Gangster from* Little Caesar *to* Touch of Evil (Chicago: University of Chicago Press, 1999), 51.

18. Recognizing the need to convince state censor boards of Warner Bros.' sincerity, Darryl Zanuck argued that *The Public Enemy* had a "strong moral tone . . . THE FUTILITY OF CRIME AS A BUSINESS OR AS A PROFIT," and a secondary theme, that, "PROHIBITION is not the cause of the present crime wave—mobs and gangs have existed for years and years BECAUSE of environment." Zanuck to Joy, January 6, 1931, *Public Enemy* file, PCA (emphasis in the original). Warners' "environmentalist" position conveniently evaded the more urgent, substantial, and politically sensitive question of the repeal of Prohibition; endorsing the wet position might have caused problems with Kansas censors, for example. The press book for *Little Caesar* explicitly warned exhibitors not to "in any way attempt to glorify the gangster or racketeer. . . . Follow the ad copy and illustrations in this press sheet to the letter and you will be on the safe side." Quoted in Andrew Bergman, *We're in the Money: Depression America and Its Films* (New York: Harper, 1971), 6.

19. *Lewistown (Maine) Sun*, April 23, 1932.

20. Robert S. McElvaine, *The Great Depression: America 1929–1941* (New York: Times Books, 1984), 210–11.

21. Pells, *Radical Visions*, 271.

22. Henry James Forman, *Our Movie-Made Children* (New York: Macmillan, 1933), 179–213.

23. The Production Code exists in a multiplicity of textual variants. For a full discussion, see Richard Maltby, "The Genesis of the Production Code," *Quarterly Review of Film and Video* 15, no. 4 (March 1995): 5–63. The text quoted here is taken from a facsimile copy of the typescript signed by the Board of Directors of the Association of Motion Picture Producers in February 1930, and by the Board of Directors of the MPPDA on 31 March 1930, reproduced on p. 55.

24. Olga J. Martin, *Hollywood's Movie Commandments* (New York: Wilson, 1937), 124.

25. Production Code in Maltby, "The Genesis of the Production Code," 53.

26. Ibid., 37.

27. Gerald Mast, *Howard Hawks, Storyteller* (New York: Oxford University Press, 1982), 81. See also pp. 89–90 for a comparable description of the death of Gaffney (Boris Karloff).

28. Lee Grieveson, "Re/forming the Audience," in *American Movie Audiences: From the Turn of the Century to the Early Sound Era*, ed. Melvyn Stokes and Richard Maltby (London: BFI, 1999).

29. This "Other Viewer," the figure of misinterpretation, has remained an archetype of the censorship argument, and is as frequently present in contemporary debates over the regulation of television and pornography as in the early

years of cinema. It has also been an important figure in high cultural critiques of popular culture. It is often identified as a child, the figure toward whom the idea of moral guardianship can most unproblematically be extended. Its essential perceptual feature is its inability to discriminate fiction.

30. In 1926 the MPPDA compiled a report entitled "Opinions of a Few Prominent People That Motion Pictures Do Not Cause Juvenile Delinquency," and circulated it widely among their public relations contacts. 1926 Influence of Screen file, Motion Picture Association of America Archive (hereafter MPA), New York. See also 1928 Influence of Screen file, 1928 Protests file, MPA.

31. Carleton Simon, quoted in Milliken to Harry A. Volz, October 22, 1928, MPA, 1928, Crime file.

32. Joy to Frank Wilstach, October 31, 1928. MPA, 1928, Crime file.

33. Bartlett Cormack, quoted in John S. Cohen Jr., "*The Racket*: Bartlett Cormack's Melodrama Arrives in Eloquent Silence," New York *Sun* (n.d.: July 1928), transcript in MPA, 1928, Caddo file.

34. Milliken, daily report, August 3, 1928; Hays to Hughes, August 15, 1928; Sidney Kent to Hughes, August 8, 1928, MPA, 1928, Caddo file.

35. M. S. Kussell to Kent, August 13, 1928, MPA, 1928, Caddo file.

36. DeBra to Kussell, August 30, 1928, MPA, 1928, Caddo file.

37. Milliken to Harry A. Volz, October 22, 1922, MPA, 1928, Crime file.

38. Milliken to Hays, October 29, 1928, MPA, 1928, Don't and Be Carefuls file.

39. "Crime Pictures Breed No Evil In Youth, Prof. Holmes Finds," *New York Herald Tribune*, April 28, 1929.

40. Roger W. Babson, "Crime Waves," *Babson's Reports Special Letter*, 8 April 1929. *Babson's Reports* was distributed to ten thousand subscribers, and also printed in newspapers throughout the United States.

41. "A Letter to Roger W. Babson from Carl E. Milliken," New York: Motion Picture Producers and Distributors of America, 1929, 18–19 and 26. Milliken's letter was dated May 7, 1929, but it was released to the press on June 26. See *Los Angeles Examiner*, June 27, 1929.

42. *The Forum*, April 1927.

43. *Recent Social Trends in the United States: Report of the President's Research Committee on Social Trends* (New York: McGraw Hill, 1933), 537.

44. Fred D. Pasley, *Al Capone: The Biography of a Self-Made Man* (1931; reprint London: Faber, 1966), 317.

45. Frederick Thrasher, *The Gang: A Study of 1,313 Gangs in Chicago* (1927; reprint Chicago: University of Chicago Press, 1936), 489–90 and 111. Lizabeth Cohen identifies many of the crimes of delinquency committed by members of this group as "crimes of mass culture," by which "deviant" youth could participate in the consumer society without any money. Lizabeth Cohen, *Making a New Deal: Industrial Workers in Chicago, 1919–1939* (Cambridge: Cambridge University Press, 1990), 144 and 422 n.159.

46. Quoted in Kenneth Alsop, *The Bootleggers: The Story of Chicago's Prohibition Era* (London: Hutchinson, 1968), 340.

47. See plot synopses for *Shooting Straight, The Widow from Chicago*, and *Yellow Contraband* in *the American Film Institute Catalog: Feature Films, 1921–1930*.

48. Michael Denning, *Mechanic Accents: Dime Novels and Working Class Culture in America* (London: Verso, 1987), 85–117; and Robert Warshow, "The Gangster as Tragic Hero," in *The Immediate Experience* (New York: Athaneum, 1970).

49. Walter Lippmann, "The Underworld as Servant," *The Forum*, January and

February 1931, reprinted in *Organized Crime in America: A Book of Readings*, ed. Gus Tyler (Ann Arbor, University of Michigan Press, 1962), 64.

50. Waldo Frank, *The Re-discovery of America: An Introduction to a Philosophy of American Life* (New York: Scribner's, 1929), 91 and 97–98.

51. Lippmann, "The Underworld as Servant," 60 and 63–69.

52. Thrasher, *The Gang*, 548.

53. Capone quoted in Allsop, *The Bootleggers*, 365.

54. For a discussion of criminals as businessmen in the 1920s, see Ruth, *Inventing the Public Enemy*, 37–62.

55. Frederick Lewis Allen, *Only Yesterday: An Informal History of the 1920s* (1931; reprint New York: Harper, 1964), 290, 293, and 295.

56. G. L. Hostetter and T. Q. Beesley, "20th Century Crime," *The Political Quarterly* 13, no. 3 (1933), reprinted in Tyler, *Organized Crime in America*, 51–52.

57. Hostetter and Beesley in Tyler, 53.

58. David Ruth notes that during the 1920s, ethnicity was more likely to be treated as a matter of style than as an explanation of criminal behavior; Michael Woodiwiss argues that during Prohibition, "no one tried to argue that organized crime was an alien conspiracy." Ruth, *Inventing the Public Enemy*, 73; Michael Woodiwiss, *Crime, Crusades, and Corruption: Prohibition in the United States, 1900–1987* (London: Pinter, 1988), 17. Arguments that criminality had an ethnic base began to resurface at the end of the 1920s, causing much concern among Italian-American organizations, who strongly protested the endorsement given to such arguments by the representation of ethnicity in gangster pictures, particularly *Scarface*. See Ruth Vasey, *The World According to Hollywood* (Exeter: University of Exeter Press, 1997), 120 and 143–44.

59. Richard Gid Powers, *G-Men: Hoover's FBI in American Popular Culture* (Carbondale: Southern Illinois University Press, 1983), 55.

60. Robert Lacey, *Little Man: Meyer Lansky and the Gangster Life* (London: Century, 1991), 88.

61. Quoted in Andrew Sinclair, *Era of Excess: A Social History of the Prohibition Movement* (New York: Harper, 1964), 229.

62. Woodiwiss, *Crime, Crusades, and Corruption*, 25.

63. Ibid., 30.

64. Fred J. Ringel, ed., *America as Americans See It* (New York: Harcourt, Brace, 1932), 175.

65. Powers, *G-Men*, xv.

66. Quoted in Allsop, *The Bootleggers*, 423.

67. Quoted in Woodiwiss, *Crimes, Crusades, and Corruption*, 41.

68. Col. Robert Isham Randolph, "How to Wreck Capone's Gang", *Collier's*, March 7, 1931. Randolph was the chairman of the Chicago Association of Commerce Subcommittee for the Prevention and Punishment of Crime, better known to the press as the Secret Six.

69. Cohen, *Making a New Deal*, 255–56.

70. *Chicago Daily Tribune*, April 9, 1931, quoted in Woodiwiss, *Crimes, Crusades, and Corruption*, 74.

71. Quoted in Allsop, *The Bootleggers*, 377.

72. Powers, *G-Men*, 4.

73. Ibid., 8.

74. Max Allen Collins and Dick Locher, eds., *The Dick Tracy Casebook: Favorite Adventures 1931–1990*, (New York: Penguin, 1990); and Powers, *G-Men*, 29.

75. Judge Samuel Seabury's investigations into civic corruption in New York filled the press with allegations of connections between Tammany Hall and organized crime during the winter of 1931–32, and led to Jimmy Walker's resignation in September 1932.

76. Memo, Lupton Wilkinson to Hays, March 31, 1931, Hays Papers.

77. PCA *Born Reckless* file.

78. Using Thomas Schatz's distinction between the classic gangster film and the diluted versions released later in the decade—that "the gangster hero's position within the genre's narrative structure [is] as the organizing sensibility through whom we perceive the urban milieu"—I can identify nineteen pictures, including program pictures from minor studios, that fit his criteria for classicism, all released between September 1930 and May 1932. This assessment approximately corresponds to that made by the Studio Relations Committee in September 1932, when Jason Joy observed that "throughout the whole period when the gangster theme was being used on the screen, only 23 pictures could possibly be classified as gangster pictures." The numbers are usually inflated by counting any picture in which a gangster appears. Thomas Schatz, *Hollywood Genres: Formulas, Filmmaking, and the Studio System* (New York: Random House, 1981), 99; and Memo, Joy to Hays, MPA, 1932, Production Code file.

79. Allen Eyles, *That Was Hollywood: The 1930s* (London: Batsford, 1987).

80. Joy to E. B. Derr of Caddo, June 4, 1931, MPA, 1932, Caddo, *Scarface* file.

81. Helen Louise Walker, "Hunting for a Hero," *Motion Picture*, July 1931, 66–67 and 116.

82. Eileen Percy, "Another Gangster Picture in the Making," unidentified newspaper clipping, February 16, 1931, *Scarface* clippings file, Margaret Herrick Library, Academy of Motion Picture Arts and Sciences, Beverly Hills.

83. Walker, "Hunting for a Hero," 66–67.

84 . *The Doorway to Hell* cast list, quoted in Robert Sklar, *City Boys: Cagney, Bogart Garfield* (Princeton, N.J.: Princeton University Press, 1992), 26; and Carleton Simon to Hays, November 15, 1930, *The Doorway to Hell* file, PCA.

85. Hays to Joseph Melillo, June 11, 1931, *Public Enemy* file, PCA.

86. Will Hays, Annual Report of the President of the MPPDA, March 30, 1931, MPA, 1931, Meetings file.

87. Sklar, *City Boys*, 31. For a discussion of ethnicity in these pictures, see Munby, *Screening the Gangster*, 39–65.

88. Maurice McKenzie to Joy, January 27, 1931. *Little Caesar* file, PCA. McKenzie also reported Carl Milliken's suggestion that "La Guardia is sore because Little Caesar looks like him."

89. Forman, *Our Movie-Made Children*, 265. The adolescents in Thrasher and Cressey's survey most frequently cited Cagney's performance in *Taxi* as the one they imitated. According to Thrasher's 1927 study of gang boys, they were frequent attenders, averaging three visits per week, with one boy in three going every day. Their favorite pictures were Westerns, other thrillers and action films, slapstick comedies, and mysteries, but they were rarely interested in society drama, news reels, or romantic pictures. Thrasher, *The Gang*, 103. *Motion Picture Herald* noted that exhibitors frequently successfully promoted gangster pictures by holding impersonation shows and awarding prizes to the best imitator. Munby, *Screening the Gangster*, 55 n.22.

90. Forman, *Our Movie-Made Children*, 264.

91. This is, in fact, the plot of a 1933 Cagney film, *Lady Killer*.

92. Draft, Special Education Section, Annual Report 1932, Hays Papers. For an

account of the genesis of the Payne Fund studies, see Garth S. Jowett, Ian C. Jarvie, and Kathryn H. Fuller, *Children and the Movies: Media Influence and the Payne Fund Controversy* (Cambridge: Cambridge University Press, 1996). For a summary of the MPPDA's measures to counter the studies, see Report by Hays to the MPPDA Board of Directors, October 8, 1931, MPA, 1931, Meetings, Board file.

93. Memo, R. B. to Hays, April 11, 1931, Hays Papers.
94. Woodiwiss, *Crime, Crusades, and Corruption*, 37–38; and Hays to Joseph Melillo, June 11, 1931, PCA *Public Enemy* file.
95. Hays to Melillo, June 11, 1931, PCA *Public Enemy* file.
96. Lupton Wilkinson, "Observations on the Association's Publicity Situation and Proposals for Remedying It," November 1, 1931, Hays Papers.
97. Trotti to Hays, April 14, 1931, PCA *Public Enemy* file.
98. Hays to Melillo, June 11, 1931.
99. Telegram, Joy to Maurice McKenzie, September 1, 1931, PCA *Scarface* file.
100. Hays to R. H. Cochrane, April 29, 1931, Hays Papers.
101. The most detailed account of the picture's production history can be found in Todd McCarthy, *Howard Hawks: The Grey Fox of Hollywood* (New York: Grove Press, 1997), 124–55. On a number of points, my account differs from McCarthy's in details of fact and interpretation. Armitage Trail, *Scarface* (1930; reprint London: Bloomsbury, 1997).
102. Joy, draft of letter to Hughes, May 1, 1931, PCA *Scarface* file.
103. Carleton Simon, report, June 1, 1931, PCA *Scarface* file.
104. Joy to Derr, June 4, 1931, MPA, 1932, Caddo, *Scarface* file.
105. John V. Wilson to Hughes, June 4, 1931, PCA *Scarface* file.
106. Joy's resume, August 20, 1931, PCA *Scarface* file; and Joy to Hays, November 3, 1931, MPA, 1932, Caddo, *Scarface* file.
107. Joy's resume, July 11, 1931, PCA *Scarface* file; and Joy to Hays, March 5, 1932, MPA, 1932, Caddo, *Scarface* file.
108. Joy's resume, July 29, 1931, PCA *Scarface* file.
109. *Christian Century*, May 13, 1931, 641.
110. *Christian Century*, August 12, 1931, 1015–16.
111. *Variety*, October 20, 1931.
112. Telegram, Joy to McKenzie, September 1, 1931, PCA *Scarface* file.
113. Memo by Trotti, September 10, 1931.
114. Trotti, draft press releases, September 1931, PCA *Scarface* file.
115. Joy's resume, September 21, 1931, PCA *Scarface* file.
116. Joy to Hays, September 30, 1931, MPA, 1932, Caddo, *Scarface* file; and draft of foreword, PCA *Scarface* file.
117. This resolution is referred to in an unsigned memo dated September 29, 1931, MPA, 1931, Production Code file. In a letter to Hays on September 5, 1935, Breen noted, "In September 1931 . . . the Board here, by formal resolution, agreed to call a halt to what was then generally referred to as 'gangster' films. The effect of this, as you know, was very satisfactory" (MPA, 1936, Production Code file). On August 7, 1939, in a letter to Hays, Breen referred to it as "the Special Agreement adopted in September 1931, against the production of gangster films" (MPA, 1939, Production Code file). The relevant wording, listed in the "Regulations re Crime adopted for a clearer and more exact interpretation of the Code" would appear to be: "Action suggestive of wholesale slaughter of human beings, either criminals, in conflict with the police, or as between warring factions of criminals, or in public disorder of any kind, will not be allowed" ("Regulations re Crime in Motion Pictures,"

December 20, 1938, MPA, 1938, Production Code file). It is, however, possible that some other wording was used to differentiate gangster pictures from crime films. Father Daniel A. Lord, who had been heavily involved in the drafting of the 1930 Production Code, suggested an amendment to the Code that read: "the action centers around gangster warfare and ruthless struggle either between rival, organized mobs, or such a mob in society and the law, with little or no implication, etc." (Lord to Joy, October 5, 1931, PCA *Scarface* file).

118. Far more disturbingly for the MPPDA, the New York board also rejected RKO's *Are These Our Children?*, a story of juvenile delinquency strongly endorsed by the association's previewing groups as "a powerful preachment against liquor, loose living and the evil consequences of bad companions." Trotti took the decision as "a real blow against what we are trying to do. . . . If [a] story with as strong preachment as this can't be made what are we going to do?" In early November, Joy succeeded in persuading the board to pass the picture with some eliminations. Trotti to Joy, October 28, 1931, PCA *Are These Our Children?* file.

119. Joy, memo, November 9, 1931, PCA *Scarface* file. McCarthy reports that Hawks had left the project in early October, after the completion of the first set of modifications. McCarthy also suggests, erroneously, that the October version was not submitted to the New York censor board. Hawks was, however, involved in the extensive discussions about modifying the October version in early November, although there is no evidence to suggest that he shot any of the material that he helped prepare. McCarthy, *Howard Hawks*, 147–48.

120. Trotti, memo, November 11, 1931, PCA *Scarface* file.

121. Joseph Breen, draft screenplay, n.d. (c. November 16, 1931), PCA *Scarface* file.

122. McCarthy, *Howard Hawks*, 141.

123. Joy to Hays, March 5, 1932, MPA, 1932, Caddo, *Scarface* file.

124. Tino Balio, *United Artists: The Studio Built by the Stars* (Madison: University of Wisconsin Press, 1976), 111.

125. *Hollywood Herald*, February 26, 1932.

126. Joseph Schenck to Hays, February 26, 1932, MPA, 1932, Caddo, *Scarface* file.

127. Telegram, Hughes to Schenck, n.d. (c. March 7, 1931), PCA *Scarface* file.

128. Joy to Hays, March 16 ,1932, PCA *Scarface* file.

129. Hays to McKenzie, March 23, 1932, MPA 1932, Caddo, *Scarface* file.

130. Censorship record, PCA *Scarface* file. Virginia passed a version with the December (execution) ending.

131. Censorship record, PCA *Scarface* file.

132. Chapin Hall, "In the Realm of Shadow Stories," *New York Times*, March 13, 1932, reprinted in *The New York Times Encyclopedia of Film 1929–1936*. Advertisements for the picture in the Los Angeles press claimed to be showing "The picture that powerful interests have tried to suppress—in its uncut, unaltered, original version." Hays complained to Joseph Schenck about these advertisements being in breach of the association's Advertising Code. *Los Angeles Times*, April 21, 1932; and Hays to Schenck, April 27, 1932, MPA, 1932, Caddo, *Scarface* file. Lewis Milestone was certainly consulted by Schenck about revisions, and may have been involved in preparing a version for censorship territories. See Hays, memo, March 21, 1932, and McKenzie, memo, March 23, 1932, both in MPA, 1932, Caddo, *Scarface* file; and Joy

to McKenzie, March 22, 1932, PCA *Scarface* file.

133. May 8, 1932, RKO Archives, Los Angeles, Censorship file; and Hughes to Hays, May 12, 1932, MPA, 1932, Caddo, *Scarface* file. Chapin Hall noted in the *New York Times* on May 22 that Hughes's "war with the censors . . . was not quite as deadly as it sounded. . . . New York has passed *Scarface* after the Hays office showed it to the censors and the apparent ease with which it went over has aroused local suspicions." Reprinted in the *New York Times Encyclopedia of Film 1929–1936*.

134. The version of *Scarface* currently in circulation bears little relation to the film seen and argued over by audiences in 1932 anywhere in the United States. It corresponds to none of the three versions of the picture completed in 1931: it appears to most closely resemble the October 1931 version, while containing some but not all of the additional material shot in November and December 1931. It is significantly different from the September 1931 version, screened for the press in Los Angeles in March 1932 and subsequently reviewed in the trade press, but never released. Moreover, these variations are not simply a matter of the contemporary version being more complete than some of the versions circulating in 1932. The New York and Pennsylvania censorship records, for instance, include deletions from scenes shot for both the September and October versions, but entirely absent from the contemporary version. Although Todd McCarthy informs us that *Scarface* was in circulation from 1932 to 1935, and that between 1936 and 1947 it grossed an additional $297,934, the picture was refused a Certificate of Approval by the Production Code Administration in April 1935, and that decision was repeated in May 1949. The figures listed by McCarthy may, however, have been overseas earnings. The contemporary version surfaced in 1979, when Hughes's Summa Corporation sold rights to it and all other Hughes productions to Universal. Censorship record, PCA *Scarface* file; McCarthy, *Howard Hawks*, 153–54; Gerald Mast, *Howard Hawks*, 75; Joseph McBride, *Hawks on Hawks* (Los Angeles: University of California Press, 1982), 44; Memo, McKenzie to Hays, June 17, 1935, and Breen to Ed Depinet, President RKO Corporation, May 26, 1949, both in PCA *Scarface* file.

135. Balio, *United Artists*, 111. McCarthy suggests that by 1935 it had grossed $905,298 for United Artists, which would have meant that Hughes made a small profit on the picture's domestic earnings. McCarthy, *Howard Hawks*, 153.

136. Henry James Forman, "To the Movies—But Not to Sleep", *McCall's* 29, no.12: 12–13 and 18–19.

137. Caddo press release, May 3, 1932, MPA, 1932, Caddo, *Scarface* file.

138. *Lewistown (Maine) Sun*, April 23, 1932.

139. Courtenay Terrett, *Only Saps Work* (New York: Vanguard Press, 1930), quoted in Tyler, *Organized Crime in America*, 5 and 8.

140. Hon. Nobile Giaccomo de Martino, Italian Ambassador, to Col. Frederick Herron, MPPDA, June 3, 1932, and Alexander Bevilacqua to Hays, April 30, 1932, both in MPA, 1932, Caddo, *Scarface* file.

141. *New York World-Telegram*, May 14, 1932, quoted in Powers, *G-Men*, 11.

142. Wingate to Hays, February 3, 1933, PCA *Gabriel over the White House* file.

143. These rulings are summarized in Martin, *Hollywood's Movie Commandments*, Appendix 3, 289–90.

144. Minutes of the MPPDA Executive Committee, March 2, 1934, MPA; Hays to MPPDA company presidents, July 28, 1934, PCA *Uncle Sam Gets His Man* file; and Hays to Albert W. Haussen (Warner Bros.), February 27, 1939, PCA *John Dillinger, Outlaw* file.

145. The ruling also specified that "there are to be no off-stage sounds of the reper-
cussions of these guns." Martin, *Hollywood's Movie Commandments*, 290.

146. Ibid., 134–35.

147. Ibid., 289–90; Breen to Edward Small, Reliance Productions, March 7,
1935, PCA *Let 'Em Have It* file; and Breen to Jack Warner, September 9,
1935, PCA *The Petrified Forest* file.

148. Martin, *Hollywood's Movie Commandments*, 132. Munby dates this decision
from a speech by Hays on July 15, 1935. Munby, *Screening the Gangster*, 19.

149. Breen to Jack Warner, December 20, 1935, and Breen, memo, January 8,
1936, both in PCA *Bullets or Ballots* file.

150. Breen to Louis B. Mayer, January 8, 1937, PCA *The Last Gangster* file.

151. Al Block, MGM, to Breen, October 25, 1937, PCA *The Last Gangster* file.

152. For an extended discussion of Hollywood's policies of ethnic and national
indeterminacy, see Vasey, *The World According to Hollywood*, 131–57.

murder's tongue:

identity, death,

and the city

in film noir

paul arthur

For murder, though it have no tongue,
Will speak with most miraculous organ.
—*Hamlet* (II.ii)

In the first three months of 1998 alone, reviewers labeled nearly a dozen new movies, or approximately a quarter of all late-winter releases, as "film noir." While it would be senseless at this late date to bemoan the transformation of "noirism" from a contentious yet relatively coherent film-historical category into a promiscuous marketing tool and signifier of eccentric criminality, it is instructive to imagine possible criteria for linking under the same banner such otherwise disparate projects as *Twilight, Dark City, Palmetto, The Big Lebowski,* and *Wild Things.*[1] Given the fashionable appeal of noir for a mind-boggling array of commodities,[2] it is perhaps not surprising to discover the term applied to films more logically classified as screwball comedies, sci-fi, or domestic melodramas. Nonetheless, it is impossible to locate either in the films themselves or in the critical discourse surrounding them a set of consistent features usually attributed to the "classical" phase of noir: the hapless private investigator, femme fatale, gritty urban settings, convoluted story structures. To be sure, recent examples of noir continue to be underwritten by relations between outlaw activity and anxious masculine codes of performance; however, the dynamics of gendered power offer shaky grounds on which to constitute generic quiddity or plausible continuity with an earlier cycle of production.

A more salient approach to what is currently considered "noir" would begin by noting affinities in the register of enacted violence, in the situations, protocols, moral ambiguities, and consequences of how bloodshed is inscribed within narrative, formal, and symbolic textual operations. Moreover, an analysis of strategies through which violent actions are generated and sustained in contemporary noir would simultaneously help to distinguish it from adjacent action genres and establish a framework for assessing the legacy of postwar depictions of the myth of criminal adventure. The problem is that despite a sizable and growing literature on the noir phenomenon, there is no systematic, or even partial, account of violence as a specific discourse in Hollywood cinema of the 1940s and 1950s. The reasons for this critical absence are varied and ultimately elusive; they include dominant trends in film theory and historiography, politically motivated attention to issues of sexual representation or bourgeois ideologies of justice, and the belated academic engagement with cultural manifestations of violence. What follows is intended as a start at filling this gap and, in a manner that parallels previous attempts to address the social implications of the noir series, it derives from a public context wherein analysis of the uses of violence has been deemed a pressing concern.

An initial contention is that different types of commercial films mobilize legible, empirically quantifiable constructions of physical brutality and death. By this view the loosely held terrain of film noir—in both old and new versions—is haunted by a spectral semiotics or textual ecology of mayhem understood as separate from idioms developed for horror, gangster, Western, or combat narratives, with a proviso for obvious instances of generic overlap and hybridization. Significantly, in the case of neo-noir what critics perceive as differences in the deployment or visualization of violence often serve to cue explicit or implicit debts to the way violence is handled in classic noir. That is, regardless of the lack of a shared vocabulary for describing modalities of violence, there exists a heuristic horizon of expectation around how this category generates, ramifies, and resolves its lethal dramas—thus we believe we know it when we see it. What is it that we see, who does what to whom, where, and under what circumstances? Finally, are there areas in which these practices intersect historically grounded discourses on violence within the broader climate of postwar society?

Out of the Past

The notion that early film noir augured a shift in Hollywood's traditional rendering of violence was a prominent, at times dominant, topic in French criticism of the late 1940s.[3] Nino Frank, credited with the first published reference to a "noir" sensibility, argued that a new type of "crime adventure" had supplanted the Western as primary vehicle for the imperatives of male action. His reckoning of a "dark" strain of detective story subtended by a "dynamism of violent death" became a flash point of heated ethical controversy over the merits of the emerging series.[4] Frank, along with Jean-Pierre Chartier, Jacques Bourgeois, and other critics, applauded Hollywood's introduction of morally ambiguous heroes as an unexpected turn toward "psychological realism" and hence toward a greater fidelity to actual conditions of American social discontent.[5] Henri-Francois Rey's claim that *Double Indemnity* and *Woman in the Window* offered shocking visions of an "unhappy and desperate" society on the verge of "chaos" exemplifies the tenor of debate.[6] Several writers seized on a local advertising slogan for *Double Indemnity*, "She kisses him, so he'll kill," as an sign of either the industry's unprecedented eroticization of violence or its principled unmasking of hidden currents of cultural misogyny.[7] The murderous schemes of, especially, women characters formed the crux of alternative views of violence as signaling reactionary attitudes or a liberatory flouting of convention.

Writing in the postwar miasma of European devastation, ideological realignment, and accelerating evidence of French collaboration in Nazi war crimes, cineastes were no doubt primed to struggle with film noir's thematics of criminal conspiracy, revenge, betrayal, and the recourse to violence by ordinary citizens. Noting what they saw as benumbed, "robotic" acts of brutality and a pathological reciprocity between killer and victim, commentators concluded that Hollywood's unalloyed veneration of male heroism had received a jolt of wartime reality.[8] Rarely were direct parallels drawn between on-screen action and the psychic mechanisms of combat; in several essays, however, there are dire warnings about how a fascination with morbidity and self-destruction feeds an appetite for political defeatism.[9] By a similar logic, violence was said to be implicated in the heedless, if somewhat soured, expression of national belligerence. Polemical assessments of the meaning of violence in noir persisted well into the following decade. Raymond Borde and Etienne Chaumeton, in the conclusion of their landmark 1955 monograph, baldly state that "Brutality serves the propaganda of war"; further, that "the presentation of massive doses of criminal films during a period of international tensions has a dangerous effect on the collective aggressiveness of the public."[10] What is at stake in these foundational responses to noir is twofold: first, that purportedly innovative and challenging indices of violence received foregrounded critical scrutiny; second, that specific practices were construed as symptoms or thinly veiled allegories of social problems induced by wartime immersion in bloodshed.

American film criticism proved equally sensitive to changes in the scope and ideological underpinnings of Hollywood's action codes heralded by a new wave of "crime melodramas" and "psychological detective films." At nearly the same moment that noir was acquiring fervent advocates and a provisional definition in France, Siegfried Kracauer was lamenting the onset of "Hollywood's Terror Films" in an essay subtitled "Do They Reflect an American State of Mind?" Having just completed his study *From Caligari to Hitler*, Kracauer was perhaps especially wary of narratives driven by brutal criminal conspiracies. His analysis, which encompasses not only film noir but *Gaslight* and other quasi-noir productions, begins with the observation that "films saturated with terror and sadism [have] become commonplace." He argues that new patterns of depicted violence, including its diffusion into quotidian settings, in tandem with a relaxed attitude toward criminal behavior mark a significant declension from gangster films of the 1930s. Far from suggesting that represented violence can lead to actual violence, he nonetheless worries that the fixation in recent films on physical brutality might produce a desensitizing effect on viewers already inured to the horrors of war. Accordingly, films laden with "the kind of horror formerly attributed only to life under Hitler" present a "real danger" by feeding the public's "emotional preparedness for fascism."[11] Rather than connecting burgeoning screen violence to any therapeutic injection of realism, as do certain French writers, Kracauer's broadside takes it as a politically malign eruption of irrational energies.

Kracauer's position, although more complex in its vision of cinema's social effects, is allied with contemporaneous condemnations of film violence in newspaper and magazine reviews. With the film industry coming under increasing public and internecine pressure to produce entertainment offering unambiguously affirmative values—as liberal producer Dore Schary, newly installed as head of MGM production, promised in 1948, "good films about a good world"[12]—individual film noir became tarred with the brush of un-Americanism. For example, Bosley Crowther of the *New York Times* found that the "unprecedented sadism" in *Brute Force* disqualified it from foreign distribution due to its distorted portrayal of the legal system.[13] In the wake of Kracauer's controversial piece, producer John Houseman wrote an impassioned denunciation of the ugliness, fatalism, and "absolute lack of moral energy" in films such as *The Big Sleep*, yet was at pains to admit that the "'tough' movie presents a fairly accurate reflection of the neurotic personality of the United States of America in the year 1947."[14] The rhetorical influence of such appraisals of noir violence is evidenced a decade later in one of the first popular surveys of film history, with Arthur Knight once again reproaching the "private eye" tradition for "a psychopathic kind of violence that recalled nothing so much as the tortures in the concentration camps and the cellars of the Gestapo."[15]

Noir came under attack from mutually hostile sectors on the political compass. Writers on the left campaigned in progressive journals against what they saw as its abuses of social realism, a sensationalism and "bourgeois decadence" in the presentation of antisocial hoodlums and innocent victims alike.[16] Amid moralistic critiques of noir's portrayal of brutality, James Agee, writing in *Time* and *The Nation*, staunchly defended the likes of *The Big Sleep* and *Kiss of Death*. Acknowledging that "more and more people who think of themselves as serious-minded, and progressive, thoroughly disapprove of crime melodramas," Agee validated their social message as a "new and vigorous trend" countering ingrained clichés about heroism and "immaculate" crime.[17] Inverting the position of colleagues on the left, he commended recent crime films for their reliance on fact-based scripts and location shooting, qualities that he compared favorably to the social agendas of Italian neorealism. In addition, he viewed the depiction of law enforcement as "an invincibly corrupt and terrifying force," a valuable response to Hollywood's benign projection of governmental authority.[18] In an article summarizing important movie trends of 1946, Agee dismissed the anti-noir polemics of Kracauer and Barbara Deming, declaring that "the most sinister thing that happened during the movie year was the emergence of just this sort of [alarmist] analysis."[19] Agee's successor at *The Nation*, Manny Farber, a sly promoter of "termite art" as antidote to pretentious "message" movies, regularly touted the cinematic pleasures and subversive thrust of postwar "sadistic epics," reveling in savage details of individual scenes as if in mockery of cinematic guardians of rectitude (hence his cheery description of Anthony Mann as a "tin-can de Sade" with "an original dictionary of ways in which to punish the human body").[20] Without overstating the centrality of film noir or the depiction of violence in popular discourse of the period, it seems safe to suggest that initial responses to a new breed of postwar crime films maintained a consistent focus on the calculus and social implications of violent images.

Despite, or perhaps because of, the intensity of previous debates, violence as a problematic receded into the background during the Anglo-American revival of noir in the early 1970s. During this second, more theoretically inclined phase of noir criticism, the series was interrogated for symbolic markers of Cold War anxieties redolent of both power struggles within the industry and the repressive measures of a national security apparatus. However, patterns of physical brutality and mayhem were no longer regarded as part of a discrete, historically grounded pathology but as surface manifestations of covert ideological or psychosexual disturbances.[21] At the risk of oversimplifying a rich spectrum of critical initiatives, the display of violence was cast as an ancillary figure in a textual system whose primary loci of signification were mapped according to formal, narratological, or metaphorical coordinates. Thus why characters commit criminal acts, what they think they know about their predicaments and what remains unspoken, superceded analysis of how or where criminal infractions occur.

There are several plausible explanations for the redirection of critical interest to elements less overtly charged with social meaning. As film studies grew increasingly institutionalized, it adopted analytical strategies—including formalism and feminist psychoanalysis—that posed peremptory challenges to supposedly outmoded sociological or "reflectionist" methods. In addition, the rediscovery of noir is entwined historically with changing industry standards for the treatment of violence. Longstanding strictures on graphic representation, as governed by the Production Code and other internal industry organs, were successively breached in the mid-1960s and replaced by a version of the current MPAA ratings system, a development galvanized by the box office success of *Bonnie and Clyde*, *Easy Rider*, and *The Wild Bunch*, among others. Thus the novel deployment of noir violence in nonritualized, frequently nightmarish patterns—a source of agonized critical opinion in the 1940s—had ceased to register as either innovative or transgressive for a younger generation of viewers. That said, it would indeed be myopic to argue that omnipresent documentary and televisual outlets for the dissemination of violent events played no role in the cultural apprehension of noir. On the contrary, the confluence in noir of political corruption and conspiratorial networks, spiraling personal insecurity, and self-abnegating carnage must have struck a resonant chord with youthful American audiences then caught in the metastasizing debacle of Vietnam and its inflamed vectors of domestic protest and extralegal government retribution.[22]

In order to revisit the question of violence in the wake of twenty years of extensive critical dissection, a somewhat different approach is required that does not lose sight of previous discursive strands but offers a more empirical, taxonomic, and inclusive account of death and destruction across a wider corpus of noir. My analysis of prominent patterns, motifs, and structures is based on a survey of almost one hundred films made between 1944 and 1956,[23] embodying a host of broad tendencies as well as emblematic instances. It is intended equally as a synthesis of and corrective to both early polemical debates and the intervening critical emphasis on "hidden" dynamics of signification. This trajectory points to, if it does not fully realize, a generatively complex view of the relationship between noir textuality and certain ideological pressures at work in American postwar society. Conceptually, what is required is a framework able to mediate notions of the symptomatically reflective with the symbolically refractive, relocating the textual activity of violence as neither blatant social index nor cryptic sanctum of unconscious desires.

Habeas Corpus

It is at once obvious and telling that film noir violence can be anatomized from several different angles. The formation of descriptive categories, definitions, and tropic models facilitates certain readings while discouraging others. What is called "empirical" here is admittedly fraught with approximations and necessary equivocations; what counts as an example of this or that motif—for example, the attribution of "suicide" or "role reversal"—is open to disagreement. Moreover, the classification of criminal acts by setting or position within a narrative system is necessarily loose if not reductive; for instance, citing the incidence of death at the "end" of a film is shorthand for "in the climactic or concluding scene or scenes." By the same token, grouping victims by age or gender masks the variegated circumstances, including the underlying narrational authority, through which a character's mortality is enacted for the viewer. Nonetheless, before examining a field of relations in what is a notoriously ambiguous territory, the enumeration of a few narrative parameters and statistical patterns is in order.

The Wrong Man is the only film in my sample without explicit diegetic reference to violent death, either as overt presentation or off-screen cues.[24] By far the most prevalent type of death is homicide, encompassing legal definitions of manslaughter and justifiable killing as well as premeditated murder. The handgun is the primary weapon of choice but it should be noted that, unlike in Westerns or combat films, most lethal confrontations take place in close physical proximity. They are not only, for the most part, intimately personal and often subjectively rendered but are lacking the ritualized narrative placements that create stable viewer anticipation in dominant action genres. While some films are structured around a single homicidal act, nearly two-thirds contain multiple deaths that are typically linked in a chain of attrition. Not surprisingly, the majority of killings are of and by male characters of roughly the same age group and social context. However, in nearly forty films a female character is fatally dispatched by a man, lending at least numerical weight to frequent assertions of an especially vindictive misogyny.

While the tantalizing figure of the femme fatale all but vanishes from film noir in the 1950s, by percentage there are as many female *victims* in the latter stages of noir production as there were in the initial, critically venerated phase. Nonetheless, of fifteen films in which women take the role of killers, eleven were made prior to 1950. Lethal women tend to target male counterparts but they also dispatch other women, often romantic rivals, in a half-dozen cases. If the series is not exactly an equal opportunity slayer, there is undoubtedly a wider distribution of violent criminal acts, as classified by gender and age, than the cottage industry of noir critical discourse would have us believe. Much has been made, and rightly so, of Oedipal currents swirling around intergenerational male conflicts. Yet there are nearly as many occasions in which middle-aged men do away with members of their own cohort (*The Woman in the Window, Force of Evil*), or women kill older women (*Gun Crazy, The Big Heat*) or dispense with middle-aged men (*The Lady from Shanghai, Where Danger Lives*). In a statistically small yet intriguing group of films, adolescents die (*On Dangerous Ground*) or kill adult figures (*The Strange Love of Martha Ivers, The Window*). Even in the psychologically charged situation of an alienated younger man slaying a powerful older character, the killing is as often motivated by financial gain or by self-defense (*The Big Clock, He Walked by Night*) as outright sexual competition. Just as there are a range of "criminal" impulses—from robbery to government undercover assignments—associated with the descent of protagonists into the underworld, those ensnared in the act of killing cannot usefully be addressed through crude binaries of age or gender or through narrative models borrowed from depth psychology, of which the sexual triangle is the most familiar and, perhaps, least comprehensive or critically useful.[25] The desire to plumb noir's textual operations of murder deserves a more nuanced account of role classifications as well as greater attention to spatio-temporal development and to the thematics of law and order.

If enactments of violent death are often positioned as central, pivotal events in the plot structure, they are also regularly deployed as catalysts for an initial task, usually an investigation, and, at the other end, routinely function as signifiers of narrative closure. Approximately two-thirds of films in my sample are resolved through the death of a main character (the remainder invariably have final scenes featuring some form of physical combat). Twenty-eight films commence on a note of mortality, of which eighteen are also bracketed by bloodshed at their conclusion.[26] Sudden death from other than natural causes is a crucial hermeneutic element in many genres and cycles other than film noir; here that idea operates mostly in conjunction with initiation and development of criminal investigations and serves as a framework for noir's singular pattern of doubled or reciprocal physical evasion and pursuit. Nonetheless, while climactic deaths conventionally signal the cessation of narrative movement, with the goal of clarifying and resolving outstanding questions of legal culpability and restoring social equilibrium, in noir such gestures typically fail to deflect the sense of ambiguous or inadequate finality. (Indeed, the problem of unsettled closure has been widely recognized and debated in noir literature.[27]) The reputedly "unsatisfying" endings are not attributable to any subversive avoidance of prescribed punishment for wrongdoing—given classical Hollywood's moral strictures, how could they be?—but because symbolic residues of mortality are so extensively embedded in iconographic, stylistic, and dialogue functions, the traditional power of death to secure a final, recuperative state of reintegration is significantly blunted or altogether vitiated.[28]

The living and the dead commingle in noir as in no other Hollywood product before or since. Although we shall return to this topic, a brief overview is indicated here. In addition to myriad tokens of the symbolic death of the subject—from near-fatal injuries to rhetorically inflated declarations of living death to prominent tropes of amnesia, dream sequences, and other markers of lapsed consciousness—protagonists assume the literal identities of dead men in nearly fifteen percent of all noir, including such otherwise disparate story constructions as *Detour* and *T-Men*. Dialogue referring to living characters as metaphorically "dead" is nearly ubiquitous (Walter Neff's memorable line in *Double Indemnity*, "I couldn't hear my own footsteps; it was the walk of a dead man," epitomizes this tendency). Moreover, the well-documented visual techniques of substituting shadows for substantive bodies, the use of mirrors, and claustrophobic framing techniques augment noir's excessive foregrounding of mortality. Divorced in one fashion or another from a stable social matrix, noir's roster of condemned men (and occasionally women) are rendered corporeally ruptured or nullified; as such they can be linked metonymically with the sepulchral spaces of tunnels and other subterranean locales that punctuate the series. Hence an insistently threnodic beat steals from the trope of climactic death a portion of its summary impact.

The problematic status of mortality as narrative terminus is a distinctive aspect of noir violence, its specificity clearly established by comparing it with the violent endings of, say, Westerns or gangster films. What is crucially absent from most noir endings is any sense of a "regeneration through violence," the consummatory act as "*necessary* and *sufficient* resolution of all the issues the tale has raised."[29] While concluding violence in Westerns contributes to the reassertion of stable personal identity, in noir it often adds to the burden of self-abnegating loss, the final stage in a process of assuming the mantle of criminal "other." Given the historical context, one might expect a socially affirmative, purgative use of violence, and the denial of that function is part and parcel of noir's ideological resistance. To be sure, the conclusions of several film noirs offer spectacularized displays of death, yet even here—as in the perceptual confusion of the amusement park shoot-out in *The Lady from Shanghai* or the nuclear explosion in *Kiss Me Deadly*—the visual authority of death as limit point of representation is to some extent effaced by the illegibility or dispersal of bodily images. That is, even in death noir characters are not visualized as radically different from their previous states of fragmentation.

If violent death arriving at the end of noir narratives summarizes an overall impression of ambiguity and instability, its eruption at the start of dramatic action is no less unsettling. As a conventional gambit, death creates that immediate gap in knowledge that sets in motion an investigative response. However, since so few noir are "whodunits" in any meaningful sense, the withholding and eventual detection of a killer's identity is seldom a crucial element in the narrative organization. Perpetrators may be known at the very outset (*This Gun for Hire*) or revealed in a following scene (*Appointment with Danger*) or figure only marginally (*Touch of Evil*) or not at all (*T-Men*) in the ensuing action. Thus the mayhem erupting in opening scenes may turn out to be less a central enigma than a signpost or avatar of a more generalized atmospheric dread. In a number of cases, killers are revealed as agents of law enforcement, invoking noir's familiar slippage between cop and criminal (*Shield for Murder*). Although the status of homicide as triggering device is unequivocal, it is often a misleading indicator of both the direction and thematic valence of criminal pursuit.[30] In retrospect, the function of incipient death within the narrative fabric is to cue anticipation of physical vulnerability rather than to raise hermeneutic questions. Trajectories of violence in film noir are subtended not by the revelation of criminal identity but by its ramifications, how immersion in an underworld adventure disrupts and ultimately voids a character's psychosocial traces of identity.

Given the blatantly self-destructive impulses exhibited by a majority of noir heroes, it is fitting that the affective boundary between homicide and suicide is tenuous at best; as Borde and Chaumeton contend, noir is underwritten by a form of male "masochism" that eventually transforms the hero into "his own assassin."[31] Violence between characters with antithetical role designations is as likely to be convulsive or self-obliterating as it is cathartic or socially redemptive. A remarkable array of character doubles—a police detective bent on eliminating a criminal alter ego (*Where the Sidewalk Ends, Cry of the City, The Big Combo*) is the most celebrated, but far from the only version—augments a wider pattern of identity exchange and alteration. Insofar as the slaying of a doppelgänger, a narrative trope in a dozen films, expresses an extreme disavowal of a killer's own internal or socially mediated contradictions, the noir series indulges in a unique and oddly displaced mode of auto-annihilation. As a character remarks in the climactic scene of *The Lady from Shanghai*, "Of course killing you is killing myself. It's the same thing, but you know, I'm pretty tired of both of us." To put it another way, the bizarre plotting of "criss-cross" proxy killings in *Strangers on a Train* reappear in the larger context of noir as a thematic template rather than an anomaly.

In a variation on the collapse of original identity as ushering in a dire and misdirected psychical violence, a group of noir characters enact their own death sentences via de facto suicides, deliberately courting mortality by refusing the opportunity to escape imminent assault or, more actively, intercepting a bullet meant for someone else. An assortment of narrative justifications are offered among the fourteen films containing this pattern: self-sacrifice for a higher cause (*T-Men*) or for a love object (*Kiss of Death*); punishment for crimes actual (*The File on Thelma Jordan*) or ambiguously assumed (*Act of Violence*). All but three de facto suicides take place in culminating scenes. Another version offers the willing death of the protagonist as an act of existential choice (*Gun Crazy, Night and the City*). Unlike other patterns of abnegation, the latter may be understood as a positive, restabilizing event that achieves a greater measure of textual closure than other film noir endings.

The principle of human expendability, of voluntary surrender of life in defense of a cause, is an appropriately affirmative gesture in late–Second World War combat films. In *13 Rue Madeleine*, for example, a military espionage officer embarks on a fatal mission not because he is disgusted with life or haunted by past misdeeds but because of an unshakable altruism. Film noir heroes bear a resemblance to wartime figures who voluntarily accept a new identity in order to penetrate an enemy network. However, lacking the ideological props of collective crisis and survival, suicide in noir is presented as a defeatist, even pathological solution to the dislocations of a criminal predicament. Protagonists in *The Killers, Out of the Past*, and other films sacrifice themselves because they are trapped, their connection to a regime of approved values and codes of behavior permanently severed. Even the ostensibly pragmatic circumstance of an undercover agent choosing to die rather than expose his cover to a gang of felons, as in *T-Men*, can be construed as misplaced institutional loyalty, a failure of self-cognizance rather than a triumphal act of selflessness. A cynical and soured individualism, however disoriented or distorted by underworld affiliations, takes precedence over communal goals. It is precisely in this sense that cops and government agents in noir are merely inverted templates of professional killers or middle-class outlaws, and why the supposedly affirmative exploits of police investigation noir, especially after 1950, carry so little patriotic conviction.

Since a number of film noirs recalibrate for domestic skirmishes the narrative trappings and male action codes of Hollywood's wartime espionage-combat genres, it is perhaps not surprising that twenty-four of fifty-three film noirs made before 1950 identify a leading character as a veteran of the Second World War. As the immediacy of wartime service fades, so does the number of ex-GIs; only nine characters in forty-four film noirs after 1950 are so designated. In historical context, references to a character's war record are arguably opportunistic, designed to capitalize on the public's veneration of returning soldiers and its anxieties concerning "readjustment."[32] In slightly more than half of the films, however, military participation is an integral element in plot construction. The uncertain social plight of returning soldiers is in one regard similar to that of private eyes, undercover agents, and rogue cops: suspended between incommensurate allegiances and value systems, they inhabit a liminal zone composed of fluid roles and motives. For film noir's former soldiers, the transition from officially sanctioned practices of violence to a furtive, outcast criminality intensifies as it annotates an overarching structure of narrative disillusionment and complication. In some cases, the stress of social reintegration is exacerbated by investigating a crime that occurred either during (*Dead Reckoning, Ride the Pink Horse*) or immediately following active service (*The Blue Dahlia*). Completion of this task is simultaneously hindered and facilitated by battlefield traumas; for instance, a lingering physical or mental impairment may be counterbalanced by an enhanced capacity for aggression (*Somewhere in the Night, The High Wall*). The haunted, disheveled appearance of film noir characters in the midst of life-threatening ordeals transmutes a recurrent image of the battle-hardened soldier common in Hollywood's late wartime production.[33] In the wider context of the industry's calculated handling of postwar readjustment, the "noir vet" may undergo extreme physical hardships, yet he is simply one member in traumatized rank of figures, "blood brothers" animated by a tenuous and confusing relationship to the ideal of social "normalcy."[34]

In the closing chapter of their study, Borde and Chaumeton cite the "fundamental contradiction" in noir as the friction between textual properties of the banal versus the *insolite*. They go on to suggest that this tension exists at various levels or filmic registers, perhaps most pointedly in the stylistic collision between heightened codes of realism—whose apogee is the Louis de Rochemont–influenced semidocumentary noir—and a florid expressionism of dream sequences, chiaroscuro lighting, and subjectivized spatial inscription.[35] The transition from soldier to embattled private citizen proffers a transparent justification for this tense mixture of visual codes, but it is important to stress that comparable interminglings of the quotidian and bizarre are evident across a range of noir narratives. If a sizable minority of protagonists start the action in an interstitial social condition, an equal number make their descent into criminal violence from a position of relative security that is uninflected by prior involvement in the vicissitudes of a "living death."

As critics at the time noted, the representation of violence in noir is not displaced from the milieu of its viewers by historical period (as in the Western), geography (war films), or supernatural causation (horror films). It is mostly perpetrated by and visited upon ostensibly ordinary individuals engaged in middle-class occupations and social pursuits—the exceptions include six private eyes and nine professional criminals (*He Walked by Night, The Asphalt Jungle*). Nearly half are employed in the private sector as salesmen, accountants, or other white-collar jobs, and apart from military service have little or no training in the violent arts; that is, they are not killers or victims by trade but by circumstance.[36] A significant group of thirty-three law officers—two-thirds of whom appear in noir made after 1950—begin their adventures already steeped in the knowledge of firearms and fisticuffs, yet in their narrative movement away from the quotidian and toward the margins of social regulation, cops undergo the same processes of intensified violence and psychic dislocation befalling figures less predisposed to mayhem. What they almost invariably have in common is an urban environment inherently coded as dehumanizing, dangerous, and infused with signifiers of mortality. Thus in a manner similar to the erosion of behavioral and role boundaries between antagonistic characters, in the underworld adventure the visual membrane separating bodies from objects or architectural settings is provisionally dissolved. Once again, the catalyst for this dispersion of identity is enacted violence.

City of Night

As distinct from studio-fabricated cities in gangster and social problem films of the 1930s, the backdrop for noir violence consists of actual, named, iconographically detailed locales frequently bolstered by the presence of extradiegetic as well as internalized guarantees of authenticity: concrete place titles (*The House on 92nd Street, 99 River Street*), quasi-official voice-over narrations (*Walk East on Beacon*), and printed texts (*Kiss of Death*) vouch for the verisimilitude of settings.[37] New York, Los Angeles, and Chicago together lay claim to the largest chunk of noir real estate, yet picturesque metropolises like San Francisco and Boston and the heartland industrial cities of Kansas City and Fort Wayne are also represented. In addition to the seemingly requisite network of generic, lower-class transient locations—diners, bars, seedy hotels—a number of films foreground recognizable architectural landmarks for the staging of dramatic action (the eponymous Union Station, the Manhattan Bridge in *The Naked City*). It is important, then, that the scenic profile of urban space is assumed as coextensive with the conditions and immediate experience of noir's contemporary audience.

Significantly, unlike other Hollywood films of the period, noir appropriates as part of its dramatic cachet pop cultural versions of urban sociology—in particular the so-called ecological dynamics of population diversity, concentration, and the distance between home and workplace, originally theorized by writers associated with the Chicago School—in the same loose fashion that it draws on realist literary and still-photographic traditions.[38] Hence naturalistic, topographical patterns of class division, ethnic enclaves, manufacturing, and commercial activity are presented as visual correlatives for the fleetingly "normal" status of the hero, or these patterns are adduced as structuring elements in a spatialized trajectory of criminal investigation. The most obvious example is *The Naked City*, in which police detectives uncover incriminating evidence while skillfully traversing a reified spectrum of social positions; more typically, investigations entail the revisiting (*Cry of the City*) or sudden revelation (*Panic in the Streets*) of an urban "lower depths."

Interwoven with traces of a determinate "aboveground" city is an equally vivid depiction of urban distress highlighted by defamiliarized, marginal landscapes that function as scenic metaphors for isolation, decay, and corporeal rupture. These familiar markers of the noir underworld amplify and are in turn penetrated by specific modalities of violence enacted on the ground of pictorial excess. The archetypal image of rain-drenched "mean streets," illuminated through the intersection of hard-boiled literary sources and the European visual flourishes advanced by the influx of refugees in wartime Hollywood, is sustained in its visual-thematic charge by the slippage from third-person detached frameworks of enunciative authority to subjectivized codes of presentation. That is, the power of urban imagery to shape the terms of dramatic action is informed by an often irreconcilable mixture of character-mediated and detached narrative discourses.[39] In this regard, it remains an open question as to whether the look of the noir city—a product of both iconographic elements and formal practices—during intensely violent scenes of dramatic action represents an externalization of a character's inner state of mind or whether that look is better understood as a subject's introjection of an overtly menacing, disorienting environment.

The tension attributed to an unstable deployment of knowledge effects is most acutely present in films containing first-person flashbacks, yet roughly the same sort of friction is operative across a range of narrational strategies including the semidocumentary format—in which the voice-over narrator's facade of absolute control over verbal exposition is contradicted by scenic or stylistic evidence of disorder. In what is arguably the first fully realized noir production, *This Gun for Hire*, a conventional third-person address centered around a lone assassin becomes increasingly infused by signs of subjective mediation. For instance, the successive appearance of physically grotesque or handicapped characters can be read as a projection of the killer's stated anxiety about his own deformity (a crooked arm mangled in childhood by a foster parent). More important, as the protagonist's twin arc of investigation ("I'm my own police") and evasion proceeds, he passes through a series of visually detailed—the amount of location shooting is unusual for 1942—but also frighteningly oneiric spaces: bloated gasworks, a cloacal drainage tunnel, a labyrinthine railroad yard. Understood as subjectivized manifestations of underworld paranoia, these spaces function as dramatized intimations of isolation, persecution, and bodily revulsion. In the throes of a legal-existential crisis, bodies and the architectural environments they inhabit are often staged as reciprocal reflections of one another.

In part because violence is an intimate, self-incriminating affair, distinctions between public and private realms are called into question, if not erased altogether. Unlike the gangster film or Western, lethal combat is seldom witnessed by nonparticipants (*Gun Crazy* and *The Undercover Man* are partial exceptions). Although forty percent of the films feature a violent confrontation set in a domestic or pseudodomestic space,[40] the majority of climactic action occurs in depopulated public or commercial arenas such as warehouses or factories (*Panic in the Streets, The Street with No Name*), office buildings (*Force of Evil, D.O.A.*), train stations (*Union Station, Pickup on South Street*), and of course street corners, docks, and roadways (*Roadblock, Pushover*). Among the most pervasive and multivalent motifs in the series is the private automobile, an image that emblematizes the confusion between a protective zone of self and the incursion of a fearful other; it is simultaneously a mobile shelter passing through public territory and an extension of the hero's body that is vulnerable to outside scrutiny (besides the obvious examples of *Gun Crazy* or *Out of the Past*, recall how in *Double Indemnity* the car functions as roving office, dining area, scene of the crime, alibi, and site of illicit sexual contact).[41]

A sizable class of architectural spaces bears the unmistakable residue of the uncanny—as in Freud's mapping of *unheimlich* for objects or places that induce in the subject a compound dread of mortality as supernatural malevolence.[42] By either grotesquely mirroring bodily structures, as in the gasworks of *This Gun for Hire*, or by generating surrogate body images, certain locations in noir foreshadow as they disperse the morbid apprehension of physical annihilation. Two flagrant examples of the latter are a mannequin factory in *Killer's Kiss*, in which antagonists do battle with assorted limbs and torsos, and a meatpacking plant in *Gun Crazy*, wherein hanging animal carcasses announce the fate of an outlaw couple. Relevant here as well are displays of taxidermy in *Raw Deal* and *Sorry, Wrong Number*. The modern city, in its intrinsic verticality and accretion of concealed or forbidden realms, provides the series with a plethora of parking garages, sewers, subway tunnels, and other subterranean areas mobilized in the course of violent action as visual harbingers of death. The point here is that impending violence is signaled across a variety of iconographic patterns, including both locations and specific objects displayed as uncanny markers of a hesitation between animate and inanimate forms. An exemplary, if statistically minor, motif involves physical, photographic, or written documents attesting to the deaths of *living* characters: in the latter group, a woman in *Laura* reads a report of her own murder, a murderer in *Scandal Sheet* writes his own newspaper obituary, and the hero of *D.O.A.* inspects what is in effect a death warrant in the form of a toxicology lab analysis.

It should be clear that the practice of doubling in noir, as index of the fragility or elusiveness of identity, entails a range of object/person exchanges in addition to the mirroring of character traits. Nowhere is the lambent flow between living and dead more pronounced than in the extraordinary and, for Hollywood movies of the period, ostensibly transgressive emphasis on physical manipulation of corpses. Where in most film genres dead bodies exit the diegesis with sanitizing alacrity, in more than fifteen noirs they tend to hang around at the center or just at the periphery of extended narrative developments. True, the examination and disposal of corpses is a staple of detective and roman noir literature, but I would argue that the dances of death performed in film noir are of a different, hauntingly visceral species.[43] For instance, in a sequence that takes up roughly one-fifth of the total running time of *The Woman in the Window*, a meek college professor rifles through the clothing of an intruder he killed in self-defense, wraps the body in a rug, hauls it down several flights of stairs to his parked car before driving the corpse to a secluded location and finally dumping it in the woods. As in other intimate encounters with the dead, the thanatopic drive is palpably heightened—the end result in this case is the killer's attempted suicide.

The overarching ordeal of disintegration experienced by all noir heroes is exacerbated by the awkward embrace of lifeless flesh in various permutations: dragged through a hotel corridor in *Dead Reckoning*, tucked under a bed in *The Dark Corner*, stuffed into a closet in *Out of the Past*, and similarly manhandled in *Where the Sidewalk Ends*. As in traditional detective stories, the dead can vanish mysteriously then reappear, complicating the process of investigation. More interesting, however, is a strategy by which bodies remain off-screen for lengthy portions of the narrative as they await discovery; in *The Window, The Big Clock*, and the semi-noir *Deadline at Dawn*, constant reference to a carefully obscured corpse serves as a locus of narrative complication. It is important to note that this tactic, in which a person's sudden disappearance fails to arouse immediate suspicion and concerted response, is difficult to imagine outside the sociospatial density, isolation, and alienation of an urban matrix.[44]

The extent to which the deceased interact with the living lends credence to the idea that rather than working to contain narrative and symbolic consequences of violence—for example, justifying it as necessary to the redress of social deviation—film noir ramifies textual effects of bloodshed through its depiction of scenic dread. Ernest Mandel, in a study of the origins and ideology of the detective story, suggests that the form "requires a particular kind of fear of death, one that clearly has its roots in the condition of [nineteenth-century] bourgeois society." The relationship Mandel sketches between "reification" of death through obsessive scrutiny of the corpse and a middle-class preoccupation with individual security and private property is given renewed historical expression along with a revised catalogue of visual tropes in film noir.[45] Just as the rapid expansion of the European industrialized city corresponded with the rise of the detective story, the massive wartime destruction of urban Europe and the projected fate of all cities in the nuclear age finds echoes in the urban violence displayed in the series. The abject unsteadiness of the noir body is directly proportional to what the city landscape affords in the way of archetypal opportunities for lethal collisions. If by its very texture and design the city creates spaces ripe with danger—secret passageways, vertiginous escarpments, vantages for ambush—it also assists the enactment of violence by compounding the range of possible situations and instruments of fatality. Characters plunge off bridges or are pushed from open windows or into empty elevator shafts in eleven film noirs, including *The Big Clock, The Dark Corner*, and *Follow Me Quietly*. The transience and anonymity associated with big cities conspire to mask the identities of a poisoner in *D.O.A.* and a plague-carrying murderer in *Panic in the Street* in ways unavailable to a small-town setting.

In a famous scene in *Double Indemnity*, an insurance claims investigator delivers a lecture on the actuarial incidence of diverse forms of suicide. A similar inventory could be constructed around film noir's reign of unconventional homicides. Like the belligerent intruder in *Woman in the Window*, death can erupt unexpectedly and from seemingly innocuous circumstances, as is the case with a lethal fistfight in *Where the Sidewalk Ends*. There are deaths by drowning (*The Naked City*), immolation (*Raw Deal*), suffocation (*Where Danger Lives*), cattle stampede (*Union Station*), and dog attack (*The Chase*). A hoodlum is beaten to death with a pair of bronzed baby shoes in *Appointment with Danger*, a criminal is asphyxiated in a steambath in *T-Men*, and a third is impaled with a window pike in *Killer's*

Kiss. The point is that practically any object, banal or exotic, can be wielded to lethal purpose. To be sure, the presentation of death tends to be less graphic or detailed than in hard-boiled novels of the period.[46] Moreover, neither the amount nor the "styles" of murder correspond to actual violence in postwar American society—murder rates, which had risen sharply during the 1930s, declined in the early 1940s and remained relatively low until the mid-1960s.[47]

It is evident that the invention of unusual, and unusually brutal, modes of violence is integral to the ordering of noir narratives and to the promotional strategies by which films of this type were marketed to the public. Examined as thematic or philosophical tendency, what matters is that the shroud of personal insecurity blanketing the noir universe is neither arbitrary in its choice of victims nor indiscriminate in its proliferation of mayhem. But it is equally important that the thematization of death is underwritten by an ambivalent erosion and dispersal of identity encompassing both human figures and landscapes. Historically operative constraints on the visualization of carnage, from the Production Code to the relative paucity of available special-effects technologies, wind up reinforcing the treatment of physical brutality as a pervasive, endlessly refractive existential crisis.

At the edges of this crisis, tropes of dis-integration flourish in the midst of technological advances associated with, and developed for, the growth of modern cities. This is undoubtedly true of a cluster of motifs that annotate problems of urban depersonalization. Within this class disembodied voices heard over the telephone, speech without the physical presence of its source, is a conspicuous device. For Abraham Polonsky, the writer-director of *Force of Evil*, the telephone serves as a direct link between the quotidian and the criminal underworld for which an unseen authority poses an ultimate threat to the protagonist's security[48] (recall, for instance, the intricate network of long-distance death threats that stretch across *The Big Heat* and *Sorry, Wrong Number*). A corollary to the blatant menace of mechanized voices hinges on recently developed technologies of sound recording. In *Dark City*, *The Prowler*, and *Touch of Evil*, implied accusations or the confessions of dead or dying characters are replayed for the living. Although the recording made by Walter Neff in *Double Indemnity* is never heard, the film itself is bracketed as a lengthy interoffice memorandum whose accumulating row of dictaphone cylinders preserve what is in effect this character's last will and testament.

Like the narrators of *Laura* and the semi-noir *Sunset Boulevard*, and in concert with the animation of corpses and willful impersonations of the deceased, these voices speak from and to a domain in which violent death is neither conclusive nor safely quarantined from the affairs of the living; in the widest sense they signify the underworld's malefic power over fixed boundaries of identity. The representational crisis that accrues to filmic bodies in the throes of death—challenging social and institutional proprieties, if not outright taboos, over what can be shown and how—is hardly unique to film noir or to postwar studio production yet is addressed in this work by a singular ensemble of narrative, thematic, and visual tropes. In brief, the inevitability or transitivity of death in noir is fueled by a continuous interpenetration of animate and inanimate, human and manmade, interior and exterior, self and mediating environment.

Coda: Postwar Necropolis

A lingering question concerns the status and meaning of noir violence in the context of postwar American society, in particular how its textual mobilization might be said to intersect, allegorize, and inform rhetorical constructions of national crisis and renewal. Mayhem performed on and by bodies operates in a reciprocal and mutually entropic relationship to the surrounding physical environment. If these films are driven by Nino Frank's gloomy "dynamism of death" rather than Richard Slotkin's "regeneration through violence,"[49] their urban settings are in part the products of a longstanding cultural discourse in which cities and criminal violence are virtually synonymous. This discourse gained in both intensity and scope in the immediate aftermath of the Second World War, and noir provided a fertile popular arena in which nightmarish fantasies and ambivalent desires could be dramatized. Although a full treatment of affinities between the noir city and the tradition of antiurban thought would require a separate essay, a brief outline of one crucial area of convergence is in order.[50]

In the throes of Cold War paranoia, public perceptions of the fate of industrialized cities were inseparable from a generalized "imagination of disaster" fusing past conflicts and future prospects. Burgeoning scenarios of nuclear annihilation, fueled by photographic documentation of European destruction and the much-discussed implications of the bombings of Hiroshima and Nagasaki, were articulated in newspapers, magazines, and radio programs as new versions of familiar jeremiads against urban life.[51] No longer merely the crucible of sexual license, criminality, proletarian upheaval, and racial atavism, newly forged images of the city— played out against a backdrop of accelerating suburbanization (nineteen of the twenty-five largest cities in the United States *decreased* in population between 1947 and 1960[52])—conspired to create a profile of harrowing danger, intractable poverty, depersonalization, and marginalized existence equivalent to the living death attributed to shell-shocked soldiers and concentration camp survivors.

The sinister cast of the urban landscape in film noir is due not simply to its nurturing of criminal conspiracies or its manifold opportunities for violence. Foreshadowing the visual depiction of cities in postapocalyptic science fiction of the 1950s and early 1960s, noir situates its ennervated, death-immersed protagonists in deserted commercial and industrial zones that mirror and transpose the projected horrors of nuclear attack detailed in popular culture of the period.[53] The pervasive physical vulnerability of the noir subject, amplified by iconographic and thematic expressions of mortality as a protean condition, renders the space of violence as preapocalyptic. Given that among the principal combatants of the Second World War, American cities escaped the bombing and massive civilian casualties suffered by its European allies, noir doubles the stakes of imagined destruction by rendering a compensatory vision of bombed-out, feral urban existence.[54] The cadre of ex-soldiers, investigators, and middle-class killers that inhabit the urban margins are in effect displaced persons, metaphoric survivors as well as the perpetrators of a violence that cannot be adequately named, that indeed must be filtered through the individual criminal ordeals of falsely, as well as justly, accused outlaws.

Jacques Ellul notes that in ancient Hebrew, the word most commonly used for *city* bears the connotation of *enemy*, and that related words suggested the emotions of vengeance and terror.[55] Cities of antiquity were given secret names known only to holy men and rulers. The secret names of the noir city, their historical dopplegängers, are Dresden, Tokyo, London, Hiroshima. There is, finally, another city whose name is even further obscured by the dramatized misdeeds of noir adventurers; indeed, the coordinates of that other, desert-bound "Manhattan" were suppressed from official maps of the period, a walled city built to the specifications of a government underworld into which private citizens disappeared with hardly a trace, whose sole product was, as J. Robert Oppenheimer lamented of his own postatomic plight, "Death itself." Los Alamos, the city to end all cities, hovers over film noir like an eschatological ghost.

Notes

1. Hollywood studios admittedly tend to issue lower-profile, more "downbeat" product during the post-Christmas season hence it seems unlikely that the noir output for any given year is more than ten percent of the total releases. Nonetheless, if one includes indie production and foreign releases, the number of recent films deemed "noir" probably equals or even exceeds that of the late 1940s. The efflorescence of "neo-noir" and the case for noir as a generalized cultural style is the focus of several recent studies: James Naremore, *More than Night: Film Noir and Its Contexts* (Berkeley: University of California Press, 1998); Richard Martin, *Mean Streets and Raging Bulls: The Legacy of Film Noir in Contemporary Cinema* (Lanham, Md.: Scarecrow Press, 1997); and Foster Hirsch, *Detours and Lost Highways: A Map of Neo-Noir* (New York: Limelight, 1999).
2. For several years I kept a clippings file of nonfilmic attributions of "noir" in reviews, publicity materials, news items, and other demotic sources of cultural description. It includes references to novels, TV episodes, poetry, avant-garde theater, postmodern dance, jazz, and pop music, to say nothing of electoral and international political intrigues. My favorite is a magazine restaurant review in which "noir" seems less evocative of the decor than the cuisine (what was on the menu, I wonder, "knuckle sandwiches"?). For more on the seepage of noir, see Naremore, *More than Night*, 36–39.
3. It should be noted that in typical Hollywood fashion a certain strain of violent action, especially violence directed at women, was an integral part of publicity campaigns for noir productions as evidenced by trailers, posters, production stills, and ads. For a selection of particularly lurid posters, see Eddie Muller, *Dark City* (New York: St. Martin's, 1998).
4. Nino Frank, "Un nouveau genre policier: L'aventure criminelle," *L'Ecran Francais* 61 (August 28, 1946): 8 (my translation).
5. Naremore provides a review of early French discussions of noir in "American Film Noir: The History of an Idea," *Film Quarterly* 49, no. 2 (winter 1995–96): 12–20. See also R. Barton Palmer's introduction to his anthology *Perspectives on Film Noir* (New York: G. K. Hall, 1996), which features translations of 1940s French criticism.
6. Henri-Francois Rey, "Hollywood Makes Myths like Ford Makes Cars (last installment): Demonstration by the Absurd: Film Noirs," in Palmer,

Perspectives, 28 and 29, respectively.

7. See Pierre Duvillars, "She Kisses Him So He'll Kill," and Jean-Pierre Chartier, "The Americans Are Making Dark Films Too," in Palmer, *Perspectives,* 25–27 and 30–32, respectively.

8. Duvillars argues, for instance, that the femme fatale in *Double Indemnity,* who murders "by proxy," is simultaneously annihilating "the instrument of her crime." Unlike the romanticized figure of the 1930s gangster, noir characters are said to be fueled by internal rather than external (acquisitive) demands. Duvillars, "She Kisses Him So He'll Kill," 31.

9. Pierre Kast, writing in 1953, cites the numerous political attacks on noir and defends its overarching treatment of brutality. Kast, "A Brief Essay on Optimism," in Palmer, *Perspectives.*

10. Raymond Borde and Etienne Chaumeton, *Panorama du film noir americain, 1941–1953* (Paris: Editions du Minuit, 1955), 189 (my translation). They are also quite clear in declaring that "In the history of cinema, film noir has led to a renewal of the theme of violence," which they then distinguish from earlier forms by its predilection for "ambushes, beatings, tortures . . . and cold-blooded executions" rather than physical battles between equals (62). Unfortunately, neither Borde and Chaumeton nor their compatriots provide an adequate conceptual framework for understanding violent imagery.

11. Siegfried Kracauer, "Hollywood's Terror Films," *Commentary* 2, no. 2 (August 1946): 132 and 135, respectively. Kracauer pressed the attack on current filmic "pathologies," on what he felt was Hollywood's retreat from a spirited defense of political liberalism, in two subsequent essays: "Psychiatry for Everything and Everybody," *Commentary* 5, no. 3 (March 1948): 222–28; and "Those Movies with a Message," *Harper's* 196 (June 1948): 567–72.

12. Quoted in Thomas Schatz, *The Genius of the System* (New York: Pantheon, 1988), 446.

13. Cited in Colin Schindler, *Hollywood Goes to War: Films and American Society, 1939–1952* (London: Routledge and Kegan Paul, 1979), 107.

14. John Houseman, "Today's Hero: A Review," *Hollywood Quarterly* 2, no. 2 (1947): 161–63. In a well-known essay, Richard Maltby skewers the logic and critical usefulness of "reflectionist" or metaphoric connections between film noir and Cold War social history, turning the tables on Kracauer, Houseman, and later commentators such as Foster Hirsch by insisting that such interpretations mask an embattled liberal bias and that noir was singularly unrepresentative of the reigning industry ethos. "*Film Noir*: The Politics of the Maladjusted Text," *Journal of American Studies* 18 (1984): 49–71.

15. Arthur Knight, *The Liveliest Art* (New York: Mentor Books, 1957), 246.

16. See Carl Richardson's informative sketch of the 1947 debate in *New Masses* over the political objectives of semidocumentary realism in *The Naked City, Autopsy: An Element of Realism in Film Noir* (Metuchen, N.J.: Scarecrow Press, 1992), 194–206. Thom Andersen provides a detailed and politically nuanced spin on the symbolic relationship between violent crime in noir and left ideology in "Red Hollywood," in *Literature and The Visual Arts in Contemporary Society,* ed. Suzanne Ferguson and Barbara Groselose (Columbus: Ohio State University Press, 1985), esp. 169–73 and 183–91.

17. James Agee, *Agee on Film* (New York: Grosset and Dunlap, 1967), 376 and 216, respectively.

18. Ibid., 199.

19. Ibid., 238.

20. Manny Farber, *Movies* (New York: Hillstone, 1971), 62 and 13, respectively.

21. Familiar touchstones of this critical revival include: Raymond Durgnat, "Paint It Black: The Family Tree of Film Noir," *Cinema* 6–7 (1970): 49–56; Paul Schrader, "Notes on Film Noir," *Film Comment* (spring 1972): 8–13; J. A. Place and L. S. Peterson, "Some Visual Motifs of Film Noir," *Film Comment* 10, no.1 (1974); and E. Ann Kaplan, ed., *Women in Film Noir*

(London: BFI, 1978). For a summary of critical positions that connect noir to the postwar zeitgeist, see Brian Neve, "*Film Noir* and Society," *Film and Politics in America* (New York: Routledge, 1992). A notable exception to the skirting of violent themes is Lawrence Alloway, *Violent America: The Movies, 1946–1964* (New York: Museum of Modern Art, 1971). Although his study does not focus solely on noir, Alloway is the first writer to suggest that a post-war shift in Hollywood's "calibration of death" could be enumerated through Hollywood's emerging technologies of lethal confrontation (39). One goal of the present essay is to, as it were, flesh out Alloway's provocative thesis. In the interim there have been sporadic, localized accounts that are duly noted in the ensuing discussion.

22. Speaking personally, I recall quite clearly how initial retrospectives and underground screenings of noir in the early 1970s struck a responsive chord with an increasingly besieged segment of the radical protest movement via romanticized identification with the plight of noir protagonists. Indeed, I trace my impassioned interest in this work from the period in which the rebellious social energies of the 1960s began to splinter and ebb.

23. The ninety-seven-film sample employed here comes from a larger work in progress. Selection procedures stipulate crime stories of contemporary society set predominantly in industrial urban locales and engaging portions of an integral set of iconographic motifs (for example, automobiles, telephones) and narrative situations (for example, opposition of pursuit and escape, mistaken or duplicitous identity). Further, films in the sample draw from an ensemble of stylistic functions expressing tropes of fragmentation, obfuscation, and spatial containment. A handful of films fail to realize one or another of four main criteria yet otherwise comport with the general profile (for example, although *Gun Crazy* lacks a strong urban presence, it resembles the bulk of film noir at narrative, formal, and iconographic levels). As restrictive and old-fashioned as this critical approach might seem, the sample contains most of the series' canonical titles and is roughly consistent in scope with samples used in other studies: Foster Hirsch cites roughly 125 films in *The Dark Side of the Screen* (New York: A. S. Barnes, 1981); J. P. Telotte lists 150 titles in *Voices in the Dark* (Urbana: University of Illinois Press, 1989). The only exceptions to the delimitation of period are *This Gun for Hire* (1942) and *Touch of Evil* (1958).

24. In *Call Northside 777* and *Abandoned*, killings are confined to the prologue or back story.

25. See, for example, James Damico, "Film Noir: A Modest Proposal," *Film Reader* 3 (1978): 48–57.

26. Admittedly, films that commence in murder rarely involve the protagonist in the initial action; most are of the police or government investigation variety (*T-Men, Appointment with Danger*).

27. Katherine Russell provides a cogent, ambitious analysis of death as concluding narrative trope in *Narrative Mortality: Death, Closure, and New Wave Cinemas* (Minneapolis: University of Minnesota Press, 1995). Although she does not treat film noir at length as a separate enunciative category, many of her insights about Fritz Lang and postwar cinema in general are relevant to this discussion.

28. Comments about the lack of conviction or ambivalence exuded by film noir endings are already evident in the earliest French and American reviews. For our purposes what is at stake is an inability to extinguish the morbid atmosphere inscribed in story and image or, in narratological terms, seal fissures sprung in the edifice of cohesive enunciative authority. Among the most sustained and useful discussions of this issue is Dana Polan's *Power and Paranoia* (New York: Columbia University Press, 1986), esp. 30–32 and 197–208.

29. Richard Slotkin, *Gunfighter Nation* (New York: Atheneum, 1992), 612 (emphasis in the original).

30. Marc Vernet proposes a very different view of film noir openings, that they begin "with an air of quietude" from which a Proppian contract emerges between investigator and victim. Vernet, "The Filmic Transaction: On the Openings of Film Noirs," trans. David Rodowick, *The Velvet Light Trap* 20 (summer 1983): 2–9. Unfortunately, the sample of six films on which his reading is based, all made prior to 1950, is far too narrow and atypical (three involve the marginal figure of the private eye) to apply to the series as a whole.

31. Borde and Chaumeton, *Panorama du film noir*, 10.

32. For a perceptive review of postwar discourse on returning soldiers, see Polan, *Power and Paranoia*, 242–48. See also Richard Maltby, "*Film Noir*: The Politics of the Maladjusted Text," *Journal of American Studies*, no. 18 (1984): 12–16.

33. See Schindler, *Hollywood Goes to War*, 79–80. This image also appears in documentaries such as *The Battle of San Pietro* (1945), directed by noir fellow traveler John Huston. Roger Tailleur was among several early French critics discerning parallels between noir and combat films; his judgment on *Ride the Pink Horse* is exemplary: for ex-GIs, the homefront is "not markedly different from what they were fighting overseas: a realm of arbitrariness and corruption." Tailleur, "The Pink Horse or the Pipe Dreams of the Human Condition," in Palmer, *Perspectives*, 42. There is also an intriguing correspondence between the hollow-eyed visage of the grunt popularized in Bill Mauldin's newspaper cartoons and the somnambulistic presence of noir heroes.

34. Because the element of criminal violence is usually absent from 1940s melodramas concerned with the after-effects of war, it is sufficient to note here the transgeneric accumulation of morbidly self-destructive men (and occasionally women): besides the obvious landmark, *The Best Years of Our Lives* (1946), examples include *Love Letters* (1945), *Till the End of Time* (1946), *Woman on the Beach* (1947), and *A Likely Story* (1947).

35. Borde and Chaumeton, *Panorama du film noir*, 190–91. Borde and Chaumeton's diagnosis of formal or perspectival friction in noir is amplified by several later commentators' employing rather different theoretical paradigms; see, for example, Telotte, *Voices in the Dark*, 22–25.

36. For more on the occupational and class slippages of noir protagonists, see my "The Gun in the Briefcase; or, The Inscription of Class in Film Noir," in *The Hidden Foundation: Cinema and the Question of Class*, ed. David E. James and Rick Berg (Minneapolis: University of Minnesota Press, 1996).

37. William Lafferty provides a useful account of the emergence of semidocumentary practices in postwar Hollywood in "A Reappraisal of the Semi-Documentary in Hollywood, 1945–1948," *The Velvet Light Trap* 20 (summer 1983): 22–26.

38. A scrupulous overview of Chicago School urban theory and its impact on American social philosophy is found in Michael Smith, *The City and Social Theory* (New York: St. Martin's, 1979). The 1940s were a period of massive cultural interest in urbanism, with fictional as well as essayistic diagnoses vying for popular attention. One example of the popularization of academic discourse is the widely seen 1939 documentary *The City* (on which the ideas of urban historian Louis Mumford had decisive influence), whose vision of industrialized chaos in many ways anticipates formal tropes in film noir. Alongside the hard-boiled literary precedents of Hammett, Cain, Chandler, and Woolrich, an outpouring of high-bourgeois novels created a bridge between the pessimistic themes of Dreiser and Dos Passos and the work of Bellow, Malamud, Mailer, and others. In this sense the ambivalent urbanism of film noir is palpably rooted in a postwar cultural movement.

39. A familiar tendency in noir criticism is to extend or recast Borde and Chaumeton's claim of a quotidian/bizarre visual antinomy as the clash of alternative forms of narrative address. See, for example, Christine Gledhill's

notion of noir as instating a "struggle between different voices for control over [story]telling," "*Klute*: A Contemporary Film Noir and Feminist Criticism," in Kaplan, *Women in Film Noir*, 15; see also Mary Ann Doane, "*Gilda*: Epistemology as Striptease," *Camera Obscura* 11 (1983): 7–27.

40. By "pseudo-domestic" I mean spaces not designed or conventionally appropriate for conjugal activity that fugitives adopt as temporary, transient residences; two examples are the model home in *Shield for Murder* and the desert ghost town in *The Prowler*. For more on the collision between domesticity and violence, see my "No Place Like Home: City versus Suburb in Film Noir," *Aura* 6 (1998): 32–37.

41. An exacting discussion of "automobility" in noir during a period of unprecedented production and purchase of private vehicles would require a separate essay. However, it is useful here to note that more than a dozen film noirs employ the car directly as a murder weapon or site of criminal violence.

42. See Sigmund Freud, "The Uncanny," in *Studies in Parapsychology* (New York: Collier, 1963). Anthony Vidler's examination of minatory spatial representation is particularly helpful in considering the magical quality of film noir locales. Vidler, "The Architecture of the Uncanny: The Unhomely Houses of the Romantic Sublime," *Assemblage* 3 (July 1987): 7–30.

43. Georges Bataille assesses the "sacramental" nature of the murder taboo and the prohibition against the touching of corpses in, among other essays, *Erotism*, trans. Mary Dalwood (San Francisco: City Lights, 1986). A classic text on the historical concept of contamination of the living by interstitial or "unclean" entities is Mary Douglas, *Purity and Danger* (New York: Praeger, 1966).

44. For an engaging treatment of the social dimensions of urban territoriality, see Robert Gurman, ed., *People and Buildings* (New York: Basic Books, 1972); especially Barry Schwartz, "The Social Psychology of Privacy." For an overview of morbid ramifications of antiurban representation, see "From Great Town to Nonplace Urban Realm," in William Sharpe and Leonard Wallock, eds., *Visions of the Modern City* (Baltimore: Johns Hopkins, 1987), esp. 6–26.

45. Ernest Mandel, *Delightful Murder: A Social History of the Crime Story* (Minneapolis: University of Minnesota Press, 1984), 41–42.

46. Detailed analysis of several dozen violent scenes failed to yield a set of identifiable, consistent practices of editing, composition, camera movement, or lighting. It is possible that visual strategies for representing violence vary according to tendencies of particular directors or cinematographers or studios, but the exact terms of differentiation are as yet unclear. Grouping of films by production budget or year of completion proved equally elusive as indicators of stylistic patterns.

47. See Jay Livingston, *Crime and Criminology* (Upper Saddle River, N.J.: Prentice Hall, 1996), 76 and 86–87.

48. Polonsky elaborates the function of telephones in Eric Sherman and Martin Rubin, *The Director's Event* (New York: Atheneum, 1969), 132. Pascal Bonitzer makes an interesting case for the morbid implications of disembodied narrators in "The Silences of the Voice," reprinted in *Narrative, Apparatus, Ideology*, ed. Philip Rosen (New York: Columbia University Press, 1986), 320–31. Joan Copjec extends and challenges Bonitzer's ideas about the mortal play of presence and absence in: "The Phenomenal Nonphenomenal: Private Space in *Film Noir*," in *Shades of Noir*, ed. Copjec (New York: Verso, 1993).

49. In *Gunfighter Nation*, Slotkin posits the Hollywood detective film and, by extension, film noir as salient revisions of the frontier myth. While certain aspects of this foundational narrative, especially the arc of "separation and regression" by which the hero merges with a savage other (11–14), may help elucidate patterns of descent into the criminal underworld, the resort to vio-

lence in noir is neither temporary nor delimited in its performance or consequences. Most important, violence is not resolved affirmatively as a necessary stage in individual or collective advancement, as Slotkin's model would dictate.

50. There is a growing body of work on film noir and urbanism whose touchstone is Mike Davis, *City of Quartz* (New York: Verso, 1990). See also Frank Krutnik, "Something More than Night: Tales of the *Noir* City," in *The Cinematic City*, ed. David B. Clarke (New York: Routledge, 1997); Edward Dimendberg, "From Berlin to Bunker Hill: Urban Space, Late Modernity, and Film Noir in Fritz Lang's and Joseph Losey's *M*," *Wide Angle* 19, no. 4 (October 1997): 63–93; Paul Arthur, "L.A. as Scene of the Crime," *Film Comment* 32, no. 4 (July–August 1996): 20–27.

51. Journalist John Hersey's *Hiroshima*, first circulated as a 1946 essay in the *New Yorker* then converted into a best-selling book and popular radio play, is an important landmark in the mass cultural dissemination of nuclear horror.

52. One of the clearest and best studies of the discursive struggles between postwar city and suburb is Kenneth T. Jackson, *Crabgrass Frontier* (New York: Oxford University Press, 1985), esp. 190–245.

53. The two best-known examinations of the cultural imagination of nuclear disaster are Paul Boyer, *By the Bomb's Early Light* (New York: Pantheon, 1985); and Spencer Weart, *Nuclear Fear* (Cambridge, Mass.: Harvard University Press, 1988). In *Hiroshima in America* (New York: Avon, 1995), Robert J. Lifton and Greg Mitchell argue that "Hollywood, no less than the press, served the official narrative" of nuclear warfare and in doing so contributed to a larger cultural process by which the realities of Hiroshima "sank, unconfronted and unresolved, into deeper recesses" of American culture (368). Although they look at films such as *Dr. Strangelove* (1963) as displaced expressions of nuclear guilt (372) they fail to consider films in which issues of atomic anxiety and guilt are even further displaced, as in the case of film noir.

54. Among the many postwar film types that in certain respects parallel or overlap with film noir, a group of thrillers (*The Third Man*) and problem films (*The Search*) set amid the devastation of European cities echo many of noir's iconographic motifs.

55. Ellul is cited in Burton Pike, *The Image of the City in Modern Literature* (Princeton, N.J.: Princeton University Press, 1981), 5.

violence in the film western

lee clark mitchell

No other popular genre asks what it means to be a man so assiduously as the Western does, which helps explain why violence is one of that genre's central features. In a given decade, of course, Westerns resolve (or fail to resolve) the same range of cultural issues that energize other popular genres—from alarm over adolescent rebellion, to consternation at changing labor patterns, to anxieties about foreign policy (and so on; the list is endless). But the Western's obsession with violence grows out of a larger fascination with what is now termed the construction of masculinity. To be a man, at least as the Western understands it, requires not only a distinctively male body but certain learned, appropriately male skills as well. Manhood, that is, forms as much a culturally conditioned experience as a blunt biological process. And the Western's characteristic eruption of violence occurs as a testing of both these assumptions—both the body that must recover its masculine features (tall in the saddle, quick on the draw) and the characteristic male response celebrated by the Western (restraint, taciturnity, endurance). Violence is the means by which men are encouraged to show their manliness, both as handsome cinematic figures that rivet the viewer's gaze, and as individuals capable of triumphing over adversity as only men are allowed to do. Unlike any other genre, then, Westerns oscillate between the conditions of sex and gender—between an essentialism that requires the flamboyant display of a male physique and a constructivism that grants manhood to men by virtue of behavior rather than bodies.

Violence in the Western begins, as it must, with the hero's body, where attention is closely paid to physical features, costumed appearance, and upright stance. The frequency with which the body is celebrated, then punished, only to convalesce, suggests something of the paradox involved in making true men out of biological men, taking their male bodies and distorting them beyond the power of self-control so that in the course of recuperation a masculinity can be revealed that is at once physical yet based on performance. In short, the Western is invariably pitched toward an exhibition of manly restraint, thereby requiring the proof of generic excess in the form of repeated violence. The first step in this process, and the basis on which everything else rests, is the body of the Western hero, situated always at center frame.

From the beginning, Western stars have been celebrated for their physical attractiveness—for clear eyes, strong chins, handsome faces, and virile bodies over which the camera lingers to disclose what it is that contributes to self-restraint. This self-conscious revelation of character through the body is parodied wittily in Mel Brooks's *Blazing Saddles* (1974), when the camera introduces the newly appointed Sheriff Bart (Cleavon Little) by focusing in close-up first on his embroidered Gucci saddle, then (to the accompaniment of nondiegetic big band music) sliding up slowly from his pearl-handled holster past his open suede shirt to his brightly smiling, handsome face. Riding away from the camera, he passes Count Basie at a white grand piano directing his orchestra. Bending from the saddle to shake Basie's hand, Sheriff Bart continues riding over the distant high plains, followed by the camera.

Not only are we allowed to gaze at men in Westerns, this gaze forms such an essential aspect of the genre that it seems covertly about just that: looking at men. To state the issue so starkly, however, suggests how problematic that process has been, and it is no surprise that the hesitations, distortions, and evasions that accompany this male-centered "look" are customarily interpreted as a deep-seated nervousness about homoeroticism. But if so, that is only part of the story. I'd like to argue instead that this concentration on male physiques feeds a broader cultural longing for renewal, which occurs in a special landscape (the American West) because that landscape is associated with personal transformation. Becoming a man (conventionally expressed as doing "what a man's gotta do") has been such a tired cliché of the Western that it hardly warrants comment. Yet this banal tag line of gender identity is tied up in the Western's focus of our gaze on the male body—a body that must be beaten, distorted, pressed out of shape so that it can paradoxically become what it already is.

The American West is thus associated with crucial transformations to an untransformed body—as if the West and only the West were a place where manhood might at last emerge yet still remain what it always was. The West is of course the region identified by Frederic Jackson Turner as the reason Americans became American, furnishing "a new field of opportunity, a gate of escape from the bondage of the past." A new society had resulted from the opportunities wrought by "conditions of frontier life," with countless experiences of individual renewal contributing to a new national character. Yet what is striking about the Western (which appeared just as the frontier closed, and as feminism gained political strength) is the way the West is associated quite specifically with masculinity. Indeed, the genre's delight in the male physique duplicates its affectionate lingering over a fantastic landscape we have come to recognize as "the Far West," a landscape defined as "western" by the absence of familiar signs encoded as female—the pastures, fields, farms, and more obviously schoolyards, church steeples, and store-window displays that signal the domestication of space. Of course, different films represent masculinity in different ways, and do so over the decades through the potential represented in quite disparate settings. As Homer Bannon (Melvyn Douglas) remarks in Arthur Penn's *Hud* (1962), "Little by little the look of the country changes because of the men we admire." The autochthonous Western hero coalesces out of the landscape and continues to be closely identified with it in whatever changing form Western films represent, whether the austere, dusty streets of Charles Swickard's *Hell's Hinges* (1916), or the Monument Valley grandiosity of John Ford's 7th Cavalry trilogy, or the nostalgically verdant Wyoming of George Stevens's *Shane* (1952), or the rain-sodden miasma of Robert Altman's *McCabe and Mrs. Miller* (1971). In short, the varying and violent conditions involved in constructing oneself as a man in film Westerns are intimately linked to a landscape that defines the essential attributes of what it is to be a man.

Just Looking?

Observers have from the beginning delighted in the picturesqueness of the cowboy, who depends more on specialized garb than almost any other modern worker. His dress is so conventional, in fact, that it has become a sort of language, signaling moral and emotional stature (the excess of two guns versus the restraint of one, or the contrasting claims made by fringe, silk, leather, and silver). As well, however, the cowboy's sign-laden costume permits the eye to roam across the male body without seeming to focus on that body as actual flesh. In Western films, the eye is trapped and held up by fetish items associated with parts of the body, as our gaze is directed from eyes, chins, chests, legs, and muscle groups to articles instead that either cover or exaggerate them. Hats of assorted shapes and tilts (few of the proverbial ten-gallon variety); handkerchiefs knotted round the neck; ornate buckles, gun belts worn low, and, of course, an array of holsters and six-shooters; pearl-buttoned shirts, fringed jackets; leather gloves carefully fitted and as carefully stripped off; leggings, chaps (with the groin area duly uncovered and framed), and tight-fitting Levi's or leather pants (in the only genre that allows men to wear them); long, stylized linen dusters; pointed, high-heeled boots and spurs: all the way up and down, the cowboy's costume invites and deflects our gaze.

Reinforcing this wavering response is the cowboy hero's self-presentation. For despite a calculated attention to costume and flamboyant self-presentation, the most notable aspect of his performance is the effort to maintain an inexpressive persona. Self-preening vies with self-effacement, exhibitionism with restraint, as the visual busyness of his demeanor is balanced by vocal inactivity, a sonic stillness that regularly offers a nearly physical pause in the narrative line (think of the narrative clefts registered by the stony faces of Gary Cooper, Alan Ladd, or Clint Eastwood). So entirely self-contained is the later Western hero that he seems to exist beyond the everyday commonplaces of talk and explanation, of persuasion, argument, indeed beyond conversation altogether. Valuing action over words, marking silence as the most vivid of actions, the cowboy hero throws us back onto the male physique, shifting attention from ear to eye in the drama of masculinity. Such an extreme laconic tic forms something of an ambivalent trait—a matter of knowing when to be silent but also an inability to make oneself known.

The restraint worn by the Western hero as part of his sign-laden costume sharply distinguishes him from other men—indeed, requires the distinction of others whose lack of restraint provides a foil to the true man's achieved coherence. Talking too much or laughing easily or expressing fear too readily are more than signs of bad form; they reveal an inability to maintain composure under the pressure of vivid sensation. And in the recurrent enactment of such scenes of emotional excess, the Western offers a silhouette that helps construct its shadow image. The exemplary instance of such inadequate men occurs in George Marshall's *Destry Rides Again* (1939), with Mischa Auer's performance as Boris "Callahan" Stavrogin, the man garrulously unable to decide "what to do, what to do" as he loses his pants in poker to Frenchy (Marlene Dietrich). Up to the end he even fails to be called by his own name, referred to instead (despite eye-rolling objections) by the name of his wife's first husband, Callahan. A similar role was played that same year by Donald Meek in *Stagecoach* (1939), as the whiskey drummer Samuel Peacock, whose name and profession no one remembers in the face of patient, repeated reminders. His obvious fear of being scalped, despite a gleaming bald pate, is played as a broad comic gag. This role of marginalized man defined by hypersensitivity, social affectation, and verbal exorbitance was represented by Walter Brennan in countless roles later in his career—as the sometimes limping, invariably toothless, always interfering friend who talks or drinks too much, in Howard Hawks's *Red River* (1948) as in Anthony Mann's *The Far Country* (1954). He enacts not so much the failed man (a role more properly defined by the villain) as an unworkable combination of masculinity and feminine excess.

Further helping to trace this silhouette of masculinity is the frequency with which the town drunk stumbles through the Western. And the stakes seem significantly higher when the drunkard is a figure of education or expertise—a doctor, say, or newspaper editor, or even a former sheriff. It is as if the rationale behind such figures of complex talents was that, unlike the hero, they fail to control their desires. Again, these professional derelicts appear most notably in *Stagecoach* and *Destry Rides Again*: Thomas

Mitchell's Doc Boone and Charles Winninger's Sheriff "Wash" Dimsdale. Driven downward by oral compulsions into ever more drunkenly reclining postures, these figures of excess are posed against the upright hero, who, in a scene multiplied countlessly in saloons across the fictional West, declines a whiskey, or orders a soda pop, or accepts a glass of milk. By withstanding the censure of a saloon full of drinkers, the hero confirms a claim on our attentions as a figure of restraint set against the chaos of non-men.

If such barroom scenes display human foils foregrounding the true man, they also dramatize the cowboy hero's sense of being watched, of creating himself as a man in a self-consciously social process. That self-construction requires him continually to observe himself, controlling behavior in a world where desire so easily leads to social disorder. The irony is that restraint can only be demonstrated through narratives of excess, since restraint takes shape as a capacity only by contrast with surrounding conditions. Without plots in which restraint can be marched out and displayed—without scenes in which this supposedly masculine virtue can be needled into action, revealed in its strength, strained to the breaking point—the blankness of the hero's countenance expresses only blankness, not the deliberateness of prudent intention or the saving power of self-control. That is the reason the villain presents the Western hero with a dramatic foil, since they share the same skills and invariably value a similar style of self-presentation. In fact, the major difference between the two has less to do with honor or ethical standing (the issues usually adduced) than with an ability to resist giving way to inner desires and outer coercions. Under the pressure of easy money, bodily pain, or adverse odds, villains simply give in. As skilled as the heroes they confront, they fall short of being true men by refusing to suffer in silence. In the long succession of notable villains that extends from, say, Trampas (Walter Huston) in Victor Fleming's *The Virginian* (1929) to Little Bill Daggett (Gene Hackman) in Clint Eastwood's *Unforgiven* (1992), restraint is ever disdained as a suitable response to a violent world.

Of course, scenes of violence are highlighted in other genres as much as in Westerns, though not primarily to provide us with conditions for self-definition. In the Western, violence poses less a social or moral dilemma than an emotional one. Even Robert Warshow, who first addressed the genre's ethical status, found himself drawn (as if despite himself) to this strange conclusion. In a powerful declaration, he claimed that the Western "offers a serious orientation to the problem of violence such as can be found almost nowhere else in our culture," and that in "acknowledg[ing] the value of violence," the Western helps us understand moral terms by which violence might ever be exercised. Yet then, in an apparent about-face, he went on to argue that

> it is not violence at all which is the "point" of the Western movie, but a certain image of man, a style, which expresses itself most clearly in violence. Watch a child with his toy guns and you will see: what most interests him is not (as we so much fear) the fantasy of hurting others, but to work out how a man might look when he shoots or is shot. A hero is one who looks like a hero.[1]

Violence in the Western, in other words, is less means than end in itself—less a matter of violating another than of constituting one's physical self as a male. The purpose is less defeat or destruction than (once again) display. And if this celebration of violence confirms it as a masculine prerogative (that is, as an activity released and controlled by men), it does so by putting the male body distinctively on display. The shoot-outs, brawls, and scenes of horse taming, the shots of riding herd as well as assorted Indian chases—each compels a man to exhibit broad shoulders and narrow waist, allowing us again to gaze at masculinity in action.

A Man Being Beaten

Given such a celebration of the male physique, it may seem surprising that violence so often destroys that body, especially since it is one of the Western's chief reasons for being. Throughout, there is an almost obsessive recurrence of scenes of men being beaten—or knifed and whipped, propped up, knocked down, kicked in the side, punched in the face, or otherwise lacerated, clubbed, battered, and tortured into unconsciousness. Countless films attest to the importance of beating scenarios in the Western's construction of masculinity, offering a vast panorama of sado-masochism that leads to even more protracted displays of the hero's convalescence. That process is usually initiated by a fistfight or brawl in settings where the primary energy of male violence can be dramatically inflated. By stepping up the volume, adding strong (often excessive) nondiegetic music to the soundtrack, and relying upon elaborate camera angles, films convert even fistfights into apocalyptic events, as though the process of assaulting bodies were being recast into realms (of sound, vision, music) having nothing to do with them. In Fred Zinnemann's *High Noon* (1952), Will Kane (Gary Cooper) is assaulted in the town's stable by his deputy, Harvey Pell (Lloyd Bridges). According to Carl Foreman's screenplay (in which Kane was originally named Doane):

> They punish each other mercilessly, nothing barred. The horses, becoming nervous, rear and whinny in their stalls. . . . Once, Doane is knocked down under a horse, and narrowly escapes being trampled. As the fight reaches a climax, the horses go completely wild. . . . Doane stands over him, panting and dazed . . . his breath whistling through his bruised lips.

What Foreman's screenplay cannot suggest is how disproportionately loud the horses' whinnying becomes or how aggressively the sequence of camera angles shifts from beneath horses to high corner angles and back again. Nor can it capture the bruised countenance of Gary Cooper on which the camera lingers as he trudges off to the emotionally overwrought, mildly feminized barber to be washed and brushed. His haggard expression (prompted, as we otherwise know, by chronic back problems, a recent hernia operation, and a painful ulcer) is at once cause and effect of his beaten state—part of the Oedipal reason why Harvey Pell feels the need to assault him (thereby, destroying the father-figure) and yet as well the direct physical consequence of that assault. The filming of such beating and recovery scenes, moreover, makes us strangely aware of the makeup artist—breaking us out of film consciousness at the very moment Cooper reclines in the barber chair, prompting us to think, "Ah, now, he's sitting in the makeup chair, waiting to be reconstructed." Self-consciously alerted to how well the wounds have been created, how easily their erasure is effected, we realize again how fully manhood is always already there, just beneath the plaster and paint.

In *Shane* (1953), George Stevens presents Alan Ladd in a pair of exaggerated brawls: the first provoked by Chris Calloway (Ben Johnson) in Grafton's saloon; the second by Joe Starrett (Van Heflin) in his own stable yard. The cinematography of both scenes relies on camera placement under animals, over swinging doors, through windows, and behind stairs, while the soundtrack is so singularly heightened that it seems like the world is coming unglued. That is the point of these hyperbolic fights, to shatter the seamless surface of masculinity by destroying the expressionless eyes and vacant glance that confirm Alan Ladd's mysteriousness. The film itself draws attention to that narrative pattern in the convalescence scene in which Marian (Jean Arthur) bandages his head, when for the sake of Joey (Brandon de Wilde) he breaks out in a (self-consciously faked, entirely uncharacteristic) expression of pain.

Other examples are rife: *Red River* presents Matthew Garth (Montgomery Clift) brawling fiercely with his foster-father, Tom Dunson (John Wayne)—a scene so dramatically powerful and at the same time so derivative that Howard Hughes successfully sued United Artists for having "copied" it from the final shoot-out of *The Outlaw* (produced 1943, released 1950). In Tom Gries's *Will Penny* (1967), the titular hero (Charlton Heston) is beaten, knifed, burned, and left for dead. Having crawled back across the winter landscape in long underwear, he finally returns to his cabin, where Catherine Allen (Joan Hackett) nurses him in a series of prolonged scenes over many days, stitching him up, bathing him, making him soup. Just as vivid is the Rojo gang's prolonged beating of the Man with No Name (Clint Eastwood) in Sergio Leone's *A Fistful of Dollars* (1964): blood trickles down his cheek, his right eye swells shut, his ribs are repeatedly kicked, his bruised hand is cruelly stepped on, and he falls unconscious. The film later tracks a painful escape as he crawls under a long boardwalk, climbs into an unfinished coffin, and is then carried out of town. Slowly, in an abandoned mine as his wounds heal, he rebuilds his strength and recovers his shooting skills.

An even more spectacular instance of abuse to the male body occurs in Marlon Brando's *One-Eyed Jacks* (1960), a strangely psychological Western that traces once again an Oedipal conflict between the Ringo Kid (Brando) and his former partner, "Dad" Longworth (Karl Malden). The paternalistic sheriff Longworth punishes Ringo in the film's central scene by lashing him to the town's hitching post, then brutally bull-whipping him before smashing a rifle down on his gun hand. Throughout, Brando remains expressionless, and even as he slips to his knees, his body retains its dignity while the camera lingers on a smooth face and unblinking eyes that stay characteristically untransformed. The rest of the film traces his slow recovery on the Monterey coast, as his lacerated back is nursed by the quiet, loyal, feminized Mexican friend, Chico Morelles (Timothy Gilman). Finally able to fit a leather thong to his gun hand, he practices shooting for long hours in preparation for revenge. The film, however, swerves from generic demands played out in Rio's brooding thoughts of revenge, as he finds his love for Longworth's step-daughter gradually transforming him. What betrays this newly pacific intention is his rejuvenated body itself, as if he could not prevent himself from carrying out the revenge against Longworth his body has so long demanded, despite a change in emotions that has finally committed him to a peaceful life.

Most clearly exposing the dynamics of the Western is Ford's *The Man Who Shot Liberty Valance* (1962). Its flashback sequence opens with Ransom Stoddard (Jimmy Stewart) being violently flogged by Valance (Lee Marvin), reduced to the same corpselike state that Tom Doniphon (John Wayne) maintains in the frame narrative. As in *One-Eyed Jacks*, the film highlights Stoddard's convalescence (at the hands of Hallie [Vera Miles]), but only to attain the status of aproned dishwasher, tripped up by Valance. Stoddard appears ever a victim of gravity, bent over, crouching, prone to fall, in a posture of feminized vulnerability that contrasts starkly with the erect bearing of Tom and Hallie. The film offers a sustained meditation on the Western's devotion to violation and recovery, in the process of preparing Stoddard for the genre's most clichéd scene of manly self-possession. And his final, limp-wristed confrontation with Valance ends in what seems an improbable triumph enforced by nothing more than sheer generic demands (the sequence of beating and recovery itself requiring a scene of physical mastery). It is Ford's ironic double perspective that masterfully attests to the impossibility yet necessity of manhood's recovery against all odds—a sequence central to the Western.

Necrology

If violence has always been central to the Western's construction of masculinity, more recent cinematic examples suggest a change in the genre's test of restraint, since by the 1960s beatings no longer confirm the hero's commitment to a set of moral values. Ford's exposure of the hypocrisy of physical violence in *Liberty Valance* can be seen as part of a transition from the morally stalwart heroes of *Shane* and *Red River* to the morally vacant spaghetti Westerns and violence-laden films of the 1970s. Indeed, in these later films all that clearly distinguishes the hero from other characters is emotional detachment—a style that seems like nothing so much as death itself, with the hero's body become a corpse, as motionless and stark as desert landscape. In particular, Sergio Leone's "reign of violence" strips character down in scenes of walking dead, in which individuals seem to come alive only once they have been shot (and either cry out or are seen to twitch), released at last into a realm where movement and vitality are once again feasible. Clint Eastwood's mechanical performance as No Name clearly parodies the genre's mysterious hero, with animation erased from his features so thoroughly that he seems deprived of life altogether. Throughout *A Fistful of Dollars*, Leone invokes the idea of the living dead as automatons, as dolls or puppets that mimic the actions of living beings—an idea that always implies something invisible animating and standing behind (whether magician, puppeteer, or God). And in this, the first of his influential spaghetti Westerns, Leone intimates that past Westerns become the master puppeteers, breathing life into dead forms, lending the illusion once again (even as that illusion is being spoofed) that Western heros are ruggedly independent, self-motivating, self-reliant individuals. Antique conventions seem, however hackneyed, to develop a life of their own, even as Leone simultaneously suggests that that appearance of vitality is nothing more than an illusion—if one of the last now available to the Western.

The parodic success of spaghetti Westerns lies in revealing how the genre regularly relies on some version of the living dead (even if characters have not always been so corpselike). The theme is nowhere better expressed than in *A Fistful of Dollars*, when No Name explains his ruse to Silvanito (Pepe Calvo) in propping up dead soldiers: "The dead can be very useful sometimes. They've helped me out of tough spots more than once. First, they don't talk. Second, they can be made to look alive if I manage it right. And third, well third, if you shot 'em there's no worry because they're dead already. Understand?" In fact, Silvanito does not understand and is openly shocked by the notion.

Oddly, however, the Western itself operates in roughly this way, tirelessly resuscitating caricatures into characters, reachieving a hold on our imaginations by revitalizing dead clichés, taking figures who "don't talk" and making them "look alive if you manage it right." Silvanito's response to this pronouncement reveals his own insufficient understanding of the way the genre has always worked: "It doesn't make a bit of sense to me, and I'm getting out. I'm alive, and I want to remain with the living, understand? And when I'm dead, I want to remain with the dead and I would be unhappy if somebody living forces me to remain with the living." The Western, on the contrary, has always celebrated a certain necrological impulse, verging ever on the edges of death, invoking violence only to show how the restrained, fetish-laden body is not to be deprived of life but made to stand as a desirable emblem of masculinity, as a self-contained, animated (if finally inanimate) object. The process of beating the hero can thus be thought of as a kind of artificial respiration, raising his temperature and bringing a bloom to his cheek—even if that "bloom" is blood on the surface rather than just beneath. And what occurs as convalescence in earlier Westerns now appears more ambiguously, as the hero "convalesces" back into the white-cheeked, frozen-faced image of death.[2]

184

Normally, recovery consists in reestablishing the hero's identification with whatever natural setting he inhabits, making him once again at home in the wilderness, familiar with its laws, capable of thriving in conditions that others find oppressive. Mastering the space around him fully as much as he does his horse, he nonetheless realizes how little mastery he actually exerts over either animal or setting, living in an intimate relationship that often defies any distinction of one from the other. To be a man, as the genre has it, is to be at one with terrain yet able to rise above it. The interconnections between landscape description and character portrayal are so closely aligned, in fact, that gender becomes a matter of defining the body vis-à-vis the earth. Narrative must ever work out the limits of masculinity by defining those who align themselves with the landscape (emerging from it, respecting its powers) against those others who simply submit to it (lying down, being put in the ground).

This link between landscape and death recurs most compellingly in the Western as a process of bodies returned to their source, forced back into the landscape from which they emerged. Such a motif helps explain the ubiquity of cemeteries in the cinematic West, as settings for the numerous funerals and burials that punctuate its narratives. Each town has its own Boot Hill not simply because violent times require it, when men who die with their boots on must be buried. Other genres, after all, are just as violent without evincing a similar regard for the recently deceased (spy movies, say, in which bodies disappear; or detective novels, in which the bodies stay inexorably put; or war movies, in which bodies simply pile up). Even in a genre like the gangster film, in which lavish funerals occur, the rituals of death confer no dignity upon the "dearly departed." By contrast, the measuring for a rude coffin, the digging of a grave, the lowering of a body into the ground, the solemn reading of a few verses, the depiction of mourners standing speechless or singing a hymn off-key, the slow turning away at last—all are part of a ceremony as central to the Western as the shoot-out or the lynching.

The more specific, gendered reason for this obsession with acknowledging death is that it serves as a liminal marker in the construction of masculine identity. After all, the hero always convalesces from his body's disfiguration, and even Leone's living dead man ultimately rises from the ground. But the process of putting bodies into the ground reminds us of what it is the hero risks and in the process reveals a key distinction between his sometimes deathlike mask and the actual fact of death itself. This distinction illuminates the frequency of cemeteries in Westerns, since they counterpoint the fetishized physique of the cowboy, identifying that signal instance when the body's supreme moment of cold self-restraint has become nothing more than rigor mortis.

From this perspective, it is clear that Western heroes are knocked down, made supine, then variously tortured so that they can recover from harm in order to rise again. Or rather, the process of beating occurs so that we can see men recover, regaining their strength and resources in the process of once again making themselves into men. The paradox lies in the fact that we watch them become what they already are, as we exult in the culturally encoded confirmation of a man again becoming a man. On the one hand, the genre advertises itself as committed to an essentialist ideology, showing how men are always already there, biologically fixed by the accident of genitals. Gender is repeatedly extolled as somehow natural and unchanging, often via an exchange between characters who defend the notion of conventional, supposedly hereditary roles for men and women. From this perspective, men (like women) are historically found, not culturally made, and even if they happen not to live up to inner potential, that potential is never in doubt. On the other hand, Westerns depend upon means that everywhere expose this ideology, relying on plots that demand instead the creation of manhood, then its re-creation. That ongoing process draws into question the assumption everywhere else reinforced—that a "man's man" always exists before the effect of cultural processes are seen.

"The Value of Violence" and the 1960s

Beginning in the 1960s, Westerns became more self-conscious about the beating scenarios that form so central a part of the genre. The decade saw the emergence of violence everywhere in popular culture rendered more explicitly than ever before, and rendered as gratuitous, irrational, unjustifiable behavior. During this same period, the Western's traditional emphasis on "the value of violence" came under scrutiny from Leone and even more from Sam Peckinpah, whose *The Wild Bunch* (1969) at once revives the traditional descriptive possibilities of the genre and nullifies conventions in its narrative content, through the venal motives of his "heroes," their vulgar behavior, and so on. This combination allowed Peckinpah to challenge the Western's persistent obfuscation of issues it had always engaged, by exposing the bad-faith gesture in the genre's conventional solicitation of violence. The very opening moments of *The Wild Bunch* deliver this challenge through the visual deception that allows the viewer to assume the Bunch are genuine American troops, until Pike Bishop finally barks a command at the end of the opening credits: "If they move, kill 'em." That eerily unofficial tone confounds our projected sympathy, as does his subsequent order about a railroad official caught in the bank: "When I kick him out, blast 'em. We'll make a run for it." The ensuing massacre—in which a woman is trampled, a sousaphone player killed, and innocent citizens wounded and maimed—disorients us, arresting the process of identification. And the rest of the scene compounds that perplexity in the squalid brutality of everyone else, whether callous bounty hunters gratuitously killing whoever happens to move, or a ruthless official ordering the massacre with no thought to public safety, or arrogant townspeople lured into a dangerous voyeurism. The later discovery that the whole was an ambush planned by Harrigan, a railroad official, and that the Bunch had succeeded in stealing nothing more than bags of washers, only underscores the scene's ghastly futility.

In contrast to the gently parodic tone of many of Leone's opening scenes, Peckinpah mounts a violent assault on the viewer, with psychological mayhem expressed through a combination of deep-focus long shots, telephoto close-ups, slow-motion sequences, and flash cuts lasting less than a second. *The Wild Bunch* has more edits than any other Hollywood film ever made, with 3,642 individual cuts in the original uncut version, some of only three and four frames (compared to 600 cuts for the average two-hour film of the period).[3] Editing is keyed not to physical events but to viewers' emotions, with a heartbeat pounding through the soundtrack, swelling gradually louder as the pulse speeds up. Especially at peak moments of violence, Peckinpah orchestrates fragments of scenes, intercutting them to suggest an incoherent immediacy—as in the slow-motion fall of an outlaw through a window, interrupted by nine other shots of random violence before he hits the ground. This "ballet of death" has the curious effect of making the viewer aware that the Western's justification of violence in terms of masculinity has always been suspect. As Peckinpah shows, the Western's secret desire has always been for violence—justified if possible, but violence nonetheless.

This point is rendered explicit by the forceful placement of the initial scene, assaulting the viewer as much by that opening status as by its studied choreography of violence. Here, Peckinpah radically inverts one of the genre's oldest conventions, which dictates that even necessary violence be a last resort, deferred long enough to allow peaceful alternatives to be imagined. And the reason for breaching that rule of deferral is to expose the rule's actual effect, which is less to encourage the impulse toward pacifism than to grant time to savor the imminence of violence that everyone knows will come. Philip French has noted this effect as it operates in even more pacific Westerns:

> Incipient violence, too, determines the structure of *High Noon*. As the clock ticks inexorably towards the final encounter, the actual scenes of physical confrontation—one fistfight, one shootout—occupy about five minutes of the picture. This very sparing use of action is dramatically admirable, and possibly socially responsible, yet it has the effect . . . of almost making the audience *will* the violence upon the characters involved.[4]

This narrative pattern emerges repeatedly in the most successful texts, making it difficult for modern audiences to watch such classics as *Stagecoach* and *Shane* in their steady deferral of the violence they solicit. William Wellman most notably anticipated this technique in *The Ox-Bow Incident* (1941), in which long conversations postpone action, eliciting a tacit desire from the viewer for the violent solution being condemned—all as a means of granting a sense of how virulent mob psychology can be, and how irrepressible.

While the unusual level of Peckinpah's cinematic violence has frequently been remarked, then, as important to its significance is that it comes so soon, flouting expectations for how violence should be unleashed in the Western. Not even Leone quite did this, though the possibility is acknowledged in *For a Few Dollars More* (1967) when a distant, whistling rider is inexplicably shot from his horse as part of the precredit sequence. Peckinpah's films raised the stakes of that agenda by imaginatively engaging a question usually relegated to narrative need: how often, how explicitly, how creatively should cinematic violence be invoked, and to what thematic end? When, that is, is violence merely gratuitous and when essential to issues at the heart of the genre?

The climax of the film's violence in General Mapache's slashing of Angel's throat is followed by a long, dramatic pause after the Bunch shoots Mapache, realizing they have "done it." When Pike Bishop then opens fire on the German advisor, the anticlimax of the massacre commences, as individuals are decimated by machine-gun fire, slit by sabers, riddled with bullets. It was this scene that led to the awarding of the first R rating for a Western, yet as David A. Cook has written, the issue was less one of violence per se than its vivid representation. Peckinpah was for the first time in the Western simply being self-conscious about what was at stake:

> As with *Bonnie and Clyde*, the violence of *The Wild Bunch was* revolutionary, *was* excessive for its time. . . . Their films introduced conventions for the depiction of violence and carnage which others exploited ad nauseam in the seventies. But both directors insisted for the first time in American cinema that the human body is made of real flesh and blood; that arterial blood spurts rather than drips demurely; that bullet wounds leave not trim little pinpricks but big, gaping holds; and, in general, that violence has painful, unpretty, humanly destructive consequences.[5]

Lucien Ballard's extraordinary photography of the final scene, with multiple cameras running at different speeds, edited by Peckinpah even more intricately than the opening massacre, assaults the viewer accustomed to sanitized and straightforward representations of violence. Even today, the film elicits an intense visceral response.

Yet few have thought to question not simply the explicitness of the violence or its cinematic "aestheticizing" by Ballard—topics that have clearly influenced imitators and viewers ever since—but the way in which the larger framing structure of *The Wild Bunch* itself compels a reconsideration of "the value of violence" in the Western. After the unsettling logic of the opening scene is clear, in other words—that those on either side of the law are equally callow and brutal—then any genuine moral distinctions among Harrigan, Mapache, the bounty hunters, or the Bunch seem simply invidious. We may side with the Bunch against the "they" ironically invoked by Freddy Sykes (Edmund O'Brien)—"Who the hell is *they*?"—but that is only for lack of any other figures with whom to identify. The world seems askew in this and other films of the 1960s, not only because no social structure is imagined capable of setting things right but also because individual morality is clearly deficient. The Western as a form appears incapable of coping with social problems it is asked to resolve, and one of its central premises—that violence is legitimate in certain circumstances, when all else fails—is gradually undone through its own excess.

In short, the two major modern practitioners of the genre share a deep ambivalence about its continuing narrative power, apparent in the self-consciousness of their films as Western films. For successful as both films are on their own terms, they also speak to the end of an era, making it difficult to know how the genre might be renegotiated and revived. In both, violence has been so split off from its traditional function as a legitimate "value"—with action reduced to little more than a passing frisson—that it is hard to imagine successors being able to have a similar striking effect, to move imaginatively beyond these directors in reinventing (rather than simply repeating) a newly revived genre. Michael Cimino's *Heaven's Gate* (1980) and Eastwood's *Unforgiven* were each the most prominent Westerns in their decades, and yet the failure of the one and the success of the other say less about the genre than the fact that neither one finds a way to transform traditional materials into something other than simply a repetition of older forms. Those earlier films that had been influential in keeping the genre alive invariably provoked a renewed consideration of the "value of violence" in the making of manhood, all within a freshly conceived western landscape and a clear set of codes. That violence, in a contemporary climate of action adventure films and postmodern pastiches, is celebrated simply for its own sake, means that the Western may well have no room to develop. In a time when screen violence has become ever more explicit and pervasive, it is hard to conceive how violent moments might be redeemed in the construction of masculinity—something the finest Westerns have always managed to do imaginatively.

Violence in the Western has never existed for itself but rather as a means of raising the question of whether a man's face and body constitute little more than a gendered mask, in need of being destroyed and reshaped to confirm that manhood exists beneath. The Western requires that masculine identity be pressed out of shape, initially deformed so as to make the "man" all but unrecognizable. Or more accurately (given the way in which masculinity itself has been constituted through the body), Westerns treat the hero as a rubber doll, something to be wrenched and contorted so that we can then watch him magically recover his shape. His convalescence reassures us in the reachievement of a form we had presumed to be static, somehow inorganic. The whole dramatic process reveals how the cherished image of masculinity we had dismissed as simply learned behavior is in fact a resilient, vital, biological process. Stretching of the body proves the body's natural essence, and all the leather, spurs, chaps, pistols, handkerchiefs, and hats may now be excused as dead talismans. In this, they are a kind of fetish to the highest power, since they "hide" a male body that has proved itself coherent. The compensatory satisfaction they offer is no longer really necessary since the physique they disguise has revealed itself as unmistakably male.

Yet the contradiction of the Western is that masculinity is always more than physical, and that in favoring an ideal of restraint well beyond bodily considerations the Western reveals how manhood is as much learned as found. Restraint, of course, is essential to our most fundamental ideals of selfhood even as it poses a concept difficult to represent. The Western therefore signals restraint always through the body, in its vacillations and hesitations under the threat of danger—in eyes alerted to peril, or shoulders stiffened against a verbal slight, or the gesture of a hand hovering over a gunbelt. Before restraint can be said to exist dramatically, in other words, it needs to be needled, stretched, otherwise exacerbated by the continuing threat of violence.

Our fascination with the Western is over those supposedly masculine forms we want to recognize as biologically fixed—forms the Western presents through scenes that can only be read on the contrary as bringing the biological into question. Of course, any balance between culture and biology is always being renegotiated, as each generation parses out what it assumes to be learned or natural behavior in the construction of race, class, ethnic, and especially gender relations. More recently, that balance would seem to have tipped away from biology toward culture, which may help explain the waning of the Western's popularity. But however true this may be, the tension between cultural and biological determinants remains central for a genre that thrives on the paradox expressed in the amount of effort it takes to remain a man, whether Shane or Hondo or even the Man with No Name—the amount of work invested in reshaping the body, relearning the skills, honing the image, mastering once again the terms of restraint. That is the reason for the recurrent narrative pattern of imperiling the body to watch it convalesce, a pattern reinforcing our ambivalent sense that masculinity has as much in common with physical therapy, say, or bodybuilding as it does with breathing or giving birth—is as much, that is, a distinct cultural effect as it is a natural cause or biological imperative.

More specifically, we come to realize how fully silence is a sovereign condition not simply and passively assumed but arduously achieved—or likewise, how restraint is a chosen mode of behavior rather than simply an automatic response, a mere psychological tic or a symptom of warped, antisocial tendencies. From this perspective, the Western hero's notorious inexpressiveness can be seen as conduct intended to focus our attention on his physical body, compelling us to heed that body as a fully constructed form uninflected by evidence of any ongoing process of fabrication. But silence has the opposite effect as well, of reinforcing our sense of the amount of continuing effort expended to maintain this state of masculinity, to ensure it as a condition not otherwise given or prescribed. Clint Eastwood's appearance as No Name, an impassive, zombielike creature, serves as only the most extreme, ironic form of this condition.

Whenever a man is being beaten in the Western, it is less to punish us for our delight in the male body than to prepare us for the process by which he becomes what he already is. We find ourselves, male and female, identifying with that subject of suffering and in that moment also identifying with the masculinizing process itself as one of American culture's most powerful (and powerfully confused) imaginative constructions. For it is the Western hero—unlike the leading men in any other genre—who is placed before us precisely to be looked at. And in that long, oscillating look, we watch men still at work in the unfinished process of making themselves, even as we are encouraged to believe that manhood doesn't need to be made.

Notes

1. Robert Warshow, "Movie Chronicle: *The Westerner*" (1954), reprinted in *The Immediate Experience: Movies, Comics, Theatre, and Other Aspects of Popular Culture* (Garden City, N.Y.: Doubleday, 1962), 151–52.

2. Ted Post's *Hang 'Em High* (1968) opens with a perfect instance of this logic: Jedidiah Cooper (Clint Eastwood) is mistakenly condemned by vigilantes, who drag him behind a horse to a hanging tree, then punch him repeatedly, cutting up his face. At the question "Are we gonna hang him, or beat him to death?" they put a noose around his neck, leaving his body to swing under the limb as the film's title and credits go by. The plot then depicts his revivification and revenge—as he repeatedly shows others his scarred neck, with close-ups of his slowly healing face—before he is again shot from behind and recovers with the help of Rachel Warren (Inger Stevens).

3. For an account of the making of the movie, see Garner Simmons, *Peckinpah: A Portrait in Montage* (Austin: University of Texas Press, 1976), esp. 101ff. The prerelease version of the film was 190 minutes, and in a sneak preview in Kansas City thirty-odd people walked out, some physically ill. The original release time was 143 minutes, while the American version was 135 minutes (eight minutes cut by Warner Bros.). See Doug McKinney, *Sam Peckinpah* (Boston: Twayne, 1979), 85–89; and Paul Seydor, *Peckinpah: The Western Films* (Urbana: University of Illinois Press, 1980), 78–79.
4. Philip French, *Westerns: Aspects of a Movie Genre* (London: Secker and Warburg, 1973), 115 (emphasis in the original).
5. David A. Cook, *A History of Narrative Film* (New York: W. W. Norton, 1981), 631–32 (emphasis in the original). See also Brian Garfield, *Western Films: A Complete Guide* (New York: Rawson Associates, 1982), 59, for an account of the film's innovations.

passion and acceleration:

generic change

in the action film

rikke schubart

Today we find the most celebrated myth of utopian masculinity in the action film. Looking back at two decades of action films we see that masculinity has changed radically: from the passion and sufferings of Rambo to the acceleration and sadism of the Terminator and into the aggravated redundancy of the action computer game.[1]

Two themes are central in the action film: passion and acceleration. The first has to do with plot, motive and myth, and psychology, identification and emotion. The second has to do with speed and spectacle, affect and exhilaration. The first theme links the hero to society, to hierarchy and the law, to martyrdom and masochism (the prototype is Christ). The second theme, acceleration, provides the reversal: now comes aggression turned into kinetic energy, sadism in the shape of vengeance, explosions, pure speed, the hard body, invulnerability, invincibility, impenetrability (the prototype is the clone machine). These two themes used to meet in the classical plot of the action film: to be an action hero was not only a question of muscles and armor, of beatings and gunfire; it was also a question of being violently beaten, sensing violence on your own flesh, suspension, suffering, passion, pain—yes, plainly speaking, torture.[2] But *Terminator* (1984) changed all that. Suddenly acceleration refused to submit to the theme of passion, it tore itself away and became a theme in its own right. In passion the element of acceleration works as a denial; its function is to transform humiliation and suffering into triumph. Conversely, in the theme of acceleration, the element of acceleration is a constant feature, not a denial of humiliation but a negation of nature, of vulnerability, of limits.

Rambo and Terminator will take us through passion and acceleration and into the future of the next generation, the action computer hero and the theme of repetition. We end in virtual reality—"after the orgy" as Jean Baudrillard has negatively termed our time—where masculinity, the male body and the pleasures of identification, are no longer the same.

Passion

> I want my country to love me as much as I love it. That's what I want!
> —*Rambo: First Blood, Part Two*

> The injury to the pride burns like a hidden wound which will not heal until the persons have had their revenge and retribution. There is nothing a masochistic character craves more than appreciation and admiration. For these he will go to any extreme.
> —*Theodor Reik*[3]

The theme of passion seems outdated today, but this is the original narrative structure of the action film, its mythical heart. It is no coincidence that Rambo is "the chosen one," that Dirty Harry is beaten and shot at the foot of an enormous cross, or that the hero is crucified in *Conan the Barbarian* (1982) and *Cyborg* (1989). The action film establishes its hero as a suffering Christ who rises from the dead as an almighty avenger.

History: Scapegoat and Idol
The film *Rambo: First Blood, Part Two* from 1985 is an exemplary version of the plot of passion: The Vietnam vet John Rambo (Sylvester Stallone) is "the best" (a decorated Green Beret), but is met with contempt by the civil world–which the audience knows from the first Rambo film, *First Blood* (1982). By his government Rambo is sent on an impossible mission, suffers incredible torture, completes his mission against all odds, punishes the guilty, saves the innocent, and in the end corrects his superior who abandoned him when he needed help ("My God, my God, why have you forsaken me?"). Central to the plot is inversion: after humiliation comes rehabilitation and now the sufferer becomes the punisher. We can say that the mythological structures of the innocent victim and the lonely avenger are joined together. Or, in the terminology of the French anthropologist René Girard, the rites of the scapegoat and the rites of the king join in the myth of the action hero.

193

Writing in such diverse fields as anthropology, philosophy, and literary theory the controversial René Girard has been criticized, and he is indeed both provocative and inspiring. With *Violence and the Sacred* and *Job: The Victim of his People*, Girard proposes his theory of the ritual slaughter of a scapegoat to avert a social crisis: from time to time any society will experience a crisis, says Girard, where everybody hates everybody.[4] Envy and dissension reigns and a civil war looms. To avoid this a scapegoat is collectively chosen to be the focus of hate; instead of everybody hating everybody, now everybody hates one. The scapegoat is sacrificed. And after sacrifice comes "the postsacrificial virginal harmony of the morning red [dawn]."[5] Aggression is purged of violence through the very act of violence. The plot of this sacrifice is tripartite: first a crisis, then the selection of a scapegoat, and finally sacrifice. When we compare the plot of passion to that of Girard's sacrifice we find parallels between the two. But where sacrifice has three parts, the plot of passion has four: marginalization, selection, sacrifice, and vengeance/resurrection.

Marginalization. The scapegoat is both fatherless and randomly chosen so that he will not be avenged after his death, says Girard. And the ideal scapegoat is a king or a hero who has worked hard to achieve success but is destroyed by an evil destiny. God giveth and God taketh. The best of scapegoats is thus a dethroned idol, a broken idol marginalized from the society he once ruled. And this is exactly what the action hero is.

Rambo is presented as the best, a king of warfare. He has "two silver stars, four bronze stars, four purple hearts, distinguished service cross and a medal of honor," and his former commander, Colonel Trautman, describes him as "the best combat vet I've ever seen. He's a pure fighting machine with only a desire to win a war that somebody else lost. If winning means he has to die, he'll die. No fear, no regrets. And one more thing: what you choose to call hell, he calls home."[6] But suddenly the unjust dethronement strikes, and the state repudiates its own creation as easily as Frankenstein repudiated his innocent monster. Rambo's medals don't "mean shit" in civil life; in fact, Rambo finally realizes that "there are no friendly civilians!" "Back there I could fly a gunship, I could drive a tank, I was in charge of million-dollar equipment. Back here, I can't even hold a job," Rambo laments at the end of *First Blood*. Girard calls this phase the social ostracization of the idol, who is slowly crushed in the very mold that shaped him. The repudiated hero is such a broken idol: Van Damme in *Hard Target* (1993), Mel Gibson in *Lethal Weapon* (1987), Steven Seagal in *Under Siege* (1992)—the action film is littered with repudiated idols, with Vietnam vets reduced to drifters, cooks, private detectives, suicidal and disillusioned cops.[7] Now they have less than nothing: the first scene of *Rambo: First Blood, Part Two* (hereafter *Rambo*) places Rambo in a quarry. In *Lethal Weapon* the crying hero takes a gun in his mouth contemplating suicide. And in *Robocop* (1987) the hero is stripped of everything: arms, legs, his family, his humanity. In short, heroism is born out of loss and crisis.

Being a marginalized and broken idol provides the hero with the strongest of all motives for undertaking a dangerous mission: the desire to remount the pedestal, to reascend his throne, to recover his lost halo. Rambo is precise in his motivation: "I want what they [POWs] want and every other guy that came over here and spilt his guts and gave everything he had, wants. For our country to love us as much as we love it. That's what I want!" No less than glorification and idolization.

Selection. Chance selects the scapegoat, says Girard, because chance is ruled by divine and not human logic. The government selects a traumatized criminal Vietnam vet because "your name was dug out of the computer as one out of three"—and three is of course a holy number. Divine chance indeed. The idea is to avoid retaliation against the system that prepares to sacrifice the hero. Rambo senses the danger: "At least here I know where I stand." However, he is comforted: "You can feel totally safe, because we have the most advanced weapons in the world available to us," "This time it's up to you," and "All this is for you." If the hero doesn't volunteer, as Lieutenant Callaghan does three times in *Dirty Harry*, he is either tempted with admittance into society or threatened with retaliation. Offering Rambo a way out of prison, Colonel Trautman does both: "There'll be a presidential pardon" and "You can't possibly want to stay here another five years."

This second part of passion usually adds a narrative motive à la Propp's fairy-tale motive numbers sixty-eight and sixty-nine: To save an object— the hero's wife, daughter, his partner's daughter, innocent people, his own life, or even world peace—or to avenge a lost object—a dead partner, a dead friend, a dead girlfriend, a dead wife. Avenging a killed partner is a specious motive—and the poster tells us "This time it is personal!"—but we must not be fooled. This motive merely covers up the true and real motive—idolization and the halo—and the system of sacrifice.

Sacrifice. The mission is to find POWs in Vietnam, but when Rambo saves an American prisoner he is abandoned in enemy country. "It was a lie, wasn't it? Just like the whole god-damned war, it was a lie. He never had a chance, did he?" Rambo's former commanding officer, Trautman, shouts at Murdock, who is in charge of the mission. Murdock is "a stinking bureaucrat who's trying to cover his ass," and more than that, "not just mine, we're talking about a nation's." Behind Murdock is the government, the state, the system, all trying to cover up the crisis. This third part of passion is reminiscent of the original religious sacrifice: a naked victim, the hating crowd, the scaffold as a setting. According to Girard the scapegoat sucks up the social crisis like a sponge. Speaking of yet another mythological collective murder, the killing of the primal father, Freud points out the relation between the primal father and the tragic hero of the drama: "Through a process of systematic distortion—one might even say, as the product of a refined hypocrisy," the primal father becomes the hero of the drama who accepts his tragic guilt. "Thus the tragic Hero became, though it might be against his will, the redeemer of the Chorus."[8] It is worth noticing that both Girard and Freud position the modern hero as the innocent victim of a social crisis.

The action hero accepts his "tragic guilt" and suffers in silence: "He was led like a sheep to the slaughter; like a lamb that is dumb before the shearer, he does not open his mouth."[9] "And these are the people you are protecting with your pain! For what?" the Russian wonders. But is the motive not clear? The pain justifies, even demands, vengeance. No one is more justified in using violence than the victim of violence.

Vengeance/Resurrection. "He will be mocked and spat upon, and flogged and killed; and three days afterwards, he will rise again."[10] Girard is quiet when it comes to the resurrection. With Christ the ritual of sacrifice disappears, he says, and prefers speaking of pre-Christian scapegoats. But resurrection and vengeance follow sacrifice as surely as night follows day. Now comes a vengeance that fully equals the sufferings, an eye for an eye and a tooth for a tooth. Girard points out how the heroic deeds of the hero are often the same as the crimes of the criminal; in *Rambo*, the Vietnamese may have killed and tortured, but now Rambo mercilessly exterminates the Vietnamese and Russian units. The hero has the "right" to level towns to the ground, kill the guilty (and innocent), bomb any target with all means. These are biblical dimensions, the hero is beyond secular law, he cannot be judged, but has himself become a figure rarely mentioned, an avenging and judging Christ: "He was robed in a garment dyed in blood, and he was called the Word of God. Out of his mouth came a sharp sword to smite the nations; for it is he who will rule them with a rod of iron, and tread the winepress of the fierce wrath of God the sovereign Lord. On his robe and on his thigh was written the title: King of kings and Lord of lords."[11]

Body: The Honorable Wound

In suffering is redemption, with sacrifice comes martyrdom. The action hero is clearly a martyr, and the martyr shares traits with the masochist. They both accept a tragic guilt, they do penance, they are tortured—and they demonstrate their wounds in public. "The honorable wound," Hemingway calls the wound that a hero receives in war. "However genuine the penitence, however voluntary the suffering, it can't do without a public. In most cases it has the character of a performance and frequently it does not dispense with a certain theatrical flavor," says the German psychologist Theodor Reik in *Masochism in Sex and Society.*[12] According to Reik the theatrical staging, the demonstrative exhibition, and the dramatic suspense are central to the masochistic drama.

The sacrifice of Rambo is indeed spectacular, demonstrative, and dramatic. "Being hung or suspended from some contraption happens to be among the favorite masochistic practices," says Reik, and Rambo hangs from a yoke wearing only a loincloth when he first faces his executioner.[13] During electric torture he is strung up on a metal bed, and the Russian interprets his silence as an invitation to perverse pleasures. "You wish to test your strength? Good. You are strong, the strongest so far!" The orgiastic vibrations of the sweating body leave little doubt as to the masochistic and homoerotic nature of the sensations, which we will be frank and call pleasures.[14] The threat of a knife cutting Rambo's face and nearing his eye is frozen into one of the photographic scenarios that the French philosopher Gilles Deleuze in *Coldness and Cruelty* finds characteristic of masochism.[15] This is man on the cross, and the pleasure is in subjecting to and subverting the threat of castration. Identification is with the hero as victim, not victor.[16] In spite of the apparently feminine position there is nothing effeminate or womanish whatsoever about the passions of the action hero. Instead of weakening the hero, the pain induces new strength. Deleuze points out this paradox: "A close examination of masochistic fantasies or rites reveals that while they bring into play the very strictest of the law, the result in every case is the opposite of what might be expected (thus whipping, far from punishing or preventing an erection, provokes and ensures it)."[17]

Girard never mentions masochism with a single word (and neither does Freud discussing the tragic guilt of the hero). However, masochism obviously has a part in this plot. Girard may find masochism effeminate and unworthy of man, but according to Reik men are not only more masochistic than women, their fantasies are also more passionate: "The masochistic phantasy of woman has the character of yielding and surrender rather than that of the rush ahead, of the orgiastic cumulation, of the self-abandonment of man."[18] Masochistic pain may be feminine but in no way is it effeminate. "You may scream. There is no shame," the Russian assures Rambo.

Pleasure: "Fucking around with the Law"

One part of the masochistic experience—and of our identification with the hero—is the element of pain. Another part is the element of rehabilitation. "Pride cometh after the fall," notes Reik, and crucial to the pleasures of passion is the story of reversal, of denial, of rebellion against the law. Halfway through *First Blood* the following conversation takes place: "I was just talking to Mitch and he was saying that Galt and a couple of deputies were a little . . . rough . . . on the guy," Deputy Lester tells Sheriff Teasle. "Assholes," comments Dave, the leader of the National Guard. "It doesn't make one god-damned bit of difference, Dave, and you know it," Teasle furiously replies. "If one of my deputies gets out of line with a prisoner, then the prisoner comes to me with it. And if I find out it's like he says, then I kick the deputy's ass. Me, the law, that's the way it's gotta be. People start fucking around with the law and all hell breaks loose." Indeed it does. Surviving the sacrifice makes the hero delirious. Now he believes himself to be the law. "I could have killed them all! I could have killed you. In town you're the law. Out here it's me!" Rambo tells Sheriff Teasle, holding a knife to his throat. Again in *Rambo*: "Find them or I'll find you," Rambo says, throwing a knife that barely misses Murdock's face. And when Dirty Harry is reproached with having used police torture to obtain a confession he arrogantly replies, "Well, I'm all broken up about that man's rights."

"Gender is determined by possessing or non-possessing of the phallus" says English film critic Anthony Easthope.[19] But there is more at stake here than possession. The hero does not possess the phallus; he believes himself to be the invincible and indestructible phallus. "Fucking around with the law" is an apt description of the hero usurping the rights of the father and the law. However, he does not want the position of the father. "Christ is not the son of God, but the new Man; his likeness to the father is abolished, he is Man on the Cross, who knows no sexual love, no property, no fatherland, no cause, no work."[20] This new man turns his back on society to return to the Vietnamese jungle to live "day by day." He does not want the responsibility of the father, he only desires the glorification. He does not want to be the law, he wants to be above, beyond, and out of reach of the law.

In the masochistic story we recognize the element of narcissism: "Masochism is never a sign of narcissism, but an expression of its being damaged and of an attempt to restore it," says Reik. "Rehabilitation in this sense would mean: compensation for the injured or offended ego, the restitution of its former rights."[21] The hero has been dethroned by the law and the father, and now he wants to return to that earlier phase in his life when he was a hero. When he was almighty. When everybody idolized him. To deny castration he must paradoxically reenact castration. And this is the pleasure of the theme of passion: in order to return to utopia, to deny the symbolic, to erase the wound of castration, the utopian masculinity transforms the scapegoat into an idol—and the masochist into a narcissist.

Acceleration

> Listen and understand. That Terminator is out there. It can't be bargained with, it can't be reasoned with. It doesn't feel pity or remorse or fear. And it absolutely will not stop. Ever. Until you are DEAD!
> —*Terminator*

> There's a gap in the freeway! What are we gonna do?
> Floor the accelerator! Floor it!
> —*Speed*

My use of the word *acceleration* has nothing to do with increase of physical velocity or number of cuts per second in a film. The theme of acceleration signifies a change of thematic, a transformation of body, a shift in desire. Utopian masculinity is now narcissistic from the outset, throughout the plot, and until the end. This is torture without pain. Body without death. And humor without irony.

History: Acceleration and Inertia

The theme of acceleration is presented for the first time in *Terminator*, from 1984. A terminator is sent back through time to kill the leader of the resistance, John Connor, before he is born. The killer machine is a T101, a cyborg—inside a machine, on the outside "living human tissue: flesh, skin, hair, blood"—and its mission is to kill John's mother, Sarah Connor, before she is pregnant. To prevent this the resistance sends a soldier, Reese, to protect the target. Reese and Sarah fall in love and before Reese is killed he becomes the future father of John, leaving Sarah to terminate the cyborg in a hydraulic press.

The plot sounds religious and romantic, but don't be fooled. What is your primary memory of this film? The holy conception or the romantic time-travel paradox? Neither one. Your primary memory is the T101 (Arnold Schwarzenegger), this figure harder than steel taking over the plot, the visual space, and the fascination of identification. Reese may be the good guy but the T101 returns as a hero in the sequel. With the robot as hero the narrative changes: torture is met with insensitivity, humiliation disappears, the scapegoat is rendered superfluous by the machine. In short, former dialectics between humiliation and rehabilitation are replaced by acceleration and vengeance.

This new plot must first be described in its negation: Gone are the first three stages of passion. Gone is the broken idol. Gone are the psychological motives for heroism—the one remaining motive is the narrative, Proppian motive, which was a fake anyway. Gone is the masochistic scene of sacrifice—which means that gone is the reenactment of castration. This lack of castration is characteristic of the theme of acceleration and binds together such otherwise diverse films as *Terminator*, *Speed*, *GoldenEye* (1995), and most of Steven Seagal's films. The heroes of these films have no past as broken idols, they have no need to reenact castration, and they are never in any danger. Seagal goes through *Out for Justice* (1991) snapping wrists, breaking arms, killing, and torturing—but is never once himself touched or threatened. Without carnal sacrifice, biblical vengeance becomes an unmotivated and unquestioned principle. This motiveless psychology is a mark of acceleration.

If there is a motive it is not located in the hero, but in the sadistic story of acceleration. Deleuze points out that sadism and masochism are not the same story with an opposite sign, they are not even parallel stories. Expiation, guilt, and shame are central to the masochist, whereas aggression, self-assurance, and activity are central to the sadist. The two perversions share elements such as violence, pain, repetition, and vengeance, but where these are used to stage the "frozen" tableaux of suffering in masochism, in sadism they are part of what de Sade calls "primary nature"—the aspiration toward pure negation, pure death, a "pure delirium of Reason." The sadist's strategy is monotony and repetition: "[The Libertine] cannot do more than accelerate and condense the motions of partial violence. He achieves the acceleration by multiplying the number of his victims and their sufferings."[22] Multiplication, condensation, acceleration. *Citius, altius, fortius*—faster, higher, stronger. The strategy requires more victims, faster speed, harder steel. The clue is not motivation, but movement. Fascination is not in the frozenness of the picture, but in the acceleration of the motion. The special effects become motivation, speed is increased, explosions are in sheer overdrive, obstacles to be overrun are multiplied. However, this excess of kinetic energy always results in stasis and inertia: the movement never moves anything, the persecution never changes anything, it only goes on and on. The emotional identification of passion is replaced by affect and the absorption of exhilaration. *Speed* is exemplary of the principle: in this plot about a bus wired with a bomb that will explode if its speed drops below fifty miles an hour, the most exhilarating moment is an unforeseen gap in the freeway. The danger of termination, of interruption of speed. The only response to this gap (the last reminiscence of castration and sacrifice) is to go faster, to accelerate.

The accelerated hero is harder than steel, invincible and almighty, and with him things begin to change. Tragedy, humanity, rebellion, passion, and emotion loose their shape, lose their content, or, in the words of the

French philosopher and sociologist Jean Baudrillard, "Things have found a way of avoiding the dialectics of meaning that was beginning to bore them: By proliferating indefinitely, increasing their potential, outbidding themselves in an ascension to the limit, an obscenity that henceforth becomes their immanent finality and senseless reason."[23] Things may look the same, but they are not. I am talking about the appearance of a principle of evil—what de Sade calls pure negation—still vague and transparent, but definitely a present ghost. One cannot but think of Baudrillard's description of hypermodern society: "We may pretend to carry on in the same direction, accelerating, but in reality we are accelerating in a void."[24]

Body: His Majesty the Ideal Ego

In the almighty hero harder than steel we recognize the soft and cuddly infant, His Majesty the Baby,[25] from the primary phase of narcissism. "Illness, death, renunciation of enjoyment, restrictions on his own will, shall not touch him; the laws of nature and of society shall be abrogated in his favor," says Freud.[26] The infant between six and eighteen months goes through a narcissistic phase in which it believes it has unlimited power, even power of thought, and it is convinced that it controls the external world. In this phase, which for Lacan is the mirror phase, the infant mistakenly recognizes itself as an ideal ego in the mirror. The omnipotent heroes that we later identify with are new versions of the old ideal ego— and our pleasurable experience is akin to what Freud calls secondary narcissism.[27] Such a fantasy would be megalomania for the adult, and identifying with the Terminator or with Steven Seagal or with any hero who is untouched by the extreme dangers that surround him is somehow megalomaniacal. This is the wonderful phase we return to when identifying with the hero who is now His Majesty the ideal ego.

The almighty hero never left the narcissistic utopia, which the hero of passion has to restage castration in order to enter. In utopia castration and humiliation have nothing to do; they are not allowed to enter when they knock on the door. At most they turn up as ghosts in the shape of a vague memory of loss—the hero in *Speed* loses his friend, Seagal in *Out for Justice* loses a friend, and so on. The vague memory of loss is the memory of castration, and often it is simply erased. History and plot also fade away and give way to the overwhelming presence of moving images, this visual excess of a speechless realm, reminiscent of the ideal ego in the mirror that is capable of physical actions that we could never perform. Motor inferior, we admire the perfect man. Or superman. Or supermachine. It is no coincidence that so many action films today deal with speed: *Under Siege II* uses an unstoppable train, *Executive Decision* (1996) a 747 airplane in motion, *Point Break* (1991) surfing and parachuting, *Drop Zone* (1994) and *Terminal Velocity* (1994) have parachuting heroes, and films such as *Mission Impossible* (1996) and *Die Hard with a Vengeance* (1995) are pure speed.

Yet this perfect ideal ego is also marked by lack. The accelerated hero resembles the biological clone, which Baudrillard discusses in *The Transparency of Evil*. The clone is not borne from a father and mother, but directly from one cell. Like the cyborg it has only one parent—the system that created it—and like the cyborg the clone is born naked and adult. "What is it like to go through space?" Sarah asks Reese. "Like being born," he says. The clone without parents and childhood becomes "a body that is no longer subject to the perspectivist space of representation, of mirrors and of discourse."[28] Because of its unnatural one-gender creation it has somehow skipped the Oedipal drama, it has not been through mirrors and languages. It does not understand tears; it must learn to speak properly, see, and feel like a human. "Can you even see anything?" John asks T101, who drives in the dark. "I see everything" is the reply of this clone machine with infrared sight, who a moment later asks the crying John, "What's wrong with your eyes?" The very lack of compassion and empathy that on the one hand makes the Terminator an ideal ego on the other hand also makes him a blind and inexperienced infant. And like an infant he has to learn: "The more contact I have with human beings, the more I learn."

The narcissistic hero is no longer a son rebelling against the father, the law, the system. How could he be, when he is himself an extension of the system? The Terminator is programmed to do what he does. Father and son are no longer on different sides of the law; they are now on one and the same side, with the son doing the father's job. The accelerated hero is either programmed by or working for the system—and in contrast to the disillusioned hero of passion he is content with the system. Sarah realizes that the Terminator is the perfect father: "Watching John with the machine it was suddenly so clear. The Terminator would never stop. It would never leave him. And it would never hurt him, never shout at him or get drunk and hit him or say it was too busy to spend time with him. It would always be there. And it would die to protect him. Of all the would-be fathers who came and went over the years, this thing, this machine, was the only one who measured up. In an insane world it was the sanest choice."

What we see is the incestuous melting together of the law and the hero, the father and the son, and, in the context of clones, Baudrillard notes that "this is still incest, but without the tragedy."

Pleasure: Supreme Certitude

The pleasure of identification with this supreme being is sadistic and narcissistic. It is in the vertigo of speed, in the admiration of power and special effects, in the unquestioned principle of sadism, in the multiplication of victims. We are presented with an almighty son/father, who protects the weak, who on the one hand represents the law and who on the other hand is untouched by the laws of nature and the reality principle—indeed, a paradoxical figure.

Gone—or at least fading away—is the element of masochism. We may find scenes of torture in acceleration, but the result is something else. "Does it hurt when you get shot?" John asks the T101 in *Terminator 2: Judgment Day* (1991). "I sense injuries. The data could be called pain," is the reply. Pain is no longer shameful torture, but "data," and this body that can be tested but not tortured is "a sensory body, but not a sensitive body."[29] The illusion of utopia is not shattered even by the final destruction of the Terminator. The elimination of the T101 (the ideal ego) in no way suspends our faith in his superiority; it only confirms his invincibility. Deleuze warns us not to mistake the apparent masochism in the theme of acceleration with the masochistic story: "The Libertine is not afraid of being treated in the way he treats others. The pain he suffers is an ultimate pleasure, not because it satisfies a need to expiate or a feeling of guilt, but because it confirms him in his inalienable power and gives him a supreme certitude."[30]

Repetition

> This is the state of simulation, a state in which we are obliged to replay all scenarios precisely because they have all taken place already, whether actually or potentially. The state of utopia realized, of all utopias realized, wherein paradoxically we must continue to live as though they had not been. But since they have, and since we can no longer, therefore, nourish the hope of realizing them, we can only hyper-realize them through interminable simulation.
> —*Jean Baudrillard*[31]

> . . . an excess of stimulation is in a sense erotic . . .
> —*Gilles Deleuze*[32]

What to dream of when utopia has been realized? What limit to cross once narcissistic limitlessness is a reality? Repetition and simulation is the only answer. Continued acceleration ad nauseam. "Aggravated redundancy," Baudrillard calls it. But even nausea holds pleasures and fascinations: vertigo, weightlessness, suspension of time.

History: Aggravated Redundancy

The pure prototype of the next generation of action is found in computer games and in video-game systems such as Sony PlayStation, Sega, and Nintendo. I am thinking of the action games that have caused furor and severe concern because of their dangerous addictiveness, hypnotic acceleration, increasing realism, and ego-weakening identification (you must have just one more game, and another, and another . . .): *Doom*, *Duke Nukem*, *Streetfighter*, *Tekken*, *Toshinden I* and *II*, and so on. These action games originate from classic arcade games and the primitive TV games from the early 1980s (the tennis game consisting of a dot beaten back and forth over the net). Monotonous, motiveless, infinite. Yet with the seed of acceleration. Today you are a person moving freely in a three-dimensional space; in *Doom* and *Duke Nukem* you fight your way through buildings (scenarios) filled with opponents, monsters, secret rooms, weapons, and equipment of all kinds. In TV games such as *Toshinden I* and *II* and *Streetfighter* you confront a number of different opponents on a battle arena, and you select your player from a number of options: young or old, man or woman, Caucasian or Asian, good or evil, sexy or repulsive. Your choice.

Comparing repetition to passion and acceleration we see radical alteration. The "plot" or "narrative"[33] is reduced to a short introductory story placed at the beginning of the game, an introduction or foreplay that can be skipped by pressing the X-button or the space bar. (In fact, each time I have had students play computer games they skipped the plot of the game—without noticing it.) The ghosts of psychology and motivation are finally put to rest by the player or avatar (the figure that is you) that can rise infinitely from the dead.

In playing you must beat opponents (human or virtual), enter a space, conquer a building. You select the level of difficulty (easy means fewer monsters), and the aim is to fulfill your mission. When you die, you simply restart. Time has lost finality and become infinite; with the option for restart and repetition game time regresses into circularity and the old dialectics of plot and motivation disappear. Being shot does not signify death, it signifies subtraction of points. And you can even cheat the restart by saving your game as you win more points and reach higher levels. In this action of the 1990s the triumphant reversal of passion has been replaced by the hyperrealization of the dominant elements of acceleration: movement, repetition, condensation.

This is not only the death of passion, it is also the death of movement: "Rigor mortis is replaced by mobilitas mortis, and the dead rider pedals on indefinitely, even accelerating, as a function of inertia." The movement continues without motive, but the movement is repeated over and over in the same spot. We are in "a transparent form of public space from which all the actors have been withdrawn—and a pure form of the event from which all passion has been removed."[34]

Body: No Point of View and Nothing to See

The avatar can be wounded and killed, as it does not have the motor perfection of the accelerated hero. But it has the advantage of infinite resurrection. Time and action does not harm it; its body has become strangely transparent. "The centrifugal force of our proliferating technologies has stripped us of all weight and transferred us into an empty freedom of movement."[35]

Having an avatar as a protagonist problematizes questions of identification and ego-building. Baudrillard points out the dilemma: "Like the practitioners of the baroque, we too are irrepressible creators of images, but secretly we are iconoclasts—not in the sense that we destroy images, but in the sense that we manufacture a profusion of images *in which there is nothing to see*."[36] What do we see when we share the point of view of our avatar? Is this avatar that we control with our keyboard or joystick a stand-in for us in the ordinary sense of identification? Or is it the locus of vertigo? The avatar is not you, but neither is it an other; it is somewhere strangely in between, "a subject purged of the other, deprived of its divided character and doomed to self-metastasis, to pure repetition."[37]

Identification means admiring your ideal ego in the mirror of the fiction. It is a projection of fantasies and desires, possibly a rebuilding of the ego. But the avatar is no ideal ego, it is not even a subject. It signifies the return to a narcissistic phase in which the individual is immersed in a pleasant (but also overwhelming and sometimes threatening) sea of vision and sound. This is a vulgar version of the imaginary or maybe even a fantasy of a return to the Lacanian real, this magic and hallucinatory phase in which subject and object were one, where object-relation did not yet exist as an external relation.

Pleasure: Simulated Stimulation

Already when speaking of *Speed* Richard Dyer pointed out that "for the male viewer action movies have a lot in common with being fellated."[38] This element of autoeroticism is taken to the extreme in repetition, where the pleasure of the computer and video game is never found in narrative closure or in the psychology of the characters, but is displaced into other areas.

Total immersion in a profusion of bright images and loud, monotonous sound is clearly pleasurable. The world of *Doom* or *Toshinden II* is markedly lacking in abstract language and dominated by the infant's experience of the world: lights, colors, sound. The game itself warns us, "Some people experience epileptic seizures when viewing flashing lights or patterns in our daily environment. These persons may experience seizures while watching TV pictures or playing video games. . . . Consult your doctor before playing video games if you have an epileptic condition or immediately should you experience any of the following symptoms during play: dizziness, altered vision, muscle twitching, other involuntary movements, loss of awareness of your surroundings, mental confusion, and/or convulsions." The second component of this infantile experience is interaction and control. You control your avatar with the tip of your finger and by repeating the action you achieve total mastery. The unleashing of aggression drives the game as you take your beatings and enjoy killing opponents, but the central pleasure and overall goal is mastery and control—to beat the game. Having beaten the game the next move is to beat your own record (to win more points or use less time), or simply to repeat the ecstasy of control. This is the addictive vice of repetitive pleasure.

This pleasure is neither sadistic nor masochistic; it is instead a pure principle of autoeroticism, of pleasure without an object, of muscle twitching. The continuous rubbing of flesh against joystick until the epileptic seizure strikes. The pleasure of the video and computer game takes the masturbatory pleasures of guns and gunfire into new dimensions. The repeated convulsion is like pornography: both dream of infinite muscle rubbing and muscle twitching, of the postponement of ejaculation, orgasm, satisfaction, stillness. Don't ever let the motion stop.

In the last two decades the action movie has slowly regressed into more ancient layers of narcissism: the original hero of passion, locked in tragic conflict with the world, became extinct when the theme of acceleration replaced his narcissistic fantasies with the even older delusions of sadistic omnipotence. And today's repetition has given up the pretence of plot, motivation, and psychology, and returned the hero to the autoerotic pleasures of his primary narcissism. This generic change may of course be shrugged off as the pragmatism of a film industry cashing in on the desire of an audience through genre formula and an excess of computer-generated special effects—especially since the disappearance of plot, motive, and psychology has transformed this B-movie genre into today's most expensive and popular blockbusters.

To do so, however, would be a mistake. Utopian masculinity was always narcissistic, but never as far removed from reality as today.[39] "John Wayne and Gary Cooper . . . were my role models during childhood, when I grew up essentially without a father," Chuck Norris writes in his autobiography. "There weren't many heroes of that type on the screen in the 1970s, and I felt that kids needed this kind of positive image. Perhaps I could become a role model for today's youth."[40] We must ask ourselves how the pure principle of repetition—images in which there is nothing to see—can present us with role models. Seeing no reflection, the spectator shifts his gaze from the mirror of identification to the frame around it. Here he notices the elaborate carvings, the light material, the vivid colors. And this is where contemporary action is located: not in heroes as role models but in fuzzy images of masculinity framed by a new attention to detail, to aestheticization, to computer-generated images. Not in narcissistic conflict, but in narcissistic pleasure—the frozenness of speed, the nostalgic memory of falling. This explains Americans' sudden acceptance of the Hong Kong action cinema in the 1990s, films from an industry that decades ago perfected the stunt, turned choreography into ballet, and experimented with visual narrativity.

The narcissistic regression of the action movie need not come to an end, at least not yet. The theme of passion was killed by boredom, acceleration stopped by exhaustion, but repetition has one step left to go: to enter the theme of the spectacle. But perhaps such an era is already here. Since the explosive vengeance of *Rambo* the action movie has become gradually more spectacular, more destructive, and more apocalyptic, culminating in the blockbusters *Independence Day* (1996), *Men in Black* (1997), and *Armageddon* (1998).[41] In the 1990s the action movie has searched desperately for generic innovation; we have seen warrior presidents (*Air Force One*, 1997), several flirtations with the disaster genre, and female action heroines. Truly innovative was *The Matrix* (1999), giving birth to a new Christ in the shape of androgynous savior hero Neo (Keanu Reeves). Neo is both old and new. Old because he is born out of the classical passion plot. New because his masculinity belongs to the immaterial bodies in cyberspace. In the new millennium the action movie is ready for new heroes, new images, new stories.

Notes

1. This paper was presented at the 1997 Society for Cinema Studies conference. It is part of my Ph.D. project "Masculinity in the Action Film, 1968–1998" at the Department of Film and Media Studies, University of Copenhagen.

2. The torture theme is also found in the Western, but is not a constitutive feature of this genre. The theme enters the action movie via Sergio Leone's spaghetti Westerns with Clint Eastwood: the Man with No Name trilogy: *A Fistful of Dollars* (1964), *For a Few Dollars More* (1965), and *The Good the Bad and the Ugly* (1966). Hereafter Clint Eastwood carries the beatings with him into his early action movies *Coogan's Bluff* (1968) and *Dirty Harry* (1971).

3. Theodor Reik, *Masochism in Sex and Society* (New York: Pyramid Books, 1976), 254.

4. René Girard, *Violence and the Sacred* (Baltimore: John Hopkins University Press, 1992), and *Job: The Victim of His People* (Stanford, Calif.: Stanford University Press, 1987). However, I have used a Danish translation of the latter book, *Job—idol og syndebuk* (Viborg: Anis, 1992), and all quotes are my translations from Danish into English.

5. Girard, *Job*, 49.

6. *Rambo: First Blood Part Two.*

7. See Susan Jeffords, *The Remasculinization of America: Gender and the Vietnam War* (Bloomington and Indianapolis: Indiana University Press, 1989), for a discussion of the scapegoat and *Rambo*.

8. Quoted in Girard, *Violence and the Sacred*, 202. For a discussion of male martyrdom and suffering see William Luhr, "Mutilating Mel: Martyrdom and Masculinity in *Braveheart*," in *Mythologies of Violence in Postmodern Media*, ed. Christopher Sharrett (Detroit: Wayne State University Press, 1999).

9. *The Revised English Bible*, Acts of the Apostles 8:32–33.

10. Ibid., Mark 10:34.

11. Ibid., The Revelation of John 19:13 and 15–16.

12. Reik, *Masochism in Sex and Society*, 85.

13. Ibid., 66.

14. For a discussion of pain, pleasure, and male masochism see Steve Neale, "Masculinity as Spectacle," *Screen* 24, no. 6 (1983): 2–16.

15. Gilles Deleuze, *Coldness and Cruelty in Masochism* (New York: Zone Books, 1991).The frozenness reminds us of Laura Mulvey's famous critique of woman as masochistic icon subjected to the two sadistic gazes of man: the fetishistic gaze freezing and fragmenting its object, and the sadistic gaze punishing woman with death and castration. See Laura Mulvey, "Visual Pleasure and Narrative Cinema," in *Film Theory and Criticism*, ed. Gerald Mast, Marshall Cohen, and Leo Braudy (New York: Oxford University Press, 1992).

16. See Kaja Silverman, *Male Subjectivity at the Margins* (New York: Routledge, 1992), for an analysis of masochism in man.

17. Deleuze, *Coldness and Cruelty*, 88.

18. Reik, *Masochism in Sex and Society*, 222–23.

19. Anthony Easthope, *What a Man's Gotta Do: The Masculine Myth in Popular Culture* (London: Paladin, 1986), 118.

20. Deleuze, *Coldness and Cruelty*, 100.

21. Reik, *Masochism in Sex and Society*, 89 and 250.

22. Ibid., 29.

23. Jean Baudrillard, *Fatal Strategies* (London: Semiotext(e)/Pluto, 1990), 7.

24. Baudrillard, *The Transparency of Evil: Essays on Extreme Phenomena* (London: Verso, 1993), 3.

25. Freud talks of His Majesty the Baby in "On Narcissism: An Introduction" (1914), in *The Standard Edition of the Complete Psychological Works of Sigmund Freud*, vol. 14, ed. James Strachey (London: Hogarth Press, 1978), and of His Majesty the Ego in "Creative Writers and Day-Dreaming" (1908), *Standard Edition*, vol. 9.

26. Freud, "On Narcissism," 91.

27. Without using the word *narcissism* but referring to the Lacanian mirror phase, Mulvey describes the identification of the male audience with a male hero thus: "A male movie star's glamorous characteristics are thus not those of the erotic object of the gaze, but those of the more perfect, more complete, more powerful ideal ego conceived in the original moment of recognition in front of the mirror. The character in the story can make things happen and control events better than the subject/spectator, just as the image in the mirror was more in control of motor coordination." Mulvey, "Visual Pleasure and Narrative Cinema," 751. See also Laura Mulvey, "Afterthoughts on

Visual Pleasure and Narrative Cinema Inspired by *Duel in the Sun*," *Framework*, nos. 15–17: 12–15, where rejection of marriage is "a nostalgic celebration of phallic, narcissistic omnipotence" belonging to "a phase of play and phantasy difficult to integrate exactly into the Oedipal drama" (14).

28. Baudrillard, *The Transparency of Evil*, 120.
29. Ibid., 120.
30. Deleuze, *Coldness and Cruelty*, 39.
31. Baudrillard, *The Transparency of Evil*, 4.
32. Deleuze, *Coldness and Cruelty*, 37.
33. In adventure games such as *Daedalus Encounter* we see an effort to unite the infinite game with the finite narration by using short film sequences with real actors. This is, however, not in action but adventure games, and the outcome is not an increase of action, but a movement towards suspense and narrativity.
34. Baudrillard, *The Transparency of Evil*, 102 and 80.
35. Ibid., 31.
36. Ibid., 17 (emphasis in the original).
37. Ibid., 122.
38. Richard Dyer, "Action!" *Sight and Sound* (October 1994): 10.
39. See, for instance, Susan Jeffords, *Hard Bodies: Hollywood Masculinity in the Reagan Era* (New Brunswick, N.J.: Rutgers University Press, 1994), for a discussion of the relation between the conservative Reagan period and the action hero.
40. Chuck Norris with Joe Hyams, *The Secret of Inner Strength* (Boston: Little, Brown, 1988), 118.
41. For a discussion of spectacle and melodrama in the action movie, see Mark Gallagher, "I Married Rambo: Spectacle and Melodrama in the Hollywood Action Film," in *Mythologies of Violence in Postmodern Media*, ed. Christopher Sharrett (Detroit: Wayne State University Press, 1999). Gallagher analyzes the turn to melodrama as a response to generic exhaustion and a search for a female audience.

Part Three:

Hollywood Violence and

Cultural Politics

black violence as cinema:

from cheap thrills

nine   to historical agonies

ed guerrero

The painful collision of comedy and history is a revealing place to start this exploration of black violence on the cinema screen. Americans living in the 1990s, a full thirty years after the end of the civil rights movement, are confronted with many unsettling paradigm shifts. As Chris Rock, the raw, funky heir to the politicized early comedic style of Richard Pryor, acidly notes in his stage act, wherever you find a boulevard named after Dr. Martin Luther King Jr. "run . . . because there's some violence going down." With racism recoding and rearticulating its hegemony and privilege in the neoconservative language of the 1990s, the ironies are sharp, sad, and very obvious. For starters, all too many black people still remain poor, disenfranchised, and trapped in urban ghettos. The only "progress," it seems, is that now the main boulevards and public schools are named after the last generation's martyrs. Moreover, the great collective ideal of liberation, across the political spectrum, from nonviolent action to "by any means necessary" militancy, has eroded into an ambivalent, self-focused consumerism of brand-name jeans and sneakers, and intracommunal annihilation through gun-drug-gang violence.

In conservative, postindustrial America, where prisons surpass public education as main lines in state budgets, black people still have too little control over their structurally determined condition at the bottom of the economic and social heap.[1] Despite the limited gains of the black middle class and the cosmetic rhetoric of "black progress," for all too many African Americans, mean ghetto streets are the lived reality, a reality that has been refracted in the hood-homeboy action flicks that have become such an influential, though now fading, staple of what critics have dubbed the "new black film wave" of the 1990s. Although hood-homeboy violence stands out, it is only one of many expressions and styles of black violence in contemporary cinema. For the purposes of this essay I would like to historicize, interrogate, and critically comment upon some of the varied social, political, and psychic conditions, along with some of the many representations, that constitute the construction of black violence on the commercial cinema screen. In the process perhaps I can address a few salient questions raised about black violence in the movies. For instance, what is the general framework within which dominant cinema violence, black and white, expresses itself? What are the origins of black violence in contemporary commercial cinema and are there variations on the theme? And is black violence held to prefigured historical codes and a double standard by the dominant movie industry and its mainstream audience?

First, it is important to note that most black-focused films or black characters in mainstream films are not unique in their expressions of violence, and that blacks got into the screen violence game late. With few exceptions, the stylistic range of black violence follows the overall configuration of mainstream white cinematic violence, which escalated in 1966 with the collapse of the Production Code and the advent of such technology-driven, stunningly violent successes as *Bonnie and Clyde* (1967), *Bullitt* (1968), and *The Wild Bunch* (1969).[2] Since then, we as a nation have become increasingly entertained by, and addicted to, ever more graphic representations of violence expressed across a broad field of commercial movies with two loosely defined categories at either end. At the most popular pole, we have action-adventure or "popcorn" violence, with its emphasis on shootouts, car chases, pyrotechnics, quadraphonic noise, and ever increasing body counts. Other than shouted threats and screams, these films are light on dialogue, character development, and intellectual or psychological complexity. In industry terms, they are "sensation driven" and are made for Hollywood's biggest and most influential audience, the young.[3] Consequently, the violent, action-adventure blockbuster delivers a jolting cinematic experience that's more akin to the thrill of a hyperkinetic amusement park ride or an action-packed computer game. At the less profitable pole are the social, psychological or political dramas, and historical epics, made for an older, baby boomer audience seeking an aesthetic or intellectual experience at the movies. These films are considered by the industry as "plot and character driven," and when violence is depicted it is aesthetically, socially, or morally edifying, erupting in such contexts as dramatic, character-focused conflicts or the broader sweep of history—in genocidal cataclysms, mass movements, political struggles, and social upheavals.

Dominant cinema productions structured on action-adventure violence abound, as exemplified by films like *True Romance* (1993), the *Die Hard* saga (1988–95), *Terminator I* and *II* (1984 and 1991), *Independence Day* (1996), *Air Force One* (1997), and *The Replacement Killers* (1998). Appealing to adolescent fantasy, this is Hollywood's biggest money-making category. At the other end of the spectrum, films that try to historicize, comment on, or dramatize the psychic, moral, social, or political consequences of violence, like *Schindler's List* (1993), *Gandhi* (1982), *Michael Collins* (1996), *Dr. Zhivago* (1965), and *The Pawnbroker* (1965), are less common industry features. However, since some sort of violence is a necessary plot ingredient for box office success these days, our polarities are not discrete, and we find a great many feature films alloyed with violent moments regardless of their themes. Moreover, in the great mix of the middle resides those films that sample graphic violence in an action-adventure style yet still strive to make an aesthetic, ideological, or psychological point, such as *Falling Down* (1993), *Boogie Nights* (1997), and *The Game* (1997). Even the industry's biggest blockbuster ever, *Titanic* (1997), which is a romantic adventure staged in a historical context, cannot escape deploying liberal doses of the popcorn disaster violence first seen in its action-adventure ancestor *The Poseidon Adventure* (1972).

To further complicate our discussion one should also consider those films that are graphically violent but claim to take an ironic view of violence, or to be statements against it, like *Natural Born Killers* (1994), or the classic mediations of the Vietnam War, the symbolic *The Wild Bunch* (1969), and the literal *Platoon* (1986). In black-focused commercial films we find a similar spectrum between the polar ends of cheap thrills and historical agonies. Features like *New Jack City* (1991), *Juice* (1992), *Menace II Society* (1993), *Trespass* (1992), *Set It Off* (1996), *Posse* (1993), and *Bad Boys* (1995) are all centered on violence as action-adventure entertainment and make up the popular end of the field. At the other end, examples of black-focused films that attempt to represent violence in a historical, moral, or epic context would include *Malcolm X* (1992), *Rosewood* (1997), *Amistad* (1997), and *Beloved* (1998). Those films that are a mix of action-adventure violence and politicized or historicized theme would include *Dead Presidents* (1995), *Boyz N the Hood* (1991), and *Panther* (1995). Moreover, both *Boyz N the Hood* and *Menace II Society*, as well as *Clockers* (1995), all make varied claims that their depictions of violence are meant to help stem black urban violence.

However we map this complex and tangled field, we find that the origins of contemporary black screen violence are located in Hollywood's blaxploitation period, which consists of sixty-something cheaply made black-focused action-adventure flicks released between 1969 and 1974. Representationally, things started to stir when, to the cheers of blacks and the applause of the mainstream white audience, star athlete turned actor Jim Brown sprinted down a line of ventilators, dropping grenades into them and blowing up a gathering of the elite Nazi German command in *The Dirty Dozen* (1967). The industry's long unspoken but strictly observed rules regarding the expression of black violence toward whites were beginning to erode under the political pressures of the civil rights movement and the surging "black power" aspirations of urban blacks. Before this defining cinematic moment, with rare exceptions, like Paul Robeson killing a prison guard (not even seen in today's prints) in *The Emperor Jones* (1933), or the obligatory threat of savage tribesmen in the Tarzan flicks or the Mau Maus in *Something of Value* (1957), black lives were expendable and spectacularly devalued. Except for the functional purposes of staging threats and challenges to white supremacy to which whites could heroically respond, nonwhites were prohibited from inflicting violence upon whites, for compared to black life, white life was sacrosanct on the cinema screen.[4]

However, it was not too long after Jim Brown's grenade attack that a black superhero outlaw with revolutionary pretensions emerged in *Sweet Sweetback's Baadasssss Song* (1971) to maim or kill several white policemen, enjoy various dubious sexual escapades, and then escape a citywide dragnet to brag about it all. Thus the blaxploitation formula, which generally consisted of a black hero out of the ghetto underworld, violently challenging "the Man" and triumphing over a corrupt, racist system, was born. What followed was a succession of detectives, gangsters, ex-cons, cowboys, dope dealers, pimps, insurgent slaves, and women vigilantes in flicks like *Shaft*, *Superfly*, *Across 110th Street*, *Black Caesar*, *Drum*, *Black Mama*, *White Mama*, and *Boss Nigger*, in which the protagonists shoot, punch, stab, and karate chop their way through a series of low-budget features that garnered mega-profits for Hollywood.[5] A couple of things are notable about the construction of violence in most blaxploitation period pieces. For one, because the technological advances of today's cinematic apparatus allow the industry to ever more convincingly represent or simulate anything that can be written or imagined, blaxploitation violence in many instances now appears crudely rendered and visually "camp" or naive in comparison to graphic blood- and brain-splashing shoot-outs in contemporary hood-homeboy action flicks. Also, the blaxploitation genre had a place for macho women in its pantheon of fierce action stars, women who echoed and upheld the cultural moment's call for a reclamation of black manhood in the most violent, masculinist terms. Pam Grier in *Coffy* (1973) and *Foxy Brown* (1974), and Tamara Dobson in *Cleopatra Jones* (1973) play sexy black women adventurers configured to the social message of the times and black male adolescent fantasies that largely determined the success of blaxploitation films at the box office.

But perhaps most important, while the genre is full of fantastic moments of popcorn violence, like Foxy Brown (Pam Grier) triumphantly displaying the genitals of her archenemy in a jar, or vampire Blacula (William Marshall) energetically dispatching several white L.A. cops in *Blacula* (1972), blaxploitation violence, in most cases, referenced black social reality, or transcoded, however fancifully, black political struggles and aspirations of the times. When outside the movie theaters urban blacks were increasingly becoming disenchanted with the limited gains of the civil rights movement, and black militancy was on the rise with insurrections in hundreds of U.S. cities, these social energies found barely containable expression on the blaxploitation screen.

Transcoding the energy of the moment, the box office hit *Superfly* (1972) exemplifies blaxploitation violence's social grounding in a variety of expressions, even though the film was considered regressive by many black critics because of its blatant celebration of cocaine use and the hero's self-indulgent, drug pushing, hustling lifestyle. In the film's opening the protagonist dope dealer, Superfly (Ron O'Neal), chases down and then brutally stomps a junkie mugger. However, the mise-en-scène is insistently socially contextualized as the foot chase winds its way through the grimy alleys and dilapidated tenements of Harlem and culminates with this hapless derelict getting the vomit kicked out of him in front of his impoverished wife and children; and all this to the over-dub refrain of Curtis Mayfield singing the hit "Little Child Runnin' Wild." No matter what we think of Superfly, or this nameless junkie, the social setting of this opening vignette forces us into a disturbing awareness of urban poverty, drugs, and the wicked symbiotic power relation between the junkie and the pusherman.

In contrast to the gritty realism of the black underworld informing *Superfly*, where, interestingly, no guns are ever fired and most of the violence wears the cool mask of macho gesture, threat, and intimidation, the movie concludes with a rather fantastic athletic explosion of fisticuffs. In a cartoonish allusion to Popeye's love of spinach, Superfly toots up on cocaine and then singlehandedly whips three police detectives (in slow motion, no less), all while the corrupt police commissioner, literally known as "the Man," holds him at gunpoint. The social issues of this violent denouement emerge when Superfly informs the Man that he's quitting the dope business, with a million dollars in drug profits. However, this retirement speech is also meant to recuperate the film's reactionary attitude and align it more closely with the political energies of the times. For Superfly dramatically tells the Man off in the collective voice and terms of the black social insurgence of the late 1960s, thus framing what would be a totally implausible scene, and the film, in the social yearnings of the historical moment. This type of politically conscious speech is fairly standard throughout the genre, from Ji-Tu Cumbuka's rousing gallows speech after an aborted slave revolt in *Mandingo* (1972), to Pam Grier's call to black unity and arms, against the backdrop of a wall-size George Jackson poster, in *Foxy Brown*.

It can be argued that society's racial power relation hasn't changed all that significantly in the past twenty years,[6] but it's clear that the psychic and social influences impelling the construction of black cinematic violence most certainly have changed. In comparison to the blaxploitation era, the hood-homeboy films of the 1990s are less obviously politically focused, and in their violent nihilism (and sometimes self-contempt) they hardly suggest the possibility of social change. Violence in the blaxploitation genre, in all of its expressions, no matter how crude or formulaic, transcoded the black liberation impulse of the 1960s. By contrast, the depiction of violence in the new black film wave, and especially the home-boy-action flick, rather than mediating black social and political yearnings, is concerned more with depicting the grim, violent struggle for individual survival left in the wake of the faded collective dreams of the 1960s. In white commercial cinema, films such as *Being There* (1979), *The Big Chill* (1983), *Wall Street* (1987), and *Running on Empty* (1988) mediate aspects of the shift away from a 1960s cultural orientation. *The Toy* (1982) and *Trading Places* (1983) certainly signal this shift for black-focused main-stream cinema as surely as the rise of their respective stars, Richard Pryor and Eddie Murphy, followed the end of blaxploitation. The concentration of Hollywood's attention and production budgets on the rise of Pryor and Murphy coincides with the political and cultural shift from "we" to "me" in mainstream culture and in representations of African Americans in com-mercial cinema. For no matter how imperfectly rendered its narratives, vio-lence in much of Blaxploitation either depicted or implied the shaking off of the oppression of "the Man," and, significantly, the movement toward the dream of a liberated future.

By contrast, violence in the new black film wave for the most part transcodes the collapse of those very hopes under the assault of the Reagan and Bush years and their rollback policies on affirmative action, black social progress, multiculturalism, and the welfare state in general. And per-haps that is the ghettocentric hood-homeboy flick's most salient political point. With black inner-city neighborhoods ringed and contained by police departments, totally deindustrialized, poisoned with abundant drugs, fortified with malt liquor, and flooded with cheap guns, ghettos have become free fire zones where the most self-destructive impulses are encouraged by every social and economic factor in the environment. Or as a white cop in Spike Lee's *Clockers* (1995) coldly analogizes, the urban ghetto has become "a self-cleaning oven." At best, then, 1990s cinematic hood-homeboy violence is socially diagnostic in an attempt to raise con-sciousness by depicting the symptoms of a failed social and racial system. These depictions amount to endless variations on scenes of black and other nonwhite people trapped in ghettos, and killing each other. Note (Ice Cube) Doughboy's "either they don't know, or they don't care" appeal for an awakening of conscience (and consciousness) at the end of *Boyz N the Hood*. The Hughes brothers, the directors of *Menace II Society*, say it another way, declaring that they are not here to give people hope but rather to depict the realities of those trapped in the urban hood.[7] Thus one can discern the great distance between the political consciousness underpin-ning even the cheapest of blaxploitation, ghetto thrillers, and the hood-homeboy flicks of the 1990s black movie boom.

Yet, as with blaxploitation, the success of any commercial black film today is still eminently configured by the tastes of its (and Hollywood's) biggest aggregate, the youth audience, which mainly consumes action-adventure and generalized comedy and eschews drama and character-focused vehicles.[8] Consequently, the popular end of the spectrum of 1990s black-focused films is crowded with those productions deploying violence very much in the style of dominant cinema, as a necessary action-adventure ingredient for box office success. Moreover, one can perceive a definite escalation or acceleration of violence from film to film. John Singleton's *Boyz N the Hood*, while punctuated with explicitly violent scenes, structures its narrative and ideology around the fates of good and bad brothers, Tre (Cuba Gooding) and Doughboy (Ice Cube). In this way the film at least holds out the possibility of escape from the hood through the time-honored, black race–building route of education. Conversely, the fates of Caine (Tyrin Turner) and O-Dog (Larenz Tate) are sealed when O-Dog brutally murders two Korean grocers in the opening moments of *Menace II Society*. From this gruesome beginning, the trajectory is straight down. And compared to *Boyz* the body count increases exponentially; the action in *Menace* is best described as sort of a gruesome hyperviolence.

Consequently, many of the issues and debates regarding the depiction of extreme graphic violence as entertainment or realism were brought into high focus with the release and box office success of *Menace II Society*. The Hughes brothers have claimed that their depiction of violence in *Menace* was a means to promote anti-violence efforts in the urban hood, telling the *New York Times*, "we wanted to show the realities of violence, we wanted to make a movie with a strong antiviolent theme and not like one of those Hollywood movies where hundreds of people die and everybody laughs and cheers."[9] However, the film's violence and impact on its audience would seem to annul this claim. As the brothers say, throughout most of *Menace* violence is handled in an ugly, brutal fashion, as in the killings of the Korean grocers that open the film. However, the narrative is saturated with so many intensely violent scenes that violent action becomes the main structuring, captivating—and thus cumulatively entertaining—device in the film. What is more, in *Menace*'s final moments, when Caine is cut down in a hail of bullets, the scene is filmed in close-frame slow motion, thus fetishizing violence and evoking a style in the grammar of representational violence going back to Hollywood's foundational *Bonnie and Clyde* (1967).[10] But perhaps more disturbing was *Menace*'s social impact, with film and media critics noting that youth audiences cheered the violent scenes—particularly the one in which the Korean grocers were killed. Because film is an intensely visual medium, audiences, whether impressionable or sophisticated, will always look past what a director says about a film's lofty intents to the visible evidence of what a film actually shows them on the big screen.

It is also important to note that ghettocentric violence is not always revealed through the lens of the hood-homeboy action formula and that in various ways some black artists have tried to counter its exploitation on the screen. When he stands up to the neighborhood bully, Ice Cube comes to a critical moment of extreme provocation in his popular hood-homeboy comedy *Friday* (1995). Flush with anger, Ice Cube pulls a gun, but instead of following the protocols of homeboy realism and "bustin' a cap" in his adversary, he pauses and reflects on the dire outcomes of such an act. Spike Lee's character-focused drama *Clockers*, about a low-level drug dealer, covers the same issues and the same deadly turf. Like Ice Cube, Lee turns his eye more to the destructive consequences and grief that violence brings to the community and people's lives. The violence in *Clockers* is minimal, low-key though realistic, and decidedly not of the action-entertainment variety. Marking the contrast between anti-violence strategies in *Clockers* and *Menace,* critic Leonard Quart comments that "Lee truly wants to turn his adolescent audience away from violence, rather than ostensibly moralize against it like *Menace* which simultaneously makes the gory spectacle of people being slaughtered so exciting that the audience could howl with joy while watching."[11]

Nowhere are the contrasts between sensation-driven and character/plot-driven films more evident than between the filmmaking practices of black men and black women, and how these gender differences are perceived by the dominant film industry. Since the breakthrough of Julie Dash's *Daughters of the Dust* (1991), which had a reflective, dreamlike surface and no action-adventure violence, Hollywood has released into mainstream distribution a meager handful of features directed or written by black women, films like *Just Another Girl on the I.R.T.* (1993) directed by Leslie Harris, *I Like It Like That* (1994) directed by Darnell Martin, and *Eve's Bayou* (1997), written by Kasi Lemmons. When it occurs, violence in all of these films is understated, it causes the protagonists a great deal of anguish, and it is used to dramatize the complexities of broader social or psychological situations. Film industry exclusion intensifies according to the number of out-groups one belongs to. So, reinforcing the bias against black women's filmmaking, Hollywood's executive offices, in general, tend to view women's narratives as "soft," centered on drama and character, and outside of their most reliable money-making formulas, which, of course, means liberal doses of action and violence. These differences in industry perception and audience consumption of black men's and women's products, especially concerning the uses of violence, in part explain the box office success of *Menace II Society* and the comparative failure of *Just Another Girl on the I.R.T.,* which were both modest-budget black films released at the same time.

It is also interesting to note that the gender hybrid originating in blaxploitation, the woman-focused action-adventure flick, has risen again in a series of variations and specific moments in films. *Set It Off,* featuring Queen Latifah, Jada Pinkett, and Vivica A. Fox, is about an all-girl gang that tries to escape the ghetto by pulling a series of increasingly violent bank jobs. In Quentin Tarantino's blaxploitation reprise *Jackie Brown* (1997), the undisputed queen of black camp violence, Pam Grier, returns to play a somewhat more subdued, middle-aged airline stewardess who rooks the streetwise gunrunner Ordell (Samuel L. Jackson) out of $500,000. One of Grier's big Freudian moments of reversal and castrating violence comes when she presses a gun to Ordell's dick and talks bad to him. And again recalling blaxploitation's sexual ideology, in Ice Cube's *The Player's Club* (1998), homosexuality, the great threat to cultural nationalism, is punished as the beautiful stripper protagonist brutally defeats the "wicked" lesbian stripper in the film's culminating woman-on-woman fistfight.

If violence is the principal and profitable cheap thrill in the hood-homeboy action flick, it also finds expression at the other end of the black cinema spectrum as historical agony in such recent films as *Malcolm X,* *Rosewood,* and *Amistad, Beloved,* and to a lesser degree in *Panther.* As Spike Lee's most ambitious and publicized project to date, *Malcolm X* grapples with a routine industry contradiction: it is a Hollywood bio-pic with crossover money-making intentions, but at the same time, it aims to portray the life of a black revolutionary hero with some historical veracity. In pursuit of the broad audience in the middle, Lee mixes his renderings of violence by first entertaining us with the adventures of Malcolm as a hoodlum with his sidekick Shorty as they pursue the transgressive adventure of the hustling life. Lee even throws in a dance-musical number in zoot suits. But in the latter half of *Malcolm X,* the mood shifts and culminates with the brutally drawn out and explicit assassination of Malcolm X before a public assembly; the moment is both stunning and ambivalent in its effects. This scene has complex crosscurrents of political meaning, first working as historiographic realism to psychically shock us into fully recognizing the sacrifice that Malcolm X (and his family) made for black liberation and social progress. Yet the graphically violent surplus of the scene also turns it, in the Foucaldian sense, into spectacle, a public execution by firing squad rendered in brutal detail, punishing Malcolm for his beliefs. Accordingly, then, his last speech can also be viewed as a gallows speech.[12]

Like Lee's *Malcolm X,* Mario and Melvin Van Peebles's *Panther* aspires to historical distinction, this time by sympathetically depicting the rise of the Black Panther Party, and the grievances of the black community that brought the party into being—police brutality, ghettoization, economic marginalization, and disenfranchisement. However, while grappling with the same recurring contradictions between commerce and politics that appeared in *Malcolm X, Panther* relies mostly on the action-adventure violence of the Hollywood heroic individual in pursuit of profits at the box office. Thus beyond the political insights about its historical moment the film articulates, like in the shoot-out in which Bobby Hutton is killed, the film's deployment of popcorn violence in other scenes tends to undermine *Panther's* claims to a historically realist style. Moreover, this tangle of issues involving varied styles of violence is certainly relevant to John Singleton's *Rosewood* and Steven Spielberg's *Amistad.* And perhaps these issues can be best explored by considering a question salient to both films: How does one make a feel-good Hollywood movie, with big box office expectations, about some of history's most wicked crimes: racism, genocide, and slavery?

John Singleton answers, in *Rosewood,* by formulating his tale about the real-life 1923 destruction of the all-black Florida town of Rosewood by a white mob as a revisionist Western, replete with an opening scene of the loner hero Mann (Ving Rhames) riding into town on a black "hoss," packing two .45 automatics, and "lookin' for a nice place to settle down." As Lee did in *Malcolm X,* Singleton opts for a mix of action-adventure moments of popcorn violence, enveloped in a more shocking overall rendering of historicized violence. In one scene depicting the former, Mann hurries out of town to escape a deputized lynch mob, but he is set upon by a gang of white men and chased deep into the woods. Finally, Mann turns, stands his ground, and opens up with both of his .45s. Cut to the whites hauling ass out of the woods, with the punchline coming when they later excitedly exclaim that they were ambushed by a gang of "ten or fifteen niggers." The audience explodes with laughter. Singleton's timing and editorial touch with this classic scene from the archives of the cinematic Old West proves just right.

Overall, however, what happens to Rosewood on that gruesome night, as rendered by Singleton, is not at all funny or entertaining. At the height of the film's action, the disturbing sight of black men and women hanging from trees and telephone poles illuminated by the flames of their burning community, seamlessly merges with those old *Life*, *Jet*, and archival photographs of the very real lynchings in America's gallery of horrors. Consequently, *Rosewood*'s panorama of violence is decidedly not escapist entertainment in the Hollywood sense. Violence here provokes the return of barely repressed collective nightmares and guilty complicities, as well as a painful examination of the national conscience. These are all things we as a national audience don't like to address, even in the darkness and anonymity of our cinemas. The historical agony of genocidal violence is brought into sharp focus in one of *Rosewood*'s culminating scenes, in which one of the mob's prime instigators, proud of his crimes, forces his young son to look at a pile of black bodies awaiting disposal. Here, all of humanity's body counts are evoked, from Auschwitz to Wounded Knee to Mylai. Singleton's obvious point is that hope resides in the next generation, as the child rejects his father's wretched path and runs away from home.

Yet, as noted, *Rosewood* is a mainstream commercial vehicle, and as such, its approach to violence is necessarily a mixed bag. If the film aspires to social conscience by shocking us with the historically repressed and oppressed, the lynch mob and its victims, it unfortunately lapses into the delusion of Hollywood formula in its portrayal of violence against women, black and white. Here we confront Hollywood's trickle-down theory of punishment, with the most powerless individuals in any hierarchy taking the rap for privileged elites hidden from critical interrogation. So, one must ask, why is it that the darkest black woman in the cast (Akosua Busia as Jewel), who opens the film with her legs spread, squealing from the pain of rape, then in the film's closure gruesomely displayed as a murdered corpse, face up, eyes open in close-up? The argument here is that the narrative chain of significations, and the visual framing of her corpse, link the spectacle of Jewel's punishment to miscegenation, but also, implicitly, to her color. The whole issue of a devaluing, color-caste hierarchy, in this instance focused on those whom Alice Walker has referred to as "*black*, black" women, continues to be a troubling reality in mainstream commercial cinema.

Rosewood ends with the camera looking down in a long shot of a shack as we hear the screams of the white woman Fannie (Catherine Kellner), who initially yelled "nigger" to set things off, being brutally beaten by her husband, mixed with an over-dub of lush, poignant cinematic music of the type used to signal narrative and ideological resolution. In Singleton's defense one can speculate that a society that could burn an entire black town on impulse would have no trouble thrashing one defenseless, lower-class white woman of loose reputation, especially one who has been set up by the narrative. Fannie does bear the historical burden of the oft-deployed false rape charge against black men. Yet with this beating the film reverts to a final cheap thrill amounting to another act of symbolic punishment that displays the sacrificial offender/victim as spectacle, while hiding the intrigues of the much more guilty and powerful. Coming in the film's closing moment, then, this beating concentrates blame for the genocide of a racial minority on yet another Hollywood out-group, disenfranchised women.[13]

In dominant cinema, moreover, the representation of black violence in the service of white narratives still circulates powerfully, animating some of Hollywood's most popular features. This is in part because the sign of blackness has become so indispensable as the implicit, negative standard in neoconservative political rhetoric and moral panics about family, education, welfare, and crime. Simultaneously, however, the stylistic inventions and expressions of black culture powerfully influence every aspect of mainstream culture, especially urban youth styles, language, music, and dance. In many ways the films of writer-directors David Lynch and Quentin Tarantino epitomize the utility and profitability of black violence, as well as the deeply rooted psychological fantasies about the sign blackness in the white popular imaginary. David Lynch's crime-action-romance *Wild at Heart* (1990) opens with the gratuitous and brutally graphic murder of a black man who gets his brains publicly stomped out for the entertainment, and perhaps wish fulfillment, of the action-adventure audience. In this scene, in fact, David Lynch treats us to a "lynching," which also happens to be a play on his name and his style as invoked by the popular press.[14] More broadly, Quentin Tarantino, in films like *True Romance, Reservoir Dogs, Pulp Fiction, Get Shorty*, and *Jackie Brown*, appears to be deeply disturbed by barely repressed, ambivalent feelings about race in general, black masculinity in particular, and the issues of violence, miscegenation, and sex. Black male delinquents, while hip and alluring in Tarantino screenplays, wind up eliminated, raped, or murdered, with black male–white female miscegenation always punished. Conversely, black women are the exotic trophies of white male desire.

Perhaps the most troubling and historically predictable of Tarantino's constructions of black violence occurs in *True Romance* (1993), with the figure of the vicious pimp, drug-dealer Drexl, played by Gary Oldman in blackface. With this character, Tarantino's construction of the violent black male criminal becomes so grotesque and caricatured that it serves as an updated version of its racist historical referent, the "renegade Negro" Gus of *The Birth of a Nation* (1915). The similarities between the two are instructive. Gus, like Tarantino's drug-dealing pimp in dreadlocks, is a blackface caricature portrayed by a white man. Most significantly, both of these figures, Gus and Drexl, represent sexual threats to white women and are ultimately punished with violent deaths. Gus's pursuit of white women becomes Griffith's rationalization for the organization and glorification of the Ku Klux Klan, which lynches Gus. Asserting the same basic threat, Tarantino evokes the rape-rescue paradigm in the actions of Clarence (Christian Slater), who, in a spectacularly violent scene, kills the black criminal Drexl to redeem his white girlfriend from sexual slavery. Considering this scene, and Tarantino's obsession with (for pleasure and profit, no less) the word *nigger*, which he says he wants to shout from the rooftops,[15] one can speculate as to how much power relations and systems of representation have changed in the dominant film industry.

The big-budget, mainstream feature at the end of the scale of black violence as historical agony and realism is Steven Spielberg's *Amistad*, weighing in with production costs totaling $75 million. *Amistad* fits into a trajectory well established by a number of films made during the blaxploitation period, like the action- and sexploitation-driven *Mandingo* and *Drum* (1976), and sustained in the 1990s with *Sankofa* (1993) and *Beloved*, which sharply reverse or debunk Hollywood's genteel sentimental depiction of slavery over the eighty-year span of its "plantation genre."[16] Because *Amistad* recounts the actual events of a slave revolt on the high seas, and the successful repatriation of the rebellious Africans after an extensive court case, the film struggles in its narrative with two issues pertaining to black violence that are not given much exposure in dominant cinema. The first concerns the right, the necessity, of the slave to rebel against tyranny. The second issue has to do with the graphic revelation of the violence and oppression routinely inflicted upon blacks by the daily operations of the slave system.

Of course it's a long way from historical actuality to the big-budget Hollywood canvas, with its ultimate imperative that everybody's story be measured by its box office potential—that is, reduced to the compromises of its commodity status. Given the pressures on any blockbuster to return a profit at the ratio of three to one on an already hefty investment, it seems that in search of the broadest audience (read: white approval), Spielberg approaches the issue of black revolt against white systems of tyranny, or even the frank depiction of those systems, with narrative restraint, to say the least. Yet, due to the inherent violent and irrepressible surplus of the subject matter, *Amistad*, unavoidably perhaps, unmasks the extreme cruelty of the slave system in historical realist terms. Consequently, as in Spielberg's *Schindler's List* (1993), as well as the work of Lee and Singleton, here again we see the containing power of delimiting form and formula aimed at ensuring the biggest audience, in direct conflict with the insurgent tendency of *Amistad*'s inherently emancipatory content.

Amistad opens with a spirited, furious, and successful shipboard rebellion that soon goes adrift, with the black rebels being recaptured, imprisoned, and put on trial in New England. From here on the Africans are enslaved by the representational chains of Hollywood liberalism as they are portrayed as confused, exotic creatures and denied all agency, voice, and centrality in what one would expect to be their story. The narrative drags, then turns into a two-hour civics lesson about noble, well-intentioned whites defining and securing black freedom.[17] When it comes to Hollywood's standard depiction of black liberation struggles, black characters tend to have no agency in the production of their own history, and are reduced to passive victims emancipated by courageous whites (like the FBI in *Mississippi Burning* or the white lawyers in *Ghosts of Mississippi*). In fact,

ed guerrero

this stratagem is so worn that Matthew McConaughey was recruited from *A Time to Kill* (1996), to play yet another dedicated white lawyer in defense of a black cause in *Amistad.* This convention is also present in *Schindler's List,* in which the narrative focus is on factory owner Oskar Schindler and concentration camp commander Amon Goeth, with the Jews mostly reduced to the passivity of a grim historical backdrop.

However, any commercial film as visual commodity bears complex, contradictory forces and meanings that are not entirely containable, and are contested by many—often opposing—social perspectives. And regarding the depiction of violence in *Amistad* this is no less the case. The slave revolt in *Amistad's* opening, a revolt of oppressed against oppressor, has considerable action-adventure impact and historical appeal. Yet its placement is a subtle form of co-optation: staging the insurrection in the opening moments of the narrative denies it any conclusive, cathartic force, thus displacing the insight that resistance against oppression in defence of one's freedom is a form of justice, one afforded every white hero from John Wayne to Gary Cooper and Henry Fonda onward. As we come to see, *Amistad's* version of justice is a weary court case that essentially celebrates constitutional definitions of *white* freedom. It is important to note that while the *Amistad* court case freed thirty-eight Africans, it did nothing to alter the fate of millions of black people enslaved in the United States, or the efficient workings of the slave system itself. If anything, the slave system was further legally entrenched and refined by such sanctions as the Fugitive Slave Act of 1850 or the Dred Scott decision of 1857. In contrast, note who has agency, and the narrative positioning of the violent slave insurrection, in Haile Gerima's *Sankofa.* Coming at the film's conclusion, this slave rebellion works as a resolution, underlining the brutality inflicted upon *Sankofa's* blacks, broadcasting that they have agency, history, and justice in their own hands. What's at issue here is how the big-budget mainstream blockbuster, regardless of what its producers claim its subject is, almost always winds up talking about whiteness, guided by the persistent refrain of Eurocentrism that subtends its narrative.[18]

In fairness, however, *Amistad* is punctuated with scenes that cannot be entirely repressed, scenes that are quite disturbing and challenging to comfortable, dominant notions of slavery, cinematic, psychic, or otherwise. As noted, Hollywood's depiction of slavery has experienced a sharp reversal of meaning since the resistant blaxploitation of the 1970s. By now, the plantation resembles the blood-soaked ground of the concentration camp more than it does the majestic site of aristocratic Southern culture and gentility. So the irrepressible horror of the slave trade comes into disturbing focus with *Amistad's* depictions of the infamous Middle Passage, and with one particularly stunning scene in which commerce and mass murder converge with brutal clarity, when the Spanish slavers discover that they don't have enough rations to keep their entire human cargo alive for the Atlantic crossing. Echoing the death camp scene in *Schindler's List,* in which the weak are culled from the strong, in *Amistad* the cargo's weak and sickly are stripped naked, chained together, and very efficiently thrown overboard. Besides the naked, chained bodies, underscoring a basic humanity, what is more disturbing about the scene's violence is the banal utility seen in the practices of maintaining human beings as slaves for profit. This insight is reinforced by other scenes of maintenance and discipline, in which slaves are fed, flogged, and washed in order to enhance their commodity value on the auction block in the New World. Very much like *Schindler's List, Amistad*'s true force resides in its visual shock value, and in those resistant images, currents, and arguments that escape the policing of Hollywood's liberal, paternalist discourse. Relevant to the fundamental problem with both *Amistad* and *Schindler's List*, one critic puts it succinctly when he asks why *Schindler's List* "is so complicit with the Hollywood convention of showing catastrophe primarily from the point of view of the perpetrators."[19]

In conclusion, I have no doubts that the cinematic depiction of black violence expressed in a variety of mixtures between the poles of cheap, pyrotechnic thrills and the collective agony of historical catastrophes, between entertainment and edification, will continue to evolve as a deeply imbricated and, often, inseparable part of Hollywood's accelerating commitment to all forms of cinematic violence as a technology-enabled, profit-driven industry strategy. Predictably, even though the genre is played out,[20] the film industry will continue to produce a certain number of popcorn violence–saturated hood-homeboy flicks like the recent *Belly*, and the more restrained and socially grounded *Slam* (both 1998). Hope resides in the more innovative ways in which black filmmakers deploy violence in the service of their takes on realism, or the revision of social or historical issues from the black point of view. Suggestions of new directions can be seen in several recent black-inspired, black-cast commercial productions, including the Spike Lee–produced *Tales from the Hood* (1995) and the Oprah Winfrey–inspired and –produced *Beloved*. A horror flick, *Tales from the Hood* makes it clear that for blacks, the horrific repressed fears returning in the form of the monster are markedly political and have to do with the great violent horrors of African-American life: police brutality, lynching, racism, and the catastrophic effects of social inequality. In its mix of popcorn and historical violence, the monsters that arise in *Tales*, are more literal than metaphorical: corrupt, brutal cops framing black citizens, criminally violent hood-homeboys bent on autogenocide, and spouses who turn into violent monsters in front of their wives and children. Similarly, *Beloved* struggles to innovate and frankly depict the reality and consequences of slavery's violence through the metaphor of scarring, both physical and psychic. The violent horror of slavery is revealed in "rememory," in a series of flame-lit, nightmarish flashbacks of hangings, whippings, and bizarre mutilations that continue to haunt and scar the psyches, the narrative present, and the bodies of the film's black cast. Ultimately, then, what will continue to subtly influence the trajectory of black screen violence and suggest new creative directions for its expression and critical understanding will be the persistent and conscientious visions of wave after wave of new black filmmakers in all of their racial and heterogeneous incarnations—as gays, women, men, subalterns, artists, intellectuals—and their ability to bring fresh narrative, social, and representational possibilities to the big screen.

Notes

1. The racial income gap is perhaps the best index of black "progress" in a nation in which social equality is dependent upon what one owns. As Andrew Hacker notes in 1975, blacks made $605 for every $1,000 that whites earned; by 1995 that figure had dropped to a black $577 for every white $1,000. Andrew Hacker, *Money: Who Has How Much and Why* (New York: Scribner, 1997) 146–47.
2. Martin Amis, "Blown Away," in *Screen Violence*, ed. Karl French (London: Bloomsbury, 1996), 12–15.
3. Neal Gabler, "The End of the Middle," *New York Times Magazine*, November 16, 1997, 76–78.
4. Ella Shohat and Robert Stam, *Unthinking Eurocentrism* (New York: Routledge, 1994), 23–25.
5. Ed Guerrero, "The Rise and Fall of Blaxploitation," in *Framing Blackness: The African American Image in Film* (Philadelphia: Temple University Press, 1993).
6. Derrick Bell, "Racial Realism—After We're Gone: Prudent Speculations on America in a Post-Racial Epoch," in *Critical Race Theory: The Cutting Edge*, ed. Richard Delgado (Philadelphia: Temple University Press, 1995), 2–8.
7. Jeff Giles, "A 'Menace' Has Hollywood Seeing Double," *Newsweek*, July 19, 1993, 52.
8. Geraldine Fabrikant, "Harder Struggle to Make and Market Black Films," *New York Times*, November 11, 1996, D1.
9. Bernard Weintraub, "Twins' Movie-Making Vision: Fighting Violence with Violence," *New York Times*, June 10, 1993, C13.
10. Paula Massood, "*Menace II Society*" *Cineaste* 20, no. 2 (1993): 44–45.
11. Leonard Quart, "Spike Lee's *Clockers*: A Lament for the Urban Ghetto," *Cineaste* 22, no. 1 (1996): 9–11.
12. Michel Foucault, *Discipline and Punish: The Birth of the Prison* (New York: Vintage Books, 1979), 42–47 and 60–61.
13. René Girard, *Violence and the Sacred* (Baltimore: Johns Hopkins Univeristy Press, 1972), 1–38.
14. Sharon Willis, *High Contrast: Race and Gender in Contemporary Hollywood Film* (Durham, N.C.: Duke University Press, 1997), 131–32.
15. Gary Groth, "A Dream of Perfect Reception: The Movies of Quentin Tarantino," in *Commodify Your Dissent*, ed. Thomas Frank and Matt Weiland (New York: W. W. Norton, 1997), 186.
16. Guerrero, *Framing Blackness*, 10.
17. Maggie Montesinos Sale, *The Slumbering Volcano: American Slave Ship Revolts and the Production of Rebellious Masculinity* (Durham, N.C.: Duke University Press, 1998), 84–86. Besides an excellent historical survey of the *Amistad* affair, Sale here gives a good account of how the *Amistad* rebels were constructed as passive "happy-go-lucky children in need of protection" at the bottom of the abolitionist defence council's hierarchy.
18. Richard Dyer, *White* (London: Routledge, 1997), 3–4.
19. Michael Andre Bernstein, "The *Schindler's List* Effect," *The American Scholar* 13, no. 3 (summer 1994): 429–32.
20. Ed Guerrero, "A Circus of Dreams and Lies: The Black Film Wave Reaches Middle Age," in *The New American Cinema*, ed. Jon Lewis (Durham, N.C.: Duke University Press, 1998), 328–52.

documenting

domestic violence

in american films

phyllis frus

The arrest of O.J. Simpson—a man with a documented history of wife
battering—for killing his ex-wife and her companion in 1994 seemed
likely to rivet national attention on domestic violence. After a brief flurry
of stories, the news media lost interest and so, apparently, did the audience.
Was it because there was no videotape of O.J. hitting Nicole Simpson to
bring the reality of this widespread crime home to us? Do we need a documentary record in order for a pattern of violence to seem real? Women
whose partners batter them or beat their children know the problem at first
hand, after all. Likewise, African Americans knew they were being targeted
by law enforcement officers before a man with a video camera documented
Rodney King being savagely beaten by cops in Los Angeles. Apparently, we
don't believe in a pattern of violence against a particular group unless we
experience it or see it for ourselves.

During the trial of O.J. Simpson there was, as documentary evidence,
the audiotape of Nicole Simpson's frightened voice telling the 911 operator, "I think you know him." Although the prosecutors played this tape,

they did not present to the jury information they had gathered about the sixty occasions on which O.J. Simpson had raped Nicole, blackened her eyes, bruised and cut her body.[1] Legal experts and the prosecution team gave several reasons for this decision not to try to convict Simpson for the murders as the culminating act in a series of brutal punishments of Nicole: the "race card" that the defense played, the limitations on character evidence, and the likelihood that the defense would counter an expert witness with its own. Above all, prosecutors seem to have despaired of being able to convince a jury of average citizens that the suave, well-dressed, rich, and personable defendant could be a savage abuser of any woman. As Myrna Raeder wrote in the *Colorado Law Review*, "despite the frequency of domestic violence, the uninformed juror runs a high risk of reaching an erroneous conclusion because popular conceptions regarding domestic violence are so often at odds with the truth."[2]

Popular Conceptions

Where do we get these notions about who is likely to batter a woman or beat a child? Because attacks are unlikely to be filmed, we cannot count on television or film documentary to make the problem of family violence real. Occasionally domestic assaults show up on the "reality" television show *Cops*, but, as in other forms of cinema vérité, a depiction may be direct without seeming real. The irony is that we get our ideas about what is real from narrative and dramatic constructions, from particular rhetorical devices and cinematic strategies that produce the effect of reality, and we judge the realism or credibility of even nonfictional representations against these conventions. Slices of life that are not produced according to the codes of realism—that have no plot, no before or after, no context in which to detect cause and effect—may not seem real. Thus Spike Lee gave meaning to the Rodney King videotape when he used it in the docudrama *Malcolm X* to show that the legacy of the failure of black militancy was continued violence against black men. Similarly, TV and film producers did some contextualizing of spousal abuse after Simpson was arrested, but it was short-lived, and O.J. Simpson did not become a plausible wife batterer to the jury.[3]

Because Hollywood films are expert at providing the illusion of reality, no matter how fantastic the story, they are an important source of our mythology about family violence. Films reinforce the view that woman battering is the victim's problem, express "commonsense" notions about how to end battering—such as the idea that women can simply leave—equate violence with sex as part of "normal" love, and in general tell these stories from the batterer's point of view, not from the woman's.[4] They are apt to depict violence against women or children in their homes as abnormal, not as the everyday reality it is, and the men who beat or torment them as psychotic or in other ways deviant. And they often sensationalize or eroticize the incidents and the victims in order to attract audiences.[5] Such strategies do not enable audiences to see the characteristics that virtually all batterers share, or how common, even mundane they are.[6] Finally, like other news and entertainment media, movies cooperate in repressing the hierarchical and gendered power relations that undergird our society. Films disseminate the ideology of the male-centered happy family and the safe and peaceful home, reinforcing as natural the man as authority figure while overlooking the reality that millions of households are unsafe places for women and children.

In films before the 1980s few scenes of men battering partners or lovers or children occur; even in the last two decades those that focus on it are rare. To anyone aware of the links between family violence and our male-dominated legal, social, and family structures it is not surprising that the subject did not get serious, focused treatment in any medium before the contemporary women's movement and battered women's defense and advocate groups brought it to the attention of the public as a specific, epidemic form of violent crime against women beginning in the 1970s.[7] Apparently woman battering was nearly invisible in films because it was rarely visible in society. More depictions occur in films since 1980, not because it has increased in actuality, but because journalists have popularized academic and feminist research on the subject, thus making it a familiar topic to the public.

One thing remains a constant, from *Public Enemy* to *What's Love Got to Do with It?:* men dominate and control women in films, just as they do in real life, even though they also fear or desire them. We can find variations on this pattern that correlate to particular sociocultural and historical realities, such as critics' identification of many characteristics of film noir with the threat to male supremacy represented by women's entry into the labor market during the Second World War and their reluctance to give up their newly won social and economic power after the war. But films do not represent overtly the mechanisms by which men enforce their power over women, despite the influence of feminism since the 1970s. Robin Wood explains why things have not changed much by noting two related phenomena: feminism was rendered nonthreatening by stripping it of its politics before it could be represented in American films; and very few women direct commercial films, for mainstream cinema is "a patriarchal industry" with "narrative conventions and genres developed by and for a male-dominated culture."[8] Films that showed woman battering as it occurs every day, in couples and families at all economic levels, could not avoid showing it as an instrument of patriarchy; that is, as a means of exercising control of women. We can imagine the response to such a film: it would be viewed as inappropriately politicizing a medium designed primarily to entertain and would be a dismal failure at the box office.

Although films about drug addiction, alcoholism, juvenile delinquency, even incest have reached large audiences (for example, the social problem films of the 1950s), Michael Wood claims they are successful because they depict characters solving these problems effectively—first identifying and then changing or creating institutions to deal with the difficulty. These problems can be solved over the course of the film because they are all variations on the same one: the problem of deviancy or otherness. Deviant behavior is corrected by returning those acting like outlaws or outside society's ordering and controlling institutions to their place within it. Because the problem solvers are male, an ordinary man acting violently in his home is unlikely to be the subject of a "problem" film, for domestic violence (as it is misleadingly called) is regarded as a woman's problem, and women's concerns, as Jackie Byars argues, are not taken seriously as social problems.[9]

Indeed, in *Come Back Little Sheba* (1952), one of the social problem films of the 1950s, when Doc Delaney, a middle class man giving a very good impersonation of a stable father and husband (his wife Lola calls him "Daddy" though they have no children), flies into a rage and threatens to kill Lola, that episode of violence is viewed as secondary to his drinking. His inability to lay off the bottle is the couple's secret, along with the fact that her pregnancy forced their marriage (she later had a miscarriage). When Doc's Alcoholics Anonymous support buddies come to take him to dry out at the hospital, they treat his waving a knife at Lola as a secondary effect of the alcohol—the "real" problem.[10]

It would be difficult to present wife battering or child abuse as deviant behavior, outside normal boundaries, for violence against family members is a crime of the hypernormal, of obsession and fanaticism. Battering a woman or a child to the point of murder is not deviant behavior; it is merely excessive—an intensification of the system that gives men control of their households.[11] And the perpetrator of the abuse cannot simply be restored to normalcy but must be driven out—by being killed or exiled from normal society. Jerry, the eponymous villain of the 1980s suspense thriller *The Stepfather*, is an example of a batterer who judges his intimates by some hidden standard of perfection; they must live up to his definition of the norm and there is no question of departing from those explicit standards. In the film, when his new neighbors are speculating about the motives of a man who has killed his whole family in a neighboring town, Jerry (that murderer in a new identity) says, "Maybe they disappointed him."[12]

Myths about Domestic Violence Communicated by Films

Guiding this survey is the question of whether films that represent woman battering in some form perpetuate or even promote various myths about domestic violence. Such myths are dangerous because they simplify the causes of wife abuse, make it easy to blame the victim, and turn stories of women trapped by socioeconomic conditions and particular structural circumstances into ones of individuals with agency, who are assumed to be able to save themselves by heroic measures. When myths dominate popular representations, the conditions under which women are abused are not clarified (the first step in changing them)—and the many "ordinary" men who beat women out of a feeling of entitlement are let off the hook because they do not resemble the madmen or animalistic brutes who commit these onerous crimes in the movies.

Myth 1: Beatings leave no permanent damage
and there are no consequences.
Surely the most famous act of aggression against a woman in a major motion picture is James Cagney's grinding a grapefruit into Mae Clarke's face in *Public Enemy* (1931), the film that made Cagney a star. Cagney

plays Tom Powers, a small-time gangster on his way up, who is living in a hotel with his girlfriend, played by Clarke. Powers is tired of his girlfriend's attempts at refined domesticity, and when she tries to keep him from drinking before he eats breakfast, he interrupts her "wish" that things could be different by first parodying her speech—"I wish you were a wishing well so I could tie you to a bucket and sink you." When she accuses him of infidelity, he picks up a grapefruit half and sticks it in her face to shut her up. This scene is cited by virtually everyone who discusses violence against women in motion pictures, formally or informally. What most people don't know, however, is that the violence was actual, rather than enacted, and it did have consequences, though they are not shown in the film.

In *Tender Comrades: A Backstory of the Blacklist,* screenwriter John Bright tells how director William Wellman got the look of "surprise and betrayal" he wanted on Clarke's face. Clarke had a bad cold that day, and at her request Cagney agreed to fake the scene, her last in the film. When Wellman heard about the arrangement, he took Cagney aside, telling him that he had to "really give it to her." Insisting that this was "the best scene in the picture" and would be "talked about for a century," he told Cagney, "it's got to be real, and if it's real . . . [it] will make you one of the biggest stars in the business." Bright says that Cagney finally agreed with Wellman, and even "added something of his own—he twisted the grapefruit," and the juice "was like a razor—it cut into her, giving her agony." Although Clarke looks stunned, the scene ends abruptly, with a dissolve to a scene later in the day. The only apparent consequence is that Tom has freed himself from the woman whom he, in true batterer fashion, doubtless blames for forcing him to hit her; representing himself as a free man, he immediately picks up a new moll, played by Jean Harlow. In real life, however, according to Bright, as soon as the scene was over, Clarke slugged Cagney, accusing him of double-crossing her, and swore never to work for Warner Bros. again.[13]

Myth 2: Batterers are not like us—they're mobsters,
or immigrants, or lower class.

Although the acting in *Public Enemy* is stylized and the gaps between scenes, with the passage of time unaccounted for, are typical of other gangster thrillers, hints of social realism are also present in the film. For example, we learn from the title cards that frame the film not only that the story of Tom Powers is based on an actual gangster's life but that it is important to see what forces lead to a public enemy like him in order to combat the evil he represents. Another element of realism is the motivation given for Tom's later misogynist behavior. In an early scene, the boy Tom and his friend Matt Doyle are shown tying a string across the sidewalk so that Matt's sister will trip on her roller skates. When Matt protests that they might hurt her, Tom says, in effect, who cares—"She's just a girl, ain't she?" Tom's father calls him inside, having heard about an episode of stealing, and beats him with a strap. Tom is afraid, but represses it under a tough guy act. His mother, who never gives up thinking the best of him even when he is a big-time gangster, here exhibits fear, but she does not interfere with her husband's discipline. We wonder, for a moment, does he beat her too? The screenplay lays the psychological groundwork for Tom to develop into a heartless, violent man, and the two establishing scenes match what we know of the role of an abusive childhood in the etiology of a batterer.[14]

Myth 3: Women enjoy rough sex and secretly want to be raped.

Nearly as famous a scene of a strong man overpowering his partner is *Gone with the Wind*'s representation of what feminists have taught us to call marital rape but audiences since 1939 have apparently regarded as what the woman wanted: Rhett Butler's seizing his wife Scarlett and carrying her upstairs to bed, where he ravishes her and leaves her pregnant. In *Holding My Own in No Man's Land* Molly Haskell discusses women's uncritical interpretation of this scene in the context of what they have in mind when they fantasize about being raped; she concludes that women mean something different by a "fantasy" of being overcome than men do. They don't desire to be raped in the sense of being forcefully and painfully penetrated when they have refused sexual relations—they know rape is an act of violence; their fantasies involve love and romance. Thus Scarlett's case matches many women's fantasies, for they assume she really did want Butler to take the initiative and insist on sex with her. Haskell says that the different scenarios men and women have in mind when they talk about rape fantasies shows the sexual divide with stark clarity: "Where a man will see territorial conquest in Gable's action, a woman will see uncontrollable longing."[15] Haskell calls this debate the "2,000-year-old misunderstanding" and views it as the crux of the war between the sexes.

A related controversy is whether films mirror reality or influence it while hiding their position behind transparent form and a supposedly neutral apparatus, so that we do not see that a gendered, class-based point of view is being presented. The two debates are related in that the assumption that women secretly want to be raped is one of the common myths that films reinforce. It is important to call attention to these myths as this survey moves into the 1940s, for when popular films began to give audiences the illusion of realism they increasingly sought through an emphasis on naturalistic (or method) acting, location filming as opposed to studio sets, and the techniques of seamless or transparent realism, their ideological effects were enhanced; they seemed to be authentic slices of life.

No one can yoke rough sex and realism without thinking of Stanley Kowalski and his wife Stella in the film version of Tennessee Williams's play *A Streetcar Named Desire* (1951). While most of the critical attention has centered on Stanley's rape of his wife's sister, Blanche Du Bois, the rape is presented as an unconscionable act of violence and so audiences are allowed their moral outrage. Also, as Peter Keough points out, this costs Kowalski in the film version, for Stella leaves him with her newborn after Blanche has been led away to a sanitarium, her loose hold on sanity finally broken by her brother-in-law's degrading violation.[16] The plot development that is more disturbing to some feminists (and to the censors, who insisted on cuts) is Stella's clear enjoyment of Stanley's violent tactics during sex (see the morning-after scene in the restored 1994 version in which Stella, still in bed, holds on to her satisfied smile while recounting to Blanche her wedding night, when Stanley smashed all the lightbulbs with her slipper). Keough protests the censors' attempt to excise the pleasure Stella takes in her husband's violent approach to sex and even his obsessive control of her—made clear in the scene of the night before, when, in response to his bellowing her name, she descends the stairs to him from her neighbor's apartment, where she has fled after his drunken beating of her pregnant body.[17] Although censorship should be resisted, feminists at least have a worthy motive for wishing that Williams's fantasy did not require Stella to forgive her husband so easily for beating her because she is in sexual thrall to him. Accounts by battered women give lie to the notion that women who suffer abuse enjoy being forced to have sex any more than they enjoy being beaten. Their testimony is no doubt what led legislators finally to acknowledge that unwanted sex from one's husband is akin enough to unwanted sex from a stranger to warrant making marital rape a crime.[18] American cinema before the 1980s seems instead to have reinforced the male fantasy that women are awakened sexually by the use of force.

One of the two love interests in the life of Dixon Steele, the screenwriter and angry protagonist of *In a Lonely Place* (1950), illustrates the myth that women find violent men attractive. A previous lover, Frances Randolph, tries to lure him back even after seeing Dix start a fight in a bar; we learn when detectives read his rap sheet (he is a suspect in the murder of a young woman) that Frances once accused him of breaking her nose, though she soon retracted the complaint. We expect his battering qualities and his violent tendencies to be downplayed because she and other characters view him as "a special and privileged being"[19]—though sinister lighting of his face and his off-center placement in some shots contradict their view of him and reinforce our suspicion that he is capable of having murdered Mildred Atkinson, who was last seen at his apartment. When the focus and point of view shift to Laurel Gray, the woman who falls in love with Dixon after furnishing him an alibi based only on his looks, contradictory versions of his character are put on view and reinforced by the mise-en-scène. For example, a menacing low-angle shot of Laurel's masseuse while she is describing Dix's history of hurting women serves as a warning. When we see Laurel putting her fears first, refusing to suppress them though she clearly would marry Dixon if he could control his rage, her action expresses the proto-feminist theme: that it is impossible for a woman to redeem a violent man by her love, because it is unlikely that such a man can change even when he has found the "right" person—the one he's been looking for, in Dixon's case, "all his life."

232

Myth 4: Women who are battered are asking for it.

It is not difficult to find in U.S. cinema reinforcement, if not the source, of a closely related male fantasy—that women regard men's force as a sign of their interest, even love. Feminist critics have noted that films of the 1940s frequently depict women who don't seem to mind being bossed around by a strong man, or who acknowledge the need for discipline in the form of a good beating or spanking. Margi McCue mentions Katherine

Hepburn in *State of the Union*, Yvonne De Carlo in *Frontier Gal*, and Greer Garson in *Adventure* as characters who interpret abuse as affection or at least regard it as beneficial to their rebellious or wild ways.[20]

In some films of this decade we find hints that some men turn to physical abuse of their wives or girlfriends out of complex feelings of fear, desire, or envy, and then rationalize it by blaming the women for their anger. This is the decade of film noir, with its femme fatale (a dangerously attractive woman) to feed the protagonist's paranoia. Although film noir has been defined based on its dark look and bleak moral vision, its themes of paranoia and betrayal, and its typical triangle of characters involved in a suspense or thriller plot, behind these films lie threats to the family resulting from changing gender roles during wartime mobilization as women assumed men's jobs and positions as heads of households, and afterward, when men returned to take up their previous roles, which had been upset by the military war and the ideological one at home.[21]

If we emphasize the noir elements of *In a Lonely Place*, we can see Dixon's propensity toward violence as readily extending to murder, for the off-center camera angles, low-key lighting, and unbalanced shots of pairs of characters reinforce our sense of the violence he keeps just under the surface;[22] and his violence against women can be explained by his status as a veteran damaged psychologically by the war. His main symptoms—his inability to write a viable screenplay and his tendency to batter—are both the results of some trauma that he has repressed (he becomes incensed at any suggestion that he should take his inner demons to counseling, where they might be revealed). Viewing Dixon as a noir character also exposes the controlling behavior that is characteristic of batterers; indeed, realizing that Laurel is leaving him—that is, escaping his control—is what finally tips him over the edge, as he begins to strangle her. Even though he is proved innocent of the murder of Mildred, this dramatic scene demonstrates Dixon's "potential for murder and his capacity for everyday violence, especially against women." As Dana Polan points out, this film "shows a violence installed within the heart of the dominant culture, ready to break out at any moment," for not only is Dixon that rare character, a batterer who is a normal man able, most of the time, to keep his rages under control, but other average men as well are shown to be capable of violence against women, including Mildred's boyfriend, who confesses to her killing, and Dixon's friend Brub, the detective, who hurts his wife while acting out Dixon's theory of how the murder was committed.[23]

Myth 5: Women are batterers too, so men are victims of "spousal violence."

This myth, reinforced by the euphemisms "family violence," "spouse abuse," even "couples who fight," is also part of a backlash against the women's movement, and may be a legacy of the fear of powerful women and of their sexuality—the same fears that perpetuated witch-hunts, made the terms *shrew* and *battleaxe* synonymous with strong women, and gave us mother-in-law jokes. The idea that both sexes batter equally may also be the result of journalism's practice of objectivity, which requires reporters to "give both sides."[24] Some women do hit their partners or boyfriends, but statistics consistently show that men are responsible for ninety-five percent of incidents of marital violence.[25]

The paranoia associated with film noir may contribute to the pop cultural myth that men are just as likely to be the victims of women's violence, for women do murder their husbands or lovers in films of this genre (see Paul Arthur's essay in this volume). While the violence sometimes does take place in the home, in the context of family life, the typical noir murder hardly resembles battering. In Hitchcock's *Shadow of a Doubt* (1943), when young Charlie murders her uncle, it is clearly in self-defense (as are most domestic partner homicides by women), whereas Uncle Charlie's attempts to murder his niece and namesake (to keep her from exposing him) are only a variation of his usual mode of killing women. There are reversals, however: rather than the male "hero" fearing a spider woman and trying to find out her secrets, this is Charlie's role—which her male name reinforces—and *he's* the "merry widow" murderer sought by the police who is dangerously attractive to Charlie. By playing on the noir conventions (having Uncle Charlie try to murder her by staging a household accident) and letting him speak his misogyny in chilling terms, Hitchcock may be reminding us of the lack of truth in common representations of women as powerful and seductive. Here a man clearly seduces his niece, convincing her not to betray him for her mother's sake.[26]

Myth 6: Ordinary men don't batter or abuse mates and children.

Raging Bull, Martin Scorsese's 1980 film based on the autobiography of boxer Jake La Motta, is pivotal because it was made after woman battering had been brought to public awareness by feminists and other advocates for the safety and health of women and children. For perhaps the first time in U.S. cinema, a film with realistic mise-en-scène treats the subject of woman battering as integral to the story of a man's life and career; what's more, the damage inflicted on the batterer's own psyche as well as on his family, particularly his second wife, Vickie, who was fifteen when they married, is clearly visible. Made by one of America's most celebrated and influential directors and featuring Robert De Niro in a tour de force of method acting, *Raging Bull* has features of documentary realism: improvised dialogue, freeze-frame sequences and stills, footage made to resemble newsreels and home movies, profanity-laced speech, and set decoration featuring items from Scorsese's family home. And yet the film's ring violence is very stylized, including slow motion, montage, abrupt cuts, extreme close-ups, and nondiegetic sound. Although La Motta was a consultant on the fight scenes, these so fetishize the blood, spittle, and sweat of De Niro's body that these scenes are surreal rather than realistic.[27]

As Frank Tomasulo notes, the documentary elements are countered by the many liberties the film takes with La Motta's autobiography and thus its failure to suggest any reason for the boxer's "lifelong rage." According to Tomasulo, La Motta's own story "provides a rather complex etiology, a combination of child abuse, poverty, and lack of education," whereas the filmmakers remove any reference to historical motives for the champion's actions on his way up or down, with the effect that his violence can be interpreted only in symbolic terms, as irrational, a sign of "personal aberrance," or as a masochistic defense against latent homosexuality.[28]

Also working against the realistic elements is the camera work that isolates certain objects for symbolic effect. In a scene in his father's empty apartment Jake and Vickie are shot looking at a picture of Jake and Joey as boys pretending to box, which is directly between them, and when Jake pulls Vickie toward the bed, the camera remains on the photograph. Also, Vickie, played by Cathy Moriarty, is given no inner life, much as directors have frequently presented women on film as vacant sites onto which men project their fantasies. Like other women who function as objects of men's desire, Moriarty's body is shown in partial images. In a bedroom scene of foreplay between the couple, between two fights with Sugar Ray Robinson in 1943, the camera moves slowly over her body from top to bottom, and we see her removing her panties, reflected in the bathroom mirror where Jake has gone to cool his erection by pouring ice water over it. Vickie is never seen as having qualities outside her sexuality (always available) and her beauty. She's an object to hit, to control, as well as to have intercourse with—or not, as La Motta fears he will spend his "fighting" energy in the sexual act. When Jake first sees Vickie at the neighborhood swimming pool, she is shot from above, her legs moving vacantly, with no succeeding shot that might indicate her thoughts; it's as if she doesn't have any of her own.[29]

Although this critically acclaimed film presents the grim facts of violence against women, it mutes the consequences (the effect of a woman batterer on the couple's children, for example), and makes these brutal acts secondary to the theme—either Jake's tragic self-destruction or his redemption through violence, depending on one's interpretation.[30] Viewers are likely to mistake the connections between boxing other men and beating up on women, assuming that they are examples of rage, of being out of control. But as Carol Adams shows in "Raging Batterer," an exhaustive analysis of the film's representations of woman battering, both are examples of controlled hitting; though boxing is sanctioned and wife abuse is not, at least overtly, both involve deliberate, measured beating as a means of asserting power over the competitor or over a woman. Adams also calls attention to the similarities between boxers' and batterers' "overinvestment in masculinity," which in the latter's case is used to build the man's superiority and the woman's subservience, ensuring male privilege. Another similarity between these two "practices" is the lack of serious consequences for brutality. Battering and rape are not considered criminal behavior unless the woman presses charges, and the batterer, like Jake La Motta when Vickie starts to leave him, often simply apologizes and promises to change. If she accepts his pleas, he is not held accountable for what he has done.[31]

Ultimately, the film conveys a grave misunderstanding of the causes and consequences of wife battering. Adams cites De Niro's comparison of the violence in *Raging Bull* to "a little domestic spat compared to what people can really do to one another." She comments, "calling a violent man's battering behavior a 'domestic spat' elides the agency of the perpetrator and trivializes the danger to the woman."[32] Another comparison is relevant here: although the ring scenes are so stylized and aestheticized that critic Morris Dickstein found them not very convincing—"Filmed in slow motion, elaborately choreographed, played at different speeds, they aestheticize the boxer's world and simplify his messy life"[33]—the domestic fights—La Motta yelling at his first wife Irma over how she has overcooked his steak, beating up his brother Joey, slapping and punching Vickie—are brutally realistic. Altogether there are many scenes of cursing, threats, and slaps by both La Motta brothers to demonstrate "who's boss" to their wives and kids.[34] As awful as the scenes are, according to Vickie La Motta, the film does not capture the sordid reality of her married life. After seeing the film she told Jake, "You were worse."[35]

It is disturbing to learn that the star and the director of *Raging Bull* (Robert De Niro and Martin Scorsese) colluded to ambush a female actor, Cathy Moriarty, for purposes of getting a realistic response, much as Cagney and Wellman surprised Mae Clarke. Moriarty describes being taken unaware by De Niro's improvised slaps and grabs. She told an interviewer, "I began concentrating so much on not getting hit or learning how to go with punches that I thought, 'I'm never going to be able to say my lines.' I would actually get bruised during those scenes, doing it that many times."[36]

Myth 7: Women can stop the abuse by leaving the batterer.

The myth that women can always get away from their violent partner is expressed in a little-known drama of 1983, *Independence Day*, in which Jack Parker (David Keith), a mechanic in a small town, suspects that his sister is being beaten by her salesman husband. When Jack seeks assurance from his girlfriend, Mary Ann Taylor (Kathleen Quinlan), that it can't be true, that no woman would stay with a man who beat her—"She'd just walk out the door, wouldn't she?"—Mary Ann answers bluntly, "And go where?" Although Mary Ann doesn't know who he is talking about, she insists, "It happens all the time. . . . It's a fact of life." Mary Ann is right: not only are most women unable to leave an abusive partner because they have nowhere to go and no money of their own to support themselves and their children, but it is also the most dangerous time for them. To leave is to rebel, and because abuse is about control, any attempt to get away frequently arouses the man to more violent acts.[37]

Independence Day (directed by Robert Mandel from a novel by Alice Hoffman) is usually described as a film about a young woman's wish to escape the town she has outgrown. Jack has dropped out of college to return to his hometown in Texas, only to get involved with the restless Mary Ann Taylor, a waitress in her family's diner who dreams of getting away to L.A. to study photography. Although this dramatic, tightly written story of Jack's depressed sister, Nancy Morgan (Dianne Wiest), totally beaten down by her husband, is a subplot, it provides the romantic plot with its most vivid dramatic scenes, as Jack and Mary Ann attempt to figure out what is going on in the Morgans' marriage and Jack attempts to rescue his sister from her abusive husband, Les (Cliff De Young). At least Jack tries; the senior Parkers appear to be in denial, which provides some insight into the ineffectual role many families play in these situations because they are reluctant to intervene in what has become a family separate from their own.[38]

Myth 8: Women who successfully escape their batterer do it all by themselves.

As a popular mode of representation, movies do not usually connect male privilege to these acts of family violence; instead, films feature particular stories of individual women resisting "monstrous," abnormal men (or boxers, as in La Motta's case), who come to stand in for the whole massive social problem. As Wendy Kozol points out, the media have "typically depicted [domestic violence] as a problem of the 'private sphere' and focused on the women involved, either blaming them for the abuse or championing them as lone heroines fighting lone villains."[39] *Sleeping with the Enemy*, Joseph Ruben's 1991 suspense thriller about a woman (played by Julia Roberts) who fakes her death in a yachting accident and flees to Iowa, highlights the implausibility of her escape by sending her husband, Martin, after her, so that she is forced to kill him in self-defense. Not only is Laura Burney fetishized as a housewife and sex object by her psychotic control freak of a husband (after lining up bathroom towels and food cans to avoid his punishment she must accommodate his lust, pretending it is lovemaking rather than rape), but Joseph Ruben directs the camera to imitate this objectification. The result is that Laura is framed as object by the plot and the cinematic form. Even Martin's pursuit of her is given from his point of view, as we learn of her secret swimming lessons only when he does, rather than seeing her planning for months to gain some control over her life by escaping from him. And as Kozol points out, "in the single scene . . . in which Martin beats Laura after she falls to the ground, the camera slowly pans up Julia Roberts's unclothed legs before focusing on her crying face . . . demonstrat[ing] the contradictions embedded in the camera's gaze at women's battered bodies."[40]

Sleeping with the Enemy is typical of thrillers in demonizing the abuser, objectifying the woman, eroticizing the victim, and sensationalizing violence. Similarly oversimplified is the abuser in *Dolores Claiborne* (1995), in contrast to the complicated plot revealed in flashbacks (it is based on a Stephen King novel). The husband and father (played by David Strathairn) who beats his wife and sexually abuses his daughter is a caricature, not a credible figure. His wife Dolores, played by Kathy Bates, is depicted as unrealistically stoical; she endures her husband's drunken attacks and hides them from her daughter, Selena (Jennifer Jason Leigh). But Selena has not only kept her father's gropings a secret from her mother, she has denied them to herself, and does not remember them as an adult. This leads to revelation in the present but contributes little to the audience's knowledge of the dynamics of families headed by ordinary abusers. This piece of the plot explains why Dolores lured her husband to his death in an "accident" twenty years before: she suddenly realized that Joe had been molesting the preadolescent Selena. Indeed, to prevent their children from suffering abuse in turn is the reason many women give for fighting back, sometimes even killing their husbands or boyfriends. The part that is not borne out by women's experience is that Dolores was not prosecuted, for the investigator, though suspicious, could not prove a crime. The part that is not borne out by battered women's experience is that Dolores does not act to help her husband to safety, but waits until he is dead to report him missing. Women who have harmed their partner while defending themselves almost always call the police; they don't want the man to die, they just want the battering to stop.[41]

Melodrama and Recent Depictions of Family Violence

Another film in which a woman has to save herself through heroic action is *What's Love Got to Do with It?*, director Brian Gibson's 1993 depiction of the love-and-battering story of popular rock duo Ike and Tina Turner. It is also the first mainstream picture by a major studio to focus on woman battering, rather than relegate the abuse to a subplot, as we follow Anna Mae Bullock from "discovery" by Ike (he changed her name before they married), through sixteen years of beatings, to her heroic escape and triumph in a solo act. Although much of the reviewers' praise went to the actors Angela Bassett, as Tina, and Laurence Fishburne, who plays Ike, critics spent a good deal of space naming the genre of this "true" story (based on the singer's autobiography, *I, Tina*). It was called a docudrama, a show-business or musical bio-pic, a tale of recovery, a heroic-survivor movie, a woman-in-jeopardy movie, and a fairytale—specifically, an "R-rated 'Beauty and the Absolute Beast.'"[42]

Critics also had difficulty with the "bone-crunching" realism of the many episodes of battering. Angela Bassett wanted these scenes to look real, but reviewer Harry Pearson was so upset by the savage beatings administered by Ike that he called it a "horror movie." Pearson argues that violence against women or children depicted at such a primitive, manipulative level is so "inherently inflammatory" that it is impossible to take the film seriously.[43] His response reveals a problem in depictions of woman battering: it is difficult not to sensationalize such scenes, but stylizing the violence carries the risk of an aesthetic response, and this may desensitize viewers by making the pain seem unreal. When the battering and its results are as vividly presented as they are here, and the story is nonfictional as well, why does the movie seem more fairytale than realistic drama? After all, no one has disputed the primary facts and interpretations—that Ike was a cocaine addict, that he abused Tina, and that she ultimately got away from him, though he menaced her afterward.

The solution lies in understanding that "entertainment genres rely on actual events for legitimacy but reshape the narrative in ways that limit rather than enlarge discussion about power and violence."[44] Narratives are commonly reshaped into melodrama, which Linda Williams calls the dominant mode of American film. *What's Love Got to Do with It?* works the way melodrama characteristically does: (1) by exaggerating the innocence of the "victim-hero" (unmentioned in the film is the child Tina had with the saxophone player in Turner's band before she took up with Ike, and the fact that she was an experienced singer when he "discovered" her); (2) by recognizing the victim-hero's virtue, which may lie simply in suffering or self-sacrifice; (3) by rendering characters as all good or all evil, which "simplif[ies] and twist[s] the real social and historical complexities of the problems" presented; and (4) by addressing underlying problems as personal, rather than social. Thus the film sidesteps the systemic problem of violent husbands as melodrama habitually does: "through a climax of pathos and action."[45]

Melodrama as conceptualized by Christine Gledhill, Williams, and others is a mode of representation and thus a way of apprehending the world. As a modality rather than a genre usually associated with "women's film," it permeates other genres such as thrillers and suspense films (including *Sleeping with the Enemy* and *Dolores Claiborne*). It also underlies many cat-. egories that we distinguish by setting (society or rural melodrama) or genre (Westerns, action melodrama).[46] Because they feature victim-heroes about whom we care, who are involved in stories that allow us to recognize their "moral value," who triumph as individuals rather than by identifying or associating with a group expressing community values and common goals, melodramatic films are complicit in the ongoing celebration of the family in its idealized form. Melodrama thus works by disguising or masking the link between many widespread social problems, such as family violence, acquaintance rape, abused and neglected children, and the ideals that depend on "male privilege"—the notion that the man or father rules his household, has the right to exclude or include members, and judges both wife and children according to his norms. This way of dramatizing stories is powerful because it fits with our national ideology of individualism and self-reliance, and dangerous because it works against radical or revolutionary social change.

Kozol finds one example of a feature film that is the exception to the usual way producers adapt feminism to melodrama (that is, ignoring "the power relations, economic factors, and social structures that shape gender relations and family dynamics"): Steven Spielberg's 1995 adaptation of *The Color Purple*. This film dramatizes Alice Walker's novel about a Southern black woman, Celie, who eventually fights back against Mister, the man who has abused her for years; she does not kill him, although she has the opportunity. Says Kozol, "Unlike other images of women isolated from a larger social context, Celie finds strength and identity through her connections with other women." Her "empowerment" is "relational and dependent on her community of women."[47] This film (like the novel) is not without controversy, however: it has been attacked for its depiction of black men as "all batterers, all the time."[48]

Several other films that depict woman battering treat it in the African-American community. Representations of blacks in film are tinged by the history of black-white relations and racism since slavery. Stories of white men raping or making concubines of black women reminds us that African-American women are oppressed by race as well as by sex, as films like *Sankofa* (1993) and *Beloved* (1998) movingly demonstrate. The one scene of woman battering in Douglas Sirk's powerful 1959 melodrama *Imitation of Life* does triple duty in reinforcing the white male as arbiter of a young woman's identity, status (her eligibility to be his girlfriend), and even her safety. When Frankie discovers that his girlfriend, Sarah Jane, is "passing," he asks her, "Is your mother a nigger?" then beats her cruelly.

His fury is aroused by his damaged standing among his peers, because he did not know her lineage, which (as it was during slavery) is determined by her mother's color, despite the fact that she looks and acts white. Rather than going to the police or asking for help in punishing him, Sarah Jane instead turns on her mother, blaming her for her victimization, as though her racial background is something her mother could "help." As Marina Heung says, by "framing the racial issue as a maternal conflict" Sirk loses the chance to comment on the racism underlying this powerful scene. By making Sarah Jane a black woman who looks white, he gives her problems with identity and with her mother rather than articulating the social problem that led to her battering: the intertwined racism and sexism of U.S. society.[49]

Straight out of Brooklyn (1991), a raw, sociologically insightful first film by nineteen-year-old director Matty Rich, depicts a woman in the projects who is regularly beaten by her husband out of his rage and resentment at the "white man's" actions toward men like him. Though the audience is more likely to think, as his son does, that it's the man's drinking that made him batter, she is so stoically accepting, even welcoming of the beatings, on the grounds that they help to alleviate her husband's frustration, that she is battered to death. Based on Rich's boyhood friend and his aunt and uncle, this tragic melodrama ends with the despair of the son (the point-of-view character); the African-American filmmaker shows the uselessness and self-destructiveness of blaming the reified white man for every trouble a black man has.

Another way to see how American films contribute to the cultural context that supports and encourages battering would be to open the lens a little wider, to include the constant depiction of misogyny and violence against women in adventure, action, thriller, and suspense films. This would be a much larger task than this survey has undertaken (though it is taken up by other essays in this volume), and the results would surely be inconclusive, for it is notoriously difficult to know the effect of such overt representations of hostile treatment of women on audiences. As Carol Clover points out in her examination of the slasher genre, audiences resourcefully identify with different characters in different parts of a movie—across gender, for example—in order to get various kinds of pleasure. Her example is the way male viewers root for the "good" character, the so-called last girl who has avenged the deaths of her friends by killing all the evil men, after disengaging from a masculine character they might have identified with earlier.[50] These more complex patterns of identification and viewing practices articulate thoroughgoing, even obsessive, male anxieties concerning gender and, especially in films of the 1970s and 1980s, feminism.

All told, recent films tend to perpetuate the myths of woman battering in the United States rather than examine these male anxieties or explore the links between them and other forms of violence against women and, in turn, to the male-dominated hierarchical structures in place in most of the world. Most recent films representing family violence rely on viewers' awareness that their stories are true, that these characters have real-life counterparts. As Leonard Maltin says about *This Boy's Life* (1993), Tobias Wolff's memoir about his struggles to get away from his abusive stepfather, "what ultimately makes it work is learning that the story is true."[51] We can only imagine how much more credibility this true story might have gained from depicting a social reality as complex as that of the set design—showing Tobias in school, at clubs, seeking help from a teacher or counselor, comparing his stepfather to other boys' fathers, and so forth. Not only do we wonder how this boy, growing up in such a flat and unrealized background, became the acutely observant writer that he is, but we are likely to see Robert De Niro's character, his stepfather, as an aberrant, sadistic figure rather than just a variation on a common paternal style of the 1950s. In other words, what movies do best is render individual stories of particular families. What they don't do is tie woman battering as a widespread problem to the social fabric.

Notes

1. Marcia Clark, *Without a Doubt* (New York: Viking, 1997), 226.
2. Myrna S. Raeder, "The Better Way: The Role of Batterers' Profiles and Expert 'Social Framework' Background in Cases Implicating Domestic Violence," *Colorado Law Review* 68 (winter 1997): 182.
3. Deborah Rhode, "Public Tunes out Battered Women," *National Law Journal* (June 5, 1995): A19.
4. See Ann Jones, *Next Time She'll Be Dead: Battering and How to Stop It* (Boston: Beacon, 1994), for criticism of the role of popular entertainment media in disseminating the ideology of "modern romance" and of journalists for adopting it in coverage of domestic homicides (ch. 4).
5. Linda Alcoff and Laura Gray, "Survivor Discourse: Transgression or Recuperation?" *Signs: Journal of Women in Culture and Society* 18 (1993): 262.
6. Alisa Del Tufo, *Domestic Violence for Beginners* (New York: Writers and Readers, 1995), 86.
7. Jones, *Next Time*, 7–11.
8. Robin Wood, *Hollywood from Vietnam to Reagan* (New York: Columbia University Press, 1986), 204 and 211.
9. Michael Wood, *America in the Movies* (New York: Basic Books, 1975), 131–35; and Jackie Byars, *All that Hollywood Allows: Re-reading Gender in 1950s Melodrama* (Chapel Hill: University of North Carolina Press, 1991), 114–16. Backlash may be an explanation here: because feminists made violence against women a public concern, it is regarded by some groups as a made-up problem, one that can be safely ignored.
10. A later, similar film, also based on a play, is Mike Nichols's version of Edward Albee's *Who's Afraid of Virginia Woolf* (1966); here, too, alcoholism is a factor in the couple's more verbal violence, and their secret is a baby who did not live.
11. Elizabeth Wilson agrees that rather than being "abnormal" male behavior, battering is "an extreme form of normality, an exaggeration of how society expects men to behave." Wilson, *What Is to Be Done about Violence against Women?* (London: Penguin, 1983), 95.
12. As the capsule summary from a fan on the Internet Movie Database (http://us.imdb.com) puts it, "Jerry has a very strict definition of the perfect family and his new family may not be making the cut."
13. Patrick McGilligan and Paul Buhle, *Tender Comrades: A Backstory of the Blacklist* (New York: St. Martin's, 1997), 135.
14. Two scenes in *Public Enemy* reinforce the myths that violence is a form of affection and that women are attracted to brutes: when Tom as an adult visits his mother, he gives her a mock punch in the face as a token of affection; and when he threatens to leaves his moll (Jean Harlow) because she hasn't given in to his

demands for sex, she keeps him there by telling him that he will ultimately win, for she is drawn to him because of his power. Other women like the polished, considerate type, but she is attracted to his strength. She says, "You don't give, you take. Oh, Tommy, I could love you to death."

15. Molly Haskell, *Holding My Own in No Man's Land: Women and Men, Film and Feminists* (New York: Oxford University Press, 1997), 131. Like so many of us who have also read Margaret Mitchell's novel, Haskell is probably using knowledge gained from the narrator's privileged point of view to interpret this movie scene. Because narrative can give expression to a character's internal point of view, the reader knows how Scarlett feels, whereas the film scene is more ambiguous since there is no way to convey Scarlett's response to being overpowered except in the pleased look on her face the next morning.

16. Peter Keough, "*A Streetcar Named Desire*," in *Flesh and Blood: The National Society of Film Critics on Sex, Violence, and Censorship*, ed. Keough (San Francisco: Mercury House, 1995), 315.

17. Ibid., 317.

18. A film reinforcing the male fantasy that marital rape isn't a crime but a sign of love is the 1973 Paul Mazursky film *Blume in Love*. Blume is so obsessed by the desire to win back his ex-wife Nina (after losing her through his womanizing) that he becomes the friend of her new lover, Elmo, as a way of being around her. Blume rapes Nina when she rejects his advances (while Elmo is out seeing *Gone with the Wind*!), but the rape ultimately brings about the couple's reconciliation, for he impregnates her; she eventually softens toward him because he wants to be a father to the baby. Another sign of male fantasy is that other characters—including Elmo—view the rape as a sign of love and treat Blume as a justifiably proud father-to-be.

19. Dana Polan, *In a Lonely Place* (London: BFI, 1993), 37.

20. Margi Laird McCue, *Domestic Violence: A Reference Handbook* (Santa Barbara, Calif.: ABC-CLIO, 1995), 20.

21. Susan Hayward, *Key Concepts in Cinema Studies* (London: Routledge, 1996), 116–17.

22. Janey Place and J. I. Peterson illustrate many of the visual elements of film noir with stills from *In a Lonely Place*. Place and Peterson, "Some Visual Motifs of Film Noir," *Film Comment* 10, no. 4 (1974); reprinted in *Movies and Methods*, ed. Bill Nichols (Berkeley: University of California Press, 1976).

23. Polan, *In a Lonely Place*, 47 and 46.

24. In her timeline of news coverage of "domestic violence" McCue notes a backlash in 1994, as conservatives and advocates for battered husbands, "the forgotten victims of domestic violence," attempted to discredit organizations supporting more aid for battered women in the weeks after the Simpson arrest. Even after the claims that too much money was being spent on women victims were in turn discredited, the stories went on. McCue says they all came from two syndicated columnists, Joe Hallinan and John Leo. McCue, *Domestic Violence*, 55.

25. Del Tufo, *Domestic Violence for Beginners*, 53.

26. Patricia Erens compares *Shadow of a Doubt* to *The Stepfather*, Joseph Ruben's 1987 film about a young woman, Stephanie, who discovers that her stepfather has killed his previous family. Ehrens, review of *The Stepfather*, *Film Quarterly* 41, no. 2 (1987–88): 51. Both Charlie and Stephanie are shown penetrating the hidden evil of their relatives—uncle and stepfather—with a knowing look; they have adopted the male gaze of classic cinema (see Hayward, "voyeurism/fetishism," in *Key Concepts*, 393–95). In her book analyzing Hitchcock's ambivalence toward women, Tania Modleski claims that men dread intelligent women, women who know "valuable secrets" about men. She cites Alice Jardine's observation that male paranoia is "fundamentally a reaction against women who know not only too much, but anything at all" and goes on to quote Charlie, who tells her namesake, "I know a secret about you, Uncle Charlie," thereby, according to Modleski, "arousing his murderous rage."

Modleski, *The Women Who Knew Too Much: Hitchcock and Feminist Theory* (New York: Methuen, 1988), 13.

27. Keyser (*Martin Scorsese* [New York: Twayne, 1992]) says that one fight sequence is based on the shower scene in Hitchcock's *Psycho*, which Scorsese studied "frame by frame, then recast . . . in the boxing ring" (113). One wonders why the director chose a scene of a woman's brutal murder by a psychopath as a model for boxing.

28. Taking a cue from other critics and from Scorsese's admission that *Raging Bull* is concerned with latent homosexuality, "sexual confusion," and "sexual ambiguity," Tomasulo interprets La Motta's woman battering in this light. He says that Jake's beating of Vickie "may have a sublimated homosexual basis, as it may portray his attempt to subconsciously attack the feminine side of his own psyche." Tomasulo, "Raging Bully: Postmodern Violence and Masculinity in *Raging Bull*," in *Mythologies of Violence in Postmodern Media*, ed. Chritopher Sharrett (Detroit: Wayne State University Press, 1999), 192 and 186.

29. David Thomson seems more exercised about *Raging Bull's* portrayal of the "emptiness" of women than with the scenes of Jake La Motta hitting his wife. He laments the fact that Scorsese gives Vickie no sense of herself, creating "the mythology that she is only a body, somehow willing to be scrutinized, and therefore innately promiscuous." As he says, the film is unable to give women any reality; it is "bewildered" by their reality. Thomson, "The Director as Raging Bull," *Film Comment* 34, no. 3 (May–June 1998): 59, 60.

30. David Denby, "Brute Force," review of *Raging Bull, New York*, December 1, 1980; reprinted in *Perspectives on Raging Bull*, ed. Steven G. Kellman (New York: G. K. Hall, 1994), 43; and Keyser, *Martin Scorsese*, 111.

31. Carol J. Adams, "Raging Batterer," in *Perspectives on Raging Bull*, 110.

32. Ibid., 111.

33. Morris Dickstein, "Stations of the Cross: *Raging Bull* Revisited," in *Perspectives on Raging Bull*, 80.

34. When Jake rushes to Joey's house, driven berserk by Vickie's defiant claim to have had affairs with, among others, his brother—as he has charged her with in his paranoia—the camera enters ahead of him, and we hear Joey telling one of his children, "Keep your fuckin' hands out of the plate. I see that one more time and I'm gonna stab you with this knife."

35. Quoted in Adams, "Raging Batterer," 114.

36. Mary Pat Kelly, *Martin Scorsese: A Journey* (New York: Thunder's Mouth Press, 1996), 138. In his study of Scorsese, Keyser describes the fear the director felt while filming the scene in *Alice Doesn't Live Here Anymore* in which Harvey Keitel as Alice's new lover becomes violent and attacks both Alice and his pregnant wife. Keitel actually became enraged (rather than simply acting enraged) and improvised one of the most intense and horrifying scenes of an abusive man out of control in films (53–54). Fortunately, the scene had been carefully choreographed and rehearsed, and Ellen Burstyn, portraying Alice in a film she chose Scorsese to direct—and herself a proponent of method acting—apparently did not get hurt.

37. According to Del Tufo (*Domestic Violence for Beginners*, 124), "Almost 80% of all serious injury and death occur when battered women try to leave . . . or after they have left."

38. Overall, it is remarkable how many of the myths—and the depictions of varieties of woman and child abuse in films—imply that women have a role in, or even bear responsibility for, domestic violence. Social workers and family crisis experts, and books like *Domestic Violence for Beginners* and *When Love Goes Wrong*, by Ann Jones and Susan Schechter (New York: Harper, 1992), insist that nothing can be done to solve the crisis of family violence until men who batter acknowledge responsibility for their actions, admit that they choose to batter, and vow to stop. In short, the batterer has to admit that he is a man who chooses to hurt women— that she didn't make him do it.

39. Wendy Kozol, "Fracturing Domesticity: Media, Nationalism, and the

Question of Feminist Influence," *Signs* 20, no. 3 (1995): 648.

40. Ibid., 663.

41. Susan Osthoff, Director, National Clearinghouse for the Defense of Battered Women, telephone interview, September 5, 2000. Dolores was never prosecuted, for the investigator, though suspicious, could not prove a crime. A widely circulated statistic, that women who kill their abusers get prison sentences three times as long as those handed down to men who kill their partners or lovers, is not accurate, according to Osthoff. Women frequently commit murder in self-defense, whereas men kill women who are trying to leave them; thus the longer sentences (an average of sixteen years compared to six for women) are appropriate. There are also cases of women sentenced to long prison terms; for interviews with eleven such women in Michigan serving disproportionately long sentences, see *From One Prison*, dir. Carol Jacobsen, documentary videocassette (Berkeley: University of California Extension, 1994).

42. Jack Mathews calls *What's Love* a "domestic violence movie," in fact, "one of the most harrowing" of 1993, but mentions no others. He apparently created the category so that he could set *What's Love* apart as "almost certainly the only one you can dance to." Mathews, review of *What's Love Got to Do with It? Newsday*, June 9, 1993, II:49.

43. Louise Gray, review of *What's Love Got to Do with It? Sight and Sound* (October 1993): 55; Harry Pearson, review of *What's Love Got to Do with It? Films in Review* (October 1993): 334.

44. Kozol, "Fracturing Domesticity," 663.

45. Linda Williams, "Melodrama Revised," in *Refiguring American Film Genres*, ed. Nick Browne (Berkeley: University of California Press, 1998), 69. As Williams asserts, "The melodramatic solution to the real issues raised by the form can only occur through a perverse process of victimization. Virtuous suffering is a pathetic weapon against injustice, but we need to recognize how frequently it has been the melodramatic weapon of choice of American popular culture" (80). Drawing on Brooks's *The Melodramatic Imagintion* and several Gledhill essays, Williams describes five features of melodrama. I have combined two of them: melodrama resolves problems for individuals, rather than dealing with them as social problems; and melodrama "offers the hope that virtue and truth can be achieved in private individuals and individual heroic acts rather than . . . in revolution and change" (67 and 74). In *I, Tina* we learn how many years it took Tina to be free of the self-pitying and menacing Ike, and how damaged their four sons were by the violence of the breakup as well as of the marriage. In the film Ike is finally punished, though not for woman battering; as the credits roll, we learn that he was jailed on cocaine charges. *I, Tina* is told only partly in first person, with friends, the Turner sons, and a third-person narrator chiming in with their stories.

46. Williams, "Melodrama Revised," 50–51.

47. Kozol, "Fracturing Domesticity," 663.

48. Cheryl Butler, "The *Color Purple* Controversy: Black Women Spectatorship," *Wide Angle* 13, nos. 3–4 (1991): 63–65.

49. Marina Heung, "'What's the Matter with Sarah Jane?': Daughters and Mothers in Douglas Sirk's *Imitation of Life*," ed. Lucy Fischer (New Brunswick, N.J.: Rutgers University Press, 1991), 313. Because of its inevitable association with black musicians, the jazz on the soundtrack during the beating is a reminder that if Sarah Jane had not deceived him about her racial background, Frankie might have dated her and earned the envy of his friends rather than their taunts. Men in this age group in the 1950s are likely to have fantasized about African-American women being more earthy and sensual than white girls because of their supposed "primitive" qualities, and thus would have been viewed as appropriate sex objects, thought not likely marriage material, out of fear of miscegenation (at least on their parents' parts).

50. Carol Clover, *Men, Women, and Chainsaws* (Princeton, N.J.: Princeton University Press, 1992).

51. Leonard Maltin, *Leonard Maltin's Movie and Video Guide* (New York: Penguin, 1999), 1408.

splitting difference: global identity politics and the representation of torture in the counterhistorical dramatic film

eleven

elizabeth swanson goldberg

The theme of unspeakability, and unknowability, is central to theories regarding the representation of pain in general, and torture in particular. Elaine Scarry asserts that "Whatever pain achieves, it achieves in part through its unsharability, and it ensures this unsharability through its resistance to language."[1] Cathy Caruth notes that "The traumatic reexperiencing of the event thus *carries with it* . . . the impossibility of knowing that first constituted it."[2] In his essay "Historical Emplotment and the Problem of Truth," Hayden White describes the position of "a number of scholars and writers who view the Holocaust as virtually unrepresentable in language."[3] The title of an essay by Peter Haidu in the same collection is "The Dialectics of Unspeakability."

This trope likewise appears in survivors' testimonials; in his *Prisoner without a Name, Cell without a Number*, Jacobo Timmerman reflects that

> During the long months of imprisonment, I thought many times about how I would be able to convey the pain that a tortured person feels, and I always

concluded that it was impossible. It is a pain that does not have a point of reference, revealing symbols or codes that could serve as a beginning.[4]

In testimonial and witness literature, however, this sense of representational impossibility coexists in a paradoxical simultaneity with the need to share stories of torture and terror (and, by extension, to find language and modes of representation sufficient to this telling). As Kali Tal asserts, "Literature of trauma is written from the need to tell and retell the story of the traumatic experience, to make it 'real' both to the victim and to the community."[5] If they are to be politically effective, then, cultural representations of pain and terror must achieve a fragile balance between the difficulty of presenting that which is too painful to think or to say aloud—and perhaps too painful to be heard—and the imperative of presenting that very material in the service of remembering those events and the people lost to them, and of resisting continued enactment of such violences.

Many authors (including survivors) strike this balance by using aesthetic strategies of "indirection"; in particular, the immersion of the unspeakable in narrative containers such as epic, tragedy, or magic realism. Saul Friedlander refers to the imperative of a distanced realism in representing the unspeakability of the Holocaust (Shoah):

> It is easier to point to literary and artistic works which give a feeling of relative "adequacy" in bringing the reader and viewer to insights about the Shoah than to define the elements which convey that sense. . . . A common denominator appears: the exclusion of straight, documentary realism, but the use of some sort of *allusive* or *distanced* realism. Reality is there, in its starkness, but perceived through a filter: that of memory (distance in time), that of spatial displacement, that of some sort of narrative margin which leaves the unsayable unsaid.[6]

The relationship to realism articulated in Friedlander's remarks is complex. In this formulation, the specific goal of representation is to bring the reader/viewer to "insights" about the traumatic event, rather than to provide survivors with space to testify to atrocity or to experience a cathartic release of terror (though this may be an important effect of such representation). Presumably the majority of reader/viewers have not directly experienced the event in question, so that their revelatory insights might include glimpses of understanding about the structural causes of such an event; recognitions of the psychological states of perpetrators, victims, and survivors; and awareness of the ongoing legacies of massive traumatic occurrences. These insights are meaningful inasmuch as they contribute to a collective consciousness about genocide and other such massive human rights violations, a consciousness that not only validates victims' and survivors' experiences, but that also provides some measure of insurance against the recurrence of such atrocities. In this case, the relative "adequacy" of images is measured by their success as both witness and deterrent, countering the deliberate certainty of authoritarian absolutism with a nuanced, resistant awareness.

In order even to attempt such goals, as Friedlander notes, art that takes atrocity as its subject must employ some form of realism so as to reference the thing itself, the historic event, the materiality of bodily experience. However, both representational extremes—of excessive abstraction, on the one hand, or a too raw realism on the other—are equally capable of diluting the force of representation, with the result that "[viewers'] capacity for comprehending and perceiving [can be] entirely blunted."[7] The objective, then, is to negotiate this fragile balance: between the necessary distancing of narrativization and genre that makes images palatable for viewers, and the equally necessary force of documentary realism, allowing fuller impact of the material conditions borne by victims and survivors. It is only in achieving this balance that images may bear ethical witness to torture and genocide. This essay is particularly concerned with the implications of generic conventions in filmic representations of atrocity, especially with regard to the relationship between narrativization and the spectacle of tortured bodies. My aim is not to police certain images as "adequate" or "inappropriate" (though I certainly may advance such assessments in the course of my argument), but rather to articulate the political ambivalences and paradoxes revealed by closer examination of such relationships, particularly in the context of global images circulated in Hollywood films.

Analysis of film spectatorship must contend with the conditions of production and circulation of the film itself, which presents a unique set of problems when considering representations of torture. For instance, what happens to "the unsayable" when the narrative or generic margins used to contain it are employed in large-scale, high-budget, mainstream Hollywood films "about" a catastrophic historical event? Rather than being mobilized (by survivors or others) to bear witness to people and events and to resist the use of torture and terror, these narrative films balance the market demands of audience appeal and box office revenues upon the point of their own often self-proclaimed imperatives to "tell the truth" about an event previously misunderstood, offering a counterhistory to the accepted official version of events. If probed, this ambivalence of purpose reveals a fundamental instability not only in the ethics of representing torture, but also in terms of the cultural work such representations ultimately perform.[8] That is, in the context of mass cultural circulation of images of wounding, torture, and death, the wounded body is at once a historical referent testifying to historical atrocity and a generic signifier of fear, suspense, desire, even humor, depending upon the interpretive signals of its narrative container, as well as the exigencies of the viewing situation and viewer.

In this regard, after such images have been widely circulated and consumed by Western audiences, how are these same audiences to negotiate the often heavy-handed "messages" in historically situated films meant to critique the use of (political) torture and terror in "other" places? Given that, as "dramatic historian" Oliver Stone asserts, "Movies have to make money, you've got to make them so they're exciting, they're gripping, people want to go see them," politically motivated message movies often borrow unabashedly from classic Hollywood techniques of genre, plot, and character, a phenomenon that drastically complicates the reception of such films by mass audiences. It is the space between "historical" films engaged in overt critique of (state) violence, and fictional films whose representations of violence are informed by imperatives of plot or genre, that interests me; that is, the gap opened by the radical shift of interpretive cues (genre, plot, context, and characterization) around the fixed spectre of rape, torture, and murder or execution. The very delicate work of representing atrocity—that which is unspeakable—is in many ways degraded before it is begun by the larger context of Hollywood filmmaking, which participates in what Dean MacCannell has in another context termed "the routinization of violence."[9]

Indeed, I would argue that the narrative strategies and cinematic techniques employed by films representing historical violence to historical bodies often participate in a degradation of those very representations, which results, in the particular category of film I will analyze here, in the prioritization of a dominant Western subject position over the other cultural and national subject positions represented. This category, which I term counterhistorical drama, crosses generic boundaries, making use of adventure, romance, suspense, high courtroom drama, and war narrative techniques. Over and above these generic classifications, however, it always calls itself "history," referring to a historic event or a "true" story. In this regard, it generally presents a counterhistory to an official version of history (or to a perceived silence surrounding a particular historical event), and it typically uses a bildungsroman form in which audiences identify with the protagonist's growth to the status of hero over the course of the movie. Such films as *The Year of Living Dangerously* (1982), *The Killing Fields* (1984), *Cry Freedom* (1985), *Salvador* (1987), *Schindler's List* (1994), *Beyond Rangoon* (1995), *Red Corner* (1997), and *Seven Years in Tibet* (1997) fall into this category.

Such films are always about an other place;[10] other, that is, than the site of Western (U.S.) freedom and democracy (though on occasion U.S. complicity in the undemocratic practices of torture and terror in another nation is critiqued). In spite of their geographic locations elsewhere, counterhistorical dramas invariably provide a white, Western protagonist who is the subject of the quest toward which audience identification is directed throughout the film; the struggle of the people or country in question provides the context within which the protagonist grows and develops, and may offer a source of alternative values or wisdom nudging that protagonist forward in his or her quest. There is a basic split in terms of plot and characterization that falls along the line of racial/cultural identity: the film traces the story of the collective struggle of the nation or people (often fleshing out more deeply one or more heroic figures from this culture as a point or points of identification) along with the story of the protagonist/hero in his or her personal, professional, or romantic growth. This split is characteristic of what David Bordwell terms "classical Hollywood cinema":

> The classical Hollywood film presents psychologically defined individuals who struggle to solve a clear-cut problem or to attain specific goals. . . . The most "specified" character is usually the protagonist, who becomes the principal causal agent, the target of any narration. . . . Usually the classical syuzhet presents a

double causal structure, two plot lines: one involving heterosexual romance, the other line involving another sphere—work, war, a mission or quest, other personal relationships. Each line will possess a goal, obstacles, and a climax.[11]

The problem with using such classical Hollywood formulae to structure a film with an overt message about an international political struggle is implicit in its definition: according to this formula, the protagonist—in this case differentiated culturally, racially, and economically from the people on whose behalf he or she protests—retains agency not only with regard to the action of the film, but also in terms of its narration. The reins of the story are wrenched from the historic "actors" and handed to a privileged observer/participant, resulting in the illusion that there is no story—no historic event—unless it is witnessed and shaped by Western eyes. Presumably, white, Western protagonists with major star appeal provide a point of recognition and identification for white, Western viewers, thereby becoming the vehicle for these viewers' identification with the struggle of the nation or people in question. Without unpacking here the psychological complexities of identification or the assumption that white, Western audiences are incapable of sustaining identification with protagonists who are racially, culturally, or nationally different (and while acknowledging that certainly such audiences are capable of sustaining a split identification and empathic response), I would argue that this doubling of plot line and characterization reveals a fundamental instability in the politics of the counterhistorical dramatic film itself. Indeed, the simple fact that the split in plot and character lies between the principles of a collective struggle (represented by non-Western characters) and an individual quest (pursued by a Western hero) exposes the films' ideological ambivalence—in spite of their emphatic enunciation of a specific, resistant political position.

The correspondence of the split plot line in the counterhistorical dramatic film to a division between individual and collective raises questions of representability in what Frederic Jameson describes as

> that new world-systemic moment which, gradually laid in place since the end of World War II, has been unveiled in discontinuous convulsions—the end of the 60s, the rise of the Third World debt, the emergence first of Japan and then of a soon-to-be united new Europe as competing superstates, the collapse of the party state in the East, and finally the reassumption by the United States of a refurbished vocation as global policeman—and which can indifferently be called postmodernity or the third (or "late") stage of capitalism.[12]

Jameson's designation of this "world-systemic moment" is precisely the site of anxiety upon which the counterhistorical dramatic film has risen as a genre, though I would supplement Jameson's citation of the events and processes commonly termed "globalization," and the rise of the United States as sole remaining superpower, with attention to the legacy of the war in Vietnam as a historical source with particular relevance to the development of this genre. Tracing the trajectory of Vietnam war films in the 1970s and 1980s, one might posit its slow dissolve into the counterhistorical dramatic film in terms of a convergence of concerns with U.S. (military) presence in "other" places; desire to tell the "real" story or reveal a repressed history; reassertion of the primacy of a democratic world order; and the construction of a heroic protagonist—this time in the new context of globalization, and this time without dread of the Red Threat.[13] Indeed, two early examples of the counterhistorical dramatic film (Roland Joffe's *The Killing Fields* and Oliver Stone's *Salvador*, set in 1970s Cambodia and 1980s El Salvador, respectively) are, historically speaking, the direct off-spring of the crisis in Vietnam, referencing it frequently in their critiques of Vietnam-related atrocity and of U.S. participation in foreign military escalation. Importantly, in the counterhistorical drama the (unsafe) soldier has now been replaced with a (safe) photojournalist or traveler.[14]

The counterhistorical drama is also related to the conspiratorial thriller, a contemporary generic category posited by Jameson, who locates its source in the detective story, which, in the context of late-stage capitalism, has metamorphosed such that the figure of the detective has now become a "social detective" (most often a war correspondent) confronting "crime and scandal of collective dimensions and consequences" in the newly globalized world.[15] Like the "terrorist film" posited by William J. Palmer as a fundamental 1980s genre that responds to the "chaos of the wide world from which America had always held itself aloof intruding upon our previously safe domestic life" in the post–Cold War era,[16] the conspiratorial thriller generally treats a contemporary political occurrence by returning "in force [to] the old narrative category of 'point of view' along with the ideological category of the 'main character' or protagonist-hero."[17] While both Jameson and Palmer include several of the films that I would classify as counterhistorical dramas in their generic analyses, the counterhistorical drama differentiates itself in two significant ways: first, its protagonist, often an "innocent" traveler or businessperson inadvertently swept into the flow of collective history, is not restricted to the "social detective" character of photojournalist.[18] Second, the counterhistorical drama as generic category is restricted to historically grounded films, excluding the purely fictional films to which Palmer refers in his analysis of terrorist films (for example, *The Delta Force* [1986], *Die Hard* [1988], or *The Naked Gun* [1988]).

The counterhistorical drama does, however, share with both the conspiratorial thriller and the terrorist film a split plot line corresponding to the division between individual and collective; as such, we might follow Jameson in asking "under what circumstances can a necessarily individual story with individual characters function to represent collective processes?"[19] For his answer, Jameson turns to the narrative possibility of allegory; for our purposes here, let us instead invoke Leger Grindon's distinction between romance and spectacle in his discussion of Hollywood's historical fiction film, another obvious precursor to the counterhistorical drama. For Grindon, the classical Hollywood split plot line may be traced in such films as *The Birth of a Nation* (1915), *The Private Life of Henry VIII* (1934), and *Gone with the Wind* (1939) to the convention of developing historical narratives within the frame of individual romance plots meant to lend emotional force to the representation of the collective:

> The recurring generic figures of the historical fiction film are the romance and the spectacle—the one emphasizing personal experience; the other, public life. Each film negotiates the relations between the individual and society and expresses the balance between personal and extrapersonal forces through its treatment of the two generic elements.[20]

Grindon's discussion of the tension between romance and spectacle, between "personal" and "public," may indeed be applied to most Hollywood genres—detective, war, Western, and so on—many of which are put to use in the counterhistorical drama. According to Grindon, however, when working properly these generic figures retain a balance; or, ideally, the individual romance plot is used to aid audience identification with the film's more abstract collective historical action. In the counterhistorical drama, it is precisely the imbalance between the two generic figures, resulting from a reduction of historical material to spectacle (essentially, background), which leads to what Jameson identifies as the "fundamental form-problem of the new globalizing representations"; that is, the "incommensurability" of the dual plot lines.[21] This incommensurability, linked to the excessive narrative weight carried by the plot line of the individual protagonist, takes on an ethical charge in the representation of torture and atrocity, and is exacerbated by the counterhistorical drama's insistent racial differentiation of its white, Western individual protagonists from non-white, non-Western collectives.

Rather than articulating a coherent stance against all human rights abuses, then, these films' loudly proclaimed opposition to international human rights violations provides instead the occasion for advancement of an idealized Western or U.S. political identity in a global context.[22] This identity, differentiated from the systems of the other nations and cultures represented, is built upon the ideal of constitutional democracy marked by romanticized notions of individual freedom and security—which, in point of fact, elide the lapses evident in these ideals as applied to the diverse populations of the United States itself. Such political differentiation is underscored by displays of cultural difference, one of which, paradoxically, is the enactment of egregious human rights violations. That is, the frame of this Western identity is built upon the spectacle of the tortured body of the national or cultural other, a spectacle that consolidates identity difference using both the figures of victim and torturer/perpetrator. The body of the victim becomes signifier of the relative safety and security of the Western body from such acts, while the acts of the torturer mark the space between (Western) citizens governed by the rule of law and morality (that is, by Christian democratic constitutionality) and the brutal irrationality of others who are neither subject to nor subjects of a written law, moral or otherwise. Thus, the use of authoritarian force represents a paradoxical combination of excess and absence of law according to the principles of democratic constitutionality. Using close readings of Richard Attenborough's *Cry Freedom,* John Boorman's *Beyond Rangoon,* and Oliver Stone's *Salvador,* I will assert that the classic Hollywood generic conventions of split story line and bildungsroman format, and especially the imperialistic conventions employed to represent the tortured body, inform a core instability in the political positioning of counterhistorical dramatic film such that the overt statement of resistance to international human rights violations masks the hegemonic assertion of a mythic Western identity and difference in a global context.

Inspired Truths and Historical Fictions

The representational instability of counterhistorical dramatic film often originates in its own self-proclaimed historical referentiality; that is, in claims to truth value using various documentary film techniques such as historical footage of an actual event (or, more insidiously, fictionalized footage made to look historical by being shot on black-and-white film), documentary-style captions identifying certain characters as real historical actors, or captions describing political events using such factual information as statistics and citing the names, dates, and places of related events. These techniques are often used in order to set up a film as corrective to dominant historical narratives or imposed silence about an event, putting the audience in the position of student to the film's didactic treatise. John Boorman's *Beyond Rangoon*, for instance, inscribes a critique of the international silence surrounding the events in postindependence Burma into several key scenes. In one, the protagonist's voice-over interior monologue describes the struggle of a photographer to get his photos out of Burma: "They were the only photos of the massacre. What the Chinese did in Tiananmen Square was televised but Burma wasn't. So for most of the world, it just didn't happen." The film, then, offers itself as a representation of that lost or silenced historical "truth." While it is not only true, but also politically meaningful, to assert that "something happened" in Burma, and that those events comprised massive human rights violations, Boorman's choice of emplotment reveals ideological instabilities that affect the production of knowledge accompanying the film's circulation.

Beyond Rangoon reveals its claim to be a representation of history in its opening notification to viewers: "This film is inspired by actual events." Similarly, Richard Attenborough's *Cry Freedom* rolls onto viewer's screens with the following message: "With the exception of two characters whose identity has been concealed to ensure their safety, all the people depicted in this film are real and all the events true." This disclosure heightens suspense and further blurs generic boundaries, evoking nightly news magazine programming, wherein identities must be changed or blocked for protection. Audiences receive the message that the danger represented in this film is not distanced by time or place; although the material is presented in a historical context, the sense of immediate danger and suspense signified by the need to protect identities will always be part of the film's viewing experience. At the same time, however, this announcement also deepens the sense of security of Western audiences, far from the danger of such state-sponsored persecution not only in place and time, but also in terms of political and cultural practice and ideology.

Just as these films emphasize their relative truth values with such notifications at the start of narrative action, they likewise reinforce this historicity with captioned passages at the end of the film, providing the viewer with information as to where the event—and characters—stand at the time of production. Generally these end captions provide statistics ("More than 700 schoolchildren were killed in the Soweto 'disturbances' that began on June 17th 1986 and over 4,000 were wounded," *Cry Freedom*); updates on the characters and events; or didactic historical information, as in *Beyond Rangoon*'s description of Aun San Suu Kyi's National League for Democracy, her house arrest, and receipt of the Nobel Peace Prize.[23] The authoritative presence of the written word preceding and following the narrative action of the film acts as a definitive set of brackets, holding audience identification within its grasp, directing and redirecting it in a manner often contradictory to what the narrative action, which has focused upon the quest of the Western protagonist, has demanded.

While the use of such captions directly evokes documentary film conventions, their wording leaves room for interpretation in considering the relationship of their respective filmic narratives to the corresponding historic referents. The statement that *Beyond Rangoon* has been "inspired" implies creative license, however deeply this verb is embedded in its more concrete object "actual events"; to be sure, a film inspired by actual events is not the same as a true story. Still, viewers are led to perceive the film as at least somewhat historically accurate given its references to actual photos of the massacres appearing in Western news journals; the interior monologues of its protagonist relating historical "facts" corresponding to the action on screen; and its closing captions offering more "facts" about the "crackdown of the Democracy Movement" in Burma. How then is an audience to read the film's representations of historic characters and events? The authority of the word appearing on screen authenticates the action of the film as "true," though it is less clear which "actual" events are being represented here. The film's blend of fictional and nonfictional conventions places it in a generic realm beyond simple mimesis or realism.[24]

At issue here is the complex relationship of these mainstream Hollywood films to the more narrowly conceived—and received—genre of documentary film, and to narrative history more generally. Allowing that both fictional and documentary films rely upon images that may maintain an indexical relationship with the profilmic world, Bill Nichols identifies the difference between documentary and fictional films as one between ethics and erotics, respectively, wherein "evidence of and from the historical world may appear in either fiction or documentary film and may have the same existential bond to the world in both. In one it supports a narrative; in the other, it supports an argument."[25] Nichols's distinction is crucial: documentary, while utilizing many of the textual strategies of the fiction film, uses its historical representations in service of an argument; hence, Nichols's identification of documentary as an ethics. Historical material in fiction film, however, is subject to "a centrifugal pull on elements of authenticity away from their historical referent and toward their relevance to plot and story," which ultimately corresponds to the erotics of narrative pleasure theorized by, among others, Laura Mulvey.[26] As such, what is most objectionable is the remarkable ease with which—after mobilizing documentary conventions of historical representation and clearly setting the terms of an argument against international human rights violations—the counterhistorical dramatic film drowns its purported ethics in the erotics of classical Hollywood emplotment. The problem with the emplotment of history in the counterhistorical drama does not arise simply from its use of certain plot types, but might more accurately be described in terms of its exaggeration of those plot types so that the content of the film shifts from the historical referent to the genre itself. The split in story line further displaces the focus of the story from the historical referent to the imaginary, tropological plot line imposed upon that referent.

In the wide-ranging debate regarding the ethical demands of historical discourse as manifested in both documentary and fiction films, it has become clear that, regardless of how difficult they may be to define, we must develop terms in which to talk about the relative adequacy of representations of atrocity, an adequacy that has most often been measured in terms of their relative truth value. In the thin atmosphere of this millennial postmodern moment it is difficult to talk about the heady subject of truth (or Truth). It does seem, however, that to accept the proposition that there are infinite perspectives upon historic events simply means accepting the existence of competing truth claims, a very different notion than the idea that we have no epistemological access to events occurring in an actual world. Thus our theories of representation must allow for ways of talking about historical events that advance claims about the truth of what happened, even if that truth is tempered by the limits of subjectivity or retrospective historicity. Further, narrativization itself—and even emplotment according to generic types—does not inherently degrade or preclude connection to those events; indeed, as Noël Carroll points out, "the basic elements of narrative structure—such as causation, influence, and rational action—correspond to actual elements of courses of events."[27]

Carroll, however, posits his rejection of "postmodern skepticist" claims that the connection between historical accounts and historical reality is inherently compromised in the process of narrativization on the premise that, while fiction and nonfiction films borrow liberally from one another's respective techniques, they are nonetheless distinct forms, recognizable by what he terms their respective "commitments." That is,

> Standardly, when one attends a film, one does not have to guess—on the basis of how it looks and sounds—whether it is fiction or nonfiction. . . . The film . . . come[s] labeled, or, as I say, indexed, one way or another, ahead of time. . . . The distinction between nonfiction and fiction is a distinction between the commitments of the texts, not between the surface structures of the text.[28]

In this case, spectators know in advance the intention of the screen images, so that even if the film's surface structures (narrativization, emplotment, technical devices, and so on) are ambiguous, it may still be clearly categorized—and thereby evaluated—as either fictional or not. Carroll's notion of indexing, however, accounts neither for the parodic effects of an intensely self-reflexive media apparatus, nor for the now commonplace blurring of generic boundaries in all forms of media, particularly those separating documentary from fiction forms. In the case of counterhistorical drama, films carrying one index (fiction) borrow freely from the conventions of another (documentary), placing the audience precisely in the position of having to "guess" whether the film is meant to be fiction or nonfiction, and about its relation to its historical referent. These techniques could simply be considered experimental or interesting in a postmodern sense if the commitment of the film (to shift the meaning of Carroll's term slightly), demonstrated by its various documentary conventions, were not to offer an alternative history of an atrocity. In this case, however, the demand for ethical representation becomes pivotal. It is the intrinsic political instability of counterhistorical dramatic film—resulting from and manifested in split plot lines and characterization—rather than its narrative emplotment or its relationship to truth that renders it inadequate to the work of historical representation it undertakes. Let me briefly provide an example, using an early counterhistorical dramatic film, before moving to a closer analysis of the problems of such generic incoherence when used to represent torture.

Early in Oliver Stone's *Salvador*, protagonist Richard Boyle and his sidekick Doc (Dr. Rock), both U.S. citizens, are stopped at an army roadblock as they cross the border into El Salvador. Lying beside them in the road is a body engulfed in flames. Increasingly nervous about entering this seemingly lawless—or, perhaps more accurately, extraordinarily *lawful*—land, Doc whispers fearfully, "Jesus, Boyle." "Relax man, it's just some guy," shrugs Boyle. Here, as in most counterhistorical dramatic films, tortured bodies stake out a danger zone through which the Western protagonist will travel, a zone that in terms of narrative emplotment heightens audience suspense regarding the physical safety of this protagonist. The presence of the burning body marks the border separating the United States and El Salvador as a margin between relative narrative calm and the rising action of the linear Hollywood plot line. Indeed, Boyle and Doc quite literally cross the border between the safe haven of bodily control (U.S. freedom) and the omnipresence of military power enacted on civilian bodies (El Salvadoran dictatorship) *over* this burning body.

Seized by the military, Doc and Boyle are confined and transported to San Salvador, their entrance to the city marked by more signs of military power in the form of mutilated bodies: a body hanging backwards over the side of a pick-up truck in the square, a student shot point-blank in the street as a "subversive." The death of this student triggers a shift in Boyle's perspective on the tortured body. Rather than dismissing him as amorphous and unremarkable, Boyle now acknowledges the symbolic weight of the tortured/executed body inasmuch as it signifies Boyle's own possible subjection to absolute authoritarian force. In shot/reverse-shot formation, Stone aligns the military questioning at gunpoint of Boyle and Doc with the simultaneous questioning at gunpoint of the Salvadoran student, so that audiences perceive the shooting of the student through the protagonists' eyes as the camera momentarily adopts their perspective.

Transcending the obscuring appellation "just some guy," the student's body—though still not considered in terms of its woundedness or loss of autonomy—is now taken into account, its injury destabilizing American immunity from such violence. Doc panics: "They're going to [. . .] kill us, Boyle [. . .] I thought you knew your way around here!" "Oh, shit," says Boyle this time.

The execution of the Salvadoran student, mediated for audiences by Boyle's parallel encounter with the Salvadoran military, momentarily dissolves the protective cloak of difference separating the U.S. protagonist from the native bodies upon whom such violence are routinely enacted— differentials based upon Boyle's U.S. citizenship, his role as journalist with contacts in the Salvadoran government, and his ability to move safely within this unsafe space using the dollar and a smarmy streetwise authority. At this moment of dissolution, the film simultaneously begins to construct a kind of definition: what it means to be American in an international context, what it means to be Not American. Viewers are made to experience the fear and vulnerability of occupying non-Western national and cultural identities as Boyle and Doc are stripped of their protection in the international danger zone.[29] This erasure of difference, however, is momentary, plot-driven. Regeneration of national difference converges with the relief of suspense in the moment the Western characters regain the safety that will be theirs for the remainder of the film—a safety delivered to viewers neatly packaged in *Salvador's* masculinist adventure narrative, easy and unthreatening (particularly to male viewers) with its typical road trip conventions. That is, fear for the bodily safety of Boyle and Doc upon their arrest is abruptly relieved when the action of the film takes a turn in the direction of a fantastical, eroticized masculine fantasy.[30] Rather than being tortured or killed, the "prisoners" are instead taken to the underground headquarters of Colonel Julio Figueroa, leader of a military "death squad" who is well-disposed toward Boyle because of a complimentary story Boyle once published about him in a right-wing Salvadoran newspaper. The tension of Boyle and Doc's imprisonment (heightened by Doc's disbelief that this could "actually happen—to *Americans!*") is released with lots of back-slapping and guffawing among the men, followed by a meal served by prostitutes who enthusiastically wash Boyle's and Doc's sweating bodies. Boyle's ego is restored, and he has now been established as a man who can make his way in this "different" country. Most important, the threat of bodily harm has been waylaid in a manner particularly satisfying to the (masculine) travel-adventure genre directing the film's emplotment.

Further generic and ideological muddle is made by the shift between "real" historical footage of the events in El Salvador and Boyle's overly dramatized photojournalistic quest narrative. Stone begins his film with documentary-style newsreel footage of the armed conflict: grainy black-and-white photos of people lying dead on the steps of the capital and being herded into military trucks apparently headed for prison or the death squads. Select "characters" introduced in the film's narrative structure are identified via large print at the bottom of the screen as "real" actors in the "real" El Salvador: "Major Maximiliano Casanova (aka 'Major Max') Presidential Candidate and Former Director of Salvadoran Intelligence," "Colonel Julio Figueroa, Commander 3rd Brigade, Infantry, Santa Ana Garrison," and so on. Stone includes pointedly ironic press clips of Ronald Reagan warning U.S. citizens about the imminent threat of communist invasion to "all of South, Central, and—I have no doubt—North America" via the El Salvadoran peasant revolution. While this documentary-style footage is clearly sympathetic to the Salvadoran opposition group Farabundo Marti Liberation Front (FMLN), the film does not tell the "story" of FMLN or of the El Salvadoran people who were "disappeared," tortured, or executed by governmental and paramilitary forces. Instead, the "real" story of Stone's film is the desperado adventuring of Boyle and his sidekick Doc. Later, Doc is replaced in the quest narrative frame by Boyle's professional compatriot, another photojournalist whose mission in El Salvador (as it was in the other war-torn nations repeatedly mentioned— and conflated—in the film, including Angola, Vietnam, Cambodia, and Nicaragua) is to capture his "one great shot of the nobility of human suffering."[31]

This redirection of audience identification from the collective story of the Salvadoran people to the narrative of the individual Western protagonist, which results in a reassuring account of Western political supremacy and individual safety, is achieved in a parallel process of lingering: on a macro level, in terms of narrative time given to the foreground adventure quest of the Western photographers, and on a micro level, in terms of relative time spent representing the pain and death of Western bodies as compared with non-Western bodies. Such coincidence between the demands of genre and the cultural differentiation achieved in part by representations of the tortured body is perhaps most prominently in evidence when considered in terms of the photographic quest, to which we are first introduced as a point of dramatic identification when Boyle and John stage a photo shoot at the dumping grounds for bodies of El Salvador's disappeared. The conventions used in this scene prepare the audience for the melodramatic horror of John's later death while taking pictures of a battle between government and FMLN forces.

Climbing the mound upon which hundreds of mutilated bodies lie rotting, Boyle and John discuss the tricks of the war journalist's trade, talking longingly about their quest for the great photo that will capture the "nobility of human suffering" (along with a Pulitzer Prize). The bodies in this scene are stripped of their power as witness to suffering as the men literally climb over them—and steady themselves upon them—in a metaphorical movement upward to the "peak" of photojournalism, the elusive signified, the most horrific of all photos of human horror. Stone's telephoto lens captures the uncertainty of John's footing as he makes his way through the bodies; the narrative takes on the suspense of the danger zone in the form of audience fear that he might fall upon this littered earth. Our fear is allayed, however, as he uses one of the bodies (an emaciated shoulder, to be exact) as a foothold and remains standing. This image, reproducing the very imperialism the film decries, is perhaps the quintessential figure for

U.S. aid to El Salvador during the war—and the moment when Stone's critique of that aid and its resulting escalation of torture and terror collapses most dramatically into itself. As the scene fades, we see the tired, heroic John, straining after his photos amid the bodies (the mound has now been made atmospheric with piped-in mist), with triumphant music and a voice-over portentously intoning, "someday . . . someday . . . someday. . . ."

This prophetic "someday" in the film ultimately materializes during the FMLN's moment of truth, the battle wherein they take the city of Santa Ana and are subsequently crushed by the military dictatorship's U.S.-imported tanks. In this scene, audience identification is still directed toward the photographers' quest, rather than to the rebels who ride exultantly into battle on decorated horses (later rendered absurd beside gargantuan U.S. tanks). John is brash during this battle, taking risks that even the foolhardy Boyle finds extreme. John's quest is fulfilled at the moment the tanks arrive, when FMLN rebels execute their prisoners at point-blank range (interestingly, these executioners are the first active female rebels portrayed in the film, and it is these women who bear the weight of Boyle's righteous diatribe that, in summarily executing their prisoners, they are no better than the death squads they battle against). This turn of events provides John with the opportunity he has waited for: a close-up of a prisoner screaming a last *Our Father* as he is shot by a female rebel, his face contorted with terror. The imperializing gesture of Stone's containment of this image of an other's suffering within the (Western) male quest for glory is exacerbated by the fact that in order to get this shot John blatantly ignores the express demand of an FMLN rebel who screams "no pictures." John is shot shortly thereafter, and Stone lingers almost lovingly over his death scene, literally slowing down narrative time to render it with more pathos and complexity than the death or mutilation of all the Salvadorans (military, civilian, and rebel) combined.

The exaggerated identification with John's death that Stone demands of his audience results from the division of characters into national, cultural, and ideological categories that determine their relative narrative weight, and thereby also the weight of the images of their pain and terror. The one-dimensionality of Stone's Salvadoran characters as either "good" political reformists or "evil" militia does not encourage the complex identification demanded by the historical situation he dramatizes: his audience never knows what forces lead some peasants to support the dictatorship, and thus to be evil, villainous, cruel, and literally ugly, while others support the FMLN, and are therefore seemingly benign, sometimes sympathetic, maybe even heroic. The personal histories—and thus the motivations or sufferings—of these characters are hidden beneath the film's use of them as fodder ("donors," to borrow from Bill Nichols) for its primary adventure narrative.

This problem results in the construction of the pain experienced by some bodies as natural, and even desirable. For instance, one Salvadoran military henchman is constructed throughout the film in conventionally villainous terms. Because he has been unrelentingly cruel and ominous throughout the film, audiences are put in the position of being glad when he dies. Taking a quick rebel bullet in the chest, he flips backward behind a desk; audiences are offered no sense of the pain he feels as the bullet enters his body, and his absence quickly relieves us of any obligation to feel for him. Indeed, the rebel who shoots him actually climbs over the desk to continue firing round after round into his body (which remains outside the camera's frame), as if for audience gratification at the death of symbolic evil characterized by this man. By contrast, when a bullet enters John's body we watch for an almost unbearable two minutes as he struggles for air through his ravaged throat and chest, slowly dying (not, however, before entrusting Boyle with the precious film containing his legacy). Partly because Stone so rigorously splits his representations of El Salvadoran people into the separate categories of the military and its supporters, on the one hand, and peasants and FMLN rebels, on the other (the latter, carrying the positive symbolic charge, corresponding to symbols of U.S. populist political identity), and partly because his Western protagonist hero remains safe and is rescued from the jaws of death any number of times by various U.S. and Salvadoran officials, diplomats, photographers, and friends, *Salvador* relinquishes its radical potential for asserting the transculturality of universal rights to the imperializing force of hegemonic (safe, free) U.S. political identity.

The representation of tortured bodies in *Beyond Rangoon* incurs similar problems resulting from the use of the historical referents (government repression in late-twentieth-century Burma, as well as the bodies of tortured and killed Burmese people) as signifiers in the film's generic coding, rather than as testimonials to their own occurrence. *Beyond Rangoon*, like most counterhistorical dramatic films, presents fascinating, potentially fruitful models of relationships between Western and native peoples even (especially) at the moment of political extremity. Indeed, the split plot line in *Beyond Rangoon* illuminates the transformation of both the Western protagonist, Laura Bowman, and her native counterpart, Aung Ko, as a result of contact in the context of state-sponsored brutality in 1980s Burma. Far from representing the flow of influence as unidirectional, from Western center to colonial periphery, the film provides ample evidence of the influence of Burmese culture and philosophy upon the Western protagonist, and of positive cultural and personal exchange between Bowman and the Burmese people she encounters. However, it undercuts the radical potential for those representations to act as models of balanced cultural contact (and for the film to act as ethical protest against the historical human rights violations central to its action) by its use of representations of terror against Burmese people as an element of the adventure emplotment used to heighten audience suspense for Bowman's safety and well-being, rather than to act as witness to the material conditions they signify. In this way, the film's narrativization ultimately gives way to the ideological construction central to counterhistorical dramatic film of Western identity as safe, superior, and separate from the rest of the world, in spite of its formal claims to represent a historic moment and to protest against human rights violations. This ideological paradox constitutes an inherent political instability that renders the film inadequate to the representation of histor-

259

ical human rights violations.

The film begins by offering the fertile premise that pain can be a means of connection between disparate peoples. Yet the potential of this empathic connection is immediately undermined by the imperialist consciousness revealed in Bowman's first interior monologue, narrated in voice-over to the image of white tourists floating through the lush landscape of Burma on a riverboat: "The trip was my sister's idea . . . she meant well. A touch of the exotic East would get me away from all the things that had happened. But it didn't . . . I thought I might find something in the east, some kind of answer. I stared at those stone statues, but nothing stirred in me. I was stone myself." The presence of orientalist discourse in Bowman's rhetoric of escape, and the specific descriptive "exotic" in relation to the generalized geographic marker "the East" (as opposed to the cultural and political specificity of Burma as independent from and interdependent with other nations and cultures in Asia), is all too familiar in dominant representations of cultural contact.[32] However, it becomes clear as the film progresses that this potentially healing exoticism is to be found quite specifically in an "Eastern" ontological approach to pain and suffering, especially as manifested in the tenets of Buddhism. As the audience is thus enlightened about Bowman's inner emotional state, the camera flashes from shots of the river to shots of a large stone Buddha carved into a hillside, reclining "just before he passed into nirvana"; to underscore the didactic significance of an "Eastern" approach to pain, the white tour guide informs his clients that "In the Buddhist world, where suffering is the accepted condition of man, the attainment of perfect detachment is the ultimate achievement." Making the connection, we must assume that the answer Bowman searches for in the East is precisely that detachment from the pain she has experienced as a result of an act of violence.

As if to complete this revelatory introduction to Bowman's wounded consciousness, the camera shifts to an aerial shot of a Western living room with a man and young boy—Bowman's husband and son—lying bloodied, shot. Thus the audience understands that Bowman is wounded in a specific way: by the loss and grief accompanying physical violence. First-world civilian violence and third-world state violence are set up early on as congruent, at least in the sense that people experiencing the effects of these different kinds of violence might find ground for an empathic connection that would bind over cultural, national, economic, and gender differences (this connection has as much to do with strategies for healing as it does with the shared experience of the violence itself). The wounded body provides that point of connection, remaining fixed in the spectre of its woundedness despite the disparate conditions that have produced it.

The wounded body also provides the occasion for Bowman's healing, the central quest of the film's bildungsroman plot formation. Trained as a physician, Bowman has been unable to practice medicine since the murder of her family because she can no longer stand the sight of blood. In addition to demonstrating the wisdom of the Buddhist ideal of detachment as a response to such earthly suffering, native bodies also provide the ground upon which Bowman is able to release the trauma that has rendered her unable to heal the wounded body. For instance, when Aung Ko receives a bullet wound that threatens to kill him, Bowman is forced to perform on-the-spot surgery to remove the bullet and save his life. In the process of healing Aung Ko, she is healed herself: his wound is redemptive to her inasmuch as she is able to pull the bullet from him as she could not from her husband or child.

At the end of the film, after a traumatic crossing into Thailand with hundreds of Burmese refugees, Bowman heads immediately for the medical tent and begins working on the injured, signifying the completion of her healing process—and thus of the main quest plot of the narrative. When the plot line corresponding to this protagonist achieves closure, the narrative field is opened to foreground the historical referent, in this case using captions over the screen images of Bowman working in the Red Cross tent (images that underscore the indispensable presence of Western aid and knowledge of Western onlookers in international crises). The caption reads in part: "Thousands of Burmese were massacred in the crackdown of the Democracy Movement. More than 700,000 fled their country. Two million more were driven from their homes and subsist in remote jungles. Torture and oppression continue in Burma to this day."

The perfect narrative closure achieved by the resolution of Bowman's healing process provides a stark contrast to this strikingly nonspecific disclosure regarding the thousands of Burmese people massacred and displaced by state terror, and especially by the simple declarative that torture and oppression continue in Burma *to this day*. Like the assertion regarding necessary identity protection at the start of *Cry Freedom*, this ambiguous and overdetermined time referent places audiences in an equivocal relationship to the assertion of ongoing torture and oppression; that is, while "this day" presumably refers to the moment the film was released, it also uncannily refers to the day an audience member views the film, which, given the circulation of film via home video, could be years hence. Apart from its referential haziness, this statement of a historical condition (ongoing oppression and brutality) is problematic not because it represents an ambiguous truth claim, but rather because of its juxtaposition with the false finitude of narrative closure imposed upon the historical referent by its classical Hollywood bildungsroman and adventure emplotment. Postcolonial theorists have argued that literary realism in general, and its tendency toward absolute closure of narrative work in particular, demonstrates an imperialist impulse toward "total representation." Following the understanding of history central to postcolonial theory as necessarily fragmented, unfinished, and even chaotic, the unity and coherence achieved by the closure of one plot line does not—cannot—extend to the other in a classical Hollywood film, and indeed such completion would, according to this view, turn out to be an "act of make-believe."[33] Certainly the closure bestowed upon the individual quest narrative of the counterhistorical dramatic film is painfully unreal when considered in relation to the ongoing collective struggle that provides the context for that narrative, and that does not itself achieve closure.[34] The imposition of perfect closure will always remain a false, imperialistic gesture in counterhistorical dramatic film because of its relationship with the extranarrative world; as Russell Reising notes with regard to the texts included in his study of narrative closure, "[some narratives] can't close, precisely because their embeddedness within the sociohistorical worlds of their genesis is so complex and conflicted."[35]

This embeddedness in an extratextual world returns us to the question of the relationship of counterhistorical dramatic films to a historical referent or truth, as well as the relationship between fictional and documentary film conventions: again we find in probing this relationship that the mode of emplotment in a text that overtly claims to rerepresent a silenced history reveals ideological instabilities at the heart of that project. The act of assigning narrative closure to the story of the white, Western protagonist, especially as that closure is achieved through the vehicle of the historical struggle of Burmese people, privileges that protagonist and reaffirms her identity as safe, secure, and separate from the ongoing, irresolvable struggles of the Burmese. It is especially significant in this context that closure is equated with healing, a healing unavailable to the Burmese, whose history is represented as an open wound, unsutured to this day. The image of Bowman, newly restored and empowered in her training as Western physician, healing the wounded Burmese, re-places her at the imperialist—if liberally altruistic—center of the indeterminate vortex of native history, and of the film.

I should add here that this security enjoyed by Bowman is also linked to her freedom of movement; that is, the Western protagonist in the counterhistorical dramatic film is safe because she or he can move out of one state into another: state meaning both nation and state of being safe. Laura Bowman can travel to the "exotic" (dangerous) East to escape the trauma of individual violence in the West and can choose, when her adventure is over, either to stay or to go; Richard Boyle can cross the border into El Salvador seeking a good time and a better photo opportunity, crossing back to the safety of U.S. territory while his Salvadoran girlfriend is remanded to the danger zone; Donald Woods in Attenborough's *Cry Freedom* orchestrates a safe escape to inform the Western world of the terror of apartheid South Africa epitomized by the torture and murder of Steve Biko in a Port Elizabeth jail. While these representations may be classified as historically "correct"—faithful to the political and geographic organization of the world and even to actual events—when cocooned within the classical Hollywood foreground of a split plot line that mimics this historical entrapment by similarly remanding non-Western subjects to the stasis of background, the films reinscribe the very imperialist oppositions of freedom/unfreedom, inside/outside, subject/object that they claim to undo with universalist protests against state violation of human rights. The collective action—chase scenes, courtroom brawls, adventure sequences, even romantic interludes—of the foreground plot composes an aria of movement for Western characters on-screen, opposed by the ensemble stagnation of non-Western characters, teleologically stuck in place and (anachronistic) time. Given that closure in the counterhistorical dramatic film means fulfillment of the excessive generic formulae of the foreground plot, non-Western characters are literally left behind in the suspended time-without-resolution of narrative danger.

Symbolic Safety and Real Harm:
The Spectacle of the Wounded Body

Beyond Rangoon's final image of Bowman, restored and hard at work in the Red Cross aid tent, is the culmination of the film's use of the wounded bodies of others to construct a Western identity defined by its difference from native people in precisely these terms of protection against bodily injury. The measure of this difference widens over the course of the film, and is especially evident in the spectacle of tortured bodies used as symbolic capital in exchange for rising audience suspense around Bowman's journey through a hazardous Burma to physical safety and emotional healing.

This use of the tortured or wounded body is related to the formal requirements of the film's classical Hollywood structure. For example, late in the film, a gruesomely stylized representation of the massacre of peaceful Burmese protestors disrupts a typical Hollywood chase scene with Bowman and compatriots narrowly escaping the shots of soldiers from behind their jeep; the wild action of the chase is abruptly truncated when they stumble upon the leisurely horror of a massacre shot in close-up. At the moment the soldiers open fire upon the crowd, the camera reverses to a shot of Bowman's face screaming "Stop it!" Slackening to a slow-motion pace, the film captures in tight close-up the spectre of men, women, and girls falling as they are shot, their bodies twisting in grisly, modern dance–like movements that are strangely aestheticized; these shots are combined with reverse shots of Bowman's screaming face throughout the sequence. And then, as abruptly as the action of the film was arrested to accommodate this baroque depiction of massacre, it bluntly snaps back to the accelerated action of the chase scene, which feels the more rapid—and *suspenseful*—as juxtaposed to the deliberate—almost *suspended*—slowness of the massacre. The representation of massacre of Burmese people is in a sense moderated by Bowman, whose horror (untamed by the gloss of aesthetic stylization, and occupying the narrative and cinematic focal point of the scene) trumps the suffering of the victims. Audience members perceive the execution of Burmese protestors from Bowman's perspective; perhaps even more importantly in this regard, Bowman's terror has the power of voice lacked by the masses of Burmese under attack, as audiences hear her individual screams distinctly over the collective (background) noise of the crowd. Ultimately, then, the interruption of Bowman's frantic chase scene with the spectre of execution heightens audience suspense and fear for Bowman's safety. The function of these representations as testimony to the historic massacre of Burmese protesters is secondary to their use in adventure emplotment.

Representations of the torture and execution of Burmese people intensify the adventure and bildungsroman formulae in similar fashion throughout the film. From the moment the film erupts into its representations of violent struggle between protestors and soldiers—the moment, that is, when the bildungsroman formula takes on the formal characteristics of adventure narrative style—Bowman's many escapes from scenes of conflict are always distinguished by the pop-pop of shots being fired and the spectre of falling Burmese bodies. Again, these background sights and sounds are used to demarcate the narrow margins of Bowman's escape: her body removes itself from the site of danger at the precise moment of arrival of soldiers firing their assault weapons in the despotic capriciousness characteristic of representations of the military in counterhistorical dramatic films. If the quest of the film involves moving through a space demarcated "dangerous" to a safe, secure space of redemptive healing and closure, then the spectre of wounded Burmese bodies provides the material(ity) of suspense for Bowman's safety as she navigates that ground.

As in most counterhistorical dramatic films, the spectacle of the tortured native body in *Beyond Rangoon* is used to cordon off space as particularly threatening, to mark the boundaries of a particularly hostile "danger zone" within the relative peril of the whole environment. The narrative time spent by the protagonist in that space, then, is a time of particularly heightened fear and suspense. Thus, the terror inspired by the spectacle of torture of a Burmese person is displaced, as audience attention is removed from that person's body, and his or her pain, to the *potential* of such pain to be enacted upon the white, Western body. As such, the question arises: Why this need for a mediating Western presence in a film that claims to be about human rights abuses in Burma, a presence that produces a fundamental incoherence in the film's politics? If one posits that the presence of Western protagonists (often played by major Hollywood stars) in counterhistorical dramatic films provides a point of identification that in turn ensures the popular appeal necessary to reach a mass audience, then, according to this model, Western audiences (a construction that elides its own racial and cultural differences) are only capable of imagining the "pain of the other" by imagining the suffering of a composite (white) Western person. This is, however, a dangerous empathy; as Saidiya V. Hartman argues, it is "by virtue of this substitution [that] the object of identification threatens to disappear."[36] This obliteration of the other's suffering constitutes the representational violence of counterhistorical dramatic film, which, unable to sustain the tension between cultural specificity and universal humanity embedded in its own protest discourse, gives way to the totalizing impulse of an imperialist resurrection of white, Western subjectivity as symbol for universal experience.

Richard Attenborough's *Cry Freedom* manages this tension between cultural specificity and universal humanity in its protest against human rights abuses in apartheid-era South Africa by providing a more complicated model of cross-cultural identification than that of *Beyond Rangoon*; however, it too ultimately manifests the ideological instability and narrative incoherence characterizing most counterhistorical dramatic films as a result of its use of a split plot line and white (Western) protagonist to render its testimony of historical human rights violations. The film distinguishes itself in this regard, however, by dramatizing only one explicit representation of torture. Rather then employing images of tortured and mutilated bodies as spectacles providing audience suspense, or as signifiers of danger to the white, Western body, here the tortured body is used to provide evidence of the "truth" against the manipulation of history by those in power. This use of images of atrocity is in keeping with an understanding of the ethical representation of human rights abuses that asserts the validity of one truth claim over another in service of an argument, as opposed to eroticizing the image as spectacle for narrative pleasure. Although its narrative is split in classical Hollywood style, *Cry Freedom* also utilizes narrative structure to radically contest the official version of what happened to Steve Biko in police custody—the manner of his death, the condition of his body—by its own representation of those events, directing the viewer's identification with Biko to shape a sense of indignation and horror at the tactics of the Afrikaner police (and by extension the whole apartheid government). It is only indirectly that what happens to Biko's body is used as motivator of suspense for the fate of white hero Donald Woods.

While the torture of Biko is not directly represented, audiences are provided evidence of it in the scenes directly following his arrest. Shot in a long, dark hallway, the camera angle is low, framing several pairs of shiny black shoes walking with a set of bare feet dragging among them. The soundtrack is empty but for the click of heels and the low gasps of labored breathing. In the next scene, Biko's body is revealed to us in parts; however, unlike the cinematic technique employed in comparable scenes in *Salvador* and *Beyond Rangoon*, the camera's perspective does not mimic the gaze of a Western onlooker. Its perspective unmediated, the audience sees first his head, then a shackled foot being lifted by a doctor who tests for a reflex. The camera pans up Biko's leg, over his naked body to his beaten, bloodied face. The soundtrack runs signifiers of torture over the voices of the doctor and guards as further evidence of the cause of Biko's injuries: the sounds of a whip or a stick banging, accompanied by agonized screams. Biko is taken out, still naked, and thrown in the back of a truck; the camera cross-cuts images of Biko's head slamming onto the truck's hard floor with images of the heavy tires bouncing over ruts in the dirt road. The final shot of Biko's body is in the morgue, where Woods has gone with Biko's wife. His face is twisted and swollen; Woods has brought his photographer to document the truth of his body's condition.

These scenes taken together act as evidence of a suppressed reality, and are used in counterbalance with scenes of Minister of Police James Kruger's formal announcement of Steven Biko's death ("Biko's death leaves me cold. He died after a hunger strike"), and the official inquest, which acknowledges Biko's brain damage but makes the absurdist pronouncement that "The cause of death was brain injury which led to renal failure and other complications. . . . On the available evidence they cannot be attributed to any act of omission amounting to a criminal offense on the part of any person." In this case—rare in the counterhistorical dramatic film—the image of the tortured body actually does bear witness to the reality of its condition. Moreover, the image provides a crucial contradiction to the vehement denials of the apartheid authorities, which constitute a secondary trauma central to the experience of torture. Elaine Scarry describes this denial, or disclaiming, as a deeply consequential, often overlooked step in the "sequence" of torture, a phenomenon that consolidates the regime's power and allows the perpetuation of torture: "This denial . . . occurs in the translation of all the objectified elements of pain into the insignia of power, the conversion of the enlarged map of human suffering into an emblem of the regime's strength."[37] *Cry Freedom* utilizes the image of the tortured body—arguably a "map of human suffering"—precisely to undo the regime's strength by reclaiming the tortured body as signifier of the regime's real brutality, as well as testimonial of its own repressed material reality. Therefore, the scene is useful to the plot only insofar as the plot presents a counterhistory to the official history asserted by South African security forces under the apartheid regime; in other words, during this scene, the film's imagery and action correspond to its proclaimed intent.

In spite of the film's clearly oppositional position in this regard, however, the incoherence in the film's rendering of torture—and thus, the instability of its proclaimed politics—hinges on the fact that Biko's death occurs approximately halfway through the film; viewers are then asked to identify with the struggle of Donald Woods to get himself, his book on Biko, and his family out of South Africa after being banned in a fashion similar to Biko himself. The generic vehicles of suspense and adventure are now mobilized in telling Woods's story, which is also the story of the making of a hero. Whatever the film's formal position, indicated by its assertion of and protest against the cause of Steve Biko's death, audiences are still asked to identify for more than half the film with a heroic figure who has benefited deeply from the apartheid system as a member of South Africa's ruling class. Viewers still see black men, women, and children being tortured and murdered and white men, women, and children escaping into the beatific sunset and orchestral crescendo of the quintessential Hollywood ending. This plot line achieves the requisite classical Hollywood closure through the dramatic gestures of border-crossing marking Woods and his family's escape from South Africa; however, the plot line corresponding to the life of Steve Biko and the struggle in South Africa remains typically open, marked as such at the end of the film by shots of military violence against Soweto schoolchildren protesting the use of Afrikaans in the schools in 1977, as well as with the list of names of those who have been killed by South African police as a result of legalized imprisonment without trial. In considering the relative adequacy of *Cry Freedom*'s representations of atrocity in South Africa, the issue is again not one of truth value; indeed, *Cry Freedom* is perhaps the counterhistorical drama most at pains to reveal the repressed truth of the historical event as opposed to the accepted, official version. The issue here is that the representations constructed to do this work are destabilized by the split in plot line that privileges the story of the white hero with the lion's share of time, resolution, safety, and closure.

Despite these compromises in the integrity of the film's representations of torture and terror, *Cry Freedom* complicates the issue of identity in the film by constructing the bildungsroman process of character growth—specifically the growth of Woods's character into a heroic protagonist—as one of cross-cultural exchange and integration. Using the strategic inter-

266

cutting of flashback shots of Biko, coupled with African music tracks and scenery, the film equates heroism with African-ness. Woods's process of becoming heroic coincides with a process of becoming more African; specifically, more *black* South African, more like Biko himself. In this way, the division of the movie into action before and after Biko's death sets up a parallel formation—reminiscent of the echoing relationship of Old and New Testament biblical parables—in which Woods's actions in the latter part of the film often evoke or repeat Biko's actions or words in the former. For instance, in an early scene with South African Security Forces, Biko resists police by interrogating them back, so to speak, as well as by actually striking a policeman who has slapped his face. Much later, when police begin harassing his family and his black maid as a result of his involvement with Biko, Woods adopts similar tactics of accosting armed policemen, facing soldiers and looking them directly in the eyes in spite of the threat posed by their power and their weapons. Audiences are reminded of Biko's example in watching Woods's newly heroic resistance.[38]

In spite of such provocative cross-cultural identifications, the political instability of *Cry Freedom*'s representations may be traced to its grounding in Donald Woods's book, *Biko: The True Story of the Young South African Martyr and His Struggle to Raise Black Consciousness*, which claims that the purpose of *Cry Freedom* was to document Biko's life and death, as well as the struggle of black South Africans against apartheid. It is only in a newly issued prologue (1991) that Woods acknowledges his own presence in the film:

> The screenplay relies on incidents from Biko's life and my writings and experiences as the "foreground," or personal interest material, for the film. Major historic events of the period serve as the documentary "background" to reveal the nature of apartheid.[39]

This reference to a plot line split into foreground and background material glosses the imbalance within *Cry Freedom*'s foreground plot; that is, audiences see relatively few incidents from Biko's life, and those that are shown are related to the development of his friendship with Woods. Indeed, well over half of the film is spent developing the classic Hollywood adventure plot of Woods's escape from South Africa after Steve's death. Despite Woods's clear commitment to anti-apartheid activism—and without minimizing the accompanying risks to himself and his family, and the great personal sacrifice of banning and exile—the narrative split in *Cry Freedom* reveals an ambiguity of purpose that slides easily into the imperialist shoring up of white, Western identity characteristic of the counterhistorical drama. Given Woods's description of the foreground plot as "personal interest" material, it is important to consider the cinematic prerequisites for personal interest, presumably that of mass audiences. Must the material supplying such personal interest focus upon the suspenseful adventures of a white protagonist hero? Was there not equally suspenseful, adventurous, and interesting material to be found in the biography of one Steve Biko, for all intents and purposes the protagonist of this story? Upon what assumptions about audience identification are writers, directors, and producers acting in their repeated decisions to wrest the story from its putative subject in the counterhistorical drama? Whether or not individual audience members maintain "dominant" or "oppositional" readings of a particular film, counterhistorical dramatic films ultimately consolidate a (white) Western identity at the expense of other cultural and national identities, leaving the stories "behind" international and domestic torture and terror in the background, as yet untold.

Notes

1. Elaine Scarry, *The Body in Pain: The Making and Unmaking of the World* (New York: Oxford Univeristy Press, 1985), 4.
2. Cathy Caruth, "Introduction," in *Trauma: Explorations in Memory*, ed. Cathy Caruth (Baltimore: Johns Hopkins University Press, 1995), 10.
3. Hayden White, "Historical Emplotment and the Problem of Truth," in *Probing the Limits of Representation: Nazism and the "Final Solution,"* ed. Saul Friedlander (Cambridge, Mass.: Harvard University Press, 1992), 43.
4. Jacobo Timmerman, *Prisoner without a Name, Cell without a Number* (New York: Knopf, 1981), 33.
5. Kali Tal, *Worlds of Hurt: Reading the Literatures of Trauma* (Cambridge: Cambridge University Press, 1996), 21.
6. Saul Friedlander, "Introduction," in *Probing the Limits of Representation*, 17.
7. Ibid.
8. This study does not purport to undertake statistical analysis of audience response to individual films, but rather to study the interpretive signals or cues embedded in films' generic imperatives, plot lines, and cinematic structure, along with broad-based audience effects. As David Bordwell notes, "Every film trains its spectator"; films adhering closely to common generic formulae are particularly overbearing in terms of the expectations and responses they seek. David Bordwell, *Narration in the Fiction Film* (Madison: University of Wisconsin Press, 1985), 45.
9. MacCannell's discussion of the routinization of violence is part of his critique of postmodern theorists' deconstruction of "the subject," which he asserts is, at worst, tantamount to a recuperation of fascism; at best, an apolitical looking away from the material conditions of violence. Dean MacCannell, *Empty Meeting Grounds: The Tourist Papers* (London: Routledge, 1992), 198.
10. *Schindler's List* is an exception in the sense that its other is located within national borders; however, it retains the format of a bildungsroman style wherein the powerful protagonist (Schindler, a member of the Nazi party) is followed as he grows and changes through his commitment to rescuing Jewish people from death.
11. Bordwell, *Narration in the Fiction Film*, 157.
12. Frederic Jameson, *The Geopolitical Aesthetic: Cinema and Space in the World System* (Bloomington: Indiana University Press, 1995), 5.
13. See William J. Palmer, *The Films of the Eighties* (Carbondale: Southern Illinois University Press, 1993), esp. chs. 2 and 3, for detailed analyses of the Vietnam War film as a genre.
14. The counterhistorical drama is indebted in formal terms to the travel narrative; for historical analysis of the travel narrative as genre, see Mary Louise Pratt, *Imperial Eyes: Travel Writing and Transculturation* (New York: Routledge, 1992); for analysis of the role of the traveler in the postmodern "globalized" world, see Caren Kaplan, *Questions of Travel: Postmodern Discourses of Displacement* (Durham, N.C.: Duke University Press, 1996).
15. Jameson, *The Geopolitical Aesthetic*, 38.
16. Palmer, *The Films of the Eighties*, 15.
17. Jameson, *The Geopolitical Aesthetic*, 39. Importantly, in a historical genealogy similar to that of the counterhistorical dramatic film, Palmer locates the

advent of the terrorist film in the "political lesson[s] learned from the Vietnam years" (132).

18. There is a subgenre of the counterhistorical drama dealing specifically with the imprisonment of U.S. or west European nationals in authoritarian countries, often on charges of drug possession: perhaps most famously, *Midnight Express* (1978), and more recently *Return to Paradise* (1998) and *Breakdown Palace* (1999).

19. Jameson, *The Geopolitical Aesthetic*, 4.

20. Leger Grindon, *Shadows on the Past: Studies in the Historical Fiction Film* (Philadelphia: Temple University Press, 1994), 10.

21. Ibid., 33.

22. My use of the term *Western* here is a nongeographic designation defined more accurately by its construction of an exceptionalist progress narrative linked to modernization and technology, as well as its economic and political hegemony in global context. As Stathis Gourgouris notes, "[the] idiomatic condition [of Western culture] is that it recognizes no geographical core, that it enjoys a continuous geographical mutation . . . characteristic of a tradition that believes itself to be founded on an exclusive sense of modernity." Stathis Gourgouris, "Enlightenment and Paranomia," in *Violence, Identity, and Self-Determination*, ed. Hent de Vries and Samuel Weber (Stanford, Calif.: Stanford University Press, 1997), 120.

23. Significantly, in Oliver Stone's *Salvador* the closing update is split according to the classical Hollywood formulaic plot line into material referencing the protagonist/hero and information about the background struggle, in this case, political events in El Salvador: "Richard Boyle is still looking for Maria and her children. . . . Salvador continues to be one of the largest recipients of U.S. military aid and the same military leaders continue in power."

24. Part of the problem is related to selectivity and specificity of historical representation; that is, how much detailed information it is possible to include in a fictionalized film history. In this case, as in many counterhistorical dramatic films, the conflict appears to be between the Burmese "military" and Burmese "people." Beyond indications that the military was particularly repressive of students, professors, and suspected communists, the characteristics of specific targets of repression are not fleshed out. No historical context is provided for this clash, and the ethnic distinctions among particular groups targeted by the military are elided.

25. Bill Nichols, *Representing Reality: Issues and Concepts in Documentary* (Bloomington: Indiana University Press, 1992), 116.

26. Ibid. See especially Laura Mulvey, "Visual Pleasure and Narrative Cinema," in *Movies and Methods*, vol. 2, ed. Bill Nichols (Berkeley: University of California Press, 1985).

27. Noël Carroll, "Nonfiction Film and Postmodernist Skepticism," in *Post-Theory: Reconstructing Film Studies*, ed. David Bordwell and Noel Carroll (Madison: University of Wisconsin Press, 1996), 290.

28. Ibid., 287.

29. In the films under analysis in this chapter, the political entity situated at the apex of international hierarchy is the United States; however, in considering the counterhistorical dramatic film as a genre, the United States might be considered synecdochically representative of "the West" more generally. This parallel is especially relevant as international images of both the United States and the West depend heavily upon political terms, and U.S. political identity is derived more broadly from a Western Enlightenment tradition. This link between the West, modernity, and the rule of law is important to my argument here.

30. The requirement of classical Hollywood cinema to depict the wounded body of a hero/protagonist is discussed in this volume by Lee Clark Mitchell, "Violence in the Film Western."

31. Part of the geopolitical differentiation of West from non-West in *Salvador* takes the form of a typically imperialist conflation of all non-Western sites of armed struggle into a massive other based upon what they offer to the Western observer and what the Western observer did while he was there. For instance, when Boyle experiences difficulty getting a news agency assignment in El Salvador John asks him why he doesn't try Angola for a photo-op; Boyle replies that Angola "has no nightlife." Also, much of Boyle's (self-constructed) currency as a photojournalist is that he was "the last man out" of Cambodia when things got too "hot" for less intrepid reporters.

32. See Edward Said, *Orientalism* (New York: Knopf, 1978), for an exegesis of the central tropes of orientalist discourse.

33. D. A. Miller, *Narrative and Its Discontents: Problems of Closure in the Traditional Novel* (Princeton, N.J.: Princeton University Press, 1988), 267.

34. The political and ideological lines dividing these separate plots correspond to a traditional vision of history as a totalizing linear system, on the one hand, and the sense of evolving, circular, chaotic history (or historical dispossession) characterizing the (neo)colonial world, on the other. See Edouard Glissant, *Caribbean Discourse: Selected Essays*, trans. J. Michael Dash, ed. A. J. Arnold and Kandioura Drame (Charlottesville: University Press of Virginia, 1992), for a discussion of such views of history and narrative in the context of Caribbean writing and identity.

35. Russell Reising, *Loose Ends: Closure and Crisis in the American Social Text* (Durham, N.C.: Duke University Press, 1996), 11.

36. Saidiya V. Hartman, *Scenes of Subjection: Terror, Slavery, and Self-Making in Nineteenth-Century America* (New York: Oxford University Press, 1997), 19.

37. Scarry, *The Body in Pain*, 56.

38. Corresponding to these parallels set up by plot elements is a strategic use of music to equate Woods's rise to heroic consciousness (itself directly linked to the narrative demands of the classical Hollywood plot) with a gradual shift to an African consciousness; that is, traditional African music rises to mark moments of particular defiance or triumph as he moves toward his final border-crossing.

39. Donald Woods, *Biko: The True Story of the Young South African Martyr and His Struggle to Raise Black Consciousness* (New York: Henry Holt and Company, 1991), 10.

holocaust film criticism

and the politics

of judeo-christian

twelve

phenomenology

terri ginsberg

It is a commonly accepted fact that the first images of the Holocaust transmitted to the European and North American publics took the form of newsreels containing select footage of concentration camp atrocities either expropriated from Nazi archives or filmed first-hand by Allied liberating forces.[1] It is also a commonly accepted opinion that the footage contained in these newsreels comprises some of the most gruesome, horrific, violent images ever to have been recorded on film. Indeed, the footage turns precisely on the sight of mounds of naked corpses numbering in the thousands, droves of skeletal prisoners crammed three to a single wooden bunk or wandering aimlessly after their liberations, scraping rubbish piles for a morsel to eat, and trainloads of displaced and uprooted persons, exhausted from countless days of journeying without food or water, lined up for selection either to be worked or gassed to death. These are the images to which historians, critics, philosophers, and theologians have referred when designating the Holocaust—the systematic, industrialized mass murder of approximately twelve million people, including Jews (who comprised a disproportionately large percentage of victims), Roma (Sinto and Lalleri "Gypsies"), Soviet prisoners of war, lesbians and gays ("homosexuals"), political resisters (communists, socialists, trade-unionists, and Freemasons), dissident religious groups (Jehovah's Witnesses, Jesuits), Slavs (Poles, Czechs, Ukrainians), and the mentally and physically infirm and disabled, under the auspices of the German National Socialist Party ("Nazis") during the Second World War. They are also the images that have helped accord the Holocaust the status as one of the most heinous, atrocious, unspeakable, unimaginable, incomprehensible, unrepresentable events of all time.

Against this backdrop, however, Holocaust cinematic culture has gradually proliferated and expanded in scope. Beginning most notably with the highly abstract poetic documentary *Night and Fog* (Alain Resnais, France, 1954), this culture moved into Hollywood melodramas[2] that aped formally and ideologically some of the very earliest, pre- and immediate postliberation films on the subject[3] and that soon after were accompanied by U.S. network television interviews with survivors and traditional, expository documentaries about the concentration camp structure and experience.[4] It then passed into the postrealist, "retro-style" and high art films of the European auteurs,[5] which eventually also were appropriated into a Hollywood aesthetic format, most notably and recently by *Schindler's List* (Steven Spielberg, U.S.A, 1993) but also earlier, by *Sophie's Choice* (Alan J. Pakula, U.S.A., 1982). Finally, after a spate of popular melodramatic docudramas and theatrical reruns aired over Hollywood network television,[6] Holocaust cinematic culture has moved into today's veritable multimedia museum spectacular-extravaganza.[7]

Not widely discussed, however, is the fact that this cinematic cultural proliferation and expansion has been accompanied by a converse movement in cultural theory. That movement relies on a general consensus—fostered and encouraged by both popular and scholarly criticism as well as by many of the films themselves—of the proverbial assignation of the Holocaust as beyond intelligibility or cultural representation. The basis of this consensus was a philosophical problematic for which the Holocaust was so monumental, so horrific, so unique, so phenomenologically sublime as to be capable neither of adequate aesthetic reproduction nor definitive historical and epistemological explanation.[8] Associated with the post-Holocaust writings of Theodor W. Adorno, this consensus consolidated an unspoken taboo against the formal academic study of Holocaust and film, the idea being that such study was tantamount to indulging in obscenity. The range of study deterred by this consensus was, furthermore, varied and included historical and critical analyses of Holocaust film culture's proliferation and expansion, the institutional sponsorship of such study, curricular development of Holocaust film courses, the funding of Holocaust film research and its publication, and the installation of Holocaust film culture and discourse at Holocaust museums. Indeed, to date, one is struck by the relative dearth of Holocaust film criticism, not to mention courses, in the contemporary academy, where Holocaust cinema studies finds its structural origin and center.[9] This contrasts the popular print media's preponderant focus on the subject both in North America and abroad and is especially ironic in that one of the most canonical, widely read and discussed, and not coincidentally controversial cinema studies texts, Kracauer's *From Caligari to Hitler*,[10] articulates its critique of Weimar cinema in terms of pervasive discursive affiliation with the Third Reich and the Holocaust.

Is there some underlying or extenuating rationale for this apparent contradiction between an expansive array of Holocaust film production on the one hand, and a relative dearth of Holocaust film scholarship on the other? After all, whether one agrees or not with the ostensibly Adornian paradigm, Holocaust films do often lend themselves to the literal definition of obscenity. Newsreel documentaries and documentaries containing newsreel footage, with their pathetic depictions of naked corpses and barely clad concentration and death camp prisoners, do meet the cultural, if not legal, criteria of "obscenity." This condition, which cultural theorist Peter Michelson has defined lucidly and candidly as "the Greek sense of bringing onstage what is customarily kept offstage in western culture," presumably entails a necessary aestheticization of the so-called un(re)presentable, "a perceptual alteration whereby the obscene, a species of the ugly, is reconstituted to a function akin to that of the beautiful." "Obscenity" is a condition that consequently takes on the simultaneous quality of the culturally offensive, perversely pleasurable, and socially threatening.[11] More figuratively and complexly, the Adornian taboo, as it is commonly interpreted, presupposes the Holocaust as a socially enabled occasioning of death so horrible, unprecedented, and historically paradigmatic that its representative artistic rendering is conceivable only as a mimesis of Nazi ideology itself. In other words, the representation of the Holocaust is considered an aesthetic reformulation of a historical phenomenon considered always already generative of mass destruction, and henceforth as *essentially* "obscene," in both structure and spectatorial effect.[12]

This perspective, widely attributed to Adorno, is in fact prototypical of Michelson. The latter's literal definition of obscenity is undergirded by a structuralist understanding of the philosophical dialectic on the sublime, for which the cultural reconstitution of what is traditionally forbidden from appearing "onstage" is likened to "the modern and especially contemporary assertiveness of . . . materialism." Michelson likens the obscene not to some romantic notion of a profound, uncannily alluring, morally restitutive truth of nature, but to those conditions and practices of capitalism that are sublimated, suppressed, dissimulated, or diverted from view. To be clear, Michelson ultimately understands such conditions and practices as fundamental and irrepressible, even while recognizing their quite visible perpetuation of social misery.[13] In his view, these conditions and practices are designated "obscene" for the threat of violence widespread knowledge of them is thought capable of posing to the status quo.

Whereas Michelson draws an ontological analogy between this structural-materialist dialectic (as an existential context for technocultural development) and the Freudian libido (as a referential axis of corporeal experience), Adorno's analysis of the Holocaust cultural problematic is more theoretical. Accessing and incorporating radical critiques of ontology by Horkheimer, Benjamin, and Marx, as well as recalling the Levinasian critique of Heidegger, Adorno foregrounds what he sees as the social institutional parameters of the obscene. He critically reorients the traditional discursive mediation and dissimulation of obscenity by relocating aesthetic concerns away from the ontological onto the class-political and -conceptual planes.[14] From this perspective, by and large ignored by Holocaust film critics but increasingly evident in Adorno's subsequent attempts to qualify his original statement,[15] no strict ontological affinity exists between the material and the libidinal registers of Holocaust cultural production: attempts to represent the Holocaust should be viewed politically rather than poetically. Holocaust representation is always in the first place historically conditioned by aesthetic ideologies, especially those associated with romantic tradition. The phenomenon of libidinal attraction to the sublime is itself likewise always preconditioned—at the level of technocultural form as well as referential content—and rooted in aesthetic philosophy; again, especially problematic, nay, "obscene," is the romantic tendency to thematize the material register across a libidinal-cultural nexus.[16]

As the relative dearth of Holocaust film scholarship over the years suggests, the Adornian taboo against comprehending the Holocaust through romanticized, rhetorically abstract lenses has been greatly misunderstood. The clear scholarly tendency has been to interpret the Holocaust according to a perspective more akin to that of Michelson, for whom the obscene is conceived phenomenologically, almost mystically, as an event that can never really be comprehended, much less known conceptually. The consequence for cinema studies is that the Holocaust can therefore never really be represented, much less understood, beyond those romantic, aesthetic-philosophical, techno-libidinal parameters misidentified with Adorno. A propos of this misidentification, Holocaust film criticism, when practiced, has not surprisingly conformed to the basic discursive parameters of phenomenology and, by extension, the ideology of Christian moral philosophy. Most texts of Holocaust film criticism have presented analyses or reviews of Holocaust films that devise an irreducibly opaque epistemological relationship across the historical, philosophical, and formal-textual registers of those films. On this tack, the only guiding question permitted is methodological: how best to ascertain, or at least to approximate, the relationship between representation and event. What this allows, however, is little more than the management and containment of any real knowledge one might acquire about that relationship, including its purported aesthetic foundations and the instability and volatility attributed to them. In short, Holocaust film criticism has disallowed radical connection between the historical generation, industrial production, technological construction, and subjective interpellation of Holocaust cinematicity itself. Much criticism tends instead toward a skilled hermeneutic decoding of esoteric rhetorical forms, a practice compelling critics to approach ostensibly inaccessible states thought to manifest protection against the perceived chaos or evil of the material, quotidian—"Jewish"—world.[17]

Even as Holocaust film criticism has moved from its earlier, ontological-existential articulations to the hermeneutic modalities informing contemporary scholarship, it has continued to uphold basic phenomenological postulates that are in line with the Christian moral foundations of aesthetic philosophy. One of these postulates is that objects, including objects of culture, can and should be known only approximately, by an inspection of their apparent forms. Another is that the binding analogy of these forms is an intentional, normative, synthetic, self-correcting, ever excessive "elsewhere" or "other." A third is that the quiddity and significance of this analogy between object and form—this structured absence—may itself only be approximated; this approximation can only be pursued, furthermore, by comparative analysis of plural, uncanny variations as these manifest self-evidently in the very object of analysis, the intended, sacralized "thing-in-itself" (*die Sache*).[18] This is to say, more plainly, that Holocaust film criticism enacts a paradigm shift from "high" philosophical to more conventional aesthetics, by which it rearticulates theological premises to a quotidian, ecumenical framework known commonly as the "Judeo-Christian."[19] From this perspective, the other of traditional aesthetics—the Jew of Christian moralism—is assimilated onto a postphilosophical, immanent, anthropological plane, where its distinguishing cultural markers are relinquished and its social stigmatization is ameliorated, but where its otherness is nonetheless retained. An abiding example is the persistent Wandering Jew myth, with its connotations of inherent or unavoidable sinfulness and eternal suffering,[20] in discourses on modern Jewish tribulation and catastrophe, including Holocaust film criticism. These essentially christo-phenomenological—or, *christological*—foundations, contextualizing a modern-day revision of christic redemption, profoundly contradict the Holocaust film criticism that on its face purports to theorize its critical difference on, inter alia, Judaically informed principles.

Suffice it to say here that the effect of this persisting christological approach has been the propagation of a relatively circumscribed perspective on Holocaust film culture. A telling characteristic of this perspective is that a refusal to merely approximate the purported, designated other, whether conceived on Christian or Judeo-Christian grounds, becomes tantamount to hubris, to the promotion of critical modalities deemed intellectually violent or totalizing.[21] Holocaust film criticism has, in effect, preempted critical theorization by implicitly adopting the conciliatory, basically Christian moral belief in the material world as an essentially fallen, inherently destructive, teleologically motivated "acceptance-phenomenon."[22] In this context, the materialist kernel of the Adornian taboo is denied. Indeed, what for Adorno is etched historically at the barbaric core of Western civilization—of capitalism and its ideological ethos—as an occurrence incomprehensible without sustained consideration of its social-institutional and especially political-economic determinants, becomes instead for Holocaust film criticism an index of human fallibility. That fallibility, moreover, lies beyond the conceptual horizon, where questions can be posed without provoking the same sorts of barbarity against which human society has historically been compelled to struggle and to seek "redemption." In the christological reading, Holocaust film criticism presents the Holocaust as but a necessary irruption and reenactment of this essential human fallibility, the social significance of which is reduced to the proverbial moral lesson: Jewish victims of the Holocaust, like Jesus "Christ" before them, are raised—resurrected—to the status of that event's defining, self-sacrificial other. By extension, the question of the Holocaust's *other* victims—not to mention the victims of other, preceding and subsequent genocides—and the question of the political and economic determinants of all these events are effectively ignored or transposed and played out in terms of christic sacrifice via the standardized dialectic of the Jewish Holocaust.[23]

One might usefully invoke in this regard the philosopher Levinas, whose Judaic phenomenological critique of ontological formulations has itself been justifiably critiqued for its contradictory reinscription of conceptual opacities ("infinity," "the Other").[24] Levinas has warned emphatically against the adoption of christo-anthropocentric notions; that is, of the mythical, phenomenological groundings that he sees dangerously precluding sustained interrogation of the means of forestalling holocaustic violence and catastrophe.[25] To Levinas, the invocation of notions such as these can only lead to an elision of the Judaic concept of sacrifice, which entails an interrogative and entirely worldly adherence to a critical, anti-authoritarian, radically differential—proto-Adornian—Judaic social promise to mend the world (*tikkun olam*). Indeed, for Levinas, as for other philosophers of Judaic discourse, the conceptualization of Judaic sacrifice is largely unconcerned with the appropriative re(an)nunciation or regenerative (re)assumption of an other, whether anthropologically or ideally conceived. Whereas Judaic texts do refer to social others, these are not conceived as exemplars of negative transcendence. When otherness is invoked in Judaic philosophy, it is in the context of a critical dialectic in which a hypothetical, second-person perspective is extended a sometimes indefinite concession in an effort to render possible a primary postulate or contention. Here the "other" refers to neither the hypothetical second person nor his or her perspective, but instead to a utopic effect that informs that perspective and whose grounds signal a seeming paradox that is nonetheless historically comprised: they hail both the not-yet and the might-have-been. This dialectical praxis is known as *le-didakh*.[26] *Le-didakh* is ultimately inseparable from the critical epistemology, familiar to Adornian critical theory and contemporary derivatives like cultural materialism and (post)structural Marxism, that works to resituate and resolve the social contradictions underlying historical and cultural dramas of differentiation. Judaic "otherness" thus refers to the possibility of an atheological—even atheistic—field of social being entailing a self-consciously problematical view to institutions and other systemic structures of social division and intelligibility such as class, gender, sexuality, ethnicity, and creed. It involves, in effect, a simultaneously *ideological* and *interrogative* praxis subtending the historical rift Jew-Gentile, which, among other things, the Judaic is obliged to repair, or mend—not by figuring a false and premature assimilation of one pole of the binarism into the other, but by cleaving to, while critically destabilizing, the deep structures of their differentiation. This historical rift, it must also be recognized, is so deeply ingrained in the global imaginary that a protracted, seemingly unresolvable, often mutually exacerbated struggle is required for its reparation actually to occur.[27]

However the "obscene" quality of Holocaust cultural representation may be conceived and dealt with, the dedicated Holocaust film scholar must inevitably struggle with these overriding aesthetico-moral contentions. These contentions position the critic as both an exemplar of "redemptive" Holo-sacrifice and a perverse purveyor of a cultural practice notable, even laudable, for marking an "embarrassment beyond intelligibility" with the extreme horror and violence it undeniably depicts and displays.[28] Keeping this in mind, I shall endeavor to pursue a serious analysis of Holocaust film culture. And in view of the phenomenological character of much Holocaust film criticism, I will focus my analysis on film critical texts that saliently exemplify this character and its christological implications. Aiming toward a historically grounded, ideologically attuned, intellectually oriented approach, my analysis will not be limited to a comparative description (explication or mimesis) of these texts. Rather, I will work to elucidate, interrogate, and critically resituate reasons the texts offer critics for resisting a sustained critique of Holocaust film onto the material institutional register that Adorno believed so crucial to an anti-holocaustic—if not necessarily peaceful—Holocaust cultural analysis.

Before doing this, however, it behooves us to acknowledge briefly that the development of Holocaust film culture has been approached in decidedly political, if not always materialist ways both outside the academy and in fields other than cinema studies. Most prominent in this regard are popular print media reviews of, and ensuing public debates over, various Holocaust films as well as significant scholarly publications on, and likewise ensuing public debates over, the relationship of the Holocaust to the contemporary study of history, social science, philosophy, and legal studies. For instance, following the onset of Holocaust historiography debates in France and Germany during the late 1970s and early 1980s, themselves responding in part to the politically provocative Hollywood television films *Holocaust* and *Playing for Time*, and to controversial developments in the scholarly critical sphere (deconstruction, cultural studies, new historicism, and critical legal theory), a wave of book-length texts on contemporary Holocaust culture and society began to be published. The primary source materials for these texts were print media reviews of and debates over Holocaust (film) culture and other public occasionings of Holocaust discourse such as those involving Holocaust denial and revisionism. The underlying if not always explicit contentions of these otherwise widely divergent texts supported the liberal notion that, for better or worse, Holocaust culture, discourse, and representation were irrevocably political—especially national-political—in both context and orientation. Moreover, attempts to argue otherwise, despite or even because of the Holocaust's irrefutable horror and violence, were themselves imbricated with dubious ideological agendas. These texts displayed and in some instances argued for a broad, interdisciplinary approach to the subject of the Holocaust, even when the scope of that subject's articulations became necessarily limited by particular methodologies and the critical, often ideological, programs associated with them.

In *The Holocaust and American Film*, for example, Judith Doneson insists upon the situation of Holocaust film criticism within a specific national-political context. Although conceding with her contemporary, Annette Insdorf, the legitimacy of the aesthetic-philosophical question, she lends priority to the historiographic question of Holocaust cinema's public presence and concern in the postwar United States. Acknowledging with Kracauer a lurid shock-effect of violent Holocaust imagery, Doneson is more interested in how Holocaust films—especially Hollywood productions—have helped to "assimilate the Holocaust into the popular consciousness," such that the Holocaust has become a paradigm of the American "immigrant" experience: "thematizing" current events, "catalyzing" the European Holocaust historiography debates, and adopting a "specific Jewishness" while also becoming "a universal message for mankind."[29] Similar in its critical effect is *Denying the Holocaust*,[30] in which the professional historian Deborah Lipstadt critiques North American Holocaust historiography debates for their imbrication with the postmodern literary theory known as deconstruction. Extending and honing Doneson's perspective, Lipstadt argues for a return to a more empirical historical practice that, by its requisite collection and specification of data, can, in her view, offer a corrective to postmodern antifoundationalism and the "relativism" with which, again in her view, it has served Holocaust denial and right-revisionism.[31]

Likewise clearly political and interdisciplinary in its approach to the problematics of Holocaust cultural and historical intelligibility is Dominick LaCapra's *Representing the Holocaust*.[32] LaCapra's work is a sustained analysis of Holocaust cultural and historiographical critique for which deconstruction is also a questionable mode of Holocaust analysis; it posits historical specificity and empirical factuality as less crucial to a serious understanding of the Holocaust and its sociocultural effects than a controlled, psychoanalytically based exposure and rehearsal of Holocaust discourse itself. A socially meaningful Holocaust cultural practice entails for him an allegorical praxis, a controlled reflection of traumatic holocaustic symptoms from their perceived manifestations in cultural and behavioral forms back onto the discursive conditions thought possibly to enable them. LaCapra's idea is that such symptoms not be understood primarily as threats to a national-political order, as would seem the case for Lipstadt, but on a transnational-political scale more akin to the ideological perspective of Doneson. In his view, holocaustic symptoms are occasions for a transferential, dialogic "exchange" between contestatory, even formerly ideologically opposed interlocutors interested in "mediating" and "modulating"—but, importantly, never closing off—their historical differences; this exchange is what LaCapra believes marks the essential, irreducible instability of Holocaust symptomaticity.[33]

The explicit attention lent by these recent works in Holocaust studies

to the transnational politicality and cross-disciplinarity of Holocaust critical and cultural discourse is not only crucial to their respective arguments
but continues the tendency of earlier, politically progressive, though persistently controversial Holocaust studies texts. *Eichmann in Jerusalem*
(Arendt), *Anti-Semite and Jew* (Sartre), *Faschismus, Rassenwahn,
Judenvervolgung* (Pätzold), *Fascism and Dictatorship* (Poulantzas), and *Why
Did the Heavens Not Darken?* (Mayer) are among texts in which Holocaust
knowledgeability is determined and comprehended sociohistorically before
aesthetically.[33] It is therefore all the more unfortunate that, unlike these
predecessors, more recent efforts take explicitly conservative positions vis-
à-vis their subject matter by accessing and employing the phenomenologically structured, christologically oriented paradigm in order to dissimulate
the very knowledge they would appear interested in exploring.

Both Doneson and Lipstadt belie their ostensible political progressivism
with qualifications consonant with a neoliberal agenda. For Doneson, this
entails designating Holocaust film culture as a viable means of projecting
and universalizing the North American ideology of a manifestly destined,
redemptive melting pot—an ideology well known to critics of the film
Western, film noir, and science fiction film[35]—to a global audience, and
hence of its advocating North American "democratization" (that is, economic expansion) abroad. Such an assertion, furthermore, has an ontothe-
ological layer, which Doneson attempts tenaciously to legitimize by
reference to the writings of Talmudic scholar Jacob Neusner: she holds that
the Holocaust, like the christological "Jew," is best represented as an allegory of universal human sin, suffering, and salvation.

> The Holocaust functions as a model, a paradigm, or a framework for history.
> It is a metaphor that teaches a lesson. . . . The more visible [it] becomes, the
> greater are its chances of being internalized by the American psyche [that]
> brings with it a tendency toward Americanization. . . . [In this way] the
> Holocaust becomes part of the American tradition . . . one of the principle
> components of the civil religion of American Jews . . . [a redemptive modality
> that] defies despair [and becomes firmly] integrat[ed] into the myth of liberty
> and equality.[36]

Celebrating the Holocaust as "Holocaust," as a concept allegorizable to
American manifest destiny, Doneson rehearses the tendency of much non-
Holocaust film genre criticism to exculpate cinematic depictions of
extreme violence against marginalities and "others" such as Native
Americans (the Western), women (film noir), and "aliens" (science fiction)
as part of a larger project of regenerating the American national mythos.[37]
She thus transcribes that tendency toward violence so emphatically into a
discourse on redemptive civil religiosity that what may at first have
appeared a critique of Hollywoodian constructions of the Holocaust is
revealed as nothing less than their dubious affirmation.

Although less blatant, Lipstadt likewise upholds the Holocaust and, by
extension, the "Jews," as exemplars of North American manifest destiny, as
she rehearses a theologically rooted transcription of that discourse onto

contemporary U.S. foreign policy practices. Ironically appropriating the very deconstructionism she has ostensibly rejected, Lipstadt selectively abandons empiricism for rationalist abstraction, thereby downplaying the centrality of the actual genocides of Native Americans and African-American slaves to North American "destiny." In the process, she dislocates the support she more explicitly offers the economic policies of Reagan and Bush from concomitant criticisms of Reagan's 1986 visit to the S.S. cemetery at Bitburg.[38] The glaring contradictory quality of these tacks is not resolved by a subsequent reference to Genesis: "God's presence can be found in many different places and made manifest in a variety of ways."[39]

Most problematic in this series of key examples is LaCapra, for it is his methodological recommendation that marks an increasingly predominant discursive tendency within an already problematic Holocaust cinema studies. Like Doneson, LaCapra supports the global dissemination of Americanism, to which he refers at different points as "pragmatism," "ethicopolitics," "creative modes of consumption," "secular sacrifice," and, most tellingly, "wizened evangelicism."[40] Like Lipstadt, he appropriates into this overtly "Judeo- Christian" ideologic the politically more progressive writings of earlier Holocaust theorists whose respective critiques of particular modalities of Holocaust intelligibility he at once rejects and coopts.[41] Unlike both his contemporaries, however, and in a move that is cannily attractive to contemporary film scholarship, LaCapra's methodological grounding in post-Lacanian psychoanalysis lends his "Judeo-Christian" appropriation of earlier Holocaust theory a decidedly *neo*phenomenological character. That is to say, LaCapra incorporates the poststructuralist psychotherapeutic concept of perpetual dialogic exchange and (counter-)transference associated with object-relations theory and articulated most prominently in film studies via the writings of Gilles Deleuze.[42] As a result, LaCapra's call for a renewed Holocaust studies remains dependent upon aesthetically mediated and theologically oriented discourses and thereby serves to preempt a sustained social-institutional interrogation of Holocaust theory and culture. Instead of basing his claims simply upon either a political-economic project (Doneson) or a rationalized empiricism (Lipstadt), that is, LaCapra actually revises the very aesthetic register along which any such preemption may occur. This revision entails a relocating of the aesthetic register from the idealist and rationalist planes on which it has traditionally been situated onto a plane of quotidian experience, wherein the operative agency of its interpretability shifts from the ethereal realm of moral feeling to the tangible activity of the human body.

In order to accomplish this, LaCapra refines a concept, the *differend,* inaugurated within contemporary literary theory by postmodern philosopher Jean-François Lyotard. For Lyotard, a performative enactment of inaudibility, rather than any reasoned discursive enunciation, is seen as the last remaining mode of authentic post-Holocaust representation. In Lyotard's view, the Adornian contention that the history and culture of the Holocaust may be ascertained and subjected to critical analysis, even judgment, through a sociohistorically reflexive philosophical praxis, is no longer relevant to or in the postmodern era. He argues, instead, that the rhetorical structures necessary to such a praxis have been detached or deflected ineluctably from any discernible, reliable hermeneutic axis that might otherwise authorize them and henceforth legitimize truth claims about the Holocaust.[43]

For LaCapra, who likewise calls for a mode of Holocaust knowledge-ability synchronous with the postmodern notion of a self-evident real, however, the liminal inaudibility signified by the performative *differend* marks an "extreme theoreticism":[44] the *differend* disallows the dialogics of witnessing and confession so central to the "Judeo-Christian" ethos he believes pervades and demarcates the Holocaust and its psychotherapeutic rehearsal as "Holocaust." So as to retain the extreme core of the Lyotardian view, LaCapra supplements *differend* with a notion of "anthropological sac-rifice" he gleans carefully and selectively from René Girard.[45] This unmis-takably christological interpolation of Judaic notions of sacrifice[46] presupposes a "primitive" economics of social determination; the repeat-edly violent, often murderous, frequently celebrated displacement and pro-jection of meaning onto designated and particular groups of subjects is deemed by Girard the central and necessary defining praxis of cultural identity and survival. For LaCapra, this theory of social foundation and regeneration, which he himself initially concedes may offer little more than a nostalgic, pseudoscientific rationale for universal social destruction, can nonetheless be culled strategically to ground and thereby ameliorate the elusiveness of the Lyotardian *differend*. The capacity to speak or to repre-sent supplies the means by which to reinscribe the *differend*'s liminality into a recognizable as well as prescriptive cultural form—namely, into a myth allegorizable to the Girardian paradigm, a myth perennially familiar to Western culture, but to which LaCapra does not refer outright as the Christian mystery play.[47]

On this line, what previously was considered the *differend*'s speculative significance, incapable by a presumed contingency of serious review, may now claim legitimacy and accountability as an accessible, realizable, *speak-able* manifestation of an essential and eternal *human* condition.[48] This claim is made, more precisely, through an allegorical rearticulation of the dominant, ever prevailing, christo-sacrificial myth. With respect to Holocaust theory, this (onto)mythological reinscription allows what Lyotard presupposes, and LaCapra does not dispute: the liminal character of holocaustic horror and violence undergoes a reenactment whose ensu-ing viability of expression and enunciation becomes proof both of "Holocaust"'s human pervasiveness and the persisting ontological necessity of its repetition.

Apparently inconsequential to LaCapra is the fact that, through this naturalizing, mythologizing process, the erroneous but persistent formula-tion of Jewish history as intrinsically self-sacrificial and beyond reasoned intelligibility remains unchallenged. The christological discourse framing LaCapra's anthropological turn ramifies an otherwise post-hermeneutic, post-theological scholarly terrain. Meanwhile the familiar phenomenolog-ical notion of the Holocaust is upheld, as is, by association, the notion of the proverbial suffering Jew as ineffable—obscene—and as an index of transhistorical truth.

LaCapra in this way implicitly overlooks the Levinasian admonition against christo-anthropological modalities, and henceforth redeploys a decidedly Christian notion of otherness—the universal and eternal recurrence of pathetic human suffering—as the fulcrum of Holocaust intelligibility. He thus disallows what might otherwise have helped enable more thoroughgoing, substantive kinds of Holocaust, not to mention Judaic, knowledgeability. This would have had the effect of opening the question so crucial within film studies of the relevance of "Holocaust" to contemporary American culture. As such, the broad interdisciplinary scope of LaCapra's post-Holocaust therapeutic must finally be seen as an elite-populist, christo-ecumenical gesture. That gesture, furthermore, not only demotes prevention of future holocausts to the status of pipe dream; it also rejects such efforts at prevention as negative examples of hubristic (read: "Hebraistic") obstinacy in the face of a presumably natural, universally manifest social-economic system that entails an American capitalist expansion served by the "Judeo-Christian" ideologic of anthropological sacrifice.

The preceding foray into the viable contradictions of three paradigmatic Holocaust studies texts not only illustrates some pervasive ideological tendencies within Holocaust scholarship but also indicates the challenge facing critics interested in something other than the simple, comparative, even performative appreciation of Holocaust film. As suggested earlier, the charge of hubris/"Hebraism" has served effectively to squelch the formulation and articulation of both a non-neophenomenological, nonchristological Holocaust film theory and a Holocaust film studies curriculum. Indeed, little significant analysis of Holocaust films has emerged that does not comprehend and understand the violence and horror—the so-called obscenity—of their subject matter in fatalistic terms, and that therefore does not consider the theorizing of that obscenity off-limits to critical intelligibility.

Within cinema studies proper, this overall absenting of a critical Holocaust intelligibility has come to bear the particular mark of a twofold neglect. The first aspect of this neglect is an apparent obstinacy toward focusing on Holocaust films that either have never achieved popular acclaim or have at one time or another become subject to widespread, even vociferous public contestation and debate. The second of these aspects comprises an apparent inability, if not refusal, to question the prevailing criteria for what counts as a Holocaust film and, in turn, what sort of genocide may be described as holocaustic. From the writings of Friedländer to Koch, Insdorf to Avisar, and Colombat to Loshitzky, one is hard-pressed to locate Holocaust film scholarship that focuses on films other than *Schindler's List*, *Shoah*, *Night and Fog*, and a few additional European art-cinema and Hollywood productions. Largely missing from the limited scholarship on the topic are analyses of *Camp de Thiaroye*, *The Killing Fields*, *Memories of Prison*, and *Come See the Paradise*,[49] whose categorizations as Holocaust films would be considered debatable in some circles because of the broader applicability this would propose of the term *Holocaust*. Sustained analyses of *Korczak, Balagan, Entre Nous,* and *The Sorrow and the Pity*,[50] which have been subject to varying degrees of censure and suppression in both the academic and popular spheres for their overt problematizations of the Jewish Holocaust, are likewise missing. Few if any Holocaust film critical texts, furthermore, ever place their analyses of Holocaust films into the sort of discursive relation to the institutionalized field of cinema studies or to the public debates over Holocaust historiography so widely engaged in other fields. References to cultural criticism are regularly confined to the fields of art and literature, while discussions of film historiography, most notably the phenomenological approaches of Béla Balasz and Kracauer, are almost completely absent.[51]

Even when attempts have been made toward more epistemologically attuned, politically oriented analysis, as in Colombat's *The Holocaust in French Film*, a resounding, overriding call to "Judeo-Christian" ecumenicism works to contain the historical contradictions and philosophical inconsistencies thereby accessed.[52] Despite referencing film history and theory and thereby engaging in an unabashed, wholehearted contextualization of Holocaust film criticism in public debates over Holocaust historiography, Colombat prematurely resolves the social contradictions opened via his analysis into an unmistakably Christian allegory. This is most demonstrable in his apparent unwillingness to concede the applicability of "Holocaust" to any but the Jewish and Roma genocides; it is also clear in his understanding of those genocides as occasions for gaining moral lessons about rescue efforts undertaken by and within Nazi-occupied France during the Second World War. *The Holocaust in French Film* does not balk at extended analyses of controversial productions such as *The Sorrow and the Pity* and *The Memory of Justice*, which, respectively, expose and critique the contradictions and hypocrisy of the French *Résistance* and the Nuremberg trials.[53] However, its ostensibly critical narrative culminates in an appreciative affirmation of the widely acclaimed film *Weapons of the Spirit*, a historical documentary about members of the Huguenot community of Le Chambon-sur-Ligne who selflessly and on solely religious grounds aided hundreds of Jews wishing to flee the Nazi Occupation.[54] Rather than delve critically into urgent political questions about anti-Nazi rescue and resistance raised by the Le Chambon phenomenon (and in a film such as *The Sorrow and the Pity*), Colombat facilely resuscitates the christological notion of the Holocaust. By extension, he rearticulates Holocaust rescue and resistance as a locus of personal sacrifice, such that the community of Le Chambon portrayed in *Weapons of the Spirit* can be interpreted and subsequently valorized as a convocation of Christian sainthood. In so doing, Colombat implicitly characterizes the Holocaust perpetrated against Jews and Roma alike as a reenactment of the christic sacrifice and, in turn, ironically reinscribes a necessity onto that event eerily reminiscent of Girard. Instead of elaborating the political questions raised by *The Sorrow and the Pity*, this culminative analysis has the counterpolitical effect of collapsing any *critical* notion of the Holocaust—including its conception as an event overdetermined by *an ideology of* sacrifice[55]—into the christological notion of the Holocaust *as sacrifice*. Such a collapse dissolves the historical factuality and residing political significance of the Le Chambon phenomenon into what Colombat actually refers to as an obscurantist allegory of "disorienting mystery."[56]

In effect, and pace the paradigm undergirding LaCapra's position as well as the imperative outlined by Lipstadt to remain truthful to the empirical facts of Holocaust history, texts of Holocaust film criticism have remained fixated upon the aesthetic-philosophical problematics of representation. On the one hand, they aspire to uphold the priority of historical experience in the analysis of Holocaust culture. On the other hand, they neglect the conceptual overdetermination of any such experience, which transposes its material significance onto an esoteric register that comprehends Holocaust culture in mystical terms—as at once an intangible mnemonic analogue of the actual Holocaust and a literal exemplification of that event's presumed "Judeo-Christian" interpretability. Even the very recent secondary literature in this area, invigorated by the dismantlement of the Eastern bloc, understands the Holocaust as both empirically self-evident and (onto)theologically predetermined. Much of this criticism relies on and recycles an ambiguous, if familiar, anthropological structure of redeemed sacrificial alterity; within this structure, the Holocaust becomes, in the context of the classic, allegorical "lost object" retrieved from potential oblivion, the proverbial "other planet" of concentration camp memoires.[57] Briefly put, these texts of Holocaust film criticism refashion the event into a broadly, if not universally, palatable commodity that befits prevailing tastes and presumed ideological needs.

In line with the liberal populism of Doneson, however, this latest series of texts articulates markedly different terms than did the philosophically informed, discursively challenging excurses of LaCapra, Colombat, and others. Indeed, a distinctly mainstream journalistic modality characterizes these texts; the glib subjectivism of this modality assumes certain knowledge or its acceptance on the part of their readership and, as with Lipstadt, seeks to achieve legitimacy by approximating empirical accuracy. This is the case even though these texts refer, atypically for Holocaust cinema studies, to contemporary and topical issues such as pornography, propaganda, humor, sexuality, popular memory, and the Israel-Palestine conflict. So despite their ostensible novelty, these texts display an inability or refusal to break with the phenomenological paradigm. Exemplary are the concluding words of the introduction to the premier Holocaust film studies anthology, *Spielberg's Holocaust*, which insist that questions about the Holocaust are "not easily answered" and are therefore best contextualized within "an ongoing, provocative debate." As if recalling LaCapra's subtle analogy of Holocaust discourse to "creative modes of consumption," these words bespeak an understandable refusal to supply easy answers to urgent questions while also running the risk of privileging Holocaust studies approaches that not only acknowledge but affirm ambivalence. While perhaps unintentionally, these works also finally condone efforts to keep the issue a lucrative one.[58]

This subtle alignment of Holocaust critical ambivalence with cultural commodification finds a blatant Christian analogue in Miriam Hansen's contribution to *Spielberg's Holocaust, "Schindler's List* Is Not *Shoah."* This text lends an imperialist twist to the problematics of critical ambivalence by conceiving Holocaust films as affirmative allegories of transnationalism that make a case "for a capitalist aesthetics and culture which is at once modernist and popular, which would be capable of reflecting upon the shocks and scars inflicted by modernity on people's lives in a generally accessible, public horizon."[59] Hansen is committed to formulating and ascribing to this pragmatic, populist, and capitalist aesthetics despite the potentially destructive, even holocaustic ramifications of the accommodation it proposes to contemporary neoliberalism. In her view, failing to do so would mean "missing a chance to understand the significance of the Shoah in the present . . . as a kind of screen allegory behind/through which the nation is struggling to find a proper mode of memorializing traumata close to home."[60]

As I have argued, a dearth is demonstrable in both substantive scholarly criticism of Holocaust cinematic culture and in criticism of that culture that could break the intellectually, politically, and economically obfuscatory pattern of christology. Still missing, then, is a sustained criticism of Holocaust culture's phenomenological interpolation that could resist and, potentially, work critically to transform the enabling conditions of anti-Judaism and pragmatic populism.

From what position could one articulate and enact such a resistance and transformation? Could we indeed initiate a Holocaust film theory that, while necessarily breaking the taboo against its formulation, does not also carry with it the stigma(ta) of hubris, mere speculation, or immanent destruction? Is it possible, that is, for traditionally sacral theologies bound up even with secular Holocaust film theory to be reconceived, on *radically secular* grounds, as nothing more than discourses among others and, as such, as subjectable to the same sorts of interrogations and critiques as are any philosophical or epistemological discourses now familiar to film and cultural studies? Is it furthermore conceivable that such a veritable profanation would not take the form of a reinscribed christology and merely replicate the naturalization and normalization of sacrificial othering on the quotidian plane? Would it be possible, instead, to develop a Judaically informed mode of analysis that would enable a distinctive, potentially radical Holocaust film criticism? And, if so, what would characterize such a *radically secular Judaic analytic?*

How would the problematics of Holocaust film criticism be altered, for instance, were the crucial Talmudic methodological concept, *le-didakh*, to be imported into film studies? Such a move might enable a rediscovery of the philosophical priority of the Judaic within the criticism of Holocaust film. It could also effect a paradigm shift whereupon the Judaic would be reunderstood as historically having both preceded and derived from the christological. The Judaic strand rediscovered via *le-didakh*, that is, could be reenvisioned not as the familiarly ideal other of, but as a philosophical system at once *other than* and *radical to*, that of the "Judeo-Christian." In this way, Holocaust film culture could be subjected to a sorely needed and thoroughgoing critique. Each layer of any particular Holocaust film, for example, could be effectively exposed: these would include the figurative layer of narrative-compositional and textual-discursive structuring and the literal layer at which this structuring becomes associable to nontextual fields of public contestation, (inter)national affiliation, and economic determination. With regard to Adorno, the importation of *le-didakh* would offer a radically reflexive reorientation of the social conditions that constitute and enable Holocaust films. Such an extensive mode of inquiry would not work to reduce, divide, and redeploy its objects of analysis; rather, it would intellectually relocate Holocaust films by at once engaging and interrogating the very contradictions and aporias that reduce their many layers into apparent coherence and viability. The aim of this intellectual relocation would thus be to pose the critical question of how *and why* these films might be theorized, produced, and received other than through phenomenological approaches that assimilate them, their means of conception and dissemination, into a christological orientation.[61]

Unfortunately, as it stands, the field of cinema studies has yet to see an actual and sustained theorization and application of *le-didakh*, and a current wave of "antitheoretical" scholarship threatens further to deter any such pursuit.[62] It is as though the supposition offered by the Holocaust historian John Weiss were true, as he remarks, in another context,

> Even today in the most liberal of nations, such truly free expression is far too strong for most, for Christians would be forced to confront powerful arguments against the idea that Jesus was the Messiah of the Jews, and this from a community well represented by learned biblical scholars who best know the original languages and texts. "Jews for Jesus" is one thing; Jews against Jesus would be quite another.[63]

Some might question whether Weiss's remarks are applicable here—that is, whether the persistent christological occlusion of Judaically informed discourse from Holocaust film criticism is merely a defense against critiques, Judaic or otherwise, of Christianity per se rather than an ideological effort to justify the pragmatic (re)generation of competing nationalisms under the rubric of neoliberal globalism. It nevertheless would be disingenuous to deny a general, political-historical connection between the outright anti-Judaism Weiss believes prevalent within contemporary society and the more subtle, philosemitic "Judeo-Christian" discourse that interpolates the problematics of Holocaust film theory and culture and evidently requires for its continued legitimacy the marginalization of the Judaic as well as the Judaically informed. On the other hand, it has been the express purpose of this essay to urge the encouragement and support of *le-didakhic* film theory—and to suggest that failure in this respect occurs only as a symptom of a much larger dissolution and collapse.

Notes

I would like to thank David Slocum and Imke Lode for their trenchant commentaries and helpful critiques of this paper.

1. For example, *Death Mills* (U.S. War Department, 1948); and *Les Camps de*

la mort (Actualités Françaises, France, 1948). See K. R. M. Short and Stephen Dolezel, *Hitler's Fall: The Newsreel Witness* (London: Croom Helm, 1988).

2. *The Diary of Anne Frank* (George Stevens, U.S.A., 1959); *Exodus* (Otto Preminger, U.S.A., 1960); *Judgment at Nuremberg* (Stanley Kramer, U.S.A., 1961).

3. *Long Is the Road* (Herbert B. Fredershof and Marek Goldstein, U.S.-Occupied Germany, 1945); *The Last Chance* (Leopold Lindtberg, Switzerland, 1945); *Murderers Are among Us* (Wolfgang Staudte, East Germany, 1946); *Somewhere in Europe* (Geza von Radvanyi, Hungary, 1947); *The Last Stop* (Wanda Jakubowska, Poland, 1948); *The Blum Affair* (Erich Engel, East Germany, 1948); and *Border Street* (Aleksander Ford, Poland, 1948).

4. *Fighters of the Ghetto* (Mira Hamermesh, Israel, 1968); *The Warsaw Ghetto* (BBC-TV, U.K., 1968); *Genocide* (Michael Darlow, Thames-TV, U.K., 1975); and *The Eighty-first Blow* (Haim Gouri, David Bergman, Jacquo Erlich, Israel, 1975). Regarding U.S. network television talk-show appearances, see Jeffrey Shandler, *While America Watches: Televising the Holocaust* (New York: Oxford University Press, 1999).

5. "Retro-style" films include: *Love Camp Seven* (R. L. Frost, U.S.A., 1968); *The Seven Beauties* (*Pasqualino settebelezzi*) (Lina Wertmuller, Italy, 1975); *The Serpent's Egg* (Ingmar Bergman, U.S.A./West Germany, 1977); *Lacombe, Lucien* (Louis Malle, France, 1974); *The Night Porter* (Liliana Cavani, Italy, 1974); *The Last Métro* (François Truffaut, France, 1980); *Das Boot* (*The Boat*) (Wolfgang Petersen, West Germany, 1981); and *Lili Marleen* (Rainer Werner Fassbinder, West Germany, 1981).

Among the "European art film" category, under which the preceding films also may be listed, we include additionally: *The Garden of the Finzi-Continis* (Vittorio De Sica, Italy, 1970); *Mr. Klein* (Joseph Losey, France, 1976); *Mephisto* (István Szabó, Hungary, 1981); *Shoah* (Claude Lanzmann, France, 1986); and *The Assault* (Fons Rademakers, The Netherlands, 1986).

For an overview of the "retro" genre, see Robert C. Reimer and Carol J. Reimer, *Nazi-Retro Film: How German Narrative Cinema Remembers the Past* (New York: Twayne, 1992). For a critical perspective, esp. as regards the French cultural scene, see Pascal Bonitzer and Serge Toubiana, "'Anti-Rétro': Entretien avec Michel Foucault," *Cahiers du Cinéma* 251–52 (July–August 1974): 5–17. Also belonging to this list are films and books that project a "retro" vision into a science-fictional or demonic-conspiratorial future: Tim Barrus, *Genocide: The Anthology* (Stamford, Conn.: Knights Press, 1988); Alan Cantwell Jr., *Queer Blood: The Secret AIDS Genocide Plot* (Los Angeles: Aries Rising Press, 1993); and, in a subtle way, the recent film *Contact* (Robert Zemeckis, U.S.A., 1997).

6. *Holocaust* (Marvin Chomsky, NBC-TV, U.S.A., 1978); *Playing for Time* (Daniel Mann, CBS-TV, U.S.A., 1980); *Skokie* (Herbert Wise, CBS-TV, U.S.A., 1981).

7. For example, U.S. Holocaust Memorial Museum, Washington, D.C. (beside the Smithsonian); Simon Wiesenthal Center Beit Hashoah Museum of Tolerance, Los Angeles (near West Hollywood); A Living Memorial to the Holocaust—Museum of Jewish Heritage in Battery Park, New York City (in view of the Statue of Liberty); New England Holocaust Memorial, Boston (along the Freedom Trail); Holocaust Museum and Learning Center, St. Louis (a city known as the "Gateway to the West"); Miami Beach Holocaust Memorial (ninety miles from Cuba); Holocaust Memorial Resource and Education Center of Central Florida, Orlando (in the vicinity of Disney World); and Museum to the Black Holocaust, Detroit (focusing on American slavery).

8. For salient examples of the argument that the Holocaust is "unique," see Nathan Rotenstreich, "The Holocaust as a Unique Historical Event," *Patterns of Prejudice* 22, no. 1 (1988): 14–20; and John K. Roth and Michael Berenbaum, eds., *Holocaust: Religious and Philosophical Implications* (New

York: Paragon House, 1989), esp. "What if the Holocaust Is Unique?"; André Neher, "The Silence of Auschwitz"; and Berenbaum, "The Uniqueness and Universality of the Holocaust."

My usage of "sublime" here is in reference to its formulation by Immanuel Kant, *Observations on the Feeling of the Beautiful and Sublime*, trans. John T. Goldthwait (1764; reprint Berkeley and Los Angeles: University of California Press, 1966).

9. The extant book-length texts are Annette Insdorf, *Indelible Shadows: Film and the Holocaust*, 2nd ed. (1983; reprint Cambridge and New York: Cambridge University Press, 1989); Judith E. Doneson, *The Holocaust in American Film* (Philadelphia: Jewish Publication Society, 1987); Ilan Avisar, *Screening the Holocaust: Cinema's Images of the Unimaginable* (Bloomington and Indianapolis: Indiana University Press, 1988); André Pierre Colombat, *The Holocaust in French Film* (Metuchen, N.J., and London: Scarecrow Press, 1993); and Yosefa Loshitzky, ed., *Spielberg's Holocaust: Critical Perspectives on "Schindler's List"* (Bloomington and Indianapolis: Indiana University Press, 1997). Most notable among short articles are: Gertrud Koch, "The Aesthetic Transformation of the Image of the Unimaginable: Notes on Claude Lanzmann's *Shoah*," trans. Jamie Owen Daniel and Miriam Hansen, *October* 48 (1989): 15–24; Koch, "The Angel of Forgetfulness and the Black Box of Facticity: Trauma and Memory in Claude Lanzmann's *Shoah*," trans. Ora Wiskind, *History and Memory* 3, no. 1 (1991): 119–34; Ora Avni, "Narrative Subject, Historic Subject: *Shoah* and *La Place de l'Etoile*," trans. Katherine Aschheim and Rhonda Garelick, *Poetics Today* 12, no. 3 (1991): 495–516; Rebecca M. Pauly, "From *Shoah* to Holocaust: Image and Ideology in Alain Resnais' *Nuit et brouillard* and *Hiroshima mon amour*," *French Cultural Studies* 3, no. 9 (1992): 253–61; Shoshana Felman, "The Return of the Voice: Claude Lanzmann's *Shoah*," in *Testimony: Crisis of Witnessing in Literature, Psychoanalysis, and History*, ed. Felman and Dori Laub (New York and London: Routledge, 1992); Lynn A. Higgins, "If Looks Could Kill: Louis Malle's *Portraits of Collaboration*," in *Fascism, Aesthetics, and Culture*, ed. Richard J. Golsan (Hanover, N.H., and London: University Press of New England, 1992); Karel Margry, "'Theresienstadt' (1944–1945): The Nazi Propaganda Film Depicting the Concentration Camp as Paradise," *Historical Journal of Film, Radio, and Television* 12, no. 2 (1992): 145–62; Gertrud Koch, "On the Disappearance of the Dead among the Living—The Holocaust and the Confusion of Identities in the Films of Konrad Wolf," trans. Jeremy Gaines, *New German Critique* 60 (fall 1993): 57–75; Daniel Mark Fogel, "'Schindler's List' in Novel and Film: Exponential Conversion," *Historical Journal of Film, Radio, and Television* 14, no. 3 (1994): 315–20; André Stein, "Humor and Irony in Two Films about the Holocaust," *Bulletin Trimestriel de la Fondation Auschwitz* 42–43 (July–September 1994): 83–94; Robert Gallately, "Schindler's List," *Central European History* 26, no. 4 (1994): 475–90; William J. Niven, "The Reception of Steven Spielberg's *Schindler's List*," *Journal of European Studies* 25, nos. 8–9 (1995): 165–80; Frank Manchel, "A Reel Witness: Steven Spielberg's Representation of the Holocaust in *Schindler's List*," *Journal of Modern History* 67, no. 1 (1995): 83–100; Susan E. Linville, "Agnieszka Holland's *Europa, Europa*: Deconstructive Humor in a Holocaust Film," *Film Criticism* 19, no. 3 (1995): 44–53; Miriam Bratu Hansen, "*Schindler's List* Is Not *Shoah*: Second Commandment, Popular Modernism, and Public Memory," *Critical Inquiry* 22, no. 2 (1995): 292–312; Jean-Pierre Geuens, "Pornography and the Holocaust: The Last Transgression," *Film Criticism* 20, nos. 1–2 (1995–1996): 114–30; Scott L. Montgomery, "What Kind of Memory? Reflections on Images of the Holocaust," *Contention* 5, no. 1 (1995): 79–103; Moshe Bejski, "Oskar Schindler and *Schindler's List*," *Yad Vashem Studies* (1995): 317–48; Geoffrey Hartman, "The Cinema Animal: On Spielberg's *Schindler's List*," *Salmagundi* 106–7 (1995): 127–45; Marguerite

Waller, "Signifying the Holocaust: Liliana Cavani's *Portiere di notte*," in *Feminisms in the Cinema*, ed. Laura Pietropaolo and Ada Testaferri (Bloomington and Indianapolis: Indiana University Press, 1995); Robert Brinkley and Steven Youra, "Tracing *Shoah*," *PMLA* 111, no. 1 (1996): 108–27; Thomas Elsaesser, "Subject Positions, Speaking Positions: From *Holocaust, Our Hitler*, and *Heimat* to *Shoah* and *Schindler's List*," in *The Persistence of History: Cinema, Television, and the Modern Event*, ed. Vivian Sobchack (New York and London: Routledge, 1996); Michael Wildt, "The Invented and the Real: Historiographical Notes on *Schindler's List*," *History Workshop Journal* 41 (1996): 240–49; Tony Barta, "Consuming the Holocaust: Memory Production and Popular Film," *Contention* 5, no. 2 (1996): 161–75; Kirby Farrell, "The Economies of *Schindler's List*," *Arizona Quarterly* 52, no. 1 (1996): 163–88; William H. Thornton, "After the Carnival: The Filmic Prosaics of *Schindler's List*," *Canadian Review of Comparative Literature* (September 1996): 701–7; Jeffrey Skoller, "The Shadow of Catastrophe: Towards an Ethics of Representation in Films by Antin, Eisenberg, and Spielberg," *Discourse* 19, no. 1 (1996): 131–59; Ingeborg Majer O'Sickey and Annette Van, "*Europa Europa*: On the Borders of *Vergangenheitsverdrängung* and *Vergangenheitsbewältigung*," in Ginsberg and Thompson, eds., *Perspectives on German Cinema* (New York and London: G. K. Hall/Prentice Hall International, 1996); Dominick LaCapra, "Lanzmann's *Shoah*: 'Here There Is No Why,'" *Critical Inquiry* 23 (winter 1997): 231–69; and the special issue of *New German Critique* 71 (spring–summer 1997) entitled "Memories of Germany." The reader will note that the majority of these texts have been published only within the last five to seven years.

10. Siegfried Kracauer, *From Caligari to Hitler: A Psychological History of the German Film* (Princeton, N.J.: Princeton University Press, 1947).

11. Peter Michelson, *Speaking the Unspeakable: A Poetics of Obscenity* (Albany: SUNY Press, 1993), xi.

12. Adorno's statement in this regard is by now proverbial: "Cultural criticism finds itself faced with the final stage of the dialectic of culture and barbarism. To write poetry after Auschwitz is barbaric. And this corrodes even the knowledge of why it has become impossible to write poetry today. Absolute reification, which presupposed intellectual progress as one of its elements, is now preparing to absorb the mind entirely. Critical intelligence cannot be equal to this challenge as long as it confines itself to self-satisfied contemplation" (*Prisms*, trans. Samuel and Shierry Weber [1955; reprint Cambridge, Mass.: MIT Press, 1981], 81).

13. Michelson, *Speaking the Unspeakable*, viii and xii.

14. See, for example, Adorno, *The Jargon of Authenticity*, trans. Knut Tarnowski and Frederic Will (1964; reprint Evanston, Ill.: Northwestern University Press, 1973). Compare Max Horkheimer, . . . *Eclipse of Reason* (1947; reprint New York: Continuum, 1974); Walter Benjamin, "The Work of Art in the Age of Mechanical Reproduction," in *Illuminations*, trans. Harry Zohn, ed. Hannah Arendt (1935; reprint New York: Schocken Books, 1968); Karl Marx and Friedrich Engels, *The German Ideology*, trans. C. Dutt, C. P. Magill, and W. Lough, ed. C. J. Arthur (1846; reprint New York: International Publishers, 1970); and Emmanuel Levinas, *Existence and Existents*, trans. Alphonso Lingis (Boston and Dordrecht: Kluwer, 1988).

15. Adorno, "Commitment," trans. Francis McDonagh, in *The Essential Frankfurt School Reader*, ed. Andrew Arato and Eike Gebhardt (1962; reprint New York: Continuum, 1982) 313; and Adorno, *Negative Dialectics*, trans. E. B. Ashton (1966; reprint New York: Continuum, 1973), 362–64.

16. For a critique of romanticism along these lines, see Mary A. Favret and Nicola J. Watson, eds., *At the Limits of Romanticism: Essays in Cultural, Feminist, and Materialist Criticism* (Bloomington and Indianapolis: Indiana University Press, 1994); also relevant is David Simpson, *Romanticism, Nationalism, and the Revolt*

against Theory (Chicago and London: University of Chicago Press, 1993).

17. Compare Erika Rummel, *The Humanist-Scholastic Debate in the Renaissance and Reformation* (Cambridge, Mass., and London: Harvard University Press, 1995); also Gary Remer, *Humanism and the Rhetoric of Tolerance* (University Park: Pennsylvania State University Press, 1996). Regarding the anti-Judaic aspect of this discourse, see Rosemary Radford Reuther, *Faith and Fratricide: The Theological Roots of Anti-Semitism* (New York: Seabury Press, 1974); and Reuther, "The *Adversus Judeos* Tradition in the Church Fathers: The Exegesis of Christian Anti-Judaism," in *Aspects of Jewish Culture in the Middle Ages*, ed. Paul E. Szarmach (Albany: SUNY Press, 1978).

18. Compare J. N. Mohanty, "Transcendental Philosophy and the Hermeneutic Critique of Consciousness," in *Hermeneutics: Questions and Prospects*, ed. Gary Shapiro and Alan Sica (Amherst: University of Massachusetts Press, 1984), 102 and 112; and Pierre Macherey, *A Theory of Literary Production*, trans. Geoffrey Wall (London and Boston: Routledge and Kegan Paul, 1978).

19. For examples of this secularized, "Judeo-Christian" philosophy, see J. H. Hexter, *The Judaeo-Christian Tradition*, 2nd ed. (1966; reprint New Haven, Conn., and London: Yale University Press, 1995); and William J. Courtenay, ed., *The Judeo-Christian Heritage* (New York: Holt, 1970). For a trenchant Judaic critique, see Arthur A. Cohen, *The Myth of the Judeo-Christian Tradition* (New York and Evanston, Ill.: Harper and Row, 1970); and for a useful, Judaically based historicization, see Mark Silk, "Notes on the Judeo-Christian Tradition in America," *American Quarterly* 36 (spring 1984): 65–85. For other, related criticisms, see Benny Kraut, "A Wary Collaboration: Jews, Catholics, and the Protestant Goodwill Movement," in *Between the Times: The Travail of the Protestant Establishment in America, 1900–1960*, ed. William R. Hutchison (London: Cambridge University Press, 1989); Walda Katz Fishman, "Right-Wing Reaction and Violence: A Response to Capitalism's Crises," *Social Research* 48, no. 1 (1981): 157–82; and Robert Boston, *Why the Religious Right Is Wrong about Separation of Church and State* (Buffalo, N.Y.: Prometheus Books, 1993), 163–64.

20. For critiques of the medieval myth of the Wandering Jew, see Galit Hasan-Roken and Alan Dundes, *The Wandering Jew: Essays in the Interpretation of a Christian Legend* (Bloomington and Indianapolis: Indiana University Press, 1986), esp. Hyam Maccoby, "The Wandering Jew as Sacred Executioner," and Paul Lawrence Rose, "Ahasverus and the Destruction of Judaism"; and, more generally, Jules Isaac, *The Teaching of Contempt: The Christian Roots of Anti-Semitism* (New York: Holt, Rinehart, and Winston, 1964), published originally as *Jésus et Israël* (Paris Fasquelle, 1959); and Joshua Trachtenberg, *The Devil and the Jews: The Medieval Concept of the Jew and Its Relation to Modern Anti-Semitism* (New Haven, Conn.: Yale University Press, 1943).

21. Compare Calvin O. Schrag, *Experience and Being: Prolegomenon to a Future Ontology* (Evanston, Ill.: Northwestern University Press, 1969), 10–11.

22. Regarding this belief and its relationship to phenomenology, see Mohanty, op. cit., 107; and Paul Ricoeur, *Fallible Man*, trans. Charles Kelbley (Chicago: Henry Regnery, 1965). Compare also the New Testament books of Corinthians and Galatians.

23. Jacques Derrida, "Violence and Metaphysics: An Essay on the Thought of Emmanuel Levinas," in *Writing and Difference*, trans. Alan Bass (Chicago: University of Chicago Press, 1978). Compare Jacob Meskin, "The Other in Levinas and Derrida: Society, Philosophy, Judaism," in *The Other in Jewish Thought and History: Constructions of Jewish Culture and Identity*, ed. Laurence J. Silberstein and Robert L. Cohn (New York and London: University of Chicago Press, 1992).

24. Corroborating this evaluation implicitly is Jon Petrie, "On the Secular Word 'Holocaust': Scholarly Myths, History, and Twentieth Century Meanings," *Journal of Genocide Research* 2, no. 1 (2000): 31–63, where a transformation of "holocaust" into christo-sacrificial "Holocaust" is traced to Cold

War–related mystification.

25. Emmanuel Levinas, "Reflections on the Philosophy of Hitlerism," trans. Seán Hand, *Critical Inquiry* 17, no. 1 (1990): 62–71. Going even further is Phillippe Lacoue-Labarthe and Jean-Luc Nancy, "The Nazi Myth," trans. Brian Holmes, *Critical Inquiry* 16 (winter 1990): 291–312, in which the problematics of "myth" as an explanatory tool vis-à-vis (post)modernity are themselves deconstructed. In *Representing the Holocaust*, LaCapra tellingly rejects Lacoue-Labarthe and Nancy shortly before appropriating Lyotard and Girard.

26. The Eastern Aramaic phrase *le-didakh* is a dialectical concept deployed most recently by Judaic scholar Yosef Hayim Yerushalmi (*Freud's Moses: Judaism Terminable and Interminable* [New Haven, Conn., and London: Yale University Press, 1991]) that occurs in the Babylonian Talmud approximately eighty-seven times. It means "according to that (opinion) which is yours"— that is, "according to your opinion." Its Hebrew equivalent is *le-daatkha*, and its definition is similar to that of the Hebrew phrase *u-le-ta 'amekh*, meaning "according to your reasoning." According to Talmudic scholar Louis Jacobs, whose position in this regard is implicitly supported by Yerushalmi, *u-le-ta 'amekh* is but one of three types of comparative or differential Talmudic argumentative methods, the other two being *ve-tisbera* ("and even according to your theory"), which entails exposing flaws in an opponent's position, and *ka-saleka da'atekh* ("you might have supposed"), which entails forwarding an argument with the intention of rejecting it. See Jacobs, *The Talmudic Argument: A Study in Talmudic Reasoning and Methodology* (Cambridge: Cambridge University Press, 1984), 14–15. In the view of another Talmudic scholar, Adin Steinsaltz (*The Essential Talmud*, trans. Chaya Galai [New York: Basic Books, 1976]), *u-le-ta 'amekh* (or, what we shall refer to in our text as *le-didakh* for the sake of linguistic ease and expedience as well as in deference to the popular-mass significance of the Aramaic) is distinguished by its tactic of *shinuya* ("argument by alternative demonstration"), which entails both the question, posed by a *makshan* (questioner), *Ve-dilma ipkha*? ("And perhaps the opposite is true?") and the hypothetical reply, offered by the *tartzan* (answerer), *Ipkha mistbra* ("The opposite holds"). See Steinsaltz, 231–41 and 270; also Robert Goldenberg, "Talmud," in *Essential Papers on Talmud*, ed. Michael Chernick (New York and London: New York University Press, 1994). The proverbial reference for this methodology is Rabbi Hillel, "Do not judge your fellow until you come to his place," from Talmudic tractate Avot 2:5–7, quoted in Jacob Neusner, *Judaism in the Beginning of Christianity* (Philadelphia: Fortress Press, 1984), 68. Compare Emmanuel Levinas, *Nine Talmudic Readings*, trans. Annette Aronowicz (1968; reprint Bloomington and Indianapolis: Indiana University Press, 1994).

27. Compare Abba Hillel Silver, *Where Judaism Differs: An Inquiry into the Distinctiveness of Judaism* (New York and London: Collier Books, 1989); Arthur A. Cohen, *The Myth of the Judeo-Christian Tradition* (New York: Harper and Row, 1970); and Jacques Derrida, *Of Spirit: Heidegger and the Question*, trans. Geoffrey Bennington and Rachel Bowlby (Chicago and London: University of Chicago Press, 1989).

28. For an elaboration of this phrase, see Max Horkheimer and Theodor Adorno, *Dialetic of Enlightenment*, trans. John Cumming (1947; reprint New York: Continuum, 1989).

29. Doneson, *The Holocaust in American Film*, 7, 9, 11, and 205.

30. Deborah Lipstadt, *Denying the Holocaust: The Growing Assault on Truth and Memory* (New York: The Free Press, 1983).

31. Ibid., 17–26.

32. Dominick LaCapra, *Representing the Holocaust: History, Theory, Trauma* (Ithaca, N.Y., and London: Cornell University Press, 1994).

33. LaCapra, *Representing the Holocaust*, 9, 37, 39 n.13, 138, 174–75, 176 n.7, 193, 215, and 220–21.

34. Hannah Arendt, *Eichmann in Jerusalem: A Report on the Banality of Evil* (New

York: Viking Press, 1963); Jean-Paul Sartre, *Anti-Semite and Jew*, trans. George J. Becker (New York: Schocken, 1965); Kurt Pätzold, *Faschismus, Rassenwahn, Judenvervolgugn: Eine Studie zur politischen Strategie und Taktik des faschistischen deutschen Imperialismus, 1933–1945* (East Berlin: Deutsche Verlag der Wissenschaften, 1975); Nicos Poulantzas, *Fascism and Dictatorship: The Third International and the Problem of Fascism*, trans. Judith White (London: New Left Books, 1974); and Arno J. Mayer, *Why Did the Heavens Not Darken? The "Final Solution" in History*, rev. ed. (New York: Pantheon, 1990).

35. See, for example, Richard Slotkin, *Gunfighter Nation: The Myth of the Frontier in Twentieth Century America* (New York: Atheneum, 1992); James M. Mellard, "Lacan and the New Lacanians: Josephine Hart's *Damage*, Lacanian Tragedy, and the Ethics of *Jouissance*," *PMLA* 113, no. 3 (1998): 395–407; and Janice Hocker Rushing and Thomas S. Frentz, *Projecting the Shadow: The Cyborg Hero in American Film* (Chicago: University of Chicago Press, 1995).

36. Doneson, *The Holocaust in American Film*, 9–10, 91, 146, 161, and 201. Neusner, of course, would be very critical of such a designation. See, for example, his *Judaism in the Beginning of Christianity*, op. cit.; and *Judaism in the Matrix of Christianity* (Philadelphia: Fortress Press, 1986).

37. This is true even for the otherwise insightful Slotkin. See his *The Fatal Environment: The Myth of the Frontier in the Age of Industrialization, 1880–1890* (Middletown, Conn.: Wesleyan University Press, 1985), for a more sustained example of this claim. For an interesting comparison, see David E. Stannard, *American Holocaust: Columbus and the Conquest of the New World* (New York and Oxford: Oxford University Press, 1992); and for a sharp contrast, see Ward Churchill, *A Little Matter of Genocide: Holocaust Denial in the Americas, 1492 to the Present* (San Francisco: City Lights Books, 1998).

38. Lipstadt, *Denying the Holocaust*, 2, 154, and 210. For an archival explication of the Reagan visit to Bitburg, see Ilya Levkov, ed., *Bitburg and Beyond: Encounters in American, German, and Jewish History* (New York: Shapolsky Publishers, 1987). For a collection of critical analyses, see Geoffrey Hartman, ed., *Bitburg in Moral and Political Perspective* (Bloomington and Indianapolis: Indiana University Press, 1986).

39. Lipstadt, *Denying the Holocaust*, ix.

40. LaCapra, *Representing the Holocaust*, ix, 7–8, 11, 14–15 n.11, 37 n.7, 105, 172 n.4, and 214–20.

41. Significant among these are Jürgen Habermas, "A Kind of Settlement of Damages: Apologetic Tendencies in German Historical Writing," in *Forever in the Shadow of Hitler: Original Documents of the "Historikerstreit," the Controversy Concerning the Singularity of the Holocaust*, ed. James Knowlton and Truett Cates (Atlantic Highlands, N.J.: Humanities Press, 1993); Arno J. Mayer, *Why Did the Heavens Not Darken?*; Zygmunt Bauman, *Modernity and the Holocaust* (Ithaca, N.Y.: Cornell University Press, 1989); and Phillippe Lacoue-Labarthe and Jean-Luc Nancy, "The Nazi Myth."

42. LaCapra, *Representing the Holocaust*, 208–10. For relevant examples of object-relations theory, see Juliet Mitchel, ed., *The Selected Melanie Klein* (London: The Free Press, 1987); Jay R. Greenberg and Stephen A. Mitchell, *Object Relations in Psychoanalytic Theory* (Cambridge, Mass., and London: Harvard University Press, 1983); Jeffrey Seinfeld, *Containing Rage, Terror, and Despair: An Object Relations Approach to Psychotherapy* (Northvale, N.J., and London: Jason Aronson, 1996); and C. Fred Alford, "Melanie Klein and the 'Oresteia Complex': Love, Hate, and the Tragic Worldview," *Cultural Critique* (spring 1990): 167–89. For the classical psychoanalytic contrast, see Sigmund Freud, "The Economic Problem of Masochism," trans. Joan Riviere, in *On Metaphysics and the Theory of Psychoanalysis*, ed. Angela

Richards (New York: Penguin Books, 1984); and for a critical historiograph-
ical appropriation, see Janice Doane and Devon Hodges, *From Klein to
Kristeva: Psychoanalytic Feminism and the Search for the "Good Enough"
Mother* (Ann Arbor: University of Michigan Press, 1992). Relevant texts of
Gilles Deleuze include *Masochism* (New York: Zone Books, 1991); *Cinema
1: The Movement-Image*, trans. Hugh Tomlinson and Barbara Habberjam
(Minneapolis: University of Minnesota Press, 1986); and *Cinema 2: The
Time-Image*, trans. Hugh Tomlinson and Robert Galeta (Minneapolis:
University of Minnesota Press, 1989). See also David Toole, "Of Lingering
Eyes and Talking Things: Adorno and Deleuze on Philosophy Since
Auschwitz," *Philosophy Today* 37, no. 3 (1993): 227–46.

43. See Jean-François Lyotard, *Heidegger and "the Jews,"* trans. Andreas Michel
and Mark Roberts (Minneapolis: University of Minnesota Press, 1988); and
Lyotard, *The Differend: Phrases in Dispute*, trans. Georges Van Den Abbeele
(Minneapolis: University of Minnesota Press, 1988). It should be noted to his
credit that LaCapra justifiably criticizes another postmodern theorist of
Holocaust culture, Shoshana Felman, for analogizing pathetic silence to an
authentic, if cryptic, mode of Holocaust explanation. Compare Felman and
Dori Laub, *Testimony: Crisis of Witnessing in Literature, Psychoanalysis, and
History* (New York and London: Routledge, 1992).

44. LaCapra, *Representing the Holocaust*, 99.

45. *Violence and the Sacred*, trans. Patrick Gregory (Baltimore and London: Johns
Hopkins University Press, 1977). Girard's theories have been linked to a
school of thought known as liminal anthropology, with which Mary Douglas
and Georges Bataille have also been associated. See Douglas, *Purity and
Danger: An Analysis of the Concepts of Pollution and Taboo* (New York and
London: Routledge, 1992); and Bataille, *The Accursed Share: An Essay on
General Economy. Vol. 1: Consumption*, trans. Robert Hurley (New York: Zone
Books, 1991). Compare Sigmund Freud, *Totem and Taboo: Some Points of
Agreement between the Lives of Savages and Neurotics*, trans. James Strachey
(New York: Norton, 1952), and Freud, *Moses and Monotheism*, trans.
Katherine Jones (New York: Vintage Books, 1939), for an analysis and cri-
tique, respectively, of notions of ritual sacrifice that differ significantly from
the ultimately Jungian, implicitly anti-Judaic approaches to the subject from
within the liminal anthropological school.

46. Compare Robert L. Cohen, "Sainthood on the Periphery: The Case of
Judaism," in *Sainthood: Its Manifestations in World Religions*, ed. Richard K.
Kieckhefer and George D. Bond (Berkeley: University of California Press,
1988); Yoram Bilu, "Dreams and the Wishes of the Saint," in *Judaism Viewed
from Within and from Without: Anthropological Studies*, ed. Harvey E.
Goldberg (Albany: SUNY Press, 1987); Ivan G. Marcus, "From Politics to
Martyrdom: Shifting Paradigms in the Hebrew Narratives of the 1096
Crusade Riots," in *Essential Papers on Judaism and Christianity in Crisis*, ed.
Jeremy Cohen (New York and London: New York University Press, 1991);
Sidney Goldstein, *Suicide in Rabbinic Literature* (Hoboken, N.J.: KTAV
Publishing House, 1989); Lawrence Fine, "Purifying the Body in the Name of
the Soul: The Problem of the Body in Sixteenth-Century Kabbalah," in *People
of the Body: Jews and Judaism from an Embodied Perspective*, ed. Howard
Eilberg-Schwartz (Albany: SUNY Press, 1992); and Eugene Weiner and Anita
Weiner, *The Martyr's Conviction: A Sociological Analysis* (Atlanta: Scholars
Press, 1990). We will discuss these Judaic notions in more detail below.

47. Here one might recall the historical proximity of the staging of mystery plays
and the perpetration of anti-Jewish pogroms during the medieval period. For
an overview of this phenomenon, see Léon Poliakov, *The History of Anti-
Semitism. Vol. 2: From Mohammed to the Marranos*, trans. Natalie Gerardi
(New York: Vanguard Press, 1973). Regarding the specific genre of the mystery play, see Robert Speaight, *The Christian Theatre* (London: Burns and

Oates, 1960), 9–36.

48. Lyotard himself encourages such a reinscription in his blatantly christological allegory "Europe, the Jews, and the Book," trans. Thomas Cochran and Elizabeth Constable, *L'Esprit Créateur* 31, no. 1 (spring 1991): 158–61.

49. *Camp de Thiaroye* (Ousmane Sembène and Thierno Faty Sow, Tunisia/Algeria/Senegal, 1987); *The Killing Fields* (Roland Joffé, U.K., 1984); *Memories of Prison* (Nelson Periera dos Santos, Brazil, 1984); *Come See the Paradise* (Alan Parker, U.S.A., 1990).

50. *Korczak* (Andrzej Wajda, Poland, 1990); *Balagan* (Andres Veiel, Germany, 1994); *Entre Nous* (Diane Kurys, France, 1983); *The Sorrow and the Pity* (Marcel Ophuls, France, 1970).

51. This is especially surprising in the instance of Gertrud Koch, one of the most prolific philosophers of Holocaust and film, whose writings on both Balasz and Kracauer and frequent references to Sartre have involved repeated insistence upon the experiential self-evidence of the sort of heightened imagery often projected in Holocaust film, without so much as a nod to its sociopolitical significance. Koch, "'Not Yet Accepted Anywhere': Exile, Memory, and Image in Kracauer's Conception of History," trans. Jeremy Gaines, *New German Critique* 54 (fall 1991): 95–109; Koch, "Sartre's Screen Projection of Freud," *October* 57 (1991): 3–17; and Koch, "Rudolf Arnheim: The Materialist of Aesthetic Illusion—Gestalt Theory and Reviewer's Practice," *New German Critique* 51 (fall 1990): 164–78. Indeed in her two published reviews of *Shoah*, this phenomenological vein translates merely into a general claim adducible to an unreferenced combination of Balasz and the later Kracauer that, through heightened and recurrent depictions of "gesture, mien and mimicry," *Shoah*'s imaging of the Holocaust transcends the empirical and conscious to "grasp the [unconscious] somatic impact of traumatic shock" and thereby figurally "proves" the Holocaust by "becom[ing] the phenomenological physiognomy of [its] fact[icity]" (Koch, "The Angel of Forgetfulness and the Black Box of Facticity," 131).

52. For example, K. L. Billingsley, "Jews Urged to Cut Ties to Liberals: New Group Seeks 'Balanced' Stance," *Washington Times*, November 13, 1995; Alexander Cockburn, "Edward Alexander, Holocaust Revisionist," *The Nation*, August 17–24, 1992, 163; Rabbi Yechiel Eckstein, "Hollywood Demeans Christianity," *Human Events*, February 21, 1997, 158; Michael Medved, "Hollywood Embraces Religion: Elite Profess Christianity, Judaism," *Washington Times*, April 26, 1995; Peter Steinfels, "Evangelicals Ask Help in Fighting Persecution," *New York Times*, January 23, 1996; Amy Vishrup, "A Jew for Jesus," *George*, October 1996, 62–65; and "Ralph Reed at the 92nd Street Y," Jews for Racial and Economic Justice Home Page, www.columbia.edu/~ljw17/jfrej/reed.htm, July 3, 1997, 3.

53. *The Memory of Justice* (Marcel Ophuls, U.S.A., 1976).

54. *Weapons of the Spirit* (Pierre Sauvage, U.S.A., 1988).

55. For an excursus on this former understanding, see Arno J. Mayer, *Why Did the Heavens Not Darken?*.

56. Colombat, *The Holocaust in French Film*, 345.

57. The classic instance of this usage is David Rousset, *The Other Kingdom*, trans. Ramon Guthrie (1947; reprint New York: Fertig, 1982), where the perpetration of the Holocaust is said to have taken place in an entirely "other" world, the *universe concentrationnaire*.

58. Loshitzky, *Spielberg's Holocaust*, 13.

59. Hansen, "*Schindler's List* Is Not *Shoah*," 97.

60. Ibid., 98–99.

61. With this theoretical possibility in mind, the contemporary film scholar may be reminded of the recent and ongoing debate in film historical circles of the role and significance of Jews in the Hollywood studio era, in relation to which a critical deconstructive methodology akin to *le-didakh* has been

deployed in efforts to comprehend and explain the phenomenon of Jewish-American complicity in anti-black racism. Notable instances of this deployment, which are in fact relevant to our discussion for their focus on a form of violent racist imagery, include Neal Gabler, *An Empire of Their Own: How the Jews Invented Hollywood* (New York: Crown Publishers, 1988); and Michael Rogin, *Black Face, White Noise: Jewish Immigrants in the Hollywood Melting Pot* (Berkeley and Los Angeles: University of California Press, 1996). In differing but related ways, these texts rationalize the prevalence of racist images of African Americans in Hollywood cinema of the studio era as the effect of a *masquerade*, a displaced allegory-effect of suppressed, often repressed, Jewish anger and indignation over historical, including American, anti-Semitism, which, in this view, continues to be necessary to the legitimation of the Hollywood studio system and the ideology of industrial capitalism in which that system was, and remains, based. This perspective has been echoed subsequently—pace the culturally more conservative Gabler—in the recent film *Hollywoodism* (Simcha Jacobovici, Canada, 1998). Important to our formulation of *le-didakh* as a Holocaust film analytic is the crucial difference it marks between "Jews" as subjects of an ethnic creed and/or as descended (*herkunft*) from that subjectivity, and the "Judaic" as the intelligibility of an ideological creed staking a hermeneutic relationship to the world that is philosophically distinct from, while critically foundational to, that of the "Judeo-Christian" mainstream into which the majority of actual "Jews," studio moguls among them, along with Christians have been interpellated. On the basis of this marked difference, and while not denying the psychology of racism effectuated via the Holocaust and other watersheds in the history of antisemitism (*The Pawnbroker* [Sidney Lumet, U.S.A., 1965] is probably the best cinematic examination to date of this phenomenon), the allegorical methodology employed by Rogin and by Gabler is only cursorily *le-didakhic*; insofar as it collapses the philosophical layer of critical praxis onto an existential layer of untheorized social groupings, it not only implicitly occludes the crux of the Jewish-Christian differentiation we are otherwise here positing, but also subtly disallows the possibility that more thoroughgoing and sustained understandings be reached, and critiques be formulated, of Jewish-American racism.

62. Beginning a decade ago with David Bordwell's conservative tract *Making Meaning: Inference and Rhetoric in the Interpretation of Cinema* (Cambridge, Mass.: Harvard University Press, 1989); and taking hold recently with Richard Allen and Murray Smith, eds., *Film Theory and Philosophy* (Oxford and New York: Oxford University Press, 1997), an ostensibly more critical collection; and Irving Singer, *Reality Transformed: Film as Meaning and Technique* (Cambridge, Mass., and London: MIT Press, 1998).

63. John Weiss, *The Ideology of Death: Why the Holocaust Happened in Germany* (Chicago: I. R. Dee, 1996), 43.

contributors

Paul Arthur is professor of film and literature at Montclair State University. He has published widely on film noir, documentary, and the American avant-garde and is coeditor of *Millennium Film Journal*.

Leo Charney is senior editor at Movies.com. He is the author of *Empty Moments: Cinema, Modernity, and Drift* and coeditor (with Vanessa Schwartz) of *Cinema and the Invention of Modern Life*. He has taught film at New York University, Northwestern University, and the University of Iowa.

Phyllis Frus teaches at the University of Michigan. She is the author of *The Politics and Poetics of Journalistic Narrative: The Timely and the Timeless* and coeditor of the New Riverside Edition of the works of Stephen Crane. She has carried her interest in the border where fiction and nonfiction overlap into three new projects: a book (with Stanley Corkin) proposing to organize American literary studies around the contingencies of history rather than a "timeless" canon; a series of essays on documentary, docudrama, and historical film; and a study of the way family violence is represented in film, television, and drama abroad as well as in the United States.

Terri Ginsberg holds a doctorate in cinema studies from New York University. She has taught film, literary, and cultural studies at New York University, Rutgers University, and Florida Atlantic University. Her publications include *Perspectives on German Cinema* (coedited with Kirsten Moana Thompson) and essays and reviews in *Holocaust and Genocide Studies*, *Textual Practice*, *Journal of the History of Sexuality*, *Mediations*, *Journal of Lesbian Studies*, and *Quarterly Review of Film and Video*. She is currently writing a book on the politics of hermeneutics in contemporary Holocaust film.

Elizabeth Swanson Goldberg is a consultant with the Professional Development Program at Northeastern University, and teaches literature and writing at Fisher College. She has just completed a manuscript on representations of torture in twentieth-century film and literature, and has published in the areas of ethnic American literature and multicultural pedagogies. She has presented her work at professional meetings including the 1995 United Nations Conference on Women in Beijing, China, the Modern Language Association, and the American Studies Association.

Ed Guerrero is an associate professor in cinema studies at New York University. He is the author of *Framing Blackness*, and has written extensively on black and emergent cinema in numerous journals and anthologies. He is on the editorial boards of *Cinema Journal* and *Cineaste*, and a member of the Library of Congress's National Film Preservation Board.

Marsha Kinder has been a professor of critical studies in the School of Cinema-Television at the University of Southern California since 1980. She is a cultural theorist specializing in narrative theory, new digital media, and children's media culture, and author of ten books, including *Blood Cinema: The Reconstruction of National Identity in Spain*, *Luis Buñuel's The Discreet Charm of the Bourgeoisie*, and *Kid's Media Culture*. She is also a multimedia producer, whose current project is an experimental website called "Dreamwaves," which presents an exhibition space for dream-based art and generates a discourse on dreams as a model of interactive database narrative.

Peter Kramer teaches film studies at the University of East Anglia (U.K.). He has published in *Screen*, *The Velvet Light Trap*, *Theatre History Studies*, *Historical Journal of Film, Radio, and Television*, *History Today*, and numerous edited collections. He is coeditor, together with Alan Lovell, of *Screen Acting*. He is the author of *The Big Picture: Hollywood Cinema from Star Wars to Titanic*, forthcoming from BFI.

Richard Maltby is a professor of screen studies and head of the School of Humanities at Flinders University, South Australia. He is the author of *Hollywood Cinema: An Introduction*, *Passing Parade: Popular Culture in the 20th Century*, and *Harmless Entertainment: Hollywood and the Ideology of Consensus*, as well as numerous articles and essays on the cultural history of American cinema.

Lee Clark Mitchell is Holmes Professor of Belles-Lettres at Princeton University, where he has served as chair of the English Department and director of the Program in American Studies. He teaches courses in

American literature and is the author of *Witnesses to a Vanishing America: The Nineteenth-Century Response, Determined Fictions: American Literary Naturalism, The Photograph and the American Indian,* and *Westerns: Making the Man in Fiction and Film.* His recent essays on Crane, James, and Twain, among others, have appeared in *Critical Inquiry, PMLA,* and *Raritan.*

William Rothman is professor of motion pictures and director of the Graduate Program in Film Studies at the University of Miami. He is the author of *Hitchcock—The Murderous Gaze, The "I" of the Camera, Documentary Film Classics,* and (with Marian Keane) *Reading Cavell's The World Viewed: A Philosophical Perspective on Film,* and series editor for the Cambridge University Press Studies in Film series.

Rikke Schubart is a lecturer in the Department of Film and Media Studies at the University of Copenhagen. She is the author of *In Pleasure and Pain: From Frankenstein to Splatter Movies,* a study (in Danish) of the horror genre, and has written articles on horror, splatter movies, action films, and serial killer cinema. She is presently finishing a Ph.D. project entitled "Masculinity in the Action Movie, 1968–2000."

J. David Slocum is assistant dean in the Graduate School of Arts and Science at New York University, where he teaches cinema studies and humanities. His writings on violence, film, and culture have appeared in *American Quarterly, Cineaste, Social Research,* and *The Times Literary Supplement.* He is currently completing *Community and Carnage: A Cultural History of Violence in American Movies, 1896–1950.*

index